HOW YIDDISH CHANGED AMERICA AND HOW AMERICA CHANGED YIDDISH

HOW YIDDISH CHANGED AMERICA AND HOW AMERICA CHANGED YIDDISH

Edited by Ilan Stavans and Josh Lambert

RESTLESS BOOKS
BROOKLYN, NEW YORK

First Restless Books Hardcover Edition January 2020

Hardcover ISBN: 9781632062628
Library of Congress Control Number: 2019943996

Cover design by Alex Robbins
Set in Garibaldi by Tetragon, London

Printed in Canada

1 3 5 7 9 10 8 6 4 2

Restless Books, Inc.
232 3rd Street, Suite A101
Brooklyn, NY 11215

www.restlessbooks.org
publisher@restlessbooks.org

This work is published with support from the Yiddish Book Center,
thanks to a gift from Lori and Michael Gilman;

David Bruce Smith, Grateful American Foundation;

And Terry Philip Segal.

To my *Tate-Mame*.

—I.S.

To my *mitarbeters* at the Yiddish Book Center, all those who came before us, and the supporters who helped to make it the institution it is today.

—J.L.

Contents

PART IV: AMERICAN COMMEMORATION

PART V: OY, THE CHILDREN!

Preface

THE OLD IN THE NEW

We have to believe in free will. We have no choice.

—ISAAC BASHEVIS SINGER

CELEBRATED AND MARGINALIZED, lionized and trivialized, Yiddish is so deeply woven into the fabric of the United States that it can sometimes be difficult to recognize how much it has transformed the world we live in today. It's a language and culture that's as American as bagels and Rice Krispies, Hollywood and Broadway, Colin Powell and James Cagney (and connected to all of these, in one way or another). Yet many Americans think of Yiddish, when they think of it at all, as a collection of funny-sounding words. *Oy gvald*, indeed!

The aim of this book is to present a very different picture of Yiddish, true to its history, as a language and culture that is—like the Americans who spoke, read, and created in it—radical, dangerous, and sexy, if also sweet, generous, and full of life. Its inception is embedded in a radical shift. Some see Yiddish not only as a language but as a metaphor. They note that unlike most other tongues, it doesn't have an actual address—a homeland, so to speak—or claim, as Isaac Bashevis Singer did when accepting the Nobel Prize in Literature, that it doesn't have words for weapons. And because of its history, it awakens strong feelings of nostalgia. But others see this as an ongoing problem. In particular, it irritates Yiddishists that the language is fetishized, especially by people who don't speak it.

Since the Second World War, many valuable anthologies have helped American audiences understand the gamut of Yiddish possibilities.

Arguably the most influential has been *A Treasury of Yiddish Stories* (1954), edited by Irving Howe and Eliezer Greenberg. It concentrated on the Yiddish literary outpouring from figures like the three so-called classic Yiddish writers, Mendele Moykher Sforim, I. L. Peretz, and Sholem Aleichem, and served as a conduit to connect an American Jewish audience to the pre-Holocaust civilization. Its publication was certainly a watershed: the volume was the manifestation of a collective longing. That anthology looked at the *shtetlekh*, or small towns, in which Ashkenazi Jews lived for centuries through an American lens, as noble, even idyllic, and with a sense of homesickness, but also as a site of contradictions, violence, and unfaithfulness. Readers simultaneously idealized what Israel Joshua Singer called "a world that is no more" and sought to understand themselves as a continuation, as well as a departure, from it.

Other anthologies of Yiddish literature in translation followed suit. Each concentrated on either a region (the USSR, for instance) or a particular literary genre (such as poetry). These volumes include *Ashes Out of Hope: Fiction by Soviet-Yiddish Writers* (1977), also edited by Howe and Greenberg; *The Penguin Book of Modern Yiddish Verse* (1987), edited by Howe, Ruth Wisse, and Khone Shmeruk; Benjamin and Barbara Harshav's *American Yiddish Poetry: A Bilingual Anthology* (1986); and *Yiddish South of the Border: An Anthology of Latin American Yiddish Writing* (2003), edited by Alan Astro. To various degrees, the objectives of these anthologies remained the same.

But in the last few decades, the position of Yiddish in the zeitgeist has dramatically changed. The study of Yiddish thrives in America, among teenagers and senior citizens, the religious and the secular, and everyone in between. Technology has made the language and culture available in wider ways. Young people are studying it. Scholarship related to it is prolific. Its musical rhythms and motifs have been borrowed by other traditions. It is part of movies, television, and radio. And the internet serves up lexicons, memes, recipes, and all sorts of surprising artifacts. Assimilation in the United States has indeed presented Yiddish with challenges, and it has responded impressively, dynamically, demonstrating its flexibility, complexity, and strength.

So what is Yiddish, exactly? First and foremost, it's a language, a Jewish one. Throughout the thousands of years of their history, Jewish people have spoken many languages, their own and the languages of the majority cultures in which they've lived. Hebrew, the language of the Torah (what Christians call the Old Testament) and an official language of the contemporary State of Israel, is one such Jewish language, and many others have arisen in other places and times as means of communications for Jewish communities. For example, Ladino, or Judeo-Spanish, has been spoken by the descendants of the expulsion from Spain in 1492, and Judeo-Arabic has been spoken by Jews throughout the Arabic-speaking world. Yiddish, meanwhile, was the primary Jewish language of Ashkenaz, which is what Jews called northern Europe.

During much of its existence, Yiddish was dismissed as a *zhargon*, not quite a language at all; this was the common fate of many vernaculars, which were seen as less prestigious than scholarly languages like Latin, and the major European languages like French, English, and German, which had state power behind them. But Yiddish was absolutely a language, one that originated somewhere in central Europe about a thousand years ago, with the oldest extant example of a printed Yiddish sentence dating all the way back to 1272. Written in the Hebrew alphabet, and drawing for its grammar and vocabulary on Germanic, Slavic, Romance, and Semitic languages, Yiddish soon became the vernacular spoken by the majority of the world's Jews for more than seven centuries, and over those centuries, a language of increasingly popular books and prayers.

In the nineteenth century, around the same time that languages like Italian and Norwegian evolved into their modern forms, Yiddish hit its stride, flowering into a language not just of commerce and community but of modern theater, journalism, literature, and even national aspiration. At that time, speakers of the dialects of Yiddish—sometimes referred to as Lithuanian, Polish, and Ukrainian Yiddish—constituted large minorities or even majorities in many European cities and in hundreds of European small towns and villages, while many more Yiddish speakers had relocated from Europe to other parts of the globe. The world's total Yiddish-speaking population just before the Second World War is estimated by scholars to have been about thirteen million people.

The language's fate would be entangled with one of the world's most brutal tragedies—millions of those Yiddish speakers were murdered by the Nazis and their collaborators in the Holocaust during the Second World War—but it also flowered almost everywhere that Jews settled, before and after the war: Yiddish newspapers and books were published in Montreal and Montevideo, Cairo and Melbourne, Paris and Cape Town (not to mention Warsaw and New York). While mostly the language has had to survive, unlike most major languages, without a government's backing, Yiddish was briefly an official language of the Soviet Union and today it is one in Sweden. It has been recognized as an irreplaceable treasure by UNESCO, and it is currently spoken, at home and in the street, by more than 400,000 people around the world.

We might never know when the very first Yiddish speaker arrived on American shores, but it's clear that a substantial number of speakers had already arrived by the middle of the nineteenth century, and that they quickly found their way to almost every corner of the developing nation. In the late nineteenth and early twentieth centuries, an enormous wave of European immigration brought hundreds of thousands and then millions of Yiddish speakers. Free from some of the strictures imposed by European governments, American Yiddish speakers created newspapers and theaters, and before long they had built one of the most vibrant centers for Yiddish culture in the world.

At the height of the language's American popularity in the 1920s, a handful of different Yiddish newspapers circulated hundreds of thousands of copies every day, and Yiddish theaters on Second Avenue, in Manhattan, seated thousands of spectators every night. Also, as the primary language of a vast immigrant community of poor laborers and their upwardly mobile children, Yiddish became a crucial part of American politics—at a moment when socialism, anarchism, and communism competed for Americans' votes with more familiar political orientations—and of American business, entertainment, cuisine, and speech.

In short, America, famously a nation of immigrants, was the site of many of Yiddish's greatest triumphs—a Nobel prize, bestsellers, and theatrical smashes, as well as political movements that changed the way people everywhere work. As specific as its history might be, like any language, Yiddish is, for all intents and purposes, infinitely capacious: you can say anything in Yiddish that you want. And of course, in America, all kinds of people have done so: factory owners and Communists, Hasidic Jews and Christian missionaries, anarchists and political fixers, scientists and quacks. To dive into the diversity and complexity of American Yiddish culture, as this book invites you to do, is one wonderful way to appreciate the wild possibilities of life in the United States.

This anthology showcases the rich diversity of Yiddish voices in America, and of the American culture influenced and inspired by Yiddish. It is made of poems, stories, memoirs, essays, plays, letters, conversations, and oral history. Many of the authors represented here were immigrants themselves who remained loyal to Yiddish in the new land. Others are their offspring, the so-called *kinder* for whom the language was a link to ancestors and a source of inspiration and provocation, or people from a variety of backgrounds, Jewish and not, who learned the language and made it their own.

Much of the material included here comes from the publications and collections of the Yiddish Book Center, a nonprofit organization working to recover, celebrate, and regenerate Yiddish and modern Jewish literature and culture, which was founded in 1980 by Aaron Lansky, then a twenty-four-year-old graduate student of Yiddish literature (and now the Center's president). In the course of his studies, Lansky realized that untold numbers of irreplaceable Yiddish books—the primary, tangible legacy of a thousand years of Jewish life in Eastern Europe—were being discarded by American-born Jews unable to read the language of their Yiddish-speaking parents and grandparents. So he organized a nationwide network of *zamlers* (volunteer book collectors) and launched a concerted campaign to save the world's remaining Yiddish books before it was too late. Since its founding, the Center has recovered more than a million books, and published *Pakn Treger* (*The Book Peddler*), an English-language magazine that features articles, works in translation, profiles, and portfolios about Yiddish culture. Drawing on that rich archive and the Center's other collections, this anthology offers landmarks and sidelights of American Yiddish culture to give readers a spirited introduction to what Yiddish America has been and can be.

The book does not attempt to present this material in chronological order or to make a single argument. Like many anthologies, this one wants to be a smorgasbord. We offer the nexus between American and Yiddish culture, in English translation—with full knowledge of how complex, and also generative, translation can be. This anthology's animating hope is that its readers will make connections between its heterogeneous content, browsing and skipping and finding surprises everywhere.

To that end, the sixty-two entries have been organized into six distinct parts. The first, "Politics and Possibility," explores immigrants' initial encounters with America. It features scenes of ritual and tradition in the Jewish ghetto of the Lower East Side and explores the ways children of immigrants ventured out into Harlem, the Bronx, and well beyond. The selections reflect how, around the turn of the twentieth century, Yiddish culture in New York emanated from a community whose first concern was survival, and who had to decide what that struggle for survival implied about politics, ethics, and culture. For example, a watershed moment in the history of Yiddish in the United States took place in 1923 when Sholem Asch's play *God of Vengeance* (written in Yiddish in 1906) opened, in English, on Broadway. The play represents a setting that was as shocking to audience members then as it would be today: a brothel operated by a Jewish pimp and offering the services of Jewish prostitutes.

The realities of Jewish participation in sex work in the late nineteenth and early twentieth centuries are complex and tragic, and what Asch's play captures, with stark symbolism, is the tension between the noble aspirations of Jews of that time to holiness and purity, and the degradations imposed on them by the struggle to earn a living under discriminatory regimes. The play included much that shocked its audiences, including a scene in which a young, supposedly innocent girl is seduced by an older, female prostitute—posing the question of what would happen and what would change when the old authority structures, derived from the rabbis and from Christianity, crumbled away. The second act of *God of Vengeance* appears in this part. So does a letter written in 1936 about a female athlete who successfully transitioned to male, written to the editor of *Forverts*, arguably the most important immigrant publication in the United States, in which readers looked for answers to daily questions about becoming American: In what way is this nation also mine? How much tradition am I ready to sacrifice on the road to gaining new rights?

A central question for Yiddish speakers in America, as for most immigrants, was precisely a question about language. Each one had to answer for herself how much she should depend upon and defend the language of her childhood and tradition, and how much she should embrace a new language—English—with its strange possibilities. Such questions had especially large stakes for writers, artists, and politicians. "The Mother Tongue Remixed," the second part of this anthology, concentrates on the vicissitudes of the Yiddish language as it adapted to the new territory. It features reflections on what happens in the classroom to make Yiddish survive, and the role dictionaries and other authoritative entities play in the continuation of life for the language.

Part two also includes appreciations of figures like Leo Rosten, a humorist who became famous for his efforts to codify "Yinglish"—the blend of Yiddish and English that became common in midcentury America—and some concrete examples of the playfulness with which Yiddish can be deployed, as in the case of Stanley Siegelman's poem "The Artificial Elephant." People often get defensive—or *prescriptive*—about the right ways and wrong ways to speak a language (and of course that kind of attitude has its value), but very often the story of Yiddish in America, even linguistically, has been a story of playfulness and irreverence.

The third part of this volume, "Eat, Enjoy, and Forget," focuses on one of the avenues through which the culture of Yiddish-speaking Jews has had the broadest impact in America: food. In an immigrant culture, assimilation in the culinary dimension is about experimenting with flavors and ingredients in order to satisfy evolving palates. Those experiments quickly moved from Jewish homes out into restaurants. In the twentieth century, delicatessens became staples of every major American city, and bagels triumphed across the country. American companies like Maxwell House and Crisco understood that they could profit by serving a hungry Jewish market. More recently, as nostalgia for Jewish cooking has found its way into haute cuisine, dishes such as latkes have fused with other ethnic flavors (say, chocolate-based Mexican mole) to create new tastes that reflect the complex families and histories of Jews in America. Over the decades, classic Ashkenazi dishes have undergone changes in the way they are cooked, in how they are presented, and in what they are accompanied with during a meal. In a 1988, 14-minute short film by Karen Silverstein called *Gefilte Fish*, three Jewish women of the same family, an immigrant grandmother and her American daughter and granddaughter, explain how each prepares the dish. The first describes the labor-intensive process of cooking it, which she learned from her own mother, starting with the purchase of a living fish—"to make sure it is fresh." The last just acquires a bottle of the Manischewitz brand before serving it on the table.

The fourth part, "American Commemoration," focuses on the wide array of Yiddish literary voices in America. It includes translations from the Yiddish of a short story and a lecture by the American Nobel laureate Isaac Bashevis Singer—still the only Yiddish writer to win the Nobel Prize in Literature—and examples of poetry, fiction, and literary essays by many equally talented but less widely celebrated Yiddish writers, including Chaim Grade, Jacob Glatstein, Anna Margolin, Blume Lempel, Peretz Fishbein, and Celia Dropkin. Almost all American Yiddish writers of that generation were born in Europe, and they naturally drew upon European models as well as Anglo-American ones in developing their verse and prose. It's not surprising that their narratives frequently take up the experience of dislocation, whether by explicitly telling stories about being an émigré in a land with little patience for the past, or more implicitly by exploring the complications faced by Jews and others in the twentieth century.

The fifth part of this anthology, "Oy, the Children!," considers the descendants of Yiddish speakers, who went on to roles of increasing prominence in American culture. Inheritors of the immigrants' pathos, their offspring built upon that legacy to make their own marks. In many cases, like Cynthia Ozick's story "Envy: or, Yiddish in America" (1968) or Joan Micklin Silver's film *Hester Street*, they did so by depicting the experiences of Yiddish speakers; artists who did so include novelist Michael Chabon and playwright Paula Vogel, both of them winners of the Pulitzer Prize. In other cases—for example, Hollywood actors Leonard Nimoy and Fyvush Finkel—they distilled the humor or charm of their Yiddish-speaking families and milieus and transformed them in one way or another for wider consumption. The section also includes a story-within-a-story by Art Spiegelman that is part of *Maus* (1991), an extraordinarily influential graphic novel about the Holocaust in which the characters are depicted as mice, cats, dogs, and pigs. Other comics by Liana Finck and Stan Mack showcase the way Jews in America have gone from being only the "People of the Book" to also being the "People of the Graphic Book." Among other things, there has been a veritable explosion in Yiddish-related children's books, to mention only one aspect of the intense creativity with which Askhenazim have married the word with the image in recent decades. This section showcases the way the torch moved on from the immigrant generation to its descendants.

Finally, the sixth and last section of the anthology, "The Other Americas," explores Yiddish as it flourished not just in the United States but through the American continent, from Canada to Argentina. (The word "America" comes from Amerigo—in Latin, Americus—Vespucci, the Italian cartographer, navigator, financier, and explorer who in 1501–02 sailed to Brazil and the West Indies.) The language thrived in these regions, too, and continued to link Jews who had come from the same communities in Europe but found themselves in very different situations after immigration. These selections help to suggest some of the ways in which the story of Yiddish in the United States wasn't unique but rather part of a larger set of phenomena that involved the establishment of Jewish communities throughout the Diaspora.

Each of the entries is introduced with a brief contextual headnote, and a time line presents some fascinating and representative historical events—but, again, this isn't a history. It's most of all meant to be a grab bag, an opportunity for readers to get a little lost and to discover something that they weren't expecting. It showcases the rich diversity of Yiddish voices in America and of the American culture influenced and inspired by, and created as a result of, Yiddish and its speakers and their descendants. They pushed Yiddish—its sound, its sensibility—to utterly unexpected regions in the continuation of its epic story. By doing so, they have changed America.

Finally, a note on style: the pieces included in this anthology come from various historical periods. In general, we follow the YIVO transliteration system unless an individual author has chosen otherwise. Yiddish words not already accepted in standardized English are italicized, except again when writers opt for an individualized approach.

ILAN STAVANS AND JOSH LAMBERT

Time Line

YIDDISH IN AMERICA

1880s Eastern European Jews begin to immigrate to America in large numbers. (The first group of Sephardic Jews settled in New Amsterdam from Brazil in 1654, and German Jews arrived in the 1840s.)

1888 Bernard Weinstein and Morris Hillquit establish the *Fareynikte Yidishe Geverkshaftn* (United Hebrew Trades) to organize Jewish labor.

1897 *Forverts*, a Socialist Yiddish-language daily published in New York City, appears. It is a successor of *Di arheter-tsaytung* (*The Worker's Newspaper*), founded seven years earlier. Abraham Cahan would become its most distinguished editor, and it would reach a circulation of over 200,000.

1899 Leo Weiner, an instructor in Slavic Languages at Harvard, publishes a pioneering study, in English, titled *The History of Yiddish Literature in the Nineteenth Century*.

1902 On May 15, 20,000 protestors, led by Fanny Levy and Sarah Edelson, protest the high price of kosher meat in New York; more than sixty women would be arrested for their part in the protest, but it was largely successful.

1909 The "Uprising of the 20,000," a major strike of garment workers, is led by the International Ladies' Garment Workers Union, inspired in part by a speech by the activist and laborer Clara Lemlich.

1911 The Triangle Shirtwaist Factory fire, on March 25, kills 146 workers, many of them Yiddish-speaking Jews, and exposes unsafe working conditions.

1916 Tens of thousands of mourners attend the funeral of Sholem Aleichem, and his will is printed in the *New York Times* and read into the Congressional Record.

1917   Emma Goldman, a Yiddish-speaking anarchist activist and the editor of *Mother Earth*, is deported to Russia for advocating against the draft.

1919   Three Yiddish poets—A. Leyeles, Jacob Glatstein, and N. B. Minkov—publish the first issue of *In zikh* (*In Oneself*), a journal dedicated to a new poetic practice, with a manifesto explaining their aims.

1923   Sholem Asch's controversial Yiddish play *God of Vengeance* (1906), which includes a scene in which two women kiss, opens on Broadway, in English translation; the cast, director, and producer are arrested on indecency charges.

1925   YIVO, *Yidisher Visnshaftlekher Institut* (Yiddish Scientific Institute) is established, with its headquarters in Vilnius, Lithuania. It will soon have branches in Berlin, Warsaw, and eventually New York, where its library will contain 350,000 books and extraordinary archival materials.

1927   The *Arbeter Ring* (Workmen's Circle), a major Yiddish organization, opens Camp Kinder Ring, a summer camp, in Hopewell Junction, New York.

1931   Stella Adler, whose acting career began in her parents' celebrated Yiddish theater troupe, joins the Group Theatre, a legendary New York–based theater company influenced by Konstantin Stanislavski.

1934   Henry Roth publishes the English-language novel *Call It Sleep*, about a boy growing up in a Yiddish-speaking family on the Lower East Side.

1935   Isaac Bashevis Singer emigrates from Warsaw to New York.

1937   A song written by Jacob Jacobs and Sholom Secunda for the Yiddish theater becomes a massive international hit in a cover by the Andrews Sisters, "Bei Mir Bist Du Schön."

1946   The English translation of Sholem Asch's novel *East River* spends more than six months on the *New York Times* bestseller list.

1953   *Partisan Review* publishes the story "Gimpel the Fool" (1945) by Isaac Bashevis Singer, in a translation by Saul Bellow.

1959 Uriel Weinreich is appointed assistant professor of Yiddish language, literature, and culture at Columbia University.

1964 *Fiddler on the Roof*, a musical by Jerry Bock, Sheldon Harnick, and Joseph Stein, and based on the Yiddish stories of Sholem Aleichem, opens in New York. It will go on to break the record for the longest-running Broadway show, be adapted into a Hollywood film, and, in 2018, run in New York for the first time in Yiddish translation, directed by Joel Grey.

1967 Chaim Grade publishes the first volume of his novelistic masterpiece, *Tsemakh Atlas*, which will appear in English translation as *The Yeshiva* in 1976.

1968 Cynthia Ozick publishes the story "Envy: or, Yiddish in America" in *Commentary* magazine, and Leo Rosten publishes *The Joys of Yiddish*.

1973 Max Weinreich's *Geshikhte fun der yidisher shprakh* is published posthumously by YIVO in New York; it would appear in English translation as *The History of the Yiddish Language*, in four volumes, in 2008.

1976 Literary critic Irving Howe publishes *World of Our Fathers: The Journey of East European Jews to America and the Life They Found and Made*. It will receive the National Book Award.

1978 Isaac Bashevis Singer is awarded the Nobel Prize in Literature, the first and so far only Yiddish writer to receive the award.

1980 The Yiddish Book Center is founded by Aaron Lansky in Amherst, Massachusetts.

1990 *Forverts* launches an independent English-language edition under the name *The Forward*.

1991 *The Wall Street Journal* publishes its first-ever Yiddish headline: "*Der letster yidisher laynotayp in Amerike*" ("The Last Yiddish Linotype in America).

2005 The *Forverts* building on the Lower East Side, with the faces of Karl Marx and Friedrich Engels carved into its historic facade, is converted into luxury condos, some of which sell for more than $3 million.

2009   On December 3, Zackary Sholem Berger, a doctor, translator, and poet in Yiddish and English, creates what are thought to be the first-ever Yiddish-language posts on the social media network Twitter.

2018   The National Yiddish Theater Folksbiene's Yiddish-language version of *Fiddler on the Roof* (*Fidler afn dakh*), inspired by the novel by Sholem Aleichem, translated by Shraga Friedman (originally performed in Israel in 1965) and directed by Joel Grey, becomes an unlikely hit on Broadway.

די גאַנצע וועלט שטייט אויף דער שפיץ צונג.

Di gantse velt shteyt af der shpits tsung.

The entire world rests on the tip of the tongue.

—YIDDISH PROVERB

HOW YIDDISH CHANGED AMERICA AND HOW AMERICA CHANGED YIDDISH

PART I

Politics and Possibility

די זון שײַנט גלײַך אױף אָרעם און רײַך.

Di zun shaynt glaykh af orem un raykh.

The sun shines the same on rich and poor.

HOWEVER IMPROBABLE it may seem, the arrival of around two million Yiddish-speaking Jews from Central and Eastern Europe in North America, between the middle of the nineteenth century and the middle of the twentieth, has turned out to be one of the most profoundly influential modern migrations. It's an astonishing story. When those Jews first arrived in large numbers in North America, they came mostly from countries in which their economic and political disenfranchisement was taken for granted, places where a Jewish man could not freely choose where to live or what profession to pursue, and where the publishing of newspapers and magazines in the language he spoke, Yiddish, was subject to harsh censorship. (Jewish women were disenfranchised doubly, as Jews and as women.) Violent attacks on Jewish civilians in their homes and businesses—which came to be known as pogroms—were frequent enough, and received enough tacit government support, to add pervasive terror to a Jew's typical experience of life. Meanwhile, as other Jews gained civil rights in western Europe, even they looked back at the still-disenfranchised, increasingly impoverished Yiddish-speaking Jews of Eastern Europe as embarrassments or as a problem to be solved.

Once they got to America, Yiddish-speaking Jews faced a vastly different set of possibilities. While prejudice against them certainly persisted among their neighbors, there was less of a threat of violence for individual Jews. Economically and culturally, these Jews had the opportunity to create businesses and institutions that could benefit their communities and the world. And they did. Jewish entrepreneurs and families created companies, political parties, banks, unions, publications, hospitals, museums, universities, and many other institutions. In less than a century, the children and grandchildren of those first Yiddish-speaking immigrants were living an entirely different existence: whereas their grandparents had been some of the poorest and most politically disenfranchised people on the planet, by the 1970s Ashkenazi Jews were among the most financially successful and educated demographic group in the world's most powerful nation.

The texts gathered in this section reflect what it was like to live through this massive transformation, showing how Yiddish-speaking Jews and their descendants have reacted to the new possibilities that America offered them. For some, this was a chance to scrimp and save, to earn a better life for themselves and their descendants. For others, it was an opportunity to advocate for new political systems and new approaches to social and economic problems. Everything was up for grabs, and the question was: what's worth fighting and sacrificing for?

FURTHER READING

Tony Michels, *A Fire in Their Hearts: Yiddish Socialists in New York* (2005)
Lara Rabinovitch, Shiri Goren, and Hannah S. Pressman, eds., *Choosing Yiddish: New Frontiers of Language and Culture* (2012)

A Ghetto Wedding

ABRAHAM CAHAN

Born in Belarus, Abraham Cahan (1860–1951) was the longtime editor of Forverts, *the most important Yiddish daily newspaper in America. He also wrote novels, in English, and was an active Socialist politician. His books include* Yekel: A Tale of the New York Ghetto *(1896), the novel* The Rise of David Levinsky *(1917), and an autobiography, translated in part as* The Education of Abraham Cahan *(1969). The following story comes from* The Imported Bridegroom and Other Stories of the New York Ghetto *(1898).*

HAD YOU CHANCED to be in Grand Street on that starry February night, it would scarcely have occurred to you that the Ghetto was groaning under the culmination of a long season of enforced idleness and distress. The air was exhilaratingly crisp, and the glare of the cafés and millinery shops flooded it with contentment and kindly good will. The sidewalks were alive with shoppers and promenaders, and lined with peddlers.

Yet the dazzling, deafening chaos had many a tale of woe to tell. The greater part of the surging crowd was out on an errand of self-torture. Straying forlornly by inexorable window displays, men and women would pause here and there to indulge in a hypothetical selection, to feast a hungry eye upon the object of an imaginary purchase, only forthwith to pay for the momentary joy with all the pangs of awakening to an empty purse.

Many of the peddlers, too, bore piteous testimony to the calamity which was then preying upon the quarter. Some of them performed their task of yelling and gesticulating with the desperation of imminent ruin; others implored the passers-by for custom with the abject effect of begging alms; while in still others this feverish urgency was disguised by an air of martyrdom or of shamefaced unwantedness, as if peddling were beneath the dignity of their habitual occupations, and they had been driven to it by sheer famine—by the hopeless dearth of employment at their own trades.

One of these was a thick-set fellow of twenty-five or twenty-six, with honest, clever blue eyes. It might be due to the genial, inviting quality of his face that the Passover dishes whose praises he was sounding had greater attraction for some of the women with an "effectual demand" than those of his competitors. Still, his comparative success had not as yet reconciled him to his new calling. He was constantly gazing about for a possible passer-by of his acquaintance, and when one came in sight he would seek refuge from identification in closer communion with the crockery on his pushcart.

"Buy nice dishes for the holidays! Cheap and strong! Buy dishes for Passover!" When business was brisk, he sang with a bashful relish; when the interval between a customer and her successor was growing too long, his singsong would acquire a mournful ring that was suggestive of the psalm-chanting at an orthodox Jewish funeral.

He was a cap-blocker, and in the busy season his earnings ranged from ten to fifteen dollars a week. But he had not worked full time for over two years, and during the last three months he had not been able to procure a single day's employment.

Goldy, his sweetheart, too, who was employed in making knee breeches, had hardly work enough to pay her humble board and rent. Nathan, after much hesitation, was ultimately compelled to take to peddling; and the longed-for day of their wedding was put off from month to month.

They had become engaged nearly two years before; the wedding ceremony having been originally fixed for a date some three months later. Their joint savings then amounted to one hundred and twenty dollars—a sum quite adequate, in Nathan's judgment, for a modest, quiet celebration and the humble beginnings of a household establishment. Goldy, however, summarily and indignantly overruled him.

"One does not marry every day," she argued, "and when I have at last lived to stand under the bridal canopy with my predestined one, I will not do so like a beggar maid. Give me a respectable wedding, or none at all, Nathan, do you hear?"

It is to be noted that a "respectable wedding" was not merely a casual expression with Goldy. Like its antithesis, a "slipshod wedding," it played in her vocabulary the part of something like a well-established scientific term, with a meaning as clearly defined as that of "centrifugal force" or "geometrical progression." Now, a slipshod wedding was anything short of a gown of white satin and slippers to match; two carriages to bring the bride and the bridegroom to the ceremony, and one to take them to their bridal apartments; a wedding bard and a band of at least five musicians; a spacious ballroom crowded with dancers, and a feast of a hundred and fifty covers. As to furniture, she refused to consider any which did not include a pier-glass and a Brussels carpet.

Nathan contended that the items upon which she insisted would cost a sum far beyond their joint accumulations. This she met by the declaration that he had all along been bent upon making her the target of universal ridicule, and that she would rather descend into an untimely grave than be married in a slipshod manner. Here she burst out crying; and whether her tears referred to the untimely grave or to the slipshod wedding, they certainly seemed to strengthen the cogency of her argument; for Nathan at once proceeded to signify his surrender by a kiss, and when ignominiously repulsed he protested his determination to earn the necessary money to bring things to the standard which she held up so uncompromisingly.

Hard times set in. Nathan and Goldy pinched and scrimped; but all their heroic economies were powerless to keep their capital from dribbling down to less than one hundred dollars. The wedding was postponed again and again. Finally, the curse of utter idleness fell upon Nathan's careworn head. Their savings dwindled apace. In dismay they beheld the foundation of their happiness melt gradually away. Both were tired of boarding. Both longed for the bliss and economy of married life. They grew more impatient and restless every day, and Goldy made concession after concession. First the wedding supper was sacrificed; then the pier-mirror and the bard were stricken from the program; and these were eventually succeeded by the hired hall and the Brussels carpet.

After Nathan went into peddling, a few days before we first find him hawking chinaware on Grand Street, matters began to look brighter, and the spirits of our betrothed couple rose. Their capital, which had sunk to forty dollars, was increasing again, and Goldy advised waiting long enough for it to reach the sum necessary for a slipshod wedding and establishment.

It was nearly ten o'clock. Nathan was absently drawling his "Buy nice dishes for the holidays!" His mind was engrossed with the question of making peddling his permanent occupation.

10

Presently he was startled by a merry soprano mocking him: "Buy nice di-i-shes! Mind that you don't fall asleep murmuring like this. A big lot you can make!"

Nathan turned a smile of affectionate surprise upon a compact little figure, small to drollness, but sweet in the amusing grace of its diminutive outlines—an epitome of exquisite femininity. Her tiny face was as comically lovely as her form: her apple-like cheeks were firm as marble, and her inadequate nose protruded between them like the result of a hasty tweak; a pair of large, round black eyes and a thick-lipped little mouth inundating it all with passion and restless, good-natured shrewdness.

"Goldy! What brings you here?" Nathan demanded, with a fond look which instantly gave way to an air of discomfort. "You know I hate you to see me peddling."

"Are you really angry? Bite the feather bed, then. Where is the disgrace? As if you were the only peddler in America! I wish you were. Wouldn't you make heaps of money then! But you had better hear what does bring me here. Nathan, darling—dearest little heart, dearest little crown that you are, guess what a plan I have hit upon!" she exploded all at once. "Well, if you hear me out, and you don't say that Goldy has the head of a cabinet minister, then—well, then you will be a big hog, and nothing else."

And without giving him time to put in as much as an interjection, she rattled on, puffing for breath and smacking her lips for ecstasy. Was it not stupid of them to be racking their brains about the wedding while there was such a plain way of having both a "respectable" celebration and fine furniture—Brussels carpet, pier-glass, and all—with the money they now had on hand?

"Come, out with it, then," he said morosely.

But his disguised curiosity only whetted her appetite for tormenting him, and she declared her determination not to disclose her great scheme before they had reached her lodgings.

"You have been yelling long enough today, anyhow," she said, with abrupt sympathy. "Do you suppose it does not go to my very heart to think of the way you stand out in the cold screaming yourself hoarse?"

Half an hour later, when they were alone in Mrs. Volpiansky's parlor, which was also Goldy's bedroom, she set about emptying his pockets of the gross results of the day's business, and counting the money. This she did with a preoccupied, matter-of-fact air, Nathan submitting to the operation with fond and amused willingness; and the sum being satisfactory, she went on to unfold her plan.

"You see," she began, almost in a whisper, and with the mien of a care-worn, experience-laden old matron, "in a week or two we shall have about seventy-five dollars, shan't we? Well, what is seventy-five dollars? Nothing! We could just have the plainest furniture, and no wedding worth speaking of. Now, if we have no wedding, we shall get no presents, shall we?"

Nathan shook his head thoughtfully.

"Well, why shouldn't we be up to snuff and do this way? Let us spend all our money on a grand, respectable wedding, and send out a big lot of invitations, and then—well, won't uncle Leiser send us a carpet or a parlor set? And aunt Beile, and cousin Shapiro, and Charley, and Meyerke, and Wolfke, and Bennie, and Sore-Gitke—won't each present something or other, as is the custom among respectable people? May God give us a lump of good luck as big as the wedding present each of them is sure to send us! Why, did not Beilke get a fine carpet from uncle when she got married? And am I not a nearer relative than she?"

She paused to search his face for a sign of approval, and, fondly smoothing a tuft of his dark hair into place, she went on to enumerate the friends to be invited and the gifts to be expected from them.

"So you see," she pursued, "we will have both a respectable wedding that we shan't have to be ashamed of in after years and the nicest things we could get if we spent two hundred dollars. What do you say?"

"What *shall* I say?" he returned dubiously.

The project appeared reasonable enough, but the investment struck him as rather hazardous. He pleaded for caution, for delay; but as he had no tangible argument to produce, while she stood her ground with the firmness of conviction, her victory was an easy one.

12

"It will all come right, depend upon it," she said coaxingly. "You just leave everything to me. Don't be uneasy, Nathan," she added. "You and I are orphans, and you know the Uppermost does not forsake a bride and bridegroom who have nobody to take care of them. If my father were alive, it would be different," she concluded, with a disconsolate gesture.

There was a pathetic pause. Tears glistened in Goldy's eyes. "May your father rest in a bright paradise," Nathan said feelingly. "But what is the use of crying? Can you bring him back to life? I will be a father to you."

"If God be pleased," she assented. "Would that mamma, at least—may she be healthy a hundred and twenty years—would that she, at least, were here to attend our wedding! Poor mother! it will break her heart to think that she has not been foreordained by the Uppermost to lead me under the canopy."

There was another desolate pause, but it was presently broken by Goldy, who exclaimed with unexpected buoyancy, "By the way, Nathan, guess what I did! I am afraid you will call me braggart and make fun of me, but I don't care," she pursued, with a playful pout, as she produced a strip of carpet from her pocketbook. "I went into a furniture store, and they gave me a sample three times as big as this. I explained in my letter to mother that this is the kind of stuff that will cover my floor when I am married. Then I enclosed the sample in the letter, and sent it all to Russia."

Nathan clapped his hands and burst out laughing. "But how do you know that is just the kind of carpet you will get for your wedding present?" he demanded, amazed as much as amused.

"How do I know? As if it mattered what sort of carpet! I can just see mamma going the rounds of the neighbors, and showing off the 'costly tablecloth' her daughter will trample upon. Won't she be happy!"

Over a hundred invitations, printed in as luxurious a black and gold as ever came out of an Essex Street hand press, were sent out for an early date in April. Goldy and Nathan paid a month's rent in advance for three rooms on the second floor of a Cherry Street tenement house. Goldy regarded the rent as unusually low, and the apartments as the finest on the East Side.

"Oh, haven't I got lovely rooms!" she would ejaculate, beaming with the consciousness of the pronoun. Or, "You ought to see my rooms! How much do you pay for yours? Or again, "I have made up my mind to have my parlor in the rear room. It is as light as the front one, anyhow, and I want that for a kitchen, you know. What do you say?" For hours together she would go on talking nothing but rooms, rent, and furniture; every married couple who had recently moved into new quarters, or were about to do so, seemed bound to her by the ties of a common cause; in her imagination, humanity was divided into those who were interested in the question of rooms, rent, and furniture and those who were not—the former, of whom she was one, constituting the superior category; and whenever her eye fell upon a bill announcing rooms to let, she would experience something akin to the feeling with which an artist, in passing, views some accessory of his art.

It is customary to send the bulkier wedding presents to a young couple's apartments a few days before they become man and wife, the closer relatives and friends of the betrothed usually settling among themselves what piece of furniture each is to contribute. Accordingly, Goldy gave up her work a week in advance of the day set for the great event, in order that she might be on hand to receive the things when they arrived.

She went to the empty little rooms, with her lunch, early in the morning, and kept anxious watch till after nightfall, when Nathan came to take her home.

A day passed, another, and a third, but no expressman called out her name. She sat waiting and listening for the rough voice, but in vain.

"Oh, it is too early, anyhow. I am a fool to be expecting anything so soon at all," she tried to console herself. And she waited another hour, and still another; but no wedding gift made its appearance.

"Well, there is plenty of time, after all; wedding presents do come a day or two before the ceremony," she argued; and again she waited, and again strained her ears, and again her heart rose in her throat.

The vacuity of the rooms, freshly cleaned, scrubbed, and smelling of whitewash, began to frighten her. Her overwrought mind was filled with sounds which her over-strained ears did not hear. Yet there she sat on the window sill, listening and listening for an expressman's voice.

"Hush, hush—sh, hush—sh—sh!" whispered the walls; the corners muttered awful threats; her heart was ever and anon contracted with fear; she often thought herself on the brink of insanity; yet she stayed on, waiting, waiting, waiting.

At the slightest noise in the hall she would spring to her feet, her heart beating wildly, only presently to sink in her bosom at finding it to be some neighbor or a peddler; and so frequent were these violent throbbings that Goldy grew to imagine herself a prey to heart disease. Nevertheless the fifth day came, and she was again at her post, waiting, waiting, waiting for her wedding gifts. And what is more, when Nathan came from business, and his countenance fell as he surveyed the undisturbed emptiness of the rooms, she set a merry face against his rueful inquiries, and took to bantering him as a woman quick to lose heart, and to painting their prospects in roseate hues, until she argued herself, if not him, into a more cheerful view of the situation.

On the sixth day an expressman did pull up in front of the Cherry Street tenement house, but he had only a cheap huge rocking chair for Goldy and Nathan; and as it proved to be the gift of a family who had been set down for nothing less than a carpet or a parlor set, the joy and hope which its advent had called forth turned to dire disappointment and despair. For nearly an hour Goldy sat mournfully rocking and striving to picture how delightful it would have been if all her anticipations had come true.

Presently there arrived a flimsy plush-covered little corner table. It could not have cost more than a dollar. Yet it was the gift of a near friend, who had been relied upon for a pier-glass or a bedroom set. A little later a cheap alarm clock and an ice-box were brought in. That was all.

Occasionally Goldy went to the door to take in the entire effect; but the more she tried to view the parlor as half finished, the more cruelly did the few lonely and mismatched things emphasize the remaining emptiness of the apartments: whereupon she would sink into her rocker and sit motionless, with a drooping head, and then desperately fall to swaying to and fro, as though bent upon swinging herself out of her woebegone, wretched self.

Still, when Nathan came, there was a triumphant twinkle in her eye, as she said, pointing to the gifts, "Well, mister, who was right? It is not very bad for a start, is it? You know most people do send their wedding presents after the ceremony—why, of course!" she added, in a sort of confidential way. "Well, we have invited a big crowd, and all people of no mean sort, thank God; and who ever heard of a lady or a gentleman attending a respectable wedding and having a grand wedding supper, and then cheating the bride and the bridegroom out of their present?"

The evening was well advanced; yet there were only a score of people in a hall that was used to hundreds.

Everybody felt ill at ease, and ever and anon looked about for the possible arrival of more guests. At ten o'clock the dancing preliminary to the ceremony had not yet ceased, although the few waltzers looked as if they were scared by the ringing echoes of their own footsteps amid the austere solemnity of the surrounding void and the depressing sheen of the dim expanse of floor.

The two fiddles, the cornet, and the clarinet were shrieking as though for pain, and the malicious superabundance of gaslight was fiendishly sneering at their tortures. Weddings and entertainments being scarce in the Ghetto, its musicians caught the contagion of misery: hence the greedy, desperate gusto with which the band plied their instruments.

At last it became evident that the assemblage was not destined to be larger than it was, and that it was no use delaying the ceremony. It was, in fact, an open secret among those present that by far the greater number of the invited friends were kept away by lack of employment: some having their presentable clothes in the pawn shop; others avoiding the expense of a wedding present, or simply being too cruelly borne down by their cares to have a mind for the excitement of a wedding; indeed, some even thought it wrong of Nathan to have the celebration during such a period of hard times, when everybody was out of work.

It was a little after ten when the bard—a tall, gaunt man, with a grizzly beard and a melancholy face—donned his skullcap, and, advancing toward the dancers, called out in a synagogue intonation, "Come, ladies, let us veil the bride!"

An odd dozen of daughters of Israel followed him and the musicians into a little side room where Goldy was seated between her two brideswomen (the wives of two men who were to attend upon the groom). According to the orthodox custom she had fasted the whole day, and as a result of this and of her gnawing grief, added to the awe-inspiring scene she had been awaiting, she was pale as death; the effect being heightened by the wreath and white gown she wore. As the procession came filing in, she sat blinking her round dark eyes in dismay, as if the bard were an executioner come to lead her to the scaffold.

The song or address to the bride usually partakes of the qualities of prayer and harangue, and includes a melancholy meditation upon life and death; lamenting the deceased members of the young woman's family, bemoaning her own woes, and exhorting her to discharge her sacred duties as a wife, mother, and servant of God. Composed in verse and declaimed in a solemn, plaintive recitative, often broken by the band's mournful refrain, it is sure to fulfill its mission of eliciting tears even when hearts are brimful of glee. Imagine, then, the funereal effect which it produced at Goldy's wedding ceremony.

The bard, half starved himself, sang the anguish of his own heart; the violins wept, the clarinet moaned, the cornet and the double-bass groaned, each reciting the sad tale of its poverty-stricken master. He began:

> Silence, good women, give heed to *my* verses!
> Tonight, bride, thou dost stand before the Uppermost.
> Pray to him to bless thy union,
> To let thee and thy mate live a hundred and twenty peaceful years,
> To give you your daily bread,
> To keep hunger from your door.

Several women, including Goldy, burst into tears, the others sadly lowering their gaze. The band sounded a wailing chord, and the whole audience broke into loud, heartrending weeping.

The bard went on sternly:

> Wail, bride, wail!
> This is a time of tears.
> Think of thy past days:
> Alas! they are gone to return nevermore.

Heedless of the convulsive sobbing with which the room resounded, he continued to declaim, and at last, his eye flashing fire and his voice tremulous with emotion, he sang out in a dismal, uncanny high key:

> And thy good mother beyond the seas,
> And thy father in his grave
> Near where thy cradle was rocked,
> Weep, bride, weep!
> Though his soul is better off
> Than we are here underneath
> In dearth and cares and ceaseless pangs,
> Weep, sweet bride, weep!

Then, in the general outburst that followed the extemporaneous verse, there was a cry—"The bride is fainting! Water! quick!"

"Murderer that you are!" flamed out an elderly matron, with an air of admiration for the bard's talent as much as of wrath for the far-fetched results it achieved.

Goldy was brought to, and the rest of the ceremony passed without accident. She submitted to everything as in a dream. When the bridegroom, escorted by two attendants, each carrying a candelabrum holding lighted candles, came to place the veil over her face, she stared about as though she failed to realize the situation or to recognize Nathan. When, keeping time to the plaintive strains of a time-honored tune, she was led, blindfolded, into the large hall and stationed beside the bridegroom under the red canopy, and then marched around him seven times, she obeyed instructions and moved about with the passivity of a hypnotic. After the Seven Blessings had been recited, when the cantor, gently lifting the end of her veil, presented the wineglass to her lips, she tasted its contents with the air of an invalid taking medicine. Then she felt the ring slip down her finger, and heard Nathan say, "Be thou dedicated to me by this ring, according to the laws of Moses and Israel."

Whereupon she said to herself, "Now I am a married woman!" But somehow, at this moment the words were meaningless sounds to her. She knew she was married, but could not realize what it implied. As Nathan crushed the wineglass underfoot, and the band struck up a cheerful melody, and the gathering shouted, "Good luck! Good luck!" and clapped their hands, while the older women broke into a wild hop, Goldy felt the relief of having gone through a great ordeal. But still she was not distinctly aware of any change in her position.

Not until fifteen minutes later, when she found herself in the basement, at the head of one of three long tables, did the realization of her new self strike her consciousness full in the face, as it were.

The dining room was nearly as large as the dancing hall on the floor above. It was as brightly illuminated, and the three tables, which ran almost its entire length, were set for a hundred and fifty guests. Yet there were barely twenty to occupy them. The effect was still more depressing than in the dancing room. The vacant benches and the untouched covers still more agonizingly exaggerated the emptiness of the room, in which the sorry handful of a company lost themselves.

Goldy looked at the rows of plates, spoons, forks, knives, and they weighed her down with the cold dazzle of their solemn, pompous array.

"I am not the Goldy I used to be," she said to herself. "I am a married woman, like mamma, or auntie, or Mrs. Volpiansky. And we have spent every cent we had on this grand wedding, and now we are left without money for furniture, and there are no guests to send us any, and the supper will be thrown out, and everything is lost, and I am to blame for it all!"

The glittering plates seemed to hold whispered converse and to exchange winks and grins at her expense. She transferred her glance to the company, and it appeared as if they were vainly forcing themselves to partake of the food—as though they, too, were looked out of countenance by that ruthless sparkle of the unused plates.

Nervous silence hung over the room, and the reluctant jingle of the score of knives and forks made it more awkward, more enervating, every second. Even the bard had not the heart to break the stillness by the merry rhymes he had composed for the occasion.

Goldy was overpowered. She thought she was on the verge of another fainting spell, and, shutting her eyes and setting her teeth, she tried to imagine herself dead. Nathan, who was by her side, noticed it. He took her hand under the table, and, pressing it gently, whispered, "Don't take it to heart. There is a God in heaven."

She could not make out his words, but she felt their meaning. As she was about to utter some phrase of endearment, her heart swelled in her throat, and a piteous, dovelike, tearful look was all the response she could make.

By-and-by, however, when the foaming lager was served, tongues were loosened, and the bard, although distressed by the meager collection in store for him, but stirred by an ardent desire to relieve the insupportable wretchedness of the evening, outdid himself in offhand acrostics and witticisms. Needless to say that his efforts were thankfully rewarded with unstinted laughter; and as the room rang with merriment, the gleaming rows of undisturbed plates also seemed to join in the general hubbub of mirth, and to be laughing a hearty, kindly laugh.

Presently, amid a fresh outbreak of deafening hilarity, Goldy bent close to Nathan's ear and exclaimed with sobbing vehemence, "My husband! My husband! My husband!"

"My wife!" he returned in her ear.

"Do you know what you are to me now?" she resumed. "A husband! And I am your wife! Do you know what it means—do you, do you, Nathan?" she insisted, with frantic emphasis.

"I do, my little sparrow; only don't worry over the wedding presents."

It was after midnight, and even the Ghetto was immersed in repose. Goldy and Nathan were silently wending their way to the three empty little rooms where they were destined to have their first joint home. They wore the wedding attire which they had rented for the evening: he a swallow-tail coat and high hat, and she a white satin gown and slippers, her head uncovered—the wreath and veil done up in a newspaper, in Nathan's hand.

They had gone to the wedding in carriages, which had attracted large crowds both at the point of departure, and in front of the hall; and of course they had expected to make their way to their new home in a similar "respectable" manner. Toward the close of the last dance, after supper, they found, however, that some small change was all they possessed in the world.

The last strains of music were dying away. The guests, in their hats and bonnets, were taking leave. Everybody seemed in a hurry to get away to his own world, and to abandon the young couple to their fate.

Nathan would have borrowed a dollar or two of some friend. "Let us go home as behooves a bride and bridegroom," he said. "There is a God in heaven: he will not forsake us."

But Goldy would not hear of betraying the full measure of their poverty to their friends. "No! no!" she retorted testily. "I am not going to let you pay a dollar and a half for a few blocks' drive, like a Fifth Avenue noble-man. We can walk," she pursued, with the grim determination of one bent upon self-chastisement. "A poor woman who dares spend every cent on a wedding must be ready to walk after the wedding."

When they found themselves alone in the deserted street, they were so overcome by a sense of loneliness, of a kind of portentous, haunting emptiness, that they could not speak. So on they trudged in dismal silence; she leaning upon his arm, and he tenderly pressing her to his side.

Their way lay through the gloomiest and roughest part of the Seventh Ward. The neighborhood frightened her, and she clung closer to her escort. At one corner they passed some men in front of a liquor saloon.

"Look at dem! Look at dem! A sheeny fellar an' his bride, I'll betch ye!" shouted a husky voice. "Jes' comin' from de weddin'."

21

"She ain't no bigger 'n a peanut, is she?" The simile was greeted with a horse-laugh.

"Look a here, young fellar, what's de madder wid carryin' dat lady of yourn in your vest pocket?"

When Nathan and Goldy were a block away, something like a potato or a carrot struck her in the back. At the same time the gang of loafers on the corner broke into boisterous merriment. Nathan tried to face about, but she restrained him.

"Don't! They might kill you!" she whispered, and relapsed into silence.

He made another attempt to disengage himself, as if for a desperate attack upon her assailants, but she nestled close to his side and held him fast, her every fiber tingling with the consciousness of the shelter she had in him.

"Don't mind them, Nathan," she said.

And as they proceeded on their dreary way through a somber, impoverished street, with here and there a rustling tree—a melancholy witness of its better days—they felt a stream of happiness uniting them, as it coursed through the veins of both, and they were filled with a blissful sense of oneness the like of which they had never tasted before. So happy were they that the gang behind them, and the bare rooms toward which they were directing their steps, and the miserable failure of the wedding, all suddenly appeared too insignificant to engage their attention—paltry matters alien to their new life, remote from the enchanted world in which they now dwelt.

The very notion of a relentless void abruptly turned to a beatific sense of their own seclusion, of there being only themselves in the universe, to live and to delight in each other.

"Don't mind them, Nathan darling," she repeated mechanically, conscious of nothing but the tremor of happiness in her voice.

"I should give it to them!" he responded, gathering her still closer to him. "I should show them how to touch my Goldy, my pearl, my birdie!"

They dived into the denser gloom of a sidestreet.

A gentle breeze ran past and ahead of them, proclaiming the bride and the bridegroom. An old tree whispered overhead its tender felicitations.

The First Shock

from **World of Our Fathers**

IRVING HOWE

Irving Howe (1920–1993), a literary critic, cultural historian, co-founder and editor of the journal Dissent, *and a prominent figure in the Democratic Socialists of America, taught at the City University of New York. He was the author of numerous books, including studies on Sherwood Anderson, William Faulkner, and Thomas Hardy, the book* Leon Trotsky *(1978), and* A Margin of Hope: An Intellectual Autobiography *(1982). An anthology of his work is featured in* Selected Writings: 1950–1990 *(1990). The following comes from* World of Our Fathers: The Journey of the Eastern European Jews to America and the Life They Found and Made *(1976), which received the National Book Award.*

IN THE EARLY EIGHTIES the Jewish quarter was still small, with much of the East Side under the control of Irish and German immigrants.

> A few Jewish families had moved into houses along East Broadway at Clinton and Montgomery Streets. Only a few years earlier this had been a purely native American section. . . . The number of Jewish families diminished as one moved away from East Broadway toward Henry to Madison, Monroe and finally to Cherry Street where there were no Jews at all. In the other direction, the Jewish quarter . . . extended north to Delancey Street. [Abraham Cahan, *The Education of Abraham Cahan*, ed. Leon Stein (Philadelphia, 1969), pp. 219–220.]

East Broadway, in those days an imposing avenue with wide sidewalks and distinguished homes, was often called *ulitsa* (the Russian word for street) because the Jewish intellectuals who made it their center felt it was more cultivated to speak Russian than Yiddish. By 1883, we hear of great over-crowding in Essex and York Streets among Russian and Polish Jews. It was said that in one house of sixteen apartments, of two rooms each, about two hundred people were quartered. . . . On the East Side the Jews have pressed up through the [whole area] driving the Germans before them."

Within a few years, the Lower East Side became the most densely populated area in the city. By 1890 it had 522 inhabitants per acre, by 1900 more than 700. The density of the Tenth Ward, reported the University Settlement Society shortly after the turn of the century, was greater than that of the worst sections of Bombay. And since many small shops were crammed into this area, the crowding by day was scarcely less extreme than by night. One of the worst spots was "the Pig Market," as the Jews called it, on Hester near Ludlow, where everything but pigs could be bought off pushcarts—peaches at a penny a quart, "damaged" eggs, eyeglasses for thirty-five cents, old coats for fifty cents—and where greenhorns would bunch up in the morning to wait for employers looking for cheap labor.

In 1890, within the small space bounded by the Bowery on the west, the river and its warehouses on the east, Houston on the north, and Monroe on the south, there were some two dozen Christian churches, a dozen synagogues (most Jewish congregations were storefronts or in tenements), about fifty factories and shops (exclusive of garment establishments, most of which were west of the Bowery or hidden away in cellars and flats), ten large public buildings, twenty public and parochial schools—and one tiny park, on Grand and East Broadway. Gangs of German boys pressed down from the north, Irish from the south, a dominant impression of the Jewish quarter, shared by immigrants and visitors alike, was of fierce congestion, a place in which the bodily pressures of other people, their motions and smells and noises, seemed always to be assaulting one. Of space for privacy and solitude there was none:

"Curse you, emigration," cried Abraham Cahan in a letter written for a Russian newspaper in 1882. "Accursed are the conditions that have brought you forth! How many lives have you broken, how many brave and mighty have you rubbed out like dust!" Such sentiments were not at all unusual in the eighties and nineties. Coming to America with inflamed hopes, some of the immigrants became demoralized and others permanently undone. Not only was their physical situation wretched—that, after all, they had long been accustomed to. Far worse was the spiritual confusion that enclosed their lives.

No controlling norms or institutions, neither rabbinical nor communal, could now be accepted as once they had been; no myths of tradition or even slogans of revolt. Those who wanted to remain faithful to traditional Judaism—and in these years many did—had now to make a special effort. Pressures of the city, the shop, the slum, all made it terribly hard to stay with the old religious ethic. The styles and rituals of traditional Judaism had been premised on a time scheme far more leisurely, a life far less harried than urban America demanded. As for the new ethic of materialist individualism, what could this mean to a garment worker who spent sixty hours a week in a sweatshop, physically present in America yet barely touched by its language, its traditions, its privileges? Those immigrants who stood fast by religion found whatever solace it could offer, those who turned to secularism gained the consolations of new theory. But the masses of immigrants, who rarely thought to call religion into question yet found it harder and harder to regard it as a system illuminating the totality of existence—what was left to them? Fragments of a culture, a parochialism bred by centuries of isolation, and a heritage of fear, withdrawal, insularity. Except for those who clung to faith or grappled toward ideology, the early immigrants consisted of people who were stranded—stranded socially, morally, psychologically. That all this was happening at the very time Jewish life in eastern Europe had begun to experience a secular renewal did not change things very much. Few immigrants in America had a close knowledge of the east European renewal; it was too far away to brighten or sustain their lives. All they could bring to their experience in America—and after the first shattering years, it would prove to be a great deal—was that shared tenacity with which Jews had always clung to life.

Letter to the Forverts Editor

YESHAYE KATOVSKI

In the summer of 1936, articles about a number of female athletes competing at the Berlin Summer Olympics appeared in the New York Times, *which reported that some of the women had, in fact, previously been men but had undergone "minor operations." Likewise, the* Forverts *reported to its Yiddish-language readership on news of an American woman who had undergone a similar procedure. In November, the editors received this letter:*

Not long ago I read a story in the Forverts that took place in America, about how a girl became a man. But that's not news to the people in the town where I'm from. Permit me to tell the story in your paper. In our shtetl of Krivozer, Ukraine, everyone knew Beyle, the girl who sold herring, geese, and other foodstuffs. She was a tall redhead and sturdily built. She also spoke with a deep bass voice and walked about with hard and heavy steps. The way she carried herself always brought forth an uncertain feeling: something like, she's not quite a woman, but also not quite a man. When she was still a child, her father would often take her to see the Tolner Rebbe, Reb Dovidl, and sometimes to the Sadigura Rebbe, to ask for help. The only answer he ever got was "God will help, God will help." The father would return home anguished and unhappy. In the meantime, the years flew by and Beyle grew, too, until she reached the age of 23. One fine morning, Beyle left for Odessa, where she was introduced to an important professor. She spent a long time under his care, under which Beyle eventually became a man. The story was well known and was in all the papers—all Russia talked of it. In the shtetl, we waited impatiently for her return. And on the day when Beyle was to arrive, half the shtetl ran to the bridge to greet her, or better said, to greet him. And she wasn't called Beyle anymore: Now she was Berel. And when we saw "her," it was as if we were stunned: Before our eyes was a handsome, healthy, redheaded man. Anyone who didn't know Beyle previously would never have known that he had been a girl. From then on in the shtetl, "she" was called Berel-Beyle. With the help of the professor, the government freed him from military service. Berel-Beyle soon learned to daven and was in synagogue every day. Later on, he got married to an old girlfriend, Black Rachel, who was a nice girl. In our shtetl, Berel-Beyle always had a good name as a fine, upstanding Jew.

Yeshaye Katovski
2817 West 32nd St., Brooklyn, New York

TRANSLATED BY EDDY PORTNOY

Against Marriage as Private Possession

EMMA GOLDMAN

Emma Goldman (1869–1940) was one of the most influential radical speakers and thinkers of the late nineteenth and early twentieth centuries. A native Yiddish speaker who was born in Kovno, Lithuania, she regularly gave speeches in Yiddish even after gaining fame as an English-language orator. Often jailed and eventually deported from the United States, she was the founder and editor of a journal, Mother Earth, *and among many other publications, wrote an autobiography in two volumes,* Living My Life *(1931 and 1934). The following is a speech she delivered in New York City, on July 1897.*

HOW MUCH SORROW, misery, humiliation; how many tears and curses; what agony and suffering has this word brought to humanity. From its very birth, up to our present day, men and women grow under the iron yoke of our marriage institution, and there seems to be no relief, no way out of it.

At all times, and in all ages, have the suppressed striven to break the chains of mental and physical slavery. After thousands of noble lives have been sacrificed at the stake and on the gallows, and others have perished in prisons, or at the merciless hands of inquisitions, have the ideas of those brave heroes been accomplished. Thus have religious dogmas, feudalism, and black slavery been abolished, and new ideas, more progressive, broader, and clearer, have come to the front, and again we see poor downtrodden humanity fighting for its rights and independence. But the crudest, most tyrannical of all institutions—marriage—stands firm as ever, and woe unto those who dare to even doubt its sacredness. Its mere discussion is enough to infuriate not only Christians and conservatives alone, but even Liberals, Freethinkers, and Radicals. What is it that causes all these people to uphold marriage? What makes them cling to this prejudice? (for it is nothing else but prejudice). It is because marriage relations are the foundation of private property, ergo, the foundation of our cruel and inhuman system. With wealth and superfluity on one side, and idleness, exploitation, poverty, starvation, and crime on the other, hence to abolish marriage means to abolish everything above mentioned. Some progressive people are trying to reform and better our marriage laws. They no longer permit the church to interfere in their matrimonial relations, others even go further, they marry free, that is without the consent of the law, but, nevertheless, this form of marriage is just as binding, just as "sacred," as the old form, because it is not the form or the kind of marriage relation we have, but the thing, the thing itself that is objectionable, hurtful, and degrading. It always gives the man the right and power over his wife, not only over her body, but also over her actions, her wishes; in fact, over her whole life. And how can it be otherwise?

Behind the relations of any individual man and woman to each other stands the historical age evolved relations between the two sexes in general, which have led up to the difference in the position and privileges of the two sexes today.

Two young people come together, but their relation is largely determined by causes over which they have no control. They know little of each other, society has kept both sexes apart, the boy and the girl have been brought up along different lines. Like Olive Schreiner says in her Story of an African Farm, "The boy has been taught to be, the girl to seem." Exactly; the boy is taught to be intelligent, bright, clever, strong, athletic, independent, and self-reliant; to develop his natural faculties, to follow his passions and desires. The girl has been taught to dress, to stand before the looking glass and admire herself, to control her emotions, her passions, her wishes, to hide her mental defects, and to combine what little intelligence and ability she has to one point, and that is, the quickest and best way to angle a husband, to get profitably married. And so it has come that the two sexes hardly understand each other's nature, that their mental interest and occupations are different. Public opinion separates their rights and duties, their honor and dishonor very strictly from each other. The subject of sex is a sealed book to the girl, because she has been given to understand that it is impure, immoral, and indecent to even mention the sex question. To the boy it is a book whose pages have brought him disease and a secret vice, and in some cases ruin and death.

Among the rich class it has long been out of fashion to fall in love. Men of society marry, after a life of debauchery and lust, to build up their ruined constitution. Others again have lost their capital, in gambling sports or business speculation, and decide that an heiress would be just the thing they need, knowing well that the marriage tie will no way hinder them from squandering the income of their wealthy bride. The rich girl having been brought to be practical and sensible, and having been accustomed to live, breathe, eat, smile, walk, and dress only according to fashion, holds out her millions to some title, or to a man with a good social standing. She has one consolation, and that is, that society allows more freedom of action to a married woman and should she be disappointed in marriage she will be in a position to gratify her wishes otherwise. We know the walls of boudoirs and salons are deaf and dumb, and a little pleasure within these walls is no crime.

With the men and women among the working class, marriage is quite a different thing. Love is not so rare as among the upper class, and very often helps both to endure the disappointments and sorrows in life, but even here the majority of marriages last only for a short while, to be swallowed up in the monotony of the everyday life and the struggle for existence. Here also, the working man marries because he grows tired of a boardinghouse life, and out of a desire to build a home of his own, where he will find comfort. His main object, therefore, is to find a girl that will make a good cook and housekeeper; one that will look out only for his happiness, for his pleasure; one that will look up to him as her lord, her master, her defender, her supporter; the only ideal worthwhile living for. Another man hopes that the girl he'll marry will be able to work and help to put away a few cents for rainy days, but after a few months of so-called happiness he awakens to the bitter reality that his wife is soon to become a mother, that she cannot work, that the expenses grow bigger, and that while he before managed to get along with the small earnings allowed him by his "kind" master, this earning is not sufficient to support a family.

The girl who spent her childhood, and part of her womanhood, in the factory, feels her strength leaving her and pictures to herself the dreadful condition of ever having to remain a shop girl, never certain of her work, she is, therefore, compelled to look out for a man, a good husband, which means one who can support her, and give her a good home. Both, the man and the girl, marry for the same purpose, with the only exception that the man is not expected to give up his individuality, his name, his independence, whereas the girl has to sell herself, body and soul, for the pleasure of being someone's wife; hence they do not stand on equal terms, and where there is no equality there can be no harmony. The consequence is that shortly after the first few months, or to make all allowance possible, after the first year, both come to the conclusion that marriage is a failure.

As their conditions grow worse and worse, and with the increase of children the woman grows despondent, miserable, dissatisfied, and weak. Her beauty soon leaves her, and from hard work, sleepless nights, worry about the little ones, and disagreement and quarrels with her husband, she soon becomes a physical wreck and curses the moment that made her a poor man's wife. Such a dreary, miserable life is certainly not inclined to maintain love or respect for each other. The man can at least forget his misery in the company of a few friends; he can absorb himself in politics, or he can drown his misfortune in a glass of beer. The woman is chained to the house by a thousand duties; she cannot, like her husband, enjoy some recreation because she either has no means for it, or she is refused the same rights as her husband, by public opinion. She has to carry the cross with her until death, because our marriage laws know of no mercy, unless she wishes to lay bare her married life before the critical eye of Mrs. Grundy, and even then she can only break the chains which tie her to the man she hates if she takes all the blame on her own shoulders, and if she has enough to stand before the world disgraced for the rest of her life. How many have the courage to do that? Very few. Only now and then it comes like a flash of lightning that some woman, like the Princesse De Chimay, has had the pluck enough to break the conventional barriers and follow her heart's desire. But this exception is a wealthy woman, dependent upon no one. The poor woman has to consider her little ones; she is less fortunate than her rich sister, and yet the woman who remains in bondage is called respectable: never mind if her whole life is a long chain of lies, deceit, and treachery, she yet dares to look down with disgust upon her sisters who have been forged by society to sell their charms and affections on the street. No matter how poor, how miserable a married woman may be, she will yet think herself above the other, whom she calls a prostitute, who is an outcast, hated and despised by everyone, even those who do not hesitate to buy her embrace look upon the poor wretch as a necessary evil, and some goody-goody people even suggest to confine this evil to one district in New York, in order to "purify" all other districts of the city. What a farce! The reformers might as well demand that all the married inhabitants of New York be driven out, because they certainly do not stand morally higher than the street woman. The sole difference between her and the married woman is, that the one has sold herself into chattel slavery during life, for a home or a title, and the other one sells herself for the length of time she desires; she has the right to choose the man she bestows her affections upon, whereas the married woman has no right whatsoever; she must submit to the embrace of her lord, no matter how loathsome this embrace may be to her, she must obey his commands; she has to bear him children, even at the cost of her own strength and health; in work, she prostitutes herself every hour, every day of her life. I can find no other name for the horrid, humiliating, and degrading condition of my married sisters than prostitution of the worst kind, with the only exception that the one is legal, the other illegal.

I cannot deal with the few exceptional cases of marriage which are based on love, esteem, and respect; these exceptions only verify the rule. But whether legal or illegal, prostitution in any form is unnatural, hurtful and despicable, and I know only too well that the conditions cannot be changed until this infernal system is abolished, but I also know that it is not only the economic dependence of women which has caused her enslavement, but also her ignorance and prejudice, and I also know that many of my sisters could be made free even now, were it not for our marriage institutions which keep them in ignorance, stupidity, and prejudice. I therefore consider it my greatest duty to denounce marriage, not only the old form, but the so-called modern marriage, the idea of taking a wife and housekeeper, the idea of private possession of one sex by the other. I demand the independence of woman; her right to support herself; to live for herself; to love whomever she pleases, or as many as she pleases. I demand freedom for both sexes, freedom of action, freedom in love, and freedom in motherhood.

Do not tell me that all this can only be accomplished under Anarchy, we must first have free women at least, those women who are economically just as independent as their brothers are, and unless we have free women, we cannot have free mothers, and if mothers are not free, we cannot expect the young generation to assist us in the accomplishment of our aim, that is the establishment of an Anarchist society.

To you Freethinkers and Liberals who have abolished one God and created many whom you worship; you Radicals and Socialists, who still send you children to Sunday school, and all those who make concessions to the moral standard of today; to all of you I say that it is your lack of courage which makes you cling to and uphold marriage, and while you admit its absurdity in theory, you have not the energy to defy public opinion, and to live your own life practically. You prate of equality of sexes in a future Society, but you think it a necessary evil that woman should suffer at present. You say women are inferior and weaker, and instead of assisting them to grow stronger you help keep them in a degraded position. You demand exclusiveness for us, but you love variety and enjoy it wherever you can get a chance.

Marriage, the curse of so many centuries, the cause of jealousy, suicide and crime, must be abolished if we wish the young generation to grow to healthy, strong, and free men and women.

from Di goldene medine

WILLIAM GROPPER

William Gropper (1897–1977) was the American-born son of Eastern European Jewish immigrants, and he showed early talent as an artist. A committed radical, he contributed over a long and distinguished career to such English-language publications as The Liberator, The New Masses, *and* Vanity Fair, *and also published many bitterly satirical cartoons in the Communist Yiddish newspaper,* Freiheit. *The following cartoons appeared in a Yiddish-language collection of his work, ironically titled* Di goldene medine (The Golden Land), *published in 1927.*

— בעקערמאַנ'ס „גייסט"

"Piecework"

צוויי קבלת פנים'ס פאר סטרייקער

נאָך זייער באַפרייאונג

אויף דער פיקעט־ליין

Two receptions for strikers:
After their release.
At the picket-line.

א טרײקע

גאנגסטער פאליטישן סקעב

גראָפּעל

פּאָליטישן: — זאָלן מיר אלע אזוי לעבן ווי מיר זיינען „א גאָלדענער סעט"...

A troika: Scab, politician, gangster.

March of the Jobless Corps

DANIEL KAHN

Daniel Kahn (1978–) is a contemporary musician and actor who performs around the world with a band, Daniel Kahn & The Painted Bird, and uses Yiddish sources as inspiration for what he calls "tradaptations," updated English versions of Yiddish songs. The following draws on "Arbetsloze marsh," written by Mordechai Gebirtig (1877–1942), a leading Polish Jewish poet and songwriter who was murdered by the Nazis. Kahn released "March of the Jobless Corps" in the wake of the 2008 financial crisis and the Occupy Wall Street movement of 2011.

MARCH OF THE JOBLESS CORPS

Well one, two, three, four, join the Marching Jobless Corps
No work in the factories
No more manufacturing
All the tools are broke and rusted
Every wheel and window busted
Through the city streets we go
Idle as a CEO, idle as a CEO

Well one, two, three, four, join the Marching Jobless Corps
We don't have to pay no rent
Sleeping in a camping tent
Dumpster diving don't take money
Every bite we share with twenty
Let the yuppies have their wine
Bread and water suit us fine
Bread and water suit us fine

Well one, two, three, four, join the Marching Jobless Corps
Worked and paid our union dues
What did years of that produce?
Houses, cars, and other shit
For the rich's benefit
What do workers get for pay?
Hungry broke and thrown away
Hungry broke and thrown away

One, two, three, four, pick yourselves up off the floor
Unemployment marches on
So we'll sing a marching song
For a land, a world of justice
Where no cop or boss can bust us
There'll be work for every hand
In a new & better land
In a new & better land

ADAPTED BY MORDECHAI GEBIRTIG

Di Freiheit,
A Personal Reflection

PAUL BUHLE

Paul Buhle (1944–) taught for many years at Brown University and is the author and editor of dozens of books, mostly on the subjects of American radicalism and popular culture.

THE FIRST TIME I VISITED the *Freiheit* office was in 1976. I had just begun to take a class in Yiddish (I was the *goyisher kop*, the only one who had never heard the language at home). I had come to interview a few old-time radicals. About six years earlier, translator-writer Sid Resnick had been determinedly sending exchange copies of the *Freiheit*'s English-language section to *Radical America*, the history magazine I was publishing for the Students for a Democratic Society. I just didn't know what to make of the *Freiheit* in 1970, and I think I failed to reciprocate. So I was a little sheepish as I entered the office: they had reached out to me, over the generational divide, and I had failed them. Now I hoped to make up for lost time.

Paul Novick seemed to me even then amazingly ancient—part of a vanished world—as he invited me into his cubbyhole office. The room was cold, and here was this eighty-five-year-old man wearing a heavy winter coat as he typed out his editorial on an antique Yiddish typewriter. I fumbled with the tape recorder.

Paul had a lot to say that went straight to my heart. The *Freiheit* represented that section of the Jewish old left that had never accepted assimilationism, which meant its loss of *Mame-loshn* and accompanying *Yidishkeyt*. It had that to be proud of. On the other hand, it had for nearly a half century accepted, and promulgated, a strategic policy that placed world leadership of the left unquestionably in the hands of the Russian Communists. A Faustian bargain—although Paul didn't quite put it that way.

But he knew that had been wrong. And here was the remarkable thing: knowing it didn't cause the *Freiheit* to give up the ship. *Yidishkeyt* triumphed over political premises. In all my hundreds of interviews with aging immigrant radicals in all varieties, I would never meet any other group of people who admitted so readily to drastic error; or who sought so earnestly to make up for that error with a democratic, dynamic vision of cultural pluralism in a cooperative world. What I learned, through years of studying the available sources, was that the unique history of Yiddish had made that triumph of will possible.

As of September 1988, the *Freiheit* published its last issue and closed its doors, amid groans of agony from its loyal staff and a few thousand octogenarian readers. Expenses had risen too high and the Social Security checks of retired garment workers yielded too little of the funds necessary. In the end, even the *Jewish Forward*—sworn enemy of the *Freiheit* for decades—expressed keen regret at the passing of a sister Yiddish publication.

By this time, I had become a bit of a house historian (the intellectual Shabbos goy, perhaps) for the paper, writing essays in the English-language section to understand and to reconcile the seemingly contradictory sides of Yiddish and radical history. In the long view, I had come to see that the ideological jumble of left and ultra-left, Socialist, Communist, Socialist-Zionist and Anarchist had disguised threads that ran through the immigrant Jewish community. The unresolvable problem lay in the immense odds against the prospect for the kind of world in which a democratic, secular Jewishness with its unique multivalent heritage could survive and flourish. Every radical group in the Jewish quarter had its own formula; each had to make, in the end, a difficult choice of allegiances and allies in the world outside. And each choice involved a difficult, even tragic decision about the future of Yiddish.

The supporters of the *Freiheit* built remarkable cultural institutions—Yiddish choruses, theatrical troupes, summer camps, and schools among others. But they also took part in a political sectarianism that continually undercut their best efforts. As they proclaimed the sanctity of Jewish existence, they refused to mourn the Palestine pogroms of 1929. As they preached anti-Fascism with an unmatched fervor, they bowed low to the Hitler-Stalin pact of 1939. As they built new Yiddish institutions with a frenzy after the Holocaust and threw themselves into the defense of the Rosenbergs, they denied the existence of a Soviet drive against Yiddish and Yiddishists, despite growing anti-Semitism and the murder of the Soviet Union's leading Yiddish writers and intellectuals in 1952.

Through all this, the *Freiheit* remained one of the best edited of the Yiddish dailies. Its journalists prided themselves upon their use of language and, if they had chosen to do so, could have prided themselves upon training many leading journalists who transferred to the *Forward* for mostly political reasons. Editor Paul Novick (who had been with the paper from the beginning, and took over the reins in 1939) was, after Abraham Cahan, the dean of the left political Yiddish editors. Illustrators of note, including William Gropper and the modernist Zuni Maud, graced its pages. After the greatest of Di Yunge writers left the paper, the melancholy genius Moyshe Nadir and the shop-poet Martin Birnbaum, among others, remained behind, as did serious Yiddish scholars and pedagogues such as Nachman Meisel and Itche Goldberg. A young Ruth Rubin contributed translations. Even Sholem Asch, out of sorts with the *Forward*, wrote for the *Freiheit*. This was serious talent.

By 1973 or a bit earlier, the ideological sacrifice had ended, and the paper declared a tardy political independence. Too late, some would say. But for its last twenty years, the paper had a distinct mission. If the test of true culture is the triumph over individual death, then the acid test of *Yidishkeyt* has been the triumph of survival, over the collective catastrophe of the twentieth century. From pogrom to Holocaust, from lesser to greater disillusionment, the destruction of cultures and political-spiritual ideas has continued and accelerated. Yet Yiddish remained, and its proponents had not lost their humane view of a world in which room will be found for all the cultures of humankind. Now the *Freiheit* is gone, the field of Yiddish literature narrowed once more. Yet Yiddishists have never been conquered by tragedy, however great. The deeper purpose survives. The message, as the *Freiheit* would say, has become ours to keep alive, from generation to generation.

from The Jewish Unions in America

BERNARD WEINSTEIN

Bernard Weinstein (1866–1946) helped to found the United Hebrew Trades, a crucially important American labor union, in 1888, as a nineteen-year-old shirt-maker. He later wrote The Jewish Unions in America *in Yiddish to explain to his fellow workers how it all happened. Maurice Wolfthal has translated work by Nokhem Shtif, Ayzik Meyer Dik, Yitzhak Erlichson, and Shmerke Kaczerginski.*

THE UNITED HEBREW TRADES was founded more than forty years ago on October 9, 1888.

The idea to form a central Jewish workers' association came from the Jewish branch of the Socialist Labor Party (SLP). In the summer of that year, Jacob Magidow, a shirt maker and a member of the Party, proposed such an association, for the purpose of building a strong trade union movement among Jewish workers in America, while also offering the possibility of spreading the ideals of Socialism among them.

The Jewish branch of the SLP, Branch 8, prepared itself for the task in September. By then, many of the existing Jewish unions had failed after a number of strikes. Their timing was poor, and the unions were not working together. They had no financial support. They all failed for lack of funds, and no one seemed to care.

Branch 8 chose Morris Hillquit and me to go to all the union halls and see if any of the unions were still hanging on.

Comrade Hillquit and I ran around in the evenings for weeks, visiting the places where Jewish workers met to see if we could find any unions to invite to a conference with the aim of forming a central association of Jewish unions.

The Jewish Bakers' Union used to meet at 68 ½ Orchard Street. When we got there one Friday evening we asked where the meeting was being held, but instead we were shown the Charter and told, "Here is the Bakers' Union."

We asked, "Where are the members?"

They replied, "They're down in their cellar bakeries underground."

When we looked for the Tailors' Union, we found Israel Barsky, whose dream it was to organize all twenty thousand tailors of America. In a hall at 56 Orchard Street hung the Charter of the Independent Cloak Makers' Union. Military Hall, at 193 Bowery, was where the few remaining members of the Cap Makers' Union used to meet. Their Charter hung there, but the union was not much more than that. That is to say: it was a union on paper only.

There had also been a Shirt Makers' Union, but that, too, had dissolved. They had pawned their charter to a contractor whom the fallen Shirt Makers' Union had owed a few dollars. When I say "charters," I mean those that were issued by the state to the unions. In those days all unions had to have a state charter, and they were afraid to hold meetings without one, but in any case they had ceased to exist. That was the state of the Jewish trade union movement by October of 1888 when the United Hebrew Trades was founded.

On October 9, a Monday evening, we held a meeting in the Socialist German Labor Lyceum at 25 East 4th Street. It was held in a little room in the attic. That was the historic garret where Branch 8 of the Socialist Labor Party used to have its heated debates, and we always used to meet there. Our German comrades who were sitting in the cellar drinking beer could hear us yelling. They would sometimes run upstairs to see what had happened. Our German comrades would not charge us money for the use of the room, because they knew that Jewish Socialists didn't have a penny.

The meeting had been called by both Branch 8 and Branch 17 (the Russian) of the Socialist Labor Party to start a central organization of "the Jewish unions." Two of those unions that were still alive were represented, the Typesetters' Union and the Choristers' Union. Also in attendance were members of the United German Trades, a progressive labor organization that had been in existence for a while, whose principal aim was to support the Socialist press, in particular the German newspaper, the *New Yorker Volkszeitung*. The United German Trades played a vital role in the labor movement, and was active in all discussions concerning trade unions. The Central Labor Union was very conservative, and many of its delegates were Democratic or Republican politicians. The German unions were big and strong, and Socialist without exception.

The unions had sent these delegates to our conference: J. Werber, founder of the Typesetters' Union; L. Lenzer and J. Krinsky from the choristers; Jacob Magidow and me from Branch 8 of the SLP; Morris Hillquit and Leon Bandes from Branch 17 of the SLP; two prominent Socialists from the United German Trades: A. Huber and M. Göricke. Also in attendance was W. Rosenberg, the editor of *Der Sozialist*, the German-language organ of the SLP. Toward the end of the conference there came a delegate from the Jewish Actors' Union that had just organized the week before, the actor Moyshe Simonov.

There were few speeches, for all the delegates agreed that the plan to form an association of all the Jewish trade unions was excellent. After a short discussion, a Socialist platform was adopted. These were the provisional principles: 1) mutual support between all the unions, 2) founding unions in those trades that were not yet organized, 3) spread Socialist ideology among all the Jewish workers.

I was chosen to be Recording Secretary. I was delighted to have been entrusted with such an important task, and I was very grateful. Morris Hillquit, who was then a shirt maker, was named corresponding secretary. The delegates from the United German Trades donated $10 to support our activities, and that contribution inspired us warmly.

At the suggestion of W. Rosenberg, we decided to name our new association the United Hebrew Trades, emphasizing that our organization was a sister to the United German Trades. We also decided to hold meetings every Monday night. The contribution from each union was set at fifty cents a month.

An organizing committee was named to help start new unions as well as to support existing ones.

That committee had a daunting task: to plow the field and clear the road of stones and thorns.

The first two unions that it started were the Shirt Makers' Union and the United Tailors' Union.

The members of the Shirt Makers' were the cream of the Jewish Socialist and anarchist movements: Morris Hillquit, Mikhail Zametkin, Louis Miller, Reuben Lewis, Jacob Magidow, Lubitsch, and others. But the Tailors' Union had only one prominent Socialist, Israel Barsky.

A bit later we organized the pants makers and the knee-pants makers.

The UHT immediately became essential to the life of all those unions. It organized them and taught the workers how to hold meetings, led their strikes, arranged contracts with the owners, showed the unions how to keep the books, and helped them in many other ways.

The needle trades in which Jewish workers were employed were run under the sweatshop system, and the UHT began right away to organize those workers. On January 1, 1889, we organized a Cloak Makers' Union that lasted only a few months. Only one organized shop remained, Friedlander's Cloak Company.

In 1888 a Knee-Pants' Union was organized by Social-Democrats and anarchists, and it joined the UHT on February 9, 1889.

On February 19 of that year the UHT organized a Silk Workers' Union. In March it formed a Musicians' Union, and in August it launched Local 24 of the Textile Workers' Union. Later that year came Local 31 of the Bakers' Union, then a Carpenters' Union, and a Bookbinders' Union that promptly joined the Knights of Labor.

In March the UHT helped revive the dying Cap Makers' Union, and then, two months later, built up the Purse Makers' Union. The UHT led a series of strikes in various Jewish trades.

A year after its founding, the UHT sent two delegates to the International Socialist and Labor Congress in Paris in July of 1889: Louis Miller and N. Barsky, a typesetter. They paid their own way to the Congress.

The following year, 1890, was the most fruitful for the UHT, and by March it included thirty-two unions. That month the UHT called a mass strike, and a union of 7,000 cloak makers was organized. Joseph Barondess, whom the UHT had selected to lead the strike, was elected Manager of their union.

Other workers also struck in March: the dressmakers, the pants makers, the knee-pants makers, the shirt makers, the seltzer water workers, and the makers of suspenders. And the UHT had led all those strikes, becoming quite prominent in only a year.

In 1890 the Socialist weekly *Arbeter-tsaytung* (*Workers' Newspaper*) was recognized as the official organ of the UHT.

In 1891 the UHT and the Yiddish sections of the SLP chose Abraham Cahan to represent them at the International Socialist Congress to be held in Brussels, Belgium. Before he sailed, Cahan sent a letter to the office that was organizing the Congress, asking that an item be placed on the agenda: "How should organized labor in all countries deal with the Jewish question?"

When he arrived there, he published and distributed a leaflet that presented facts and figures about the Jewish labor movement in America, about the UHT, its unions, and its strikes. It was the first time that Jewish labor was in the public eye of the international labor movement.

The delegates from various countries were interested in the leaflet that Cahan distributed. It was a novelty: there was such a thing as Jewish workers! There had been a perception in most countries that all Jews were bankers, manufacturers, or businessmen.

But there were heated debates with Cahan when he proposed that the Congress adopt a resolution to welcome the Jewish labor movement in America and to condemn anti-Semitism everywhere. His proposal occupied the attention of the Congress for quite a while, and it even received press coverage in several countries.

The UHT had begun to write a new chapter in the history of the Jewish people.

TRANSLATED BY MAURICE WOLFTHAL

The Triangle Fire

MORRIS ROSENFELD

Known as "the poet laureate of the slums and the sweatshop," Morris Rosenfeld (1862–1923) worked as a tailor and diamond cutter but made his name in literature. He was the editor of the New Yorker Morgenblatt. *His books include* The Bell *(1888),* The Chain of Flowers *(1890), and* Book of Songs *(1897). On March 25, 1911, a fire broke out at the Triangle Shirtwaist company in New York City. Almost 150 workers, mostly young Italian and Jewish immigrant women in the Lower East Side, died in the flames or jumped ten stories to their deaths. The tragedy became a galvanizing symbol of industrial capitalism's excesses and the pressing need for health and safety reforms. This poem appeared in* Forverts. *It was reprinted in* The Triangle Fire *(1962). Leon Stein (1910–2002) was a Chicago-based composer and musician.*

Neither battle nor fiendish pogrom
Fills this great city with sorrow;
Nor does the earth shudder or lightning rend the heavens,
No clouds darken, no cannon's roar shatters the air.
Only hell's fire engulfs these slave stalls
And Mammon devours our sons and daughters.
Wrapt in scarlet flames, they drop to death from his maw
And death receives them all.
Sisters mine, oh my sisters; brethren
Hear my sorrow:
See where the dead are hidden in dark corners,
Where life is choked from those who labor.
Oh, woe is me, and woe is to the world
On this Sabbath
When an avalanche of red blood and fire
Pours forth from the god of gold on high
As now my tears stream forth unceasingly.
Damned be the rich!
Damned be the system!
Damned be the world!
Over whom shall we weep first?
Over the burned ones?
Over those beyond recognition?
Over those who have been crippled?
Or driven senseless?
Or smashed?
I weep for them all.
Now let us light the holy candles
And mark the sorrow
Of Jewish masses in darkness and poverty.
This is our funeral,

These our graves,
Our children,
The beautiful, beautiful flowers destroyed,
Our lovely ones burned,
Their ashes buried under a mountain of caskets.
There will come a time
When your time will end, you golden princes. Meanwhile,
Let this haunt your consciences:
Let the burning building, our daughters in flame
Be the nightmare that destroys your sleep,
The poison that embitters your lives,
The horror that kills your joy.
And in the midst of celebrations for your children,
May you be struck blind with fear over the
Memory of this red avalanche
Until time erases you.

TRANSLATED BY LEON STEIN

from God of Vengeance

SHOLEM ASCH

Sholem Asch (1880–1957) was a best-selling, polemical Yiddish novelist, essayist, and playwright who lived in Warsaw, Nice, New York, Tel Aviv, and other places. His novels include Motke the Thief *(1916),* Kiddush ha-Shem *(1919),* East River *(1946), and a sequence of Christian narratives made of* The Nazarene, The Apostle, *and* Mary *(1939–49). His play* God of Vengeance *(1906), which opened on Broadway in 1923, was the first depiction of a female same-sex kiss on stage. For its daring in representing Jews involved in prostitution and their sexual behavior, it became extremely controversial, prompting the production to be closed. The far-reaching effects of such controversy include Paula Vogel's play* Indecent, *which opened on Broadway in 2017. The following is Act II of* God of Vengeance. *The action takes place in the present in a provincial town of Russian Poland. Joachim Neugroschel (1938–2011) was a prolific translator from Yiddish, Russian, French, German, and Italian.*

YANKL TSHAPTSHOVITSH, the "Uncle," a brothel owner
SORRE, his wife (a former prostitute)
RIVKELE, their daughter, a young girl of about seventeen
HINDL, first girl in the brothel, thirty-something years old, showing her age
MANKE, second girl, still quite young
REYZL, third girl
SHLOYME, a pimp, Hindl's bought fiancé, a handsome guy of twenty-six
ELI, a matchmaker and go-between for Yankl
AARON, an orthodox Jew, a scribe
A STRANGER looking for a bride for his son
A JEWISH WOMAN WITH ONE EYE (among the paupers)

TIME: The present.
PLACE: A large provincial town in Russian Poland.

A large basement room with a deep, vaulted ceiling, in an old house. Right under the ceiling, two small, deep-set, curtained windows with flowerpots on the sills are open, letting in the rain. A staircase leads up to a Dutch door, its top half open to the night and the drizzle. In the back, there are several tiny cubicles separated from one another by thin partitions and hung with thick, black drapes. One set is open, revealing a bed, a washstand, a mirror, makeup implements and a colored night lamp. The basement itself is furnished with several couches, a table, benches, and card tables. The walls are covered with mirrors, cheap decorations, and pictures of women in seductive poses. Shloyme is asleep, stretched out on a sofa, his long boots reaching all the way to a chair. Spring night. The room is lit by a big lamp suspended from the ceiling.

(Hindl enters, stands on the stairs for several minutes, gazing at Shloyme. She wears a light shawl; her sexy dress is too short for a woman of her age. She then walks around the basement loudly to wake up Shloyme.)

SHLOYME: *(Wakes up, peers around.)* You? Why aren't you out?

HINDL: It started rainin'.

SHLOYME: *(Sits up on the sofa.)* You're talkin' to me again, Your Highness? Did we make up?

HINDL: I wasn't angry at you.

SHLOYME: Really? Well, you can stay angry, I don' give a damn. *(Lies down again.)*

HINDL: *(Glances around, hurries over to a curtain and eavesdrops, then hurries back to Shloyme.)* Shloyme, I'm not leavin' here. Look, we're alone now, no one's listenin'. Tell me, as God is your witness, tell me. Do you really intend to marry me?

SHLOYME: Go on, Your Highness, put your shekels in your piggy bank, and then complain to Uncle Yankl that I grab all your money. Tell him you ain't even got enough to buy yourself a hat.

HINDL: Yeah, I told him. I was hurt. It was a low blow. You steal the shirt off my back and then you go sneakin' over to that redheaded slut. I'm gonna throw acid in her face. Her breath stinks. How can you stand her? You sure got yourself a nice piece of work!

SHLOYME: You wanna back out? Try it, I'll kick the livin' shit outta you!

HINDL: Go ahead, beat me, cut me to ribbons. *(Shoves up her sleeve and points to her arm.)* Ya already pinched me black and blue. *(Shoves up her other sleeve.)* Go on, pinch me, cut me, but tell me, right here and now, as sure as you remember your dead father and say kaddish for him, do you really and truly intend to marry me?

SHLOYME: *(Lying down again.)* I wanted to once. But now I don't.

HINDL: Fine with me. That's great. But don't try to pull a fast one. You want money? Say so. A coat? There. But what do you get outta lyin' to me? *(Moves away from him.)*

SHLOYME: Don't worry. There's a lotta single guys out there. You'll hook some sucker, all right.

HINDL: *(Opens the drapes of her cubicle.)* You don't have to wear your brains out for my sake.

SHLOYME: If you don' wan' me to I won't. (*Pause.*) Well, why dontcha pour me a glassa tea?

HINDL: (*Brings him a glass of tea from her cubicle, puts it on the table, then heads back to her cubicle, sits down by her trunk, and rummages through it. Another brief pause. Then, from her cubicle.*) I get it, so you like her. . . . Well, well. . . . Now you'll have your hands full buyin' towels to stuff in your dear little wifey's blouse, gettin' her a set of teeth, and puttin' her on stilts. And you'll buy yourself a hurdy-gurdy and lead her around through the courtyards and show off your fabulous creation. A fine organ grinder, I swear. I'll toss you down a few coins myself.

SHLOYME: Shut the hell up, I tell ya.

HINDL: And if I don't, whatta ya gonna do about it?

SHLOYME: Slap the shit outta you.

HINDL: Uh, uh. There's no slapping now. Today you'll get a knife for your slaps.

SHLOYME: (*Stands up.*) You and what army? (*Hindl goes into her cubicle. She quickly hides something in her trunk.*) Whatcha got there? Whatcha hidin' in ya silk blouse?

HINDL: Nonna your business.

SHLOYME: Show me, damn it! (*Struggles with her, grabs a red blouse from her hand. He emerges from the cubicle.*) Well now, let's have a look. (*He rips up the blouse, a photo drops out.*) Aha, Moyshele the locksmith—so he's the lucky guy? When did you two get so chummy? (*Goes back into her cubicle.*)

HINDL: Nonna ya business.

SHLOYME: I'll make it my business. . . . (*He slaps her around, she collapses on the bed, crying.*) There, you get chummy with Moyshele, you trade pictures—start makin' weddin' plans, and keep me in the dark? (*Pause. Returns to table.*) And keep me in the dark. (*Drinks some tea, stands up, walks up the steps to the door.*) And keep me in the dark. (*Stands by the door.*) Hindl! (*She doesn't answer.*) Hindl, get ya butt over here. (*She doesn't answer.*) Hindl! (*Stamps his feet, angrily runs back down the steps.*) Get the hell over here, ya hear?

HINDL: *(Gets up from her bed, walks over to him, shrouds her face in a shawl.)* Whattaya want?

SHLOYME: Did you talk to Manke? *(Hindl is crying.)* Well? What'd she say?

HINDL: *(Still crying.)* If we set up our own brothel, she'll come'n work fer us.

SHLOYME: Definitely?

HINDL: *(Wipes her eyes.)* Yeah. But she don' wanna come alone, she wants to bring a girlfriend.

SHLOYME: Of course. One girl won't take in enough—even to pay the rent.

HINDL: We gotta have a girl who's fresh. . . .

SHLOYME: She'd bring in a lotta cash. But where d'we find her?

HINDL: I've got my eye on a girl, as slender as a sapling, she's still a kid. . . .

SHLOYME: *(Curious.)* Can we make a lotta money offa her?

HINDL: And how!

SHLOYME: A kid? Is she already in some house?

HINDL: Naah, she's in a respectable family.

SHLOYME: Where d'ya know her from?

HINDL: She visits Manke every night, she sneaks down from her father's home. No one sees her. She's drawn here. She's so eager. . . .

RIVKELE: *(Sticks her head with its wet hair through the window, waves to Hindl.)* Psst, is my father here? *(Hindl shakes her head. Rivkele vanishes from the window.)*

SHLOYME: *(Winks at Hindl.)* Her—Uncle Yankl's daughter? She's a gold mine!

HINDL: Shhh, quiet. She's comin'.

RIVKELE: *(Slender and beautiful. Dressed respectably, wrapped in a black shawl. Silently steals in, and hurries down the steps fearfully, speaks more with her hands than her lips.)* Where's Manke? There? *(Points to a draped cubicle.)* There . . . with? *(Hindl winks "yes." Rivkele walks over to the curtain, listens passionately, keeps glancing around fearfully.)*

SHLOYME: *(Quietly, to Hindl.)* Tomorrow we gotta check out the apartment on Pivne Street.

HINDL: When are we gettin' hitched?

SHLOYME: First we gotta have a place to live.

HINDL: Who knows how much the rabbi'll charge for the ceremony?

SHLOYME: So long as there's enough money left over for furniture. The place hasta look decent.

(The door bursts open. In walks Yankl.)

YANKL: *(His face is still marked with traces of his wild youth. His clothes are somber. He shakes the rain off his hat.)* What a business—and rain to boot. *(Suddenly spots Rivkele. Angrily.)* What? You here? *(Grabs her by the collar and shakes her, grinding his teeth.)* What are you doing here?

RIVKELE: Mama told me to . . . call. . . . (Weeps.) Papa, don't hit me!

YANKL: Mama? Mama told you? Here? *(Yells.)* Mama! *(Drags Rivkele by the collar up the stairs to the door.)* She's gonna ruin you with her upbringing! It's like a magnet! She wants her daughter to end up the way her mother used to be!

RIVKELE: *(Weeps.)* Papa, don't hit me. . . .

YANKL: I'll teach you to disobey your father! *(Drags her out. Her weeping can be heard from outside.)*

SHLOYME: What a bastard! He don' think it's proper for his daughter to be a hooker. *(A commotion can be heard from out on the balcony— stamping feet, a weeping woman.)* Does he have to tear up his boots on account of his wife? Oh God . . . oh God. . . .

HINDL: He's perfectly right. A mother should keep an eye on her daughter. Whatever she used ta be, that's in the past now. Once you're a wife and mother, you oughtta keep an eye on your girl. You'll see, if we have kids, God willing, I'll know how ta bring 'em up. Any daughter of mine is gonna be as pure as a saint, her cheeks'll be rosy. No man's gonna make eyes at her. And she'll get married, yes, to a fine, decent man—a real weddin'. . . .

SHLOYME: *(Slaps Hindl on the butt.)* We'll see, we'll see. But talk to Rivkele, work on her, baby. Otherwise we're done for.

HINDL: Don't worry, I'll figure somethin' out.

SHLOYME: We'll see. *(Pause, silence.)* Once you catch her, bring her over to me right away, ya know.

YANKL: *(Enters, angry.)* Time to call it a night, it's raining. Not even a dog's gonna have a sniff here on a night like this. *(Looks at Shloyme.)* You've had enough bliss for a guy who's engaged. Call it a night. *(Goes up the steps and shouts.)* Reyzl, bedtime! Basha, bedtime!

GIRL'S VOICE: *(From outside.)* Coming! Coming! *(Hindl winks at Shloyme regarding Uncle Yankl and waves at him to go home. Shloyme mounts the steps. As he leaves, he crosses paths with Yankl. They exchange looks.)*

YANKL: Move, move, time to call it a night. You've been whispering sweet nothings long enough.

SHLOYME: *(Thrusts his hands into his trouser pockets, looks at Yankl.)* Just when did you become a pillar of society?

YANKL: Get going, get going. I'll clue you in later. Shloyme. Go ta hell. . . .

HINDL: *(Runs up the stairs to Shloyme.)* Shloyme, go home. Ya hear me? Go home, I tell ya!

SHLOYME: *(Exits, staring at Yankl.)* Creep!

YANKL: Who needs him here! *(Points to Hindl.)* You can take the old bag along and start your own business with her.

HINDL: You don' start a business with old bags. An old bag is good for restin' up. But with young dolls. . . .

YANKL: *(Calls into the hallway.)* Reyzl! Basha!

(Two hookers come scurrying in. Water is dripping from their wet, flimsy, transparent dresses. Drops of water run down from their loosened hair. Both girls are in a cheery mood, laughing as they talk. Yankl slams the door behind him.)

BASHA: *(A provincial girl—fat, with rosy cheeks. Naive, has a sharp country accent.)* The rain smells so good. *(Shakes the rain off herself)* Like apples back home, dryin' in the attic. This is the first May shower. . . .

HINDL: It's crazy standin' out in the rain. Tryin' to get every john in the world. No fool's gonna show up anyway, in this downpour. *(Steps into her cubicle with its open curtain, sits down near her wicker trunk, packs up her scattered belongings.)*

REYZL: *(Shaking off the rain.)* They can all go ta hell. I paid up my book the day before yesterday. We were standin' under the drainpipe, the rain smells so fresh. . . . It washes the entire winter outta your hair. *(Goes over to Hindl.)* Look. *(Shows her soaked hair.)* Look how fresh it is . . . it smells so good. . . .

BASHA: The first sorrel must be coming in now, back home in our shtetl. Back home, by the time the first May shower starts, they're already cookin' borsht with sorrel. . . . The goats must be grazin' in the pastures by now. . . . And the lumber rafts must be floatin' down-stream. . . . And Franek is roundin' up the peasant girls and dancin' with 'em in the tavern. . . . And the women must be bakin' cheese buns for Shavuos. . . . *(Pause.)* Know what? I'm gonna buy myself a new summer cape and visit my parents for Shavuos. *(Hurries into her cubicle, brings out a wide-brimmed summer hat with a long veil, puts it on her wet hair, and stands in front of the mirror.)* You know, if I go home for Shavuos and stroll down to the train station in this hat. . . . Ah, they'd be plotzin' with envy, wouldn' they? But I'd be terrified of my father.

REYZL: Why? Would he hit ya?

BASHA: He'd kill me on the spot. He always goes lookin' for me with an iron rod. One time he found me dancin' with Franek at the tavern, he took a stick and he banged my arm so hard, here *(shows her arm)* that I still have a scar. *(Pause.)* I come from a respectable home, my papa's a butcher. You can't imagine how many proposals I turned down. *(Speaks in a lowered voice.)* They tried to talk me into marryin' Notke—he was a butcher too. I still have this gold ring from him. *(Holds up a finger.)* He gave it to me during Succos. Damn, did he ever wanna marry me, but I didn't wanna.

REYZL: Why didn'tsha wanna?

BASHA: I jus' didn'. He stank of beef. Ughhh. People nicknamed him "Medicine." Imagine getting hitched with him and havin' a little "Medicine" every year. Ughhh.

REYZL: And whattaya got here?

BASHA: Why, here I'm a free person, I got my basket of beautiful linen, I got decent clothes, damn it—better clothes than the richest wife in town. *(From her room she brings in a light-colored frock.)* When I wear this out on Marshalkovska Street, people gape and gawk. They positively sizzle! Ohh, if I could ever wear this dress in my little shtetl *(she slips on the frock)* I'd stroll right down to the train station. *(She struts elegantly through the room, slightly lifting the back of her frock, putting on urban airs.)* They'd burst with envy. . . . They'd have fits right there. *(Struts around the room in her frock, with a grandiose expression on her face.)*

REYZL: *(Smoothes out the creases in Basha's frock from behind and readjusts her hat.)* There you are, just hold your head a little higher. No one has to know you work in a brothel. You can say you work in a store, a count fell in love with you.

HINDL: *(From her cubicle.)* And what's wrong with working in a brothel? Aren't we just like the shopgirls? The whole world's like that today, the modern world requires it. Nowadays middle-class girls are no better. This is our profession, but when a girl like us ties the knot, she's more faithful to her husband than they are. We know what a good man is worth.

BASHA: *(Still strutting about the room.)* Oh, sure! You think they couldn' tell the difference? A person can sense it. And it killed my mother. She couldn' deal with it. I've never visited her grave. . . . *(Halts abruptly in the middle of the room.)* Sometimes she comes to me . . . at night, in a dream. I see her, she comes to me in her shroud, covered with thorns and prickles, because of my sins, and she rips out my hair.

REYZL: Oh God, your mother! You actually saw her? What does she look like? A dead mother? Is she pale?

HINDL: Shut up, you two! It's nighttime, stop talkin' about the dead, no dead people can get in here, our boss has a Torah scroll upstairs in his home. *(Breaks off. Pause.)* Well, so his wife spent fifteen years workin' in a brothel, and then she got hitched. Isn't she a decent little wife now? Doesn't she observe all the laws that a Jewish woman has to follow? Isn't their daughter a pure, decent Manke child? And isn't our boss a fine man? Doesn't he behave respectably? He makes the most fabulous contributions. And he commissioned a scroll of the Torah. . . .

REYZL: But they say you shouldn't read such a Torah, and the daughters of such mothers end up the same way. They can't help it, temptation drags them through the mud.

HINDL: *(Terrified.)* Who said so?

REYZL: An old granny told me, a witch. It's like witchcraft.

HINDL: That's a big, fat lie. Where is she, the Gypsy? I'll scratch her eyes out. There is a God in the universe. We have a great God in the universe.

MANKE: *(Emerges from her curtained cubicle, half in nightclothes, draped in a lightweight shawl. Her high, colored stockings show through, her hair is disheveled. Her body is lithe, her long face lovely, her expression impudent. She is still relatively young. A lock of hair dangles over her forehead. While speaking, she blinks, and her entire body shudders as if her bones were caving in. She looks around in surprise.)* What, nobody here?

REYZL: *(Upon spotting Manke, Reyzle cheers up.)* Is that you, Manke? It's good you've come in. *(Points to Hindl.)* She's practically turned me into a rabbi's wife. Where'dya leave your john?

MANKE: He fell asleep. So I snuck away.

REYZL: Is he a big spender? You think he'll treat us to a round of beer?

MANKE: Some kind of crazy Litvak. This is the third time he's come to me. But he keeps grillin' me. Who's your dad? Who's your mom? Like he wants to get married or somethin'. When he kisses me, he buries his face in my boobs, closes his eyes, and smiles, like a baby in its mommy's arms. *(Looks around, whispers to Hindl.)* Has Rivkele been here?

HINDL: *(With a cajoling chuckle.)* She was here. . . . But she ran into her father. Boy, did he have a fit!

MANKE: Oh my God! When was it?

HINDL: Some time ago. He must be asleep by now. *(Whispers.)* She'll be comin' back soon.

REYZL: *(Cheerfully, to Manke.)* C'mon, Manke, let's go outdoors. It's raining, the raindrops are like pearls. The first May shower. Who wants
to go out with me and stand in the rain?

MANKE: *(Goes over to the window.)* It is rainin'. Ah, what a soft drizzle. . . .
And it's so fragrant. . . . Let's go.

BASHA: Back in my shtetl, when it comes pourin' down like this, the
gutters overflow, and the narrow streets get flooded, and people go
out barefoot and they dance around in the rain. . . . Who's gonna
take off their shoes? *(Removes her shoes and stockings. To Manke.)*
C'mon, Manke, take off your shoes, we're gonna go dancin' in
the rain.

MANKE: *(Takes off her stockings, lets down her hair.)* The rain'll soak us
from head to foot. You grow taller when you stand in a May shower,
don'tcha?

BASHA: *(Runs over.)* C'mon, we'll pour water over each other, we'll splash
each other like crazy. *(She lets down her hair.)* We'll wash our hair like
the trees do. . . . C'mon.

HINDL: Wait, wait. Uncle Yank isn't asleep yet, he'll hear us. *(They all
listen, checking out the ceiling.)*

REYZL: Let's go! Don'tcha hear 'im snorin'?

MANKE: Wait, let's signal Rivkele quietly. *(Basha and Reyzle exit. Manke
takes a stick and very softly taps a corner of the ceiling. We can hear the
girls outside hopping around in the puddles, taking handfuls of water and
tossing it into the room, crying, "C'mon out! C'mon out!")*

RIVKELE: *(Sticks her head with its black hair through the small window.
She's wearing a nightgown and a flimsy shawl. She calls softly.)* Manke,
Manke, did you call me?

MANKE: *(Takes a chair, puts it under the window, climbs on the chair, and
takes hold of Rivkele's hands.)* Yes, Rivkele, I called you. C'mon, let's
go out 'n stand in the May shower and pour water on each other
and grow taller. . . .

RIVKELE: *(From the window.)* Shhh, speak more softly. I sneaked out of
bed so Papa wouldn't hear me. . . . I'm scared he'll beat me.

MANKE: Don't be scared of your father, he won't wake up that soon. C'mon, let's stand out in the rain. I'll loosen your hair. (*She undoes Rivkele's black braids.*) There, and now I'll wash your hair in the rain.

RIVKELE: I'm only wearing a nightgown. I've been lying awake all night waiting for Papa to fall asleep, so I can sneak down to see you. I heard you tapping and I slipped out of bed. I tiptoed very softly, on my bare feet, so Papa wouldn't hear me.

MANKE: (*Hugs her passionately.*) C'mon, Rivkele. I'm gonna wash your eyes in rainwater. The night is so sweet, the rain is so warm, and everything is so fragrant in this air. C'mon.

RIVKELE: Shush.... Shush.... I'm scared of my father. He beat me.... He locked the door and he hid the key near the Torah scroll. I've been lying awake all night. I heard you calling me. You called me so softly. I was so anxious to see you. So I stole the key from the Ark of the scroll. My heart kept pounding so loudly ... pounding so loudly....

MANKE: Wait, Rivkele.... Wait.... I'll come out to you. (*Jumps down from the chair, leaves the basement.*) I'm coming out to you.... I'm coming to you.

(*She exits. Rivkele vanishes from the window.*)

HINDL: (*Through her cubicle curtain she has been listening with great curiosity to the conversation between Manke and Rivkele. Now she noisily walks up and down the room, lost in thought, greatly excited, talking to herself very slowly.*) If I can just catch 'em together, with God's help, Rivkele and Manke tonight. I'll take 'em both to Shloyme. They'll be our bread 'n butter. We'll rent an apartment and get married, we'll be respectable, as good as anyone else. (*Halts in the middle of the room. Brooding, lifts her arms toward the ceiling.*) Father in heaven, you're a father to orphans. Oh, Mama in your grave, please help me. Help me find a snug harbor! Help me find a settled life! (*Pause.*) Now if God helps me, I'll sponsor a Torah scroll in the synagogue. I'll donate three pounds of candles to the synagogue every Shabbos. (*A long pause. She remains absorbed in her fantasy of happiness.*) God is good, isn' he? He is góod. Father in heaven. . . . Mama, Mama, don't be silent. . . . Don't be silent. . . . Speak to Him for me. . . . Move heaven 'n earth for me. . . . (*She goes to her cubicle, starts energetically gathering up her belongings and packing them in her wicker trunk.*) First I'd better get ready. . . .

(*A long pause, the stage remains empty. Then Manke enters, snuggling with Rivkele. They are both wrapped in a wet shawl. Their hair, washed in the rain, is disheveled. Water drips to the floor from their soaked clothing. They are both barefoot. Hindl stands behind her cubicle curtain, eavesdropping on them.*)

MANKE: (*Speaks with restrained love and passion, her voice is soft, but deep and resonant.*) Are you cold, Rivkele? Snuggle with me. . . . Snuggle up close to me. Warm up against me, that's so nice. . . . C'mon, let's sit down here on the sofa. (*Leads her over to a sofa, they sit down.*) That's right, that's right. . . . Press your face against my breasts. . . . That's right, that's right. . . . And caress me with your body. . . . It's so cool, like water running between us. . . . (*Pause.*) I uncovered your breasts and I washed them in rainwater that ran over my hands. . . . Your breasts are so white and firm. . . . And the blood in your breasts becomes cool under my hand, like white snow . . . like frozen water. . . . And they smell like grass in the meadows. . . . And I loosened your hair. . . . Like this. . . . (*Runs her fingers through Rivkele's hair.*) I held your hair like this in the rain and I washed it. . . . And your hair smells so good . . . like the rain. (*She buries her face in Rivkele's hair.*) It smells so sweetly of May showers . . . so light, so soft . . . and so fresh . . . like the grass in the meadow . . . like apples on a tree. . . . Cool me like this with your hair. . . . (*She washes her face in Rivkele's hair.*) Cool me like this. . . . No, wait. . . . Let me comb your hair like a bride's hair, parted down the middle with two long black braids. (*Combs Rivkele's hair.*) Do you want to, Rivkele? Yes? Do you want to?

RIVKELE: (*Nods.*) Yes, yes.

MANKE: You'll be the bride. A beautiful bride. Friday evening, you're sitting at the Shabbos table with your papa and your mama. I'm the bridegroom, your bridegroom visiting you. . . . Do you want me to, Rivkele? Do you want me to? No?

RIVKELE: *(Nods.)* Yes, Manke.

MANKE: Wait, wait. Your parents have gone to bed. . . . The bride and groom have met here at the table, we're embarrassed. . . . Do you want to? No?

RIVKELE: *(Nods.)* Yes, Manke.

MANKE: Then we huddle together: You're my bride after all, and I'm your bridegroom. We hug *(hugs her)* very tight and we kiss very quietly, we kiss like this. . . . *(They kiss.)* We blush so deeply, we're so embarrassed. . . . Isn't it good, Rivkele, isn't it good?

RIVKELE: Yes, Manke. Yes.

MANKE: *(Lowers her face, whispers into Rivkele's ear.)* And then we lie down in one bed, nobody knows about it, only you and I, like this. *(Hugs her tight.)* Would you like to sleep with me all night, like this, in one bed? Would you like to?

RIVKELE: *(Hugging her.)* I do. . . . I do. . . .

MANKE: *(Embracing her.)* Come to me, come to me.

RIVKELE: *(Very softly.)* I'm scared of Papa. . . . He's going to wake up.

MANKE: Wait, Rivkele, wait. *(Thinks for a while.)* Do you want to come away with me? We'll be together, all day long, all night long. There'll be no father, there'll be no mother. No one will yell or hit. We'll be alone all day long. It'll be so much fun—would you like that, Rivkele? Would you like that?

RIVKELE: *(Closes her eyes.)* Papa won't know?

MANKE: No, we'll run away together, this very night, to Hindl's place. She's got a room in Shloyme's apartment. She told me so. You'll see how good it'll be. Young men will visit us, officers. We'll be alone all day. We'll dress up like the officers and ride around on horses. C'mon, Rivkele, would you like to? Would you like to?

RIVKELE: *(Her heart pounding.)* Papa won't hear us?

MANKE: No, no. He won't hear us, he's dead to the world. Listen, you can
hear him snorin'. *(Hurries into Hindl's cubicle, grabs her hand.)* Do you
have a place? Quick, take us there!

HINDL: *(Jumping up.)* Yes, yes, quickly, to Shloyme. *(She grabs a dress, tosses
it over to Rivkele.)* He'll take care of us.

MANKE: *(Quickly dresses Rivkele.)* You'll see, it's gonna be so good, it's
gonna be so much fun.

*(They get dressed, putting on anything they happen to grab, a shawl, a coat.
Then they slowly go up the stairs. At the door they run into Reyzle and Basha,
who have finished washing their hair. They gaze in surprise at Manke and
Rivkele.)*

REYZLE AND BASHA: Where are you off to?

HINDL: Don't make a fuss, don't make any noise. We're gettin' some beer
and lemonade.

(Hindl, Manke, and Rivkele leave. Reyzle and Basha gape at one another.)

REYZL: I don't like it.

BASHA: Me neither.

REYZL: Somethin' weird's goin' on!

BASHA: (Looks at her in alarm.) What could it be?

REYZL: What do we care? Let's put out the light and go to bed. We don'
know from nothin'. *(Turns off the lamp. The stage is left in semidarkness,
each girl goes into her cubicle.)*

REYZL: *(Leaving.)* Oh God, the fortune-teller was so right, she was so right.

*(Exits. The stage is empty for several seconds, dark. Basha, half undressed, dashes
wildly from her cubicle, sobbing and shouting.)*

REYZL: *(Opens the curtain of her cubicle.)* What's wrong, Basha?

BASHA: I'm scared of goin' to sleep. I keep seein' my dead mother wan-
derin' around my room with thorns and prickles.

REYZL: The Torah scroll has been defiled, and nobody has any reason to protect us now.

BASHA: I'm scared that this is not gonna be a good night, my heart's pounding. *(Suddenly a commotion can be heard from above, a scraping of chairs and tables. The girls listen, gawking in terror. Soon we hear something heavy falling down the stairs.)*

YANKL: *(Yelling.)* Rivkele, Rivkele, where are you?

REYZL: *(To Basha.)* We'd better get to bed. We don' know from nothin'.

(They both lie down and pretend to be fast asleep.)

YANKL: *(Comes dashing in, holding a candle, his hair disheveled, a coat thrown hastily over his nightshirt. He yells wildly.)* Rivkele! Is Rivkele here? *(No one responds. He yanks aside the curtains of the cubicles.)* Rivkele! Where is she? *(Wakes up Basha and Reyzle.)* Where is Rivkele? Where the hell is Rivkele?

REYZLE AND BASHA: *(Rubbing their eyes with their sleeves.)* Huh? How should we know!

YANKL: You don't know? You don't know? *(Dashes out. He can be heard taking the steps at one leap. A pause. Next, someone comes tearing down the stairs. The door bursts open. Yankl barrels in, dragging Sorre by her hair. Both are in nightclothes. He pulls Sorre down to the floor, points to the brothel.)* Where is your daughter? Your daughter?

(Basha and Reyzle both hug the wall, trembling. The curtain quickly falls.)

CURTAIN

TRANSLATED BY JOACHIM NEUGROSCHEL

On Zuni Maud

EDDY PORTNOY

Eddy Portnoy, a scholar of Yiddish popular culture, is the author of Bad Rabbi: And Other Strange but True Stories from the Yiddish Press *(2017).*

A BREEZY, LATE SEPTEMBER DAY in Warsaw, 1929. There is a stranger in the chess room at the Literatn-fareyn, the Jewish Literary Union at Tlomatski 13—a short, swarthy man chain-smoking and wearing a curly wool coat so long that its hem touches the floor. He has an odd look on his face, somewhere between anger and sadness. His fingers are rough and stained with ink. Without uttering a word, he has managed to beat everyone in the room at chess. The Union's housekeeper approaches several times to ask who he is and what he's doing there, but he doesn't answer. Instead, he growls at her like a bear, she says. Frightened, she runs to the Union's secretary, Meylekh Ravitsh, who jumps up and says, "Aha! That has to be Zuni Maud! He should have been here days ago." Ravitsh hurries to greet him, the "American," who had come to Warsaw to present the puppet theater he created along with fellow artist Yosl Cutler.

Zuni Maud (1891–1956) was one of the most creative personalities in the Yiddish culture of his time. An artist, writer, and performer, Maud illustrated dozens of Yiddish books and periodicals, his calligraphy graces the covers of hundreds of book covers and title pages, he painted and built sets for the Yiddish theater, drew cartoons in multiple Yiddish periodicals, and founded the only professional Yiddish puppet theater in America. A uniquely Yiddish bohemian, Maud had unusually close working and personal relationships with major Yiddish literary figures in the United States and Europe.

As a child growing up in the shtetl of Vashlikov, near Bialystok, Maud's interest in drawing was seen more as a detriment than an advantage. In his khadorim and yeshivas, he became known for "illustrating" mishnayes, stories of the Mishna, which earned him threats and occasional beatings from his rabbi-teachers. It got worse when he began to whittle characters and designs into the tables and shtenders. As a result, he had to switch yeshivas at least four times before turning fifteen. In spite of his obstreperous nature and inability to stop drawing, Maud forged a connection with Jewish tradition that informed his work for the rest of his life.

He arrived in America in 1905 as sixteen-year-old Yitzhok Moyed and became Isaac Maud at Ellis Island. After working as a delivery boy on the Lower East Side, where he was constantly called "sonny," he kept the name, "Zuni." Among the many jobs he held as an immigrant kid in New York City were cigar roller, errand boy, and jack-of-all-trades in clothing sweatshops. Zuni never kept these jobs for long, since his real interest was in the arts. He attended night classes at the National Academy of Art, Cooper Union, and the Ferrer School, which were packed with other eager young immigrants.

By all accounts, Zuni Maud was extremely bright, quick-witted, and cruelly funny with a deep sense of the absurd. He also appears to have had a deeply melancholic side, which imposed itself on much of the art that he produced. In spite of his morose nature, his deadpan sense of humor, delivered stone-faced in his deep bass voice, cracked up his colleagues. Gershn Einbinder recounts how denizens of the Yiddish literary hangout Cafe Europa were robbed at gunpoint in a holdup that netted $4.50. Zuni was the first to comment: "Yiddish literature in America is of no value even for holdupniks! People come in and threaten you with your life and what do they come away with? Nothing! Now even thieves in America will avoid Yiddish literature! They'll say, bums, losers, derelicts tfu!" This was the kind of self-deprecating gallows humor that his literary colleagues loved.

Maud drew the cover illustration for the small journal *Di yugend* (*The Youth*), the 1907 literary debut of a group of dilettantes dubbed Di yunge (The Young Ones) by the mainstream Yiddish press. The group included Mani Leib (Brahinsky), Moyshe Leyb Halpern, Yosef Opatoshu, Ruvn Ayzland, Y. Y. Shvartz, and Isaac Raboy, among others. Collectively they represented the interests of a younger generation of Yiddish writers who wanted to break away from the sweatshop and labor-oriented poetry of Morris Rosenfeld and Dovid Edelshtadt. Shortly thereafter, two more popularly oriented journals appeared, *Der kibitzer* and *Der groyser kundes*, whose mission became to satirically attack the Yiddish press and other Jewish institutions in prose, verse, and image.

Zuni Maud was one of the early staff cartoonists at the *Kibitzer* and later at the *Kundes*. At these magazines he began to hone his skills as a visual satirist, launching his career as one of the most published cartoonists in the history of the Yiddish press. His cartoons and drawings can be found in the *Kibitzer*, the *Kundes*, *Forverts*, *Di tsayt*, *Der hamer*, *Morgn-frayhayt*, *Kanader odler*, and dozens of other smaller literary and political journals. His artistic output provides a fascinating though heavily editorialized look into American Jewish life and reflects his love of the absurd, his interest in modernism, and his deep connection to the Jewish past.

Attempting to mimic the popular "funny pages" of the English-language American press, the *Forverts* hired Maud to redesign the humor section of its newly expanded Sunday edition in 1916. He created *Dos shtifkind* (The Stepchild), a full page of cartoons, humorous stories, jokes, and anecdotes. The page, seen by hundreds of thousands of readers each week, had some of the most artistic and complex cartoons in the Yiddish press, all created by Maud. In 1920 Maud quit to work at *Di tsayt*, a short-lived but memorable Labor Zionist daily. It was in *Di tsayt* that he created "Charlie Howyadoin,'" a vaguely autobiographical work about a Yiddish bohemian on the Lower East Side. When *Di tsayt* collapsed in 1921, the peripatetic Maud hopped right back to the *Kundes*.

In 1922, at the behest of satirist Moyshe Nadir, the *Kundes* hired one Yosl Cutler, another innovative young artist. He and Zuni Maud became fast friends. They opened a studio together in Union Square where they sold unusually painted furniture, knick-knacks, and drawings. Maud and Cutler were seen as a kind of inseparable Mutt and Jeff team who lived together, worked together, and were outrageous together. Two jokers, they were known to quickly sketch diners in restaurants in unflattering caricatures and hand them off as they left. They also drew on everything, from ceilings to floors and everything in between, and were known for frequently drawing pairs of hands on chair seats that would seem to grab people's rear ends as they sat down.

The New Year's cartoon of 1922 from **Der groyser kundes** is described thus: "Little boy, if you want to comb out my tangles, you can only do it with this comb." The comb is labeled "The new world order."

Literary reminiscences describe the team of Zuni Maud and Yosl Cutler as best friends and polar opposites. Poet Meylekh Ravitsh recalled, "Truly, if there was anyone who ever doubted that a pair is prearranged in heaven, he should take a look at Zuni Maud and Yosl Cutler. Such an artistic duo, each complementing the other so wonderfully, is truly a rarity in this world. Maud is short, Cutler is tall. Maud has a deep bass, a murky, dark bass; Cutler has a bright, cheeky, boyish tenor. Maud is full of Jewish folkloric tradition, Cutler is an expressionist, but when they're together there is no contrast whatsoever."

Their reputation grew. In 1924, Yiddish Art Theatre director Maurice Schwartz hired Maud and Cutler to design the set for his upcoming production of Avrom Goldfaden's *Di kishef-makherin* (*The Sorceress*). At the time, puppetry was undergoing a renaissance in New York, and Schwartz requested marionettes for the show. The pair created two somewhat bizarre Jewish characters, which were rejected as too small to be seen from the seats of a big theater.

Unfazed, Maud and Cutler practiced "shtik" with the puppets back in their studio and began taking their creations to literary cafes and to parties, where the Yiddish-speaking puppets were a hit. A year later the two rented a second-floor space on Twelfth Street and Second Avenue, a former children's clothing factory near the Yiddish theater district. They set up a puppet stage, brought in some wooden benches, and left the cutting tables in place to provide some local sweatshop flavor. Tickets were sold around the corner at Moyshe Nadir's "Communist Cafe" (where you could get a glezl tey—a glass of tea—at "proletarian prices").

They named their theater Modicut, after themselves. Lower East Siders packed the little 150-seat theater for nine shows weekly throughout 1926 and 1927, and even the usually cantankerous theater critics of the Yiddish press were impressed. When Modicut's landlord, at the end of 1926, took them to court to try to get them evicted, Zuni and Yosl showed up in the courtroom with their gear and had their puppets plead their case, which so impressed the Irish judge that he proposed establishing a private Modicut Club, thus avoiding the illegality of operating the rented space as a public theater.

In their Modicut plays, Zuni and Yosl brought *Der groyser kundes* caricatures to life by fusing fantasy, satire, politics, and Jewish tradition. Though puppets were not part of Jewish tradition, Maud and Cutler adapted the genre by featuring Jewish folk themes and characters. The exaggerated faces of their puppets leaned to the grotesque, and Modicut's sets later tended toward the surreal, which led to many comparisons with Chagall. Their repertoire included original plays, Purim-shpiln composed in rhyming couplets, and parodies of S. Ansky's *The Dybbuk*.

Modicut's audience, culled mostly from the millions of Yiddish speakers in the New York area, found the theater's combination of literary parody, social satire, and slapstick engaging and hilarious. The two toured Jewish communities in the United States and Canada to great acclaim. During the summers, they worked at Zumeray, a Poconos resort that belonged to Zuni's brother and sister-in-law. Many of the journalists connected to the *Frayhayt* spent time at this center for left-wing artists and writers, as did celebrities and political activists like Paul Robeson and Earl Browder. Zuni's job at Zumeray was to teach art and drama and to serve as a kind of morose *tumler*, though he was generally regarded as an eccentric character who dressed outlandishly and always went barefoot, causing his feet to remain excessively dirty. He was known to walk about wearing a long glove in place of a necktie or with a large wooden watch chain with no watch at the end. When someone would ask him why he wore a watch chain with no watch, he would reply, "Maybe you want to know what time it isn't?" Zuni and Yosl festooned the resort's dining hall with giant surrealist murals and once turned the main house into a giant rooster. Zumeray was clearly not like most of the Jewish summer resorts.

In 1929, Modicut's success carried the two artists to Europe. They performed in London, Paris, and Brussels before heading to Warsaw, where they played two hundred sold-out shows in the Jewish Literary Union's auditorium. Not only were they a huge hit with tens of thousands of Warsaw's Jews, the two puppeteers found friends among the city's Yiddish literary elite. A hastily organized tour of Jewish Poland resulted in more packed shows all over the country. After two weeks of performances in Vilna, writer Zalmen Reyzen mounted the stage and begged them to stay. Shortly after they performed there, a new Yiddish puppet theater, "Maydim," began appearing in Vilna.

The following year, Modicut was invited to perform in the Soviet Union, where the artists were received with equal enthusiasm. They did, though, retool their plays to conform to Soviet cultural reality, understanding that their performances would have to walk the Party line. Their plays began to focus more on sweatshop realities, the evils of Wall Street, and of nefarious Western politicians, all acceptable themes in the USSR. Invited by the government to remain in the country as heads of a Yiddish performance organization, they stayed for about six months, spending their time with

leading Yiddish literary figures. Then, as Maud recounted, they grew
bored and returned to New York in mid-1932.

Although they continued performing together, the act broke up the
following year, apparently the result of a dispute. No one knew the reason,
but many Yiddish writers considered it a tragedy. Eventually each pup-
peteer hired a new partner and began performing on his own. In early
1935, Cutler made a short film, *Yosl Cutler and His Puppets*, intended as a
teaser to attract funding for a full-length screen version of his *Dybbuk*.
Having completed the film, Cutler set off on a road trip to Hollywood.

Tragically, he was killed en route by a drunk driver in Iowa. Maud was too devastated to go to the funeral or attend the memorial services. As testament to the popularity of Modicut, an estimated ten to fifteen thousand people marched in Yosl Cutler's funeral procession.

After Yosl's death, Zuni's life declined. He continued drawing, painting, sculpting, writing, and performing with puppets as well. But his time had passed. In the end, he lived off the largesse of his brother and sister-in-law and their success with Zumeray, supporting himself in part by drawing cartoons for the *Frayhayt* and the *Daily Worker*. He also continued to illustrate Yiddish books.

By the 1950s, Zuni had practically retired, living with his sister and her family after his brother and sister-in-law died. Still connected to the *Frayhayt*, he spent much of his time in its offices. In April 1956 there was talk about what had happened to the Yiddish writers in the Soviet Union. While the *Forverts* had alleged that the writers had been imprisoned or executed, the *Frayhayt*, staunch supporter of the USSR, consistently refuted these claims. But on April 25, *Frayhayt* editor Pesach Novick called a meeting of the paper's inner circle and told them that the stories were true: the Yiddish writers had been imprisoned and executed on Stalin's orders. Zuni, who was at the meeting, had befriended many of these writers when he was in the USSR in 1932. Hearing of their executions made him physically ill. Shirley Novick, Pesach's wife, drove Zuni home after the meeting and said that he looked awful, "as black as dirt." Zuni Maud died that night of a heart attack, at the age of sixty-four.

The Bitter Drop

from **Der groyser kundes,** *December 17, 1915*

LOLA

Der groyser kundes *was a weekly Yiddish humor magazine published in New York from 1908 to 1927. Known in English as "The Big Stick," the Kundes combined high artistic standards with humor, satire, and biting political commentary. The magazine was also famous for its cartoons. LOLA was the pen name of Leon Israel (1887–1955), a prolific and talented cartoonist. The cartoon below offers a prophetic commentary on America's imminent entry into the First World War.*

דער ביטערער טראָפּען

אָנקעל סעם: אַ, לאָז מיך; בלויז איין שנעפּסעל.
פריעדען: נאָו סער, איך לאָז ניט! ווען אָנפֿאַנגען טרינקען, וועסטו ניט וויסען ווען אויפֿצוהערען!

"Uncle Sam" is shown in a bar, where he is served drinks by "Saloon
Keeper Mars," the god of war. Bottles are labeled "Militarism,"
"Imperialism," "Chauvinism," and "Preparedness." As Uncle Sam drinks,
a woman called "Peace" tries to pull him from the bar. Uncle Sam: "Aw,
leave me alone. Just one more shot of schnapps." Peace: "No Sir! I won't
allow it! Once you start drinking you won't know when to stop!"

PART II

The Mother Tongue Remixed

ווערטער זאָל מען וועגן און ניט ציילן.

Verter zol men vegn un nit tseyln.

Words should be weighted, not counted.

YIDDISH IS, ABOVE ALL, simply a language. Not a *zhargon*—a dialect—
or *kholile!*—a collection of funny phrases—but a daily vernacular that
served millions of people over hundreds of years as a means to express
just about everything that they needed to say, and also, of course, a
language perfectly fit for plays, songs, films, journalism, comic strips,
radio, television, and social media. One usually doesn't need to make
such statements about major languages—does anyone think you can't
write a TV episode in Russian or that it's strange to propose marriage
in Hungarian?—but smaller languages do often get stereotyped or cari-
catured, and Yiddish has been subject to more caricature than most. In
fact, the language has been stereotyped even by its greatest exponents and
practitioners. In an early version of his celebrated poem "Monish," I. L.
Peretz mused that Yiddish (as one translation phrases it) "has no words
for sex appeal / and for such things as lovers feel," while Isaac Bashevis
Singer, accepting his Nobel Prize in Literature almost a century later,
remarked that Yiddish "possesses no words for weapons." (If either of
those fanciful statements had been strictly true, it would be pretty difficult to imagine how Yiddish speakers could have survived for a week,
let alone for centuries.)

From its beginnings Yiddish was a language that, like most, drew on
others for its building blocks, taking grammatical and lexical elements
from Romance, Germanic, and Semitic languages. In that sense it is,
like English, well-suited to the modern world, in which languages, and
people, are in constant movement. As the people who spoke Yiddish had
new encounters and experiences, the language more or less kept up with
them. Again and again, faced with new circumstances, it has adapted,
expanded, and transformed itself.

The texts gathered in this section delve into the resourcefulness and
variety of the Yiddish language from myriad perspectives. A few explore
the stereotypes people apply to Yiddish, and others reflect the painstak-
ing work of Yiddish linguists and lexicographers. Still others present a

window into the many different ways Yiddish has been used for fun and for profit, whether in early modern Europe or on the contemporary streets of New York City. The language is, and always will be, as infinite as the imaginations and desires of the people who speak it.

FURTHER READING

Neil G. Jacobs, *Yiddish: A Linguistic Introduction* (2005)
Max Weinreich, *History of the Yiddish Language* (2008)

Is Hebrew Male and Yiddish Female?

NAOMI SEIDMAN

Naomi Seidman is Chancellor Jackman Professor in the Arts at the University of Toronto. The following essay is excerpted from A Marriage Made in Heaven: The Sexual Politics of Hebrew and Yiddish *(1997).*

WHAT INTERESTS ME PARTICULARLY about Hebrew and Yiddish are the ways in which the linguistic relationship reflects and reinforces the gender order of the dual-language community.

Among the ways to begin thinking about Hebrew-Yiddish as a sexual-linguistic system is to recognize the historical connections and psychological associations of Yiddish and women. In this respect, my research does not have to start from ground zero. In 1912, the Yiddish literary critic Shmuel Niger (pseudonym of S. Charney) published his groundbreaking essay "Yiddish Literature and the Female Reader." Niger's essay traces the influence of women readers on Yiddish literature over a period of three hundred years and a range of literary genres. The late sixteenth and early seventeenth centuries saw the beginnings of what would become a flourishing literature of Yiddish religious texts, including a number of well-known translations and reworkings of the major works of the Hebrew library. Such Yiddish texts would typically open with an apologetic introduction explaining the necessity of writing in Yiddish for those who were ignorant of Hebrew, a social category often referred to in some variation of the phrase "women and simple people." Weinreich records a few examples: "for women and men who are like women, that is, they are uneducated," "for men and women, lads and maidens," and "for women and men."

A few authors explicitly linked Yiddish with women and reserved Hebrew for men; for example, one eighteenth-century Hebrew-Yiddish legal guidebook provides two prayers to be recited at a deathbed, one for each sex: "Men should recite the following prayer for a dying person in the Holy Tongue while women should use the Yiddish version." Niger argues that the historical ties between women and Yiddish literature, which go beyond readership to include women's writing, publishing, and patronage of Yiddish texts, gave the older Yiddish literature a distinctively feminine cast. Not only are Yiddish literature and Yiddish writers seen as feminine, so is the God addressed in women's Yiddish prayers:

"God, in the personal Yiddish prayers, becomes feminized, as it were. Just go into the women's section of a synagogue—they're praying to a feminine God."

Niger's provocative arguments insist on the essential femininity of large parts of Yiddish literature. This characteristic even extends, as if by contagion, to male writers in Yiddish, such as the composer of the famous *Tsene-rene*, the enormously popular seventeenth-century reworking of the Bible and midrashic material on the Bible for women.

> Without a doubt [Rabbi Jacob Ashkenazi] had a feminine character, otherwise he would not have been able to write his feminine book . . . I am sure that when rabbis feared Yiddish, it was not only because of the way educated men avoid the uneducated, but also because of the opposition of the manly character to femininity, such as the feminine garrulousness of a Jacob ben Isaac of Yanov [Ashkenazi] and other writers of Yiddish religious books.

In Niger's view, the femininity of Yiddish—evidenced by the "garrulous-ness" of Rabbi Ashkenazi's expansive text—applies not only to female speakers or readers of the language but also to Yiddish literature itself and to its male writers. The passage explains the conflict over the legitimacy of Yiddish as motivated by fear, and by a psychosexual fear, arising not so much between men and women as between two types of men—the manly and the feminine. The opposition Niger notes, after all, is between "the rabbis" and one of their own who writes in the feminine tongue. Thus Niger's stereotypical views of masculinity and femininity are both essen-tialistic and strangely indeterminate, floating free from their attachment to men and women respectively.

Niger does not end his essay with an investigation of the genres sometimes referred to as "women's literature," that is, works like the *Tsene-rene* or the *tkhines*, the personal prayers composed for women and often by them as well. His analysis extends beyond the older reli-gious genres to include the beginnings of secular Yiddish literature in the nineteenth century, detecting women's continuing influence even on those (nearly always male) writers who considered their didactic novels, popular romances, and adventure stories worlds apart from the premodern "women's literature." For instance, Niger provocatively reads the prolific mid-nineteenth-century Enlightenment novelist Ayzik Meyer Dik in the light of his "feminine" literary antecedents, declaring that "despite his negative attitudes toward Yiddish feminine folk-creativity, Dik was actually the inheritor of the feminine premodern Yiddish style, the style of the *ivre-taytsh*."

Niger never revised or expanded his essay, as he had planned, nor did he publish its promised sequel, "Yiddish Literature and the Folk." Niger's failure to return to his own early research is unfortunate, but there is a sense in which I am grateful for the still open invitation and challenge implicit in his unfulfilled promise. For all the problems of Niger's stereotypical and unexamined use of terms like "femininity," my debt to his work remains great: Niger's research into the history of Yiddish as a women's literature laid the groundwork for all later explorations of this history, my own included. Niger recognized the unique importance of the audience for Yiddish literature, not as an abstract "ideal reader" or as a statistical phenomenon, but as a historically specific determining force that took shape *within* as well as outside of literary texts. Niger also opened the question of the longevity of "feminine" Yiddish traditions, exploring the possibility that Yiddish literature's distinctive heritage had lingering effects. My own study not only begins with the historical period in which Niger left off, the mid-nineteenth century, it also attempts a corrective to those of Niger's concepts that have not stood the test of time. Finally, Niger's work, even at its most inaccurate and outmoded, has a claim on our attention in its status as the fullest elaboration of the "myth of Yiddish femininity" to date.

Some concrete examples:

In 1926, a cartoonist for a New York Yiddish humor magazine wished to arouse the public's rage about what he saw as the hypocrisy of the Hebrew writers in Palestine: while these writers were protesting the state-sanctioned suppression of Hebrew in the Soviet Union, Yiddish institutions continued to be attacked in the Hebraist environment of Palestine. The cartoonist made his point through the graphic shorthand of caricature, drawing a suited male figure and labeling it "Hebrew writers in Eretz Israel." The man holds a sign aloft that reads, "We protest the Soviet suppression of Hebrew," seemingly heedless of the barefoot and supine woman on whose back he stands.

The cartoon's caption, "A Weak Position for a Strong Complaint," works on two levels. First, it exposes the hypocrisy of the Hebraists who complain about the mistreatment of the language they hold dear while they themselves suppress Yiddish. Second, the caption cleverly suggests that the Hebrew writers not only have "strong" complaints but are also the "strong" while their standpoint is weak not only because their actions have lost them the moral high ground but also because they are standing on a weak and helpless woman.

נייז, ס'איז א רעכטע ליבע

העברייאיש : מה זה, חיים נחמן, א לינקע ליבע ?
אידיש : מה רעש, מאראם, חיים נחמן קאָן מיך נאָך פון קינדווייז אָן !

The drawing shows Bialik walking arm-in-arm with an unsmiling young woman in flowing (presumably biblical) garb, with "Hebrew" written across her headdress; Hebrew looks rather haughtily at two figures standing by the side of the road, a woman dressed in the bonnet of a servant girl with "Yiddish" written across her apron and a child, who is shouting the Yiddish word for father, "*tate*." Bialik, in waistcoat and tails, is the image of bourgeois respectability. The caption reads, in Hebrew, "Who's that,

92

Hayim Nahman, an illegitimate [or 'left'] love?"; and in Yiddish, "Don't get upset, madame, Hayim Nahman knows me since he was a child!" The street drama is designed to create the maximum amount of sympathy for the young mother. She isn't trying to create a scene, the cartoonist implies; Yiddish holds her son back, and attempts to placate the annoyed and snobbish Hebrew. "No, It's a Legitimate [or 'right'] Love Affair," the cartoon is entitled.

The title of the cartoon is "Y. L. Peretz's folkstimlikher roman" (Y. L. Peretz's Popular Novel). The caption reads,

THE MISSUS (Hebrew) says, "Woe to me that I have lived this long! To see my Peretz, who is in his sixties, going off with the servant girl!"

PERETZ: The poor old thing! . . . It breaks the heart . . . she says! . . . and me? . . . My heart is breaking too . . . nevertheless she's a noble-woman . . . but my child! . . . love! . . . a young heart . . . young blood—don't take notice . . . it rages . . . fire and flame . . . torches! you are mine . . . come! we will ride in the chariots of time . . . we will spin gold and silver . . . we will build palaces of marble—come!

This cartoon shows Peretz moving from Hebrew to Yiddish, the reverse of Bialik's abandonment of Yiddish for Hebrew. The title cleverly plays with the double meaning of the Yiddish word *roman*, meaning both "novel" and "love affair." Peretz's turning to folk or popular motifs in his writing, the cartoonist implies, is equivalent to his turning from the elitism of Hebrew to a love for the Jewish folk.

I reject the proposition that Hebrew should be considered a masculine language or Yiddish a feminine one. The sexualized perceptions about Hebrew and Yiddish must be traced in large part to their respective literary audiences rather than to some quality intrinsic to the respective languages. After all, the perception that Yiddish was feminine certainly arose only after a substantial body of Yiddish literature addressed to women began to form. Thus Yiddish femininity antedates the rise of the Hebrew-Yiddish linguistic system by four or five centuries.

Nevertheless, the gendered associations of Hebrew and Yiddish are not simply or primarily a historical phenomenon. By the mid-nineteenth century . . . the myth of Yiddish femininity had taken on a powerful inde-pendent existence out of all proportion to the circumstances of Yiddish literary history and general knowledge of these circumstances. . . . Whether this ideology still holds is debatable, but something very like a myth of Yiddish "femininity," usually negatively valenced, was certainly ubiquitous in the mid-nineteenth century, and among people who may have had only the vaguest conception of Yiddish literary history.

The Maximalist's Daughter

AARON LANSKY AND GITL SCHAECHTER-VISWANATH

It took Mordkhe Schaechter, a linguist and teacher, a lifetime to collect a million Yiddish words and phrases. It took his daughter, the poet and activist Gitl Schaechter-Viswanath, sixteen years to turn them into a dictionary, published by Indiana University Press in 2016. Aaron Lansky is founder of the Yiddish Book Center and the author of Outwitting History: The Amazing Adventures of a Man Who Rescued a Million Yiddish Books *(2004). What follows is a fragment of his conversation with Schaechter-Viswanath about her lexicographic achievement.*

AARON LANSKY: There have been many Yiddish dictionaries over the years, starting with Harkavy in 1898; the multivolume *Groyser verterbukh* (*The Great Dictionary*), which never got beyond the letter *alef*; Weinreich's *Modern English-Yiddish/Yiddish-English Dictionary* in 1968; and most recently Beinfeld and Bochner's *Comprehensive Yiddish-English Dictionary*, based on Yitskhok Niborski's excellent Yiddish-French Dictionary. How is your dictionary—which you co-edited with Paul Glasser—different from all other Yiddish dictionaries?

GITL SCHAECHTER-VISWANATH: The most recent dictionary [by Beinfeld and Bochner] is Yiddish-English. Ours is English-Yiddish. Why did we need it? Because the most recent English-Yiddish dictionary was Uriel Weinreich's, in 1968. That was more than fifty years ago. Several generations have come and gone in that time. The dictionary itself only had 20,000 words. A little-known fact about Weinreich's dictionary is that this was supposed to be a first edition: Weinreich had every intention of expanding it, of adding more words. Unfortunately, he died at a very young age and he didn't even live to see his dictionary in print, so it was never expanded. It was stuck in 1968, so to speak. We live in a time now where there are thousands of words that didn't even exist back then. And there were tens of thousands of words that never made it into Weinreich's dictionary in the first place. Our new dictionary has about 50,000 entries and 33,000 subentries, for a total of 83,000 words and expressions!

You knew my father, Mordkhe Schaechter, on whose work this new dictionary was based?

LANSKY: Of course, he was my teacher.

SCHAECHTER-VISWANATH: Well, he was a maximalist, and I drank that in with my mother's milk. I also am a maximalist, which is probably why it took sixteen years to complete this dictionary. I couldn't let go until I'd included everything. Of course, it doesn't have *everything*, but I went as far as I could go with it. It has words that you could find in literature a hundred years ago that never made it into a dictionary. You'll find words that were in the Yiddish textbooks that were used in the Yiddish schools of Eastern Europe between the two world wars, words about science and sports and the military and all those words that were used in Eastern Europe that never made it into an English-Yiddish dictionary before.

LANSKY: There have been many press accounts about the dictionary, and they all seem to focus on the neologisms, the dictionary's newly coined Yiddish words. For some reason or another, reports seem to love "*blitspost*," the Yiddish word for "email." Out of 83,000 words, how many are newly coined, and why do people find them so fascinating?

SCHAECHTER-VISWANATH: When you write an article, you need a hook. The *New York Times* ran a great article on the dictionary; its hook was new words, and that's why it went viral. Journalists started calling us from all over the world, and everybody loved the neologisms. Approximately seven percent of the words are new coinages. You have to ask yourself, what is a new coinage? Is it a word that was coined in the last five years? Is it a word that was coined in the last sixty years? There were people who were very upset with Weinreich fifty years ago because he included a couple hundred neologisms in his dictionary. He also believed in coining words when we need them. But other people, they're not happy with it, for whatever reason: conservatism, or a lack of optimism about the future. Neologisms are tough to define. Take the car, the automobile. We needed to have a word for car in 1873 when the first car was produced, so is that a neologism? It's a tough question, but a huge percentage of words in our dictionary, at least ninety percent, existed previously. We didn't invent them.

LANSKY: Can you give me an example of a few of the more interesting neologisms?

SCHAECHTER-VISWANATH: A word in a new language, in any new language, whether it's created by the Académie française or any other language institute, has to not just translate the meaning of the word but to embody the flavor of the language. We tried as much as possible to use Yiddish constructions, grammatical structures, prefixes, suffixes, diminutives, Slavic endings, Germanic endings, all the word forms and roots that we have in Yiddish that we can combine to make a word that we would consider *yidishlekh*, that has that special Yiddish something. There were a number of words that Hershl [Paul Glasser] and I banged our heads against the wall about and some we ended up leaving out. This is an example that I coined, and it was one of the most recent ones, which is why it's in my head: the Yiddish word for "binge watch."

LANSKY: I barely know what that word means in English. It means to watch a ton of episodes of a TV show, is that right?

SCHAECHTER-VISWANATH: All in one sitting. You record them and then you watch them all at once. It's very popular where I live. I guess it's not popular where you live.

LANSKY: We haven't owned a TV set for forty years, so I'm not the best person to ask.

SCHAECHTER-VISWANATH: In Yiddish we have an expression, *shlingen bikher*, meaning a person who's a bookworm, who loves to read, who swallows or devours books. So we were thinking, what exactly is binge watching? It is essentially devouring episodes of a particular series. I just came up with *shlingen epizodn*. The people who are involved in the dictionary liked it, and we included it.

LANSKY: I read both of Simon Winchester's books on the making of the Oxford English Dictionary. Compiling the first edition took seventy-one years! You and your colleagues, Hershl Glasser and [associate editor] Chava Lapin, completed this dictionary in, what, sixteen years?

SCHAECHTER-VISWANATH: Yes, sixteen, but I can't compare it to the *OED*.

LANSKY: We'll let our readers decide that. Of course, you didn't exactly start from scratch. This was based on your father's lifetime of research. Can you tell me a bit about your father? Who was he, and why was he so committed to collecting and defining Yiddish words?

SCHAECHTER-VISWANATH: Mordkhe Schaechter came from a strongly Yiddishist home. His father walked by foot to attend the historic Yiddish conference in Czernowitz in 1908, where Yiddish was declared a national language of the Jewish people. My father earned a PhD in linguistics. He came to America after the war and became a Yiddish professor at Columbia. He loved to collect words. As a field researcher for the *Kulturatlas*, the *Atlas of Yiddish Language and Culture*, he would go out in the field with a huge tape recorder and record people who had come from Europe. He would speak to the tailor and the shoemaker and the former soldier and the former weightlifter and people who did all sorts of different things in Eastern Europe, and my father would record how they spoke and what they said and the words they used. He would tape record it, and he then subsequently transcribed [the interviews] onto index cards.

Anyone who knew my father never saw him without an index card and a pen. Whenever he spoke to you, he was always writing down words, words that were interesting to him, words that he had never heard or that he had heard from his grandmother but hadn't heard for the last thirty years. All words were fascinating to him, all Yiddish words. He ended up with eighty-seven card catalogs and shoe boxes full of index cards.

His goal, among many others—too many—was to create terminological dictionaries: one for this topic and one for that topic. In the end they all were . . . what's the word I'm looking for? They were aggregated into one, and it was going to come out as a dictionary. But he didn't get to it until the year 2000. I worked with him on it. I actually computerized those cards during the 1990s.

LANSKY: Is it true there were a million cards?

SCHAECHTER-VISWANATH: Oh, yes.

LANSKY: Really?

SCHAECHTER-VISWANATH: You know what, I believe there were a million words. There could have been several words on a card. Some cards could have eight words on them, words that were related in some way.

LANSKY: Still, it's astonishing, Gitl. I remember going to your family's house. In 1977 I was a student in the *zumer-program*, the YIVO summer program at Columbia, and your father was my teacher. Oh, my God, what an experience that was! One evening he invited the whole class over to your house [on Bainbridge Avenue in the Bronx]. I remember sitting there, and someone pointed to an adjacent room. I seem to remember an old wooden card catalog. Someone explained in a hushed tone, "*Ot zenen di kartlekh*—there are the cards." Was your whole house taken over by the *kartlekh*?

SCHAECHTER-VISWANATH: No. I think my mother made him keep them in the den in his workspace. But my father was a voracious reader—*er hot geshlungen tsaytungen* [he devoured newspapers]. Every single Yiddish newspaper or magazine that was being published was in our house. My father read them all, looking not for the news but for words. You can't imagine what our childhood dining room table looked like. It was full of newspapers and clippings, and those also made it into the card catalog. He and I started working on it in 2000. He unfortunately became ill two years later, and he was really not able to continue with it. I had already been working with him on it, and I was one of his right hands over several decades. He never asked me directly, but I felt that at this stage of the game, we couldn't not do something with all this. At the time, I had a husband and three young children and a day job as a nurse. Every evening, whenever I could get an hour or two, I would sit at the dining room table and work, editing and adding words. This went on pretty much for sixteen years.

As each of my children left the nest, I had more time. When I came home from work I would grab a cup of coffee and something to eat, then sit down at the dining room table and work until I dropped. When I look back on it, I don't know how I didn't become ill myself. There were times when I was very, very, very upset because I didn't feel the dictionary would ever be published.

I'll tell you one example. We started this on an old iMac. When I upgraded the software, the fonts we were using from the 1990s were no longer compatible. That I think was my low point because we had the manuscript and I had no idea how we were going to publish it. We resolved the issue. A young man named Jamie Conway came into my daughter's life and subsequently married her. He's a math PhD with great computer skills. I showed him the file, and he was able to convert it into another computer language, and then he reconverted it into Yiddish and made PDFs. From that point onward, all the editing was done on PDFs rather than text.

LANSKY: That's difficult, though, right?

SCHAECHTER-VISWANATH: This really is a *nes min hashomayim*—it was a miracle from heaven because I was in constant fear of the iMac dying on me. It never died, by the way. I still have it. I don't know what to do with it. I don't know which unique museum would want an iMac.

LANSKY: It sounds like a museum piece. You could exhibit it next to your father's card catalog.

SCHAECHTER-VISWANATH: That's how the project ended up being finished.

LANSKY: Fantastic. Had your father ever made the leap to technology?

SCHAECHTER-VISWANATH: He wrote emails. He was able to write emails, yes, in the last years of his life, but beyond that. . . . He died in 2007. I think after 2003, he wasn't even using the computer anymore. There was no Facebook and Twitter and all that, which I don't do, either. He was capable of communicating by email.

LANSKY: Was he supportive of your efforts to digitize this material, to put it online?

SCHAECHTER-VISWANATH: Oh, yes, no question. He understood that
we needed to do that.

LANSKY: So he was forward-looking?

SCHAECHTER-VISWANATH: Yes, no question. You couldn't have the
kinds of words that he had on his cards (and we have in the dictionary) and not be forward-thinking. He wanted to include the
terminology for astronomy and sciences and everything future—
everything present, past, and future—because for him, and for me
as well . . . some people might say we stick our heads in the sand,
but we see a future for Yiddish. Yiddish might look different than
what we're speaking or writing now, but we don't see it dying anytime
soon, and I'm sure you understand that.

LANSKY: Of course.

SCHAECHTER-VISWANATH: Yes. We're forward-speaking, forward-
looking, forward-searching.

Shopping for Yiddish in Boro Park

JEFFREY SHANDLER

Jeffrey Shandler is Chair and Distinguished Professor of Jewish Studies at Rutgers University, and author of a number of books, including Adventures in Yiddishland: Postvernacular Language and Culture *(2005);* Jews, God, and Videotape: Religion and Media in America *(2009);* Shtetl: A Vernacular Intellectual History *(2014); and* Holocaust Memory in the Digital Age: Survivors' Stories and New Media Practices *(2017). With J. Hoberman, he co-edited* Entertaining America: Jews, Movies, and Broadcasting *(2003). Shandler is also the translator of Jacob Glatstein's* Emil and Karl *(2006).*

ACCORDING TO OSCAR ISRAELOWITZ'S *Guide to Jewish New York City*, the "Jerusalem of America" can be reached by taking the BMT subway to Brooklyn and getting out at Utrecht Avenue. There visitors will find themselves in Boro (also spelled Borough) Park, which, among New York's many neighborhoods, boasts the city's largest Jewish population. In addition to its role as the spiritual center of several major Hasidic communities, Boro Park is home to non-Hasidic Orthodox Jews; some non-Orthodox Jewish residents, who made up the majority of the neighborhood's Jews before the influx of Hasidim that began in the late 1950s, still live there. But Boro Park's concentration of yeshivas, separate day schools for boys and girls, and synagogues large and small primarily serve tens of thousands of Belzer, Bobover, Muncaczer, and other Hasidim.

Indeed, the Hasidic parodists known as the "Rechnitzer Rejects" have written a mock anthem for the neighborhood (set to the tune of "New York, New York"), celebrating it as the center of an observant American Jewish universe:

> It's high time now,
> I'm coming back,
> Back to you, dear Boro Park.
> My heart isn't heavy,
> I no longer worry,
> I'm coming back to you, my Boro Park.
> There, where the Sabbath and holidays are strong,
> Where Jews study a page of the Talmud day and night.

Boro Park is a decidedly balebatish, or well-heeled, Hasidic neighborhood, with an elaborate and distinctive consumer culture. Eve Jochnowitz, who is a PhD candidate at New York University researching contemporary Jewish life in Brooklyn and who conducts walking tours of Boro Park, notes that the dress and comportment of the local Hasidim are governed by a uniquely urban aesthetic that combines the laws of tsnies (modesty) with concern for balebatish respectability. "You could dress sloppily and still be sufficiently covered to be considered tsniesdik," she explained on a recent visit to the neighborhood, "but Hasidic dress in Boro Park also requires an attention to detail that shows respect for oneself and others." Indeed, the wide array of goods and services available here testifies to the considerable level of comfort Hasidim enjoy in this Brooklyn neighborhood, as do its large new school and synagogue buildings and the growing number of residential blocks occupied exclusively by haredi (ultra-Orthodox) families. Here is an extensive community that, within a half century, has established itself both spiritually and materially in its new home.

For scholars and enthusiasts of Yiddish culture, whatever their religious convictions, Boro Park holds a special attraction, as it is one of the best places to shop for Yiddish. By this I mean not only buying books, periodicals, sound recordings, and videos in Yiddish, but also encountering Yiddish in the public sphere: on signs, posters, and advertisements, as well as through the spoken word. Here Yiddish is a language of the marketplace, albeit a very different one from those of Jewish Eastern Europe before the Second World War. In his 1979 study of the neighborhood, sociologist Egon Mayer cautioned visitors that, while "shtetl-like" in some respects, this part of Brooklyn is not "a recreated East European shtetl." Those who visit Boro Park today will discover it is a twenty-first-century American neighborhood as much as it is a Hasidic one, as revealed by the use of Yiddish they find there.

Though other Jewish shopping strips to the east and west mark the expansion of Orthodox settlement in the neighborhood, Thirteenth Avenue, from about 40th to 55th Streets, remains the commercial hub of Boro Park. In addition to groceries, butchers, bakeries, pharmacies, and other small shops that typically line commercial streets throughout Brooklyn, are businesses catering to the particular needs of the haredi community: wig stores and hat stores, their wares enabling married women to observe rules of modesty in public appearance; shops that sell satin bekeshes (long robes) and shtraymlekh (fur-trimmed hats), the holiday garb of Hasidic men. Some local dry cleaners offer the services of a shatnez inspector, who will check the composition of clothes to make sure they do not contain a mix of linen and woolen fibers, which is unacceptable according to rabbinic law. And there are signs advertising the services of sofrim (scribes), who copy sacred texts onto pieces of parchment that are placed in mezuzes and tfiln, as well as penning torah scrolls and megiles.

Yiddish appears on signs above a number of Boro Park storefronts. Typically, these signs feature two or three languages; besides Yiddish, English, and Hebrew, some signage is Boro Park is in Russian, for the benefit of recent immigrants from the former Soviet Union. In Boro Park, Yiddish on a shop's sign serves not so much to identify what sort of business is within as it does to indicate that the business is, in local terminology, heymish, meaning, in this context, that it is not only local and familiar but also appropriate to the specific needs and sensibilities of Brooklyn's Hasidim. Yiddish is widely employed throughout Boro Park, as well as print, to signify what is considered heymish. Even some of the local ATMs offer the option of banking in Yiddish.

As in haredi neighborhoods in Israel, posters play a strategic role in Boro Park, informing, exhorting, and enticing members of the community. They transform the street into a constantly updated bulletin board or want-ad section of a newspaper, announcing events, goods, and services. Posters change with the season: in the early fall, for example, they advertise temporary sites for performing the ritual of shlogn kapores in the days before Yom Kippur. "Ale unzere tshikens hobn pampers" ("All our chickens have Pampers") one recent sign boasted, in a typical mix of Yiddish and English, thereby assuring shloggers that the kapore-hindl (sacrificial fowl) will not soil them during the ritual of atonement; this involves raising a hen or rooster above one's head while reciting a prayer that symbolically transfers one's sins for the past year to the bird, which is then slaughtered. Soon thereafter, signs appear announcing places to buy skhakh, lulavim, and esrogim for the holiday of Succos. The end of winter brings news of upcoming purim-shpiln (Purim plays), followed soon thereafter by posters for sales of Passover foods and special amusements for the period of kholhamoyed peysekh, during which schools are closed.

A landmark of Boro Park's main commercial street is the newsstand on the corner of Thirteenth Avenue and 49th Street, with its bilingual sign: "Newspapers/*Tsaytungen*." Prominent among the newspapers and magazines available here are Orthodox and Hasidic publications: *The Jewish Press*, *Jewish Action* (a magazine published by the Orthodox Union), *Hamachne Hachareidi* (an English/Hebrew newspaper), *Der algemeyner zhurnal* (a Yiddish weekly published by Chabad), *Di tsaytung* ("The Yiddish Paper of Record"). Also sold at this newsstand are the major Israeli dailies. Not available are the *New York Times*, the *Wall Street Journal*, or the *Forward* in any of its languages. But there is a sampling of mainstream English-language magazines for sale, including *Fortune*, *Newsweek*, and *Martha Stewart Living*.

The newsstand is just a few doors from Mostly Music (4815 Thirteenth Avenue), one of several stores that cater to the community's audiovisual interests. This small shop offers an extensive and wide-ranging selection of sound recordings, including vintage Yiddish vocals by the likes of Molly Picon and Pesach'ke Burstein, classic cantorial performances, as well as the latest klezmer and avant-garde Jewish recordings, Israeli artists, and contemporary American spiritual recordings from Debbie Friedman and New York congregation B'nai Jeshurun. There is also a less extensive selection of videotapes for sale, with some classic Yiddish films among the children's videos (lots of Uncle Moishy, Torah Tots), Hasidic musicians in concert, Israel travelogues, and the occasional Orthodox exercise video featuring modestly clad instructors. But Mostly Music devotes pride of place to recordings by Mordechai Ben David (locally known simply as MBD), Shlomo Carlebach, Avraham Fried, the Miami Boys Choir, and other mainstays of Brooklyn's Orthodox popular music scene. Many of the vocal recordings feature selections in Yiddish as well as English and Hebrew. Yiddish names are also given to some contemporary instrumental pieces, an indication that this music is heymish—as are labels warning listeners not to play recordings on the Sabbath and Jewish holidays, and that duplication of the recording is "against halakha" as well as a violation of copyright law.

Two blocks from Mostly Music is another important destination for the Yiddish consumer: Eichler's bookstore (5004 Thirteenth Avenue). Claiming to be "The Largest Judaica Store in the World," Eichler's is certainly the largest of the neighborhood's several Jewish bookstores (and there appears to be no other kind of bookstore in the area). A visit to Eichler's provides an overview of Jewish literacy as it is understood in Boro Park. The store's vast inventory has little in common with the Judaica section of a Barnes & Noble or other mainstream bookstore or, for that matter, with many an American synagogue library. You will not find the novels of Cynthia Ozick or Philip Roth at Eichler's, nor the philosophical writings of Heschel or Levinas; likewise, there are no works of modern secular Yiddish or Hebrew authors (in original or translation). The store's most extensive offerings are sforim, including handsomely bound sets of the Talmud and makhzorim. Secular books include kosher cookbooks as well as a few familiar titles dealing with the Holocaust or Israel. Biographies, though, appear to deal exclusively with the lives of Hasidic and rabbinic sages.

Like other Judaica bookstores (not to mention the itinerant moykhersforim of bygone days), Eichler's also offers other goods, ranging from ritual objects and clothing to recordings and children's games. The ritual items in Eichler's testify to the elaborate haredi domestic culture that has evolved in Boro Park. The store boasts a wide selection of ornately decorated boxes for storing bentsherlekh (small booklets with the text for grace after meals) at the dinner table, all manner of ewers and basins for ritual handwashing, and kiddush fountains, which allow one to bless one large goblet of wine and then pour it simultaneously into eight or more small cups for family and guests (more hygienic, if less traditional, than passing one wine goblet from person to person around the table, notes Jochnowitz). Though these ritual items are much more likely to bear Hebrew inscriptions, some are labeled in Yiddish.

For the Yiddish reader, Eichler's offers titles that testify to the language's role in maintaining traditional cultural literacy among haredim. One can find Yiddish anthologies of Bible commentaries, selections from the Shulhan Arukh, and instructional volumes on Jewish holidays and sages of the past. Some works maintain the long-standing association of Yiddish with the pious female reader. For example, *Der kroyn fun tsnies* (*The Crown of Modesty*, published in Brooklyn in 2000), a guide to conduct for the modern Hasidic woman, explains the mores of proper dress and restrictions on activities ranging from riding a bicycle to talking on a cell phone in public.

A very recent development—apparently only within the last few years— is a spate of entertainment literature written in Yiddish that meets the haredi community's exacting concerns. Some of these works are suspense novels—such as *Der shpion vos iz antlofn* (*The Spy Who Escaped*) by F. Royz, published in Monroe, New York, in 2000; the book's title page describes it as "a suspenseful story, with many stormy moments and dramatic descriptions, with lively scenes of a Russian spy under Communist rule." Other titles fall into the category of historical fiction, such as *Antdekt Amerike* (*America Discovered*) by Y. Sh. Gros, "a suspenseful, dramatic, and instructive story that takes place during the time of the search for America by the explorer 'Columbus the Jew,'" published in Kiryas Joel, New York, in 1997. Typically, these books open with *haskomes*, letters of endorsement from rabbinic authorities; some include prefaces from the publisher offering a rationale for this new literary genre. The introduction to *Der shpion vos iz antlofn* explains that "dramatic books" such as this are a product of modern times, and that reading fiction has become an important part of life not only for gentiles, but for Jews as well. It goes on to describe how these Jews—assimilationists and followers of the Jewish Enlightenment—turned at first to books in other languages, but then began reading secular books in Yiddish. Such works by "Yiddishists," with their "false knowledge," created upheaval among traditionally observant Jews, we are told. And now there are similar books in modern Hebrew and English to contend with as well. To alleviate this problem, rabbis have turned to "trustworthy authors" to write works of fiction in Yiddish that are "worthy of being brought into respectable Jewish homes."

To the scholar of Yiddish literature, this argument sounds strangely familiar. Centuries ago, similar prefaces appeared in some of the first published Yiddish books, such as vernacular translations of the Bible and compendia of morally instructive tales and fables, which strove to locate a place for this innovative literature in the Jewish world. These books occupied a new middle ground in what the linguist Max Weinreich described as the "levels of holiness" that codify traditional Ashkenazi culture. As works of vernacular culture, Yiddish books were lower in status than canonical sforim written in *loshn-koydesh*, yet they ranked above books by gentiles written in German and other Christian vernaculars. Pious Yiddish books, then as well as now, offer the Jewish reader texts whose contents are culturally familiar and morally appropriate within the appealing form of popular entertainment genres.

Another contemporary rendering of the traditional use of Yiddish to create works that entertain as well as edify is found on the shelves in Eichler's media section, which sells both audio and audiovisual recordings of recent performances in Yiddish "durkh heymishe yingelayt," "by our own young people." These purim-shpiln and other plays are performed to amuse the rebbe (and, secondarily, his community of followers) on special occasions during the year when such activities are permitted. The repertoire features all-male casts, in keeping with Hasidic notions of female modesty in public, and includes dramatizations of episodes from Jewish history in which Jews triumphed over persecution by anti-Semites, as well as Mekires Yoysef, the classic purim-shpil recounting the biblical story of the selling of Joseph into slavery by his brothers and ending with their reunion in Egypt.

The beginning Yiddish reader of any age will find plenty of Yiddish titles among Eichler's sizable inventory of children's books. Most are designed to introduce young readers to the mores of a traditionally pious life, describing daily routines or holiday observance; other children's books relate stories of Hasidic sages of the past. There are a few Yiddish titles that deal with the secular world, notably a multivolume *Entsiklopedye far yugnt* (*Encyclopedia for Young People*), printed in Israel in 1999. Especially interesting are the readers and workbooks for the young student of Yiddish, most published by Hasidic girls' schools, such as the Satmar community's Beys Rokhl schools. The incorporation of Yiddish into American Hasidic school curricula, which began about a generation ago, is a telling sign of what sociolinguist Miriam Isaacs sees as a shift in the character of Yiddish among postwar Hasidim from an "immigrant language" to a "minority language." Today, Yiddish primers, activity books, and even stickers (teachers can reward students with a colorful "Zeyer gut!" or "Gevaldig!" or "Geshmak!") both teach the language to haredi children and imbue it with meaning as a signifier of piety in daily life.

Eichler's also sells a variety of games and puzzles that incorporate Yiddish into children's play activities. Among the more elaborate games is *Handlerlikh* ("Deal honestly"), a knock-off of Monopoly that replaces the streets of Atlantic City with place names of importance to the Hasidic world, past (Cracow and Lublin) and present (London, Montreal, and, of course, Boro Park). As players work their way around the board, buying and renting properties, they are taught lessons in piety as well as proper social and business conduct. The game's instruction booklet explains in Yiddish that Handlerlikh will "implant in children good character and reverence for God. Whoever deals honestly will have much success." Players must tithe all their income, and khezhbn-hanefesh (personal reckoning) cards penalize players for disobeying one's parents, forgetting to recite a brokhe, watching television—or for speaking either English or modern Hebrew.

This implicit endorsement of Yiddish as the Hasidic vernacular of choice should not be mistaken for Yiddishism, which the haredi community typically regards with great suspicion. In fact, a recent letter to the editor in *Mayes*, a monthly Yiddish magazine for Hasidic families published in Monsey, New York, criticizes the journal for what the reader considers a tendency toward Yiddishism, evinced by its efforts to explain Yiddish grammar and provide glossaries of Yiddish terminology. ("Who says that there has to be a Yiddish word for everything?" asks the letter's author. "Not all languages are equally rich.") Indeed, Hasidim who speak Yiddish do not celebrate the language as the fountainhead of a wide-ranging, thousand-year-old Ashkenazic heritage that embraces labor movements and avant-garde poetry as well as Hasidism, and they are suspicious of efforts to cultivate Yiddish for its own sake. Instead, they value Yiddish both as a traditional vehicle of Hasidic lore and for its new role—one that has emerged in the post-Holocaust era—of distinguishing Hasidim from other Jews. Not surprising, then, that the non-Hasid who goes to Boro Park hoping to try out his or her Yiddish on the locals may find such efforts frustrated. Some Hasidim will refuse to respond to an outsider's Yiddish in the language but will answer in English instead. Literary scholar Richard Fein wrote of his largely unsuccessful efforts to engage Lubavitcher Hasidim in Yiddish, when he visited the community in Crown Heights, another Brooklyn neighborhood, in the late 1970s:

> Only later did I realize that the members of the family did not speak to me in Yiddish because Hasidim don't want to advance the presence of a secular Jew who speaks Yiddish. . . . Yiddish, for the Hasidic family, is the daily part and parcel of a religious way of life. It is not a language that one cultivates for personal or intellectual or cultural reasons, as they correctly saw me doing. Yiddish was certainly not simply a language like any other that one might help someone else to learn. While Yiddish was basic to me, they saw it as merely incidental in my life, merely "an interest." Yiddish was basic to them, but in a completely different way.

Like Fein, many devotees of Yiddish have come to it as a "discovery" (or, in Fein's case, a rediscovery of a language he had heard and even briefly studied as a child, as he explains in his memoir, *The Dance of Leah*). They encounter Yiddish in classrooms, festivals, and other venues where lovers of the language convene—places removed from their daily routines, in which they generally use other languages. For Fein and many other

Yiddishists, the appeal of seeing Yiddish in situ, materialized in an environment in which the language is indigenous—the desire to pay a visit to Yiddishland—cannot be underestimated. Boro Park isn't Yiddishland; indeed, some Yiddishists deplore the state of Yiddish among contemporary Hasidim, complaining that it isn't regarded as a full or "pure" language and that Hasidim regularly flout linguistic standards, or even the idea of standards. Nevertheless, the neighborhood offers an encounter with Yiddish that other settings cannot provide.

Whatever their religious convictions, Yiddish enthusiasts should not shrink from visiting Boro Park or other Hasidic neighborhoods in New York and elsewhere, but they should bear in mind that their attraction to places where Yiddish thrives in the marketplace does not conform to the communities' own commitments, including their commitment to Yiddish. Such encounters not only pose challenges; they can enrich one's awareness of cultural creativity among Jews today, and expand one's concept of the possibilities of Yiddish in its second millennium.

O, R*O*S*T*E*N, My R*O*S*T*E*N!

ILAN STAVANS

Leo Rosten (1908–97) is the self-appointed Scholar of Yinglish, the controversial hybrid tongue mixing Yiddish and English that remains popular among descendants of Yiddish-speaking immigrants from Russia, Poland, and other parts of Eastern Europe. A novelist, essayist, humorist, and scriptwriter, his stamp is as a lexicographer, a discipline he used to study this jargon as an example of American assimilation. Rosten is the author of three H*Y*M*A*N K*A*P*L*A*N novels (1937, 1959, 1976), as well as The Joys of Yiddish *(1968)*, Leo Rosten's Treasury of Jewish Quotations *(1977), and* The Joys of Yinglish *(1988). This essay by Ilan Stavans explores his place in American-Jewish culture.*

SHORTLY AFTER LEO ROSTEN'S *The Joys of Yiddish*, a hilarious lexicon of colloquialisms and locutions, was published in 1968, Irving Howe, the deacon of Jewish culture in the United States, irritably reviewed it in the pages of *The New York Times*. In Rosten's book, Howe said, "Yiddish is torn out of its cultural context, its integral world of meaning and reference." He described the book as a catalog of kitsch. He was troubled by the way Yiddish had become distant and unknown among secondhand third-generation Jews, a sign of false nostalgia and lack of authenticity.

Needless to say, Howe wasn't Rosten's only critic. Accusations of inaccuracy were published in periodicals such as the *Forverts*. Even Isaac Bashevis Singer, who himself was often accused of misrepresenting Yiddish and who, upon accepting the Nobel Prize, said that the *mame-loshn* is the only language on earth that has never been spoken by men in power, in private conversations derided *The Joys of Yiddish* as impure, just as he derided mainstream phenomena like the musical *Fiddler on the Roof*. One periodical even nominated Rosten for a "shanda award." (*Shanda* in Yiddish means shame, scandal.)

Impurity is precisely what Rosten wanted to embrace. Born in Poland in 1908, he immigrated to America with his family at the age of two. Yiddish was his mother tongue. He was educated in the Chicago public schools, where he became not only proficient in English but a zealot of his newly acquired linguistic knowledge. In a trajectory spanning sixty years, Rosten was constantly attracted to the struggles of acquiring a second language. What goes on in a child's mind as one grammatical system is superimposed on another? If, as linguists suggest, language betokens thought, how does our *Weltanschauung* change? Do certain minorities have more trouble with pronunciation than others? For instance, is it easier for a French speaker to learn the English language than, say, for a Russian, Arabic, or Spanish one?

After receiving his bachelor's degree in 1930, Rosten studied at the London School of Economics. He then finished a PhD at the University of

Chicago. His doctoral dissertation was on the relationship between politicians and the media in Washington. He was thinking about pursuing an academic life. But while doing graduate work, at the age of twenty-four, he wrote a short story based on his experience teaching in a night school. It was published in *The New Yorker* under the pseudonym Leonard Q. Ross because Rosten didn't want his teachers to be aware of this lighthearted side of his career.

The protagonist was Hyman Kaplan, "a plump, apple cheeked gentleman with blondish hair and merry blue eyes, who always had two fountain pens clipped to the breast pocket of his jacket." His "bland, bright, rather charitable smile" rarely left his face. Kaplan (his first name was pronounced "Human" by some of Rosten's fans), forty-something, was a Jewish immigrant struggling to learn English at the American Night Preparatory School for Adults (A.N.P.S.A.), where the students entered through the doors "because of the world's political upheavals: a revolution in Greece, a drought in Italy, a crisis in Germany or Cuba, a pogrom in Poland, or a purge in Prague—each convulsion of power on the tormented world was reflected, however minutely, in the school's enrollment and departures."

In the next couple of years Rosten produced fourteen more short stories about Kaplan. They dealt with his errors in speech or spelling or grammar. As one of the stories puts it, Kaplan "seemed to take pride in both the novelty and the number of his mistakes." For instance, "blast" for him is the past tense of "blass." He says "lidder," not "leader." And his *w*'s come out as *v*'s, as in Voodrow Vilson. Kaplan is able to write words; he just doesn't seem able to pronounce them properly.

In 1937 Rosten gathered all the stories in between the covers of a book called *The Education of H*Y*M*A*N K*A*P*L*A*N*. They became hugely popular. Rosten would get fan letters from places as far away as Turkey, Hong Kong, and Egypt congratulating him for having invented complex, lovable characters. The book's title was given to him by a publisher infatuated with Henry Adams's autobiography. For strategic reasons mainly, as he argued, to "universalize" the cast, Rosten moved the scene from Chicago to New York. He conflated elements from relatives and people he had come across (uncles, neighbors, grocery store owners, seamstresses, spinsters, ice-cream vendors) to shape not only Kaplan but also Miss Mitnick, Fanny Gidwitz, Gus Matsouka, Norman Bloom, and the rest of the exuberant students, and especially their teacher, Mr. Parkhill. Once, when asked if he resembled Parkhill, Rosten answered: "Alas, only in function: I have nowhere near the patience, kindness, and fortitude with which Mr. Parkhill is either blessed or afflicted."

To be sure, the A.N.P.S.A. pupils are the type of immigrants one came across before the Second World War: expatriates, exiles, emigres, refugees, settlers, laborers, ingenues, and other white-skinned neophytes from the Old World. They looked like vintage Americans except that they were poorer, uneducated, and didn't always have a grasp of Shakespeare's tongue. America was theirs for the taking. Committed as they were to start again in life, these newcomers ended up reconfiguring the social texture of the country. And the country changed with them also. Rosten's episodic narrative, in spite of the students' advanced ages, is a window through which to appreciate the making of a new America.

To this day the Kaplan stories, focusing as they do not on plot but on delivery, remain a favorite among audiences driven by verbal athletics. For such readers a typical Sunday morning is spent completing *The New York Times Magazine* crossword puzzle, which is no surprise given that they're saturated with what Dr. Seuss called "wordzardry." If you're the type of person who has memorized, as I have, Lewis Carroll's poem "Jabberwocky," and if you are amazed that it's been translated into more than forty different languages (including Yiddish), these immigrant tales of confusion and knowledge, arrival and acclimatization, language and silence are a sheer delight. But those who are interested in realistic fiction or who have a predilection for intrigue, psychological insights, and a good twist at the end of their reading will find them morose, repetitive, and completely uneventful. As Rosten himself put in the preface to a sequel of sorts, *The Return of H*Y*M*A*N K*A*P*L*A*N* (in 1976, the two volumes, with a total of twenty-nine stories, were compressed into one after Rosten fundamentally rewrote the majority of them): "Grammar, Spelling, and

Pronunciation," all starting with capitals, "are hardly dramatis personae; and the locale could scarcely be less inspiring: a classroom, a classroom of a beginners' grade, a classroom of a beginners' grade in a night school, a classroom of a beginners' grade in a night school for adults, a classroom of a beginners' grade in a night school for adults presided over not by a rich, juicy character, such as Samuel Johnson or Scaramouche, but by a terribly staid teacher named Parkhill." Still, Rosten had discovered his unequivocal obsession: language.

From the fifties on, he pursued a number of different professional directions, among them screenwriting. His Hollywood credits include *The Dark Corner*, with a cast that included a then-unknown Lucille Ball, as well as *Double Dynamite*, with Frank Sinatra and Groucho Marx, who became a friend. (Years later Rosten wrote that upon being introduced, Groucho told him, in that "glum, astringent tone" of his: "Hymie Kaplan is funny.") And in the sixties he wrote *Captain Newman, M.D.*, a popular war drama about a psychiatrist, with Gregory Peck, Tony Curtis, and Angie Dickinson. He taught at Yale and Berkeley, among other academic institutions, and also wrote a couple of thrillers about Sid "Silky" Pincus, a detective who is also an ex-cop and Vietnam vet and whose partner is an Irish guy with "a better grasp of Yiddish than most New York Jews."

Rosten was already sixty when *The Joys of Yiddish* came out. He shaped it as a semi-scholarly endeavor and consulted luminaries like Maurice Samuel, Louis Finkelstein, and Felix Kaufmann. But his eye was on accessibility. He didn't want a full-fledged dictionary listing words alphabetically, but an almanac wherein every aspect of Jewishness (folklore, medicine, rabbinical debates, finances, exorcism, cuisine, metaphysics) would be featured. He not only quoted the Talmud and Sholem Aleichem but also goyim like Samuel Johnson, Mark Twain, and James Thurber. His scholar's credentials and his penchant for entertainment finally seemed to come together. He was constantly asked to comment on cultural affairs. He lectured widely and his contributions to various periodicals multiplied. In short, Leo Rosten became a household name.

Howe, I'm convinced, was wrong in scornfully portraying Rosten as a symbol of the misbegotten path taken by Yiddish across the Atlantic. It is true that contact with the Anglo-Saxon environment changed the language almost beyond recognition, to the point that Mendele and Peretz would have turned over in their graves if they had heard the malapropisms speakers used then, as they do now, on these shores. Is that the result of laziness or a consequence of natural forces? Does the immigrant lose his conscience the moment he loses his tongue?

Actually, *The Joys of Yiddish* is a benchmark. It isn't groundbreaking in its research. That quality belongs to Max Weinreich, the Latvian founder of the YIVO Institute of Jewish Research. He was responsible for a multivolume history of the Yiddish language and was, along with his son Uriel, one of the most distinguished linguists in America of the twentieth century. Yet Rosten's stew is very much his own creation. He's a humorist fully aware that writing jokes is far harder than telling them, especially when it comes to re-creating dialect. As he argued, "to elicit laughter instead of confusion, dialect cannot be a literal transcription of 'funny talk.' Nothing is lamer than a passage of mangled pronunciation recorded in accurate phonemes. Any yokel in the Ozarks can try to be a thigh-slapper by writing 'We wuz shure surprised by Maw's coolinary conkukshun': The sounds are authentic enough, and enough to make [one] wince."

Rosten's phrasebook is a thermometer showing how "cool" American Jews can be, how successful their journey from immigration to assimilation has been. From Adonai, its first entry, to the last on Zohar, the vast majority of its entries are common knowledge for Americans. Is there someone who doesn't know what a schnorrer is? How about a nosher, chutzpah, and shlep? For the few shmendriks still unaware of these terms, Rosten's manual is at their disposal. It has gone through so many editions as to mutate into a trademark, as is clear from the most recent version, edited by Lawrence Bush and illustrated by R. O. Blechman, published a few years after Rosten's death in 1997. "It is a remarkable fact," Rosten explains in his introduction, "that never in its history has Yiddish been so influential among gentiles. (Among Jews, alas, the tongue is running dry.)" He adds:

We are clearly witnessing a revolution in values when a Pentagon officer, describing the air-bombardment pattern used around Haiphong, informs the press: "You might call it the bagel strategy." Or when a Christmas (1966) issue of *Better Homes and Gardens* features: "The Season's Delightful Jewish Traditions and Foods." Or when the *London Economist* captions a fuss over mortgage rates: "HOME LOAN HOO HA." Or when the *Wall Street Journal* headlines a feature on student movements: "REVOLUTION, SHMEVOLUTION." Or when a wall in New York bears this eloquent legend, chalked there, I suppose, by some derisive student of English: "Marcel Proust is a Yenta."

Rosten's approach to language is, in my view, savvy and dynamic. He doesn't perceive it as an isolated, self-sufficient, enclosed human activity. Instead, he pushes for a more dynamic, functional conception, recognizing the constant effect politics, education, sports and entertainment, and other realms of life have on it. In other words, language is never static; it's in permanent change, adapting to unforeseen circumstances by lending and borrowing terms and expressions from the environment. His approach, obviously, came from Yiddish itself, a stunningly resilient code whose principal source of sustenance was its flexibility and improvisational nature. To find health in the Pale of Settlement, Yiddish speakers for centuries made their lingo suit the needs of the time. They were polyglots, looking at language not only as a home but also as a way of escape: if one couldn't do the trick, another one would. Plus, they were adept at the art of translation. To translate is to overcome the barriers of language, to cope with the circumstances by doing what chameleons do: make oneself part of an alien turf.

London's *Times Literary Supplement* described Rosten as a fellow "who has carried on a lifelong affair with the English language." It becomes clear after careful scrutiny that Rosten was less interested in Yiddish than in its effects on English. In his introduction he shows the way Yiddish affects colloquial English. "[W]ords and phrases are not the chief 'invasionary' forces Yiddish has sent into the hallowed terrain of English," he argues.

"Much more significant, I think, is the adoption by English of linguistic devices, Yiddish in origin, to convey nuances of affection, compassion, displeasure, emphasis, disbelief, skepticism, ridicule, sarcasm, scorn." He lists these examples:

Blithe dismissal via repetition with a sh- play-on-the-first-sound: "Fat-shmat, as long as she's happy."

Mordant syntax: "Smart, he isn't."

Sarcasm via innocuous diction: "He only tried to shoot himself."

Scorn through reversed word order: "Already you're discouraged?"

Contempt via affirmation: "My son-in-law he wants to be."

Fearful curses sanctioned by nominal cancellation: "A fire should burn in his heart, God forbid!"

Politeness expedited by truncated verbs and eliminated prepositions: "You want a cup coffee?"

Derisive dismissal disguised as innocent interrogation: "I should pay him for such devoted service?" The use of a question to answer a question to which the answer is so self-evident that the use of the first question (by you) constitutes an affront (to me) best erased either by (a) repeating the original question or (b) retorting with a question of comparably asinine self-answeringness.

That is, not only Yiddish but English, too, is a concoction, a fact that certainly contributes to its world domination. In a 1967 article for *Look* magazine, Rosten showed how the English sentence "The pistol in our bungalow is stuffed with taffy" contains elements from six sources: Slovak, Czech, Hindustani, Tagalog, Old French, and English via Old Frisian. Again, his approach isn't new. Dictionaries, as lexicons are called nowadays, have always been buffers, describing the changes undergone by the language but also prescribing its patterns and rules. Some, like Doctor Johnson in his *A Dictionary of the English Language*, published in 1755, recognize the encounter of various sources affecting English (Norman, Saxon, Greek, Latin, French, Italian, etc.) while fiercely fighting their invasion. Others, like the American Civil War writer Ambrose Bierce in *The Devil's Dictionary*, written as a weekly newspaper column from 1881 to 1906, acknowledge that lexicography cannot contain the verbal mutations taking place at all times. Bierce defined "dictionary" as "A malevolent literary device for cramping the growth of a language and making it hard and inelastic." But he added, wisely no doubt: "This dictionary, however, is a most useful work."

Humorists have an anarchic nature. They make it their business to defy authority and ridicule morality. Think of Errol Flynn, the Marx Brothers, Lenny Bruce, and Monty Python. Rosten believed humor to be "the affectionate communication of insight." He thought it was "the subtlest and chanciest of literary forms" and believed that "it is surely not accidental that there are a thousand novelists, essayists, poets, journalists for each humorist." Just as Ambrose Bierce used sarcasm in his definitions, Rosten stuffed *The Joys of Yiddish* with anecdotes, stories, and jokes, along with spelling and pronunciation devices and definitions. In fact, the humorous ingredient is the book's selling point. For instance, in the entry for "mazel tov!," he writes:

> "How am I doing?" The writer answered his friend. "You have no idea how popular my writing has become. Why, since I last saw you, my readers have doubled!" "Well, mazel tov! I didn't know you got married."

And the one for nu—also spelled nu?, nu!, nu-nu?, and noo-ooo—lists various examples of usage, including these:

> "I need money . . . Nu?"
> "And you're supposed to be there by noon. Nu?"
> "She accused him, he blamed her. Nu, it ended in court."

The widespread relevance of *The Joys of Yiddish* is confirmed by the endless references that are still being made to it in American culture. Some time ago I came across one quoted in Wikipedia about the 1998 New York Senate race between Charles Schumer and Alphonse D'Amato. Apparently, at one point D'Amato referred to Schumer as a putzhead. A reporter for the *New York Times* looked up the word in Rosten's volume and realized that it didn't exclusively mean "fool," as was obviously intended, but "dickhead," too, a misunderstanding that might have cost D'Amato the election.

The lexicon is also a Rorschach test. It allows us to understand America's current dilemma. For sociologists, Jews are a model of acculturation. Their arrival in the United States coincided with a period of expansion. There were other immigrants from Europe in the second half of the nineteenth century and throughout the early decades of the twentieth: the Irish, the Germans, the Italians, the Scandinavians, etc. Ethnically, all were Caucasian. Did their language undergo a similar metamorphosis, from private code to treasure trove of public locutions? There might be remnants of these tongues in Standard English but spotting them today doesn't appear to be a sport that generates much joy. By contrast, identifying the plethora of Yiddish expressions found in novels, comic strips, speeches, radio, and TV shows is an endless occasion for pride.

Since the sixties a major wave of people from the so-called Third World, from Mexico to Africa, from Korea to the Caribbean Basin, has arrived on these shores. These immigrants have not only reconfigured the texture of metropolitan centers but also redefined rural life everywhere, from Maine to Vermont, from Wyoming to Arkansas. A fierce debate about their status as citizens is rattling all quarters of society. Will they be able to assimilate like previous immigrants did? Are they learning English fast enough? How will their linguistic patterns revolutionize the country's identity in the twenty-first century? Mexicans constitute the largest group of newcomers, altogether some thirty-five million living north of the Rio Grande. An onslaught of Spanish words is increasingly recognizable in English, from taqueria to telenovela. The average A.N.P.S.A. student today is likely to come from Oaxaca, and be an illegal worker in his twenties, single, ready to board along with a dozen pals in a cramped one-bedroom apartment in Queens. He says "chess" instead of "yes," "weeth" instead of "with." For him, as for the original Kaplan, acquiring the skills to use the English language fluently, not to say flawlessly, is a nightmare. After all, this is a language that, as Rosten argued, enjoys confusing—or shall I say dismaying?—foreigners by telling them "that the sound 'sh' is required for such different spellings as 'shimmer,' 'passion,' 'lotion,' 'ocean,' 'sure,' 'suspicious,' 'patient,' 'chaperone,' 'tension,' 'conscientious,' 'Schick.' Or that 'rats' takes a closing sound quite different from 'nails' ('z') or 'roses' ('ez') or daisies ('eez')." Oy gevalt!

My own interest in Spanish in the United States is nurtured by a deep admiration for *The Joys of Yiddish*. In the late nineties, while studying the process of assimilation undergone by millions of Latinos, I focused my attention on Spanglish, the "interface of Shakespeare and Cervantes." I traveled from coast to coast recording neologisms, terms accepted by neither the *Oxford English Dictionary* nor the *Diccionario de la Real Academia*. Eventually, I released a dictionary of approximately 6,000 Spanglish terms and phrases, each with its corresponding definition, words like *hanguear* (to hang out), *marqueta* (supermarket), and *wátchale* (watch out), and expressions like *Hola, mi amigo!* and *Hasta la vista, baby!* It opened with a seventy-plus-page introduction placing Spanglish in historical context. Although in my definitions I inserted double entendres and secret messages to perspicacious readers, I'm not a comedian. Like Rosten, I believe that lexicography cannot be a reactive science. It needs to define the context from which it springs. To reflect this view, I included a Spanglish translation of the first chapter of *Don Quixote*. My publisher subtitled the book "the making of a new American language."

Before it disappeared as the domestic language of secular Jews in America, Yiddish gave place to a middle step, an in-between vehicle of communication known as Yinglish, on which Rosten prepared another, far inferior lexicon in 1989. In his estimation, Yinglish, also called Ameridish, resulted from "the speed with which Yiddish words, phrases and phrasing have become a part of demotic English, and the speed with which distinctively Jewish styles of humor and wit, irony and paradox, sarcasm, derision and mockery have infiltrated every level of English." Through my considerations of Spanglish, I've learned that, in equal measure, there have been other distinctively American hybrids, like Chinglish, Franglais, and Finglish. Each of these has produced its own type of culture. For instance, "The Star-Spangled Banner," much in the news recently after it was rendered into Spanglish as proof of patriotic loyalty by Latino artists, was also adapted into other mixed tongues, including Yinglish. ¡Viva la polución! "The existing phrasebooks are inadequate," Mark Twain said once. "They are well enough as far as they go, but when you fall down and skin your leg they don't tell you what to say." Leo Rosten had the khokhme to document in amusing detail the nuances of a minority as it moved from the periphery of culture to center stage.

In retrospect, it was Irving Howe who was the yenta. In his kvetching, he failed to see the superb qualities of The Joys of Yiddish. "No, not everything written about Yiddish need be dry, solemn, or scholarly," he wrote in his review. "There should be room for tasteful popularization, as in the work of Maurice Samuel. But something about the Broadway-cum-TV tone of Mr. Rosten's book—the tone of elbowing, backslapping 'local color'—gives me the chills." Howe's allergy to schmaltz culture kept him from realizing it is an homage to American individualism and creativity. If the lexicon might be said to have an overall message, it is not about selfishness but about human flexibility. We are what we speak . . . kitsch and all. Fittingly, the best quote I know by Rosten isn't about language but about perception: "We see things as we are, not as they are."

A Guide to Yiddish Sayings

SHIRLEY KUMOVE

The following draws on columns titled "Words Like Arrows" by Shirley Kumove in Pakn Treger, *collected in her books* Words Like Arrows: A Collection of Yiddish Folk Sayings *(1984) and* More Words, More Arrows: A Further Collection of Yiddish Folk Sayings *(1999). Based in Ontario, Canada, Kumove has also published translations in* Found Treasures: Stories by Yiddish Women Writers *(1994).*

A vort iz vi a fayl: beyde hobn groyse ayl.
A word and an arrow are alike: both make a speedy strike.

THE IDEA THAT WORDS have great power and potential to inflict harm is implied in the following: *Verter darf men vegn, nit tseyln*. Words should be weighed, not counted. From time to time, this column will look at folk sayings, shprikhverter, and the ideas, beliefs, and values expressed in them. It seems appropriate to begin with the subject of words themselves.

Yiddish folk sayings open a window on the rich and varied Jewish experience in Eastern Europe and immigrants in America. What is a folk saying? Generally, it is a terse expression, transmitted orally, containing a summation of spiritual, cultural, and ethical values or just plain common sense.

These expressions come out of the needs and experiences of daily life. Folk sayings, though woven into the fabric of normal, everyday conversation, are also used as formal or ritualized statements invoked on special occasions. While some sayings are derived from biblical, Talmudic, or liturgical sources, most have neither rabbinic nor secular authority. Their influence derives mainly from their widespread acceptance and use.

Jews, the People of the Book, are also People of the Word:

Ven men kumt zikh tsunoyf dabert men.
When people meet, they jabber.

Talking was a major sport and hobby of Jews in Eastern Europe and immigrant North America. It was a playfulness in a world with limited leisure. No distinction could be made between male and female, rich and poor, young and old. Everyone was accorded equal respect for the ability to call up a terse, pithy, and well-placed saying or witticism, a glaykhvertl. Most people agreed that:

A guter oysdruk makht a gutn ayndruk.
A fitting expression makes a good impression.

Jews admired the person who could sum up complicated ideas in a few choice words, who could hold their own or get the better of an argument. But if the discussion became too abstract, the speaker would be admonished with:

Fun a kleyner petrishke makht er a gantsn gortn!
From one little parsley he makes a whole garden!

Conversely, a long-winded explanation could be cut short effectively with this curt command:

Makh es kaylekhdik un shpitsik!
Make it round and to the point!

Or as we say in English: Make it short and sweet! If the nudnik, the bore, insisted on belaboring the issue, an appropriate response would be:

Er molt gemoln mel!
He's grinding already-ground flour!

A thrice-told tale invites the comment:

Di mayse hot shoyn a bord!
This story has already grown a beard!

If the speaker got carried away altogether and his talk became intemperate, he could be brought back to reality with:

Az m'iz tsu fray mit der tsung krigt men matnes yad!
If you're too free with your tongue, you'll get smacked!

128

Matnes yad brings a Hebrew twist to the Yiddish sentence. It literally means a gift—a present delivered by hand.

Yiddish speech was often argumentative and peppered with an arsenal of clever quips, retorts, salvos, and wisecracks, fired off swiftly and with zest. While many sayings are funny, others are caustic, hostile, ironic, irreverent, and downright sarcastic. They can give a shtokh (a stab), a zets (a whack), or they can just plain grizhe (gnaw) away at your kishkes (innards). We are cautioned to choose our words carefully because:

> *Di gantse velt shteyt oyf der shpits tsung.*
> The entire world rests on the tip of your tongue.

This is reinforced by the reminder that:

> *A patsh fargeyt, a vort bashteyt.*
> A blow subsides, a word abides.

More oblique is the following:

> *A shtokh makht a lokh.*
> A stab makes a hole; or colloquially, a prick makes a nick.

Ostensibly, this saying refers to the puncturing of a sack causing the contents to trickle out, but it really means that words have power to inflict wounds.

At the same time, people were advised not to take all the talk too seriously because:

> *Fun a vort vert nit keyn lokh in kop.*
> From a word you don't get a hole in the head.

This recalls the familiar playground [taunting response] of childhood: "sticks and stones may break my bones but words can never harm me."

For Jews, a world without lively discourse is beyond understanding. In fact:

> *Oyb dos ferd volt gehat vos tsu zogn volt es oykh geret.*
> If the horse had anything to say, it would also speak up.

And a handful of sayings about Yiddish food:

> *Geshmak iz der fish af yenems tish.*
> The grass is always greener on the other side.

> *Az men vil gut boydek zayn, khazer iz alts treyf!*
> If you check thoroughly, pork is still treyf.

> *Beser a kosherer groshn eyder a treyfener gildn.*
> Better a kosher penny than a treyf nickel.

> *Az men est khazer, zol shoyn rinen iber der bord.*
> If you're going to eat pork, you might as well let the juices soak your beard.

> *Der derekh hayosher iz ale mol kosher.*
> The path of righteousness is always kosher.

The Artificial Elephant

from **Der Winkl**

STANLEY SIEGELMAN

Der Vinkl *was a widely popular column in the* Forverts. *This poem was written by Stanley Siegelman, described as possessing "an incomparable ability to unearth a rare bit of news and then make his poetic commentary on the event in both English and Yiddish." The news in question was an Asian elephant conceived through artificial insemination at Jerusalem's Biblical Zoo, the first time such a birth was achieved in Israel. The column stated that "worldwide only eleven Asiatic elephants have been born through artificial insemination." It was published on January 30, 2006.*

DER KINSTLEKHER HELFAND

In eretz Yis-ro-el m'kvelt!
Aza pasirung! Zogt di velt!
Vi lebedik di visnshaft!
Vi vunderlekh ir koyakh, kraft!
An helfand makht men, eyns un tsvey!
(Der kolir alemol is "gray").
Ze vi azoy a pitsl "sperm"
Makht shoyn a groyse "pachyderm"!
Mir shepn nakhes fun der "zoo"
Zey hobn dort gemakht a "coup"!
In Tel Aviv, der act's bagrist:
Zey yoyvlin dortn gor umzist.
M'helft di khayes—eyns, tsvey, dray.
Bashaft kinder ("multiply")
Di velt dervart a bisl nayes
Fun mer kinstlekhe vilde khayes.
Nu, zol a Sabra zayn tsufridn?
M'fregt zikh: iz dos gut far yidn?

For Israel, another first!
With overwhelming pride we burst.
Technology, now procreant,
Gives rise to infant elephant!
One marvels that a man-aimed sperm
Can yield a fleeing pachyderm.
Will this success induce a spate
Of urges to inseminate?
Now many people smile becuz
The baby has a "langeh nuz,"
The deed is hailed in Tel-Aviv,
Such breakthrough they can scarce conceive.
It gives new meaning to the cry,
"Be fruitful now and multiply!"
With bated breath the world awaits
More quadrupedal neonates.
And while the world awaits more news
We wonder, "Is this good for Jews?"

PART III

Eat, Enjoy, and Forget

וואָס העלפֿט כּבֿוד אַז מען האָט ניט צו עסן?

Vos helft koved az men hot nit tsu esn?

What use is honor if you have nothing to eat?

AT ONE POINT in Beatrice Bisno's prizewinning 1938 novel, *Tomorrow's Bread*, we learn that a future labor organizer named Sam Karenski "flopped weakly into a chair at the kitchen table, and broke a fresh *Begel* in two." The author, not sure that her readers would be familiar with this strange food, decided to include that term in a glossary at the end of the book, explaining there that a *begel* is a "round roll." Eighty years later, there may be some Americans who have never met a Jewish person, and who might never meet one, but it's hard to imagine that there could be any Americans who haven't by now encountered Jewish food, and specifically the cuisine that was created by Yiddish-speaking immigrants from Eastern Europe who settled in the United States. Whether they discover it at a delicatessen or appetizing store, at a kosher restaurant, or—more likely—frozen in their supermarket or at a fast food chain, they have certainly at least once in their lives been offered a bagel.

Of course, most of those Americans probably have no idea that when they order a bagel with lox, they're speaking Yiddish. There aren't, to be clear, any "essentially" Jewish foods; there are foods that developed in Poland, Russia, Hungary, Ukraine, and elsewhere in Europe, which Jews embraced, brought with them to America, transformed, and then marketed successfully to American consumers. (In some cases, they transformed them specifically by adapting non-Jewish recipes to work within the strictures of *kashrut*, religious Jewish laws around eating.) As widely known as some Jewish dishes have become—challah, babka, pastrami, matzo ball soup—many other Yiddish delicacies remain relatively unknown pleasures enjoyed largely by insiders: some Americans may, in fact, never enjoy *kreplach*, *tsimmes*, or *tsholnt*. But the food of Yiddish-speaking immigrants to America continues, against the odds, to resonate for new generations, and chefs and cookbook authors seem to keep rediscovering and renewing them. No wonder: for those who know and love them, these foods offer more than simple nourishment; they are also a powerful means of cultural expression and provide people with a feeling of connection to their ancestors and to *landslayt* (co-religionists) around the world.

The texts that follow in this section reflect the exuberant, insatiable affection that Jewish immigrants and their descendants have felt for their culinary traditions, and the fascinating ways in which those culinary traditions became integrated into American life, thanks to companies and entrepreneurs that understood that there was a hungry Jewish market to serve. Meanwhile, recipes for some of the more iconic Yiddish dishes will allow readers to try them at home.

FURTHER READING

Joan Nathan, *Jewish Cooking in America* (1994)
Gil Marks, *The Encyclopedia of Jewish Food* (2010)

Kosher Chinese?

MATTHEW GOODMAN

Matthew Goodman is the author of five books, including Eighty Days: Nellie Bly and Elizabeth Bisland's History-Making Race Around the World *(2013).*
The following is a fragment from Jewish Food: The World at Table *(2005).*

THE JEWISH STORY IN AMERICA—immigration, acculturation, assimilation—is amply reflected in that quintessential Jewish activity: eating (in the Yiddish, *esn*). In the first decades of the twentieth century, we see American manufacturers reaching out to Eastern European Jews as one of the largest immigrant communities: products are marketed in Yiddish as well as English, to appeal to new Jewish consumers in their native language. Jewish cookbooks—again, in Yiddish as well as English—instruct housewives in the proper preparation of traditional Jewish delicacies and also American favorites previously unknown to these immigrants.

Before long Eastern European Jews have established delicatessens, restaurants, bakeries, and hotels in America, offering foods too elaborate or time-consuming to be readily prepared at home, while kosher wineries produce a distinctively thick, sweet variety of wines. These Jewish immigrants also begin to explore the wonders of a new and exotic type of restaurant, one with such a strong appeal that it would eventually become almost a second Jewish cuisine: Chinese food. By the latter decades of the twentieth century, Jewish food manufacturers are increasingly marketing their products to a mainstream audience, the confident ethnic assertions in their advertisements reflecting the Jewish community's feeling of having successfully assimilated into the broader American society.

Still, the long debate about balancing acculturation with Jewish identity continues. Even if discussions about this process no longer take place over stuffed derma and a glezele tey, they are still an essential part of the ongoing conversation about the Jewish past, present, and future. I. B. Singer described this long debate:

> For a number of years while I worked at the *Jewish Daily Forward* as a journalist the Garden Cafeteria was my second home. I ate there and discussed literature with my literary chums, gossiped about publishers, editors, and especially about the critics who didn't like us and whom we disliked. We also questioned the very purpose of

literature. What can it do? What has it done in the past? What can one expect it to do in the future? To strengthen our arguments we ate mountains of rice pudding and drank countless cups of coffee.

Between 1880 and 1914, more than two million Yiddish-speaking Jews immigrated to the United States from Eastern and Central Europe. Most made their new homes in urban enclaves, where they attempted to recreate much of the Old World food tradition even while partaking of the new and exotic ingredients (bananas! squash! salmon! cream cheese!) offered by America. An 1899 survey of New York's Lower East Side found more than six hundred food purveyors within only a few square blocks, including 131 butcher shops, thirty-six bakeries, ten delicatessens, seven herring stands, ten sausage shops, twenty soda-water stands, and twenty-eight wine shops.

Jews also began to discover the pleasure of eating in restaurants; a new Yiddish word, *oysesn* (eating out), appeared in the *Jewish Daily Forward* in 1903. New York restaurants such as Manny Wolf's, the Cafe Royale, the Monopole, and Moskowitz & Lupowitz, and cafeterias such as the Garden Cafeteria offered Jewish immigrants convenient and inexpensive meals that could be enjoyed while schmoozing with friends and neighbors and, in so doing, participating in the communal life of the city.

Recent Jewish immigrants created a huge new consumer market that was quickly seized upon by food manufacturers. Scores of products appeared with labels in both English and Yiddish to catch the eye of the Jewish housewife as she did her shopping. Probably the most successful marketing was done by the Maxwell House coffee company, which began producing Passover Haggadot in 1933. A kit produced by Maxwell House for American grocery stores directed the stores to advertise and display the free Haggadot, and thereby promote the sales of Maxwell House coffee.

Many large food companies issued free recipe books intended to familiarize Jewish housewives with the company and its products. The Hecker's Flour company, for instance, produced a Yiddish-language brochure with recipes for traditional Jewish foods such as challah, knishes, and honey cake; all the recipes called for the use of Heckers *mel*, Heckers flour. A somewhat later Yiddish-English recipe book produced by the Manischewitz Wine company similarly featured traditional Jewish foods such as khremzlekh, kneydlekh, and matzo kugel but now included recipes for American fare like cream puffs (translated as the Yinglish *kriem-pofs*) and strawberry shortcake (*stroberi shortkeyk*).

Today, eating Chinese food on Christmas is a mainstay of Jewish life in the United States, but the love affair between Jews and Chinese food is a long one, stretching back to the earliest years of the Eastern European Jewish arrival in America. For these immigrants, Chinese restaurants represented the openness and diversity of their new American life; by eating Chinese food, they were implicitly rejecting the provincialism and orthodoxy of the life from which they had fled.

To Eastern European Jews, Chinese cuisine was both exotic and familiar, using chicken broth, lots of garlic and onions, vegetables cooked to a melting softness, and sweet-and-sour flavors reminiscent of those of Ashkenazic cooking. Some Chinese restaurants went so far as to describe wonton soup on their menus as "chicken soup with kreplach." Meals began with a steaming pot of tea, served the Eastern European way, with sugar and no milk. As Chinese cuisine uses no dairy products, there was no mixing of meat and milk; and although the cuisine does feature forbidden foods such as pork and shellfish, these items were usually served in such a way as to disguise their presence on the plate. "Suddenly even the pig is no threat," recalls Philip Roth's Alexander Portnoy, describing his childhood meals in Chinatown, "though, to be sure, it comes to us so chopped and shredded, and is then set afloat on our plates in such oceans of soy sauce, as to bear no resemblance at all to a pork chop, or a ham bone, or, most disgusting of all, a sausage. . . . "

Though Jews had been flocking to New York's Chinese restaurants since the late nineteenth century, the city had no kosher Chinese restaurant until 1959, when deli owner Sol Bernstein opened Bernstein-on-Essex ("Where kashrut is king and quality reigns"). Located at 135 Essex Street on the Lower East Side, Bernstein-on-Essex or "Schmulka Bernstein's," as the restaurant was popularly known, offered both Eastern European deli food and Cantonese-style favorites such as moo goo gai pan and "lo mein Bernstein" (prepared with chicken livers), served by waiters wearing tasseled Chinese skullcaps. The restaurant closed in the mid-1990s, the victim of changing neighborhood demographics and the tastes of a younger generation that preferred spicy ginger chicken to chicken chow mein and egg foo yung.

By the 1930s the delicatessen had become one of the central culinary institutions of the American Jewish community, providing the beloved Eastern European smoked and cured meats that were too time-consuming to prepare at home. Though New York had far more delis than any other city—by one count the city boasted more than 5,000—they were by no means solely a New York phenomenon. Delicatessens could be found in Jewish urban enclaves around the country, including Cohen's in Los Angeles, Batt's in Chicago, and Morrison & Schiff in Boston. They featured sandwiches stuffed with smoked meats and fish along with homemade soups, Old World delicacies such as pickles, knishes, and chopped liver, and for dessert (at least in the non-kosher delis), huge slabs of incredibly rich "New York-style" cheesecake, made with cream cheese rather than the farmer cheese of the Eastern European variety. Cream cheese itself had been popularized in America by the merchants Joseph and Isaac Breakstone—né Breghstein—two Jewish immigrants from Lithuania.

Among the largest and most popular deli-style restaurants was Lou G. Siegel's (most often called just "Lou G.'s"), which opened in New York's garment center in 1925. In contrast to the Formica tables and fluorescent lights of most delicatessens, Lou G. Siegel's was decorated with oil paintings and wrought-iron chandeliers. For several generations the restaurant was a regular meeting spot for garmentos and power brokers alike. During the 1992 Democratic Convention, Senator Daniel Patrick Moynihan hosted a dinner for twenty-eight US senators there. It finally served its last plate of stuffed derma in 1996. Said one heartbroken patron, "It's like they're knocking down Yankee Stadium."

Jews looking for a respite from the city often vacationed in the Catskill Mountains of upstate New York, where a trademark of the hotels was the sheer abundance of the meals. Most of the food served in Catskills hotels was of the heymish variety, with a Sabbath menu from Brown's Hotel in Loch Sheldrake featuring flanken, stuffed cabbage, potato pudding, and tsimmes. At the Concord Hotel, where the clientele was more upscale, pickled tongue was "Langue de Boeuf" and French fries were "Pommes de Terre, Frites."

Just as Eastern European Jewish immigrants established delicatessens, restaurants, and bakeries that offered their patrons food like that of the "old country," so, too, did they create their own wineries, producing wine under strict rabbinic supervision. Notable among these were the Mogen David winery of Chicago; the Kedem, House of David, Crystal, and Belmont wineries of New York City; and Manischewitz of Brooklyn, which eventually established itself as the country's leading producer of kosher wine. And just as Jewish food purveyors adapt traditional menus to the new ingredients available in America (this is, for instance, how salmon replaced carp as the Jews' favorite fish), the new kosher wineries turned to the only variety of grape readily available on the East Coast: the Concord grape. The result was a distinctively thick, sweet wine, dismissed by some Jews as redolent of cough syrup but celebrated by many others as reminiscent of the homemade wines of Eastern Europe. Even today, for many Jewish families, sweet Concord grape wine is as much a fixture of Passover Seders as potato latkes are on Hanukkah.

Founded in 1899 on New York's Lower East Side with the unlikely name of the California Valley Wine Company, the Schapiro Wine Company, as it was later known, quickly became one of the largest and most recognizable of the kosher wineries. Far from attempting to downplay its wines' syrupy sweetness, the company celebrated it with the famous slogan, "Wine so thick you can almost cut it with a knife." For generations Schapiro's crushed grapes in a series of cellars that ran an entire block beneath Rivington Street on the Lower East Side; the wine was sold in its flagship store at 126 Rivington (during Prohibition the store was granted an exemption to stay open to sell "sacramental wine"), as well as in wine shops and liquor stores around the country. The company also produced a line of wines that leading Catskills hotels such as the Concord, the Nevele, and Kusher's sold under their own labels.

In 2000, the owners of Schapiro's sold the building on Rivington Street, and the company now produces its wine in Monticello, NY. In another instance of the gentrification that has overtaken the Lower East Side, the site of the former Schapiro Wine store is now a trendy cupcake bakery called Sugar Sweet Sunshine.

By the end of the 1960s the Jewish community was assimilating into American life, and earlier uneasiness about assertions of Jewish identity had made way for more confident assertions of ethnicity. Large national food corporations continued to appeal to Jewish consumers, as in advertisements from soda companies such as Coca-Cola for products made kosher for Passover. In an even more striking phenomenon, venerable Jewish companies began to reach out to a mainstream audience. Hebrew National touted its hot dogs as superior because "We're kosher, and have to answer to a higher authority," while the makers of Levy's rye bread rolled out an advertising campaign assuring Americans, "You don't have to be Jewish to love Levy's." So, too, did kosher wineries seek to expand into the broader American market, with advertisements suggesting that kosher wine was, in the words of one Manischewitz ad, "everybody's wine."

Today, the mainstreaming of Jewish food shows no signs of abating. One recent study estimated that nearly half the products in a typical American supermarket bear a kosher stamp, while some market researchers estimate that as much as nine-tenths of kosher food is purchased by non-Jews (many of them believe, often mistakenly, that it is healthier or of higher quality than other food). At the same time, traditional Jewish foods are fast disappearing or becoming deracinated. Nowhere is the latter trend more evident than in the case of that most iconic Jewish food, the bagel. Bagels are now sold as "breakfast sandwiches" at McDonald's, often with ham and cheese, and the largest purveyor of bagels nationwide is Dunkin' Donuts. As bagel shops offer varieties including blueberry, jalapeño, and sun-dried tomato, it is fair to surmise that many Americans no longer identify the bagel as a Jewish food.

Even the most observant Jews are now free to eat kosher sushi, waffles, and gummy bears. Traditional Jewish delicatessens and bakeries are increasingly scarce, and very few of the dishes found in those early Jewish cookbooks are still being made at home. Surveying the assimilation of Jewish food in America in the early twenty-first century, one might wonder what has been gained and, just as surely, what has been lost.

A Little Taste

AARON LANSKY

In Outwitting History: The Amazing Adventures of a Man Who Rescued a Million Yiddish Books *(2004), Aaron Lansky describes how, from the 1980s onward, he traveled around the US accepting donations of Yiddish books from anyone who could spare them. In this brief segment, he describes one of the particular challenges of the collections process: being constantly invited to eat.*

I TRIED WHENEVER POSSIBLE to travel in a team of three: two to do the schlepping and the third to be the Designated Eater. The latter was the really hard job: While the others carried boxes, you had to sit with the host at the kitchen table, listening to stories, sipping endless glasses of tea, and valiantly working your way through a week's worth of dishes cooked "special," just for you—gefilte fish and *khreyn* (horseradish), kashe varnishkes, blintzes and sour cream, potato latkes, and *lokshn kugl*. Given a choice, I preferred to shlep: better to strain muscles, I figured, than to sit at the table, watching your arteries harden before your eyes. And that's not to mention the care packages: So many people gave us a "little something for the road" that we had to unload the van with great care, lest a bag of onion bagels or a Tupperware container of chopped herring end up buried in our warehouse. Eventually we devised an "emergency kit" that we carried with us on every trip: an old Boy Scout knapsack packed with Bengay ointment and Ace bandages for the shleppers, and, for the Designated Eater, a roll of Tums, a jar of salted Japanese umeboshi plums (great after too much sugar), a canteen of water, and six packets of Alka-Seltzer.

Carp, Rugelach, Egg Creams

ARTHUR KLEIN, ALICE AHART, LISA NEWMAN, ALBERT BERKOWITZ, DANIEL OKRENT

The following are a series of reminiscences of joyful Yiddish-speaking eaters, collected by the Yiddish Book Center through its Wexler Oral History Project and its magazine, Pakn Treger. *Arthur Klein is a Brooklyn-born Navy veteran and retired hairdresser. Alice Ahart is a a retired speech-language pathologist. Lisa Newman is the director of communications at the Yiddish Book Center and co editor of* Pakn Treger. *Albert Berkowitz was a docent at the Yiddish Book Center. Daniel Okrent (b. 1948) is a journalist. He was the first public editor of* The New York Times. *His books include* The Guarded Gate: Bigotry, Eugenics, and the Law That Kept Two Generations of Jews, Italians, and Other European Immigrants Out of America *(2019).*

ARTHUR KLEIN

My grandmas did the typical cooking that a Jewish housewife would do in those days. You know, like kugels, and tsimmes, and they went shopping and they bought the chickens and they plucked the chickens. And my grandma always used to cook with chicken fat—she'd use chicken fat and gribenes.

You know what that is? The gribenes was the rendering of the chicken, with the chicken fat—there were little pieces of, I guess, fat—we used to call it gribenes. And we used to put it on matzo and smear it like we would smear butter, and it was absolutely delicious. Actually, until I was about seventeen or eighteen, I thought heartburn was a natural thing to have, because after eating all that gribenes and chicken fat it left me with that—but I thought it was just natural.

ALICE AHART

My father would not eat fish unless he saw it alive first. Now, how in the world my mother ever brought home this big fish from the market I never knew, but we'd come home from school and there would be a carp in the bathtub.

And then, after my father had seen it in the bathtub, my mother would take care of it and fix it. So anyway, I thought we were kind of peculiar, but apparently other people had carp in the bathtub.

LISA NEWMAN

If asked what I think is the most Jewish food, I would answer rugelach. Unlike matzo ball soup, kasha with bow-tie noodles, or challah, my mother and grandmother never made rugelach, so it doesn't have to live up to my memories of those homemade dishes. No matter where it's purchased, rugelach tastes familiar—buttery dough rolled around raisins and walnuts and caramelized with a rainfall of sugar on top. Its Jewishness lives on in my memories of its presence at holidays, bar and bat mitzvahs, and funerals. Sometimes it was the treat offered after Sunday school, and it often arrived with grandparents visiting from New York. This little palm-size pastry remains my reliable Jewish treat—one that I can seek out anywhere when I want to be transported back to days long gone.

ALBERT BERKOWITZ

I always remember coming home on a Friday and smelling challah being made. One other dish that I remember was called salata, which I think must have been Rumanian for "salad." You took an eggplant and you put it over a flame—a gas flame. My mother even had a small gas stove put in the basement of our new house to cook eggplant over a flame. You peeled all of the black skin off it, and then you put it on a cutting board tilted over the sink. All the liquid—the "poisons," the sour stuff—would drain out of it. And then the next day you chopped it up very fine and chopped an onion in it, and then you served that with olive oil.

They also made something with the Rumanian name mamaliga. Mamaliga was a standard peasant dish. It's made with corn—it's cornmeal mush. My parents used to eat it with some stuff called brindze, which was a kind of goat cheese. My brother and I always preferred scrambled eggs on this, and that's how we would eat it. But what you did is, you took a great big pot and you cooked up this cornmeal mush until it stiffened. Then you turned it over on a platter or on a board, and then you cut it with a very fine piece of thread, because it was still damp inside and was very tough getting through with a knife. I always remember them cutting the mamaliga with a string and then having their goat cheese or scrambled eggs with it.

DANIEL OKRENT

The standard definition of an egg cream is a negative: it doesn't contain eggs, and it doesn't contain cream. This is not any more helpful than saying a Ford Mustang isn't a horse. The ingredients do matter, but not as much as the ambient aura that, in combination, they evoke. After the tall glass (never plastic) accepts its whole (never skim) milk, its spoonful of Fox's U-Bet (never Hershey's) syrup, its blast of seltzer (ideally from a siphon), and a few flutters of a long mixing spoon, you've conjured up more than a drink. You've stepped back into the pre-assimilation era that now seems so distant it's barely even a memory.

When the immigrant East European Jews and their children escaped the urban ghettos of the new world, they placed bagels, smoked fish, dill pickles, and other signifying staples on the American table. But for some reason the egg cream—the least ethnic of these foods, when you think about it—stayed behind. As such, it's an anchor of sorts: each time I drink one, it takes me back to the old neighborhood.

The Baker and the Beggar

KADYA MOLODOWSKY

Kadya Molodowsky (1894–1975) was one of the most admired of twentieth-century Yiddish writers. Born in present-day Belarus, she immigrated to the US in 1935. She was a prolific author of poetry, fiction, and children's literature, and the founder and editor of a journal, Svive. *The following story appeared in a collection of her writings for children,* Martsepanes (Marzipans, 1970). *Miriam Udel teaches Yiddish language, literature and culture at Emory and is the editor of* Honey on the Page: An Annotated Anthology of Yiddish Children's Literature *(2020).*

ONCE UPON A TIME, there was a baker with his own bakery who made bread, rolls, pretzels, bagels, and challah for Shabbos.

His wife would tie up her hair in a scarf and knead the dough, and the children would twist the bagels into circles.

The whole town delighted in their pretzels and bagels. Even the birds would come down from the heavens in order to catch the crumbs and twitch their tail feathers with pleasure.

Every Friday, poor Jews would come to the bakery to beg food for Shabbos. That was the custom of the time, the time of our grandparents. The baker would give them a roll, a bagel, a pretzel, whatever he could spare. And no one left empty-handed.

One of the poor Jews had very special eyes, so radiant that they sent forth beams of light. The baker liked him best of all, and each Friday, he would give him an entire challah for Shabbos.

So it was week after week, Friday after Friday, over many years. The baker became so accustomed to his visits that he would look forward to them. He would hand the beggar the challah personally and say, "Eat in good health, and may all be well with you."

The man never thanked him; he just smiled with his bright eyes and replied, "May you live long, and may God repay you."

One Friday that happened to also be the eve of a holiday, the bakery was crowded with customers, who pushed and crushed against each other. This one wanted a challah with poppy seeds, that one, a loaf of white bread ("but make sure it's sweet!"). . . . The baker, his wife, and their children were so busy that by day's end, they could hardly stand.

Along came the bright-eyed man. He saw the great rush, so he didn't want to bother the baker just then. He stood for a while and then left without saying so much as a word.

After that Friday, the beggar stopped coming. A week passed, and then two and three. The baker thought of him many times and asked the other poor people about him—but eventually he forgot about him. Who keeps thinking about a poor man? And perhaps God had helped him so that he no longer needed to beg.

The bakery was prospering. The baker had built a fine house with a large oven for baking. His wife had sewn herself a new woolen jacket, and their children now wore shoes without holes and flannel jackets. They had bought drinking glasses and spoons by the half-dozen, and they thanked God for providing these little luxuries.

But no one's good luck lasts forever. One Friday, a fire broke out in the bakery. And the fire burnt up the sacks of flour, the shelves, and the whole house; everything the baker possessed disappeared with the smoke.

The baker stood there slumped with worry, staring at the embers of the burnt-up walls. And near him stood his wife and the children like lonely sheep. The baker thought, "God in Heaven, why have You brought such a punishment upon us? Why must I endure such a bitter blow? Shabbos is coming and we're left without a roof over our heads."

And the neighbors came and echoed the baker's sadness: "Really, why should this have happened to the baker? He's such an honest man!"

While the baker was standing there worried and despondent, not knowing what to do—*just then*, along came the poor man who had not come to the bakery in a long time.

The baker was dumbfounded. Of all times to return, the poor man had to come now and see him in the midst of this great misfortune? He ran up to him and said with a broken spirit, "You see, sir, what has happened to me! Everything burnt, lock, stock, and barrel! Now I don't even have challah for Shabbos for myself."

With his eyes beaming, the man said, "I didn't come to ask you for challah. God has changed my luck and freed me from poverty. Now I have what I need and can repay the debts of what I have borrowed from good people."

From his pocket, the man took out a bundled kerchief and handed it to the baker, who was astonished. "Here," said the man, "you have the repayment for all the challahs you gave me week after week, from Friday to Friday, over many, many years. I have added it all up and thought of everything, and my calculations are right. You may be certain I've made no error."

And it was enough for a house and an oven and a bakery, and even for a woolen jacket for the baker's wife, and for flannel jackets for the children. And the baker's wonder was very great: the price of each and every challah was recorded. Each and every challah, from week to week, from Friday to Friday, from year to year—and not a crumb was missing.

TRANSLATED BY MIRIAM UDEL

On Bagels, Gefilte Fish, and Tsholnt

ASYA VAISMAN SCHULMAN

Asya Vaisman Schulman is the Director of the Yiddish Book Center's Yiddish Language Institute in Amherst, Massachusetts. She holds a PhD in Yiddish language and culture from Harvard University.

FOOD IS LANGUAGE: each ingredient, each dish is referred to by a word. Where those words come from is, in and of itself, a wonderful culinary story.

BAGELS

Probably the best-known baked product with a Yiddish name is the bagel (beygl). This doughnut-shaped bread roll is such a common food item that many Americans probably aren't even conscious of its Yiddish origins. While the exact etymology is difficult to trace (various sources suggest that it comes from the Middle High German Bougel, meaning "ring"), it is clearly related to the verb beygn—"to bend." If we consider how the bagel is made—a roll of dough is bent into a circle until the two ends connect—the term makes perfect sense.

GEFILTE FISH

It entered Jewish cuisine in medieval Germany and became a staple among Ashkenazi Jews in Eastern Europe in the seventeenth century. The name means "stuffed fish" in Yiddish and reflects the preparation process, which involves filleting the fish, chopping the flesh, mixing in various ingredients—such as matzo meal, onions, salt, and eggs—and stuffing the mixture back into the fish skin. The "stuffed fish" is then grilled, baked, or simmered over a low flame and served intact, often with a garnish of carrots and onions. Some swear to the superiority of "gehakte," or "chopped," fish, which is made by hand with a special chopping knife, while others prefer the faster method of putting the flesh through a meat mincer.

Perhaps even more contested is the flavor of the fish: Evgeniia Krasner, from Shpykiv, Ukraine, for instance, states in no uncertain terms that she prefers her fish savory, going so far as to claim that sweet gefilte fish makes her queasy. This sweet versus savory distinction goes deeper than simply being a matter of personal preference: scholars have discovered that there are discrete geographical areas in which each type of fish [was] prepared. The "gefilte fish line" that divides the sweet from the savory regions of Europe happens to trace almost precisely the line that divides the Central Yiddish dialect (spoken primarily in the region roughly corresponding to present-day Poland) from the Southeastern and Northeastern dialects (spoken primarily in the regions corresponding to present-day Ukraine and Lithuania/Belarus, respectively). As the Yiddish linguist Marvin Herzog, among others, has noted, "sweetened fish, also called pojlise fis ('Polish fish'), is generally unpalatable to those east of the indicated [dialect] border, who prefer their fish seasoned only with pepper."

TSHOLNT

A savory stew, called *tsholnt* (more commonly spelled "cholent" in English), has been a way for observant Jews to enjoy hot food on Shabbos, the day of rest, for centuries. *Al pi halokhe*, according to religious laws, it is forbidden to light a fire and cook food on the Sabbath day. How, then, does one keep food warm in the cold winter months? The raw ingredients are assembled in a pot on Friday afternoon, before sundown, and then left in the oven to cook over a low flame overnight, providing a hot meal the following day.

There are almost as many theories about the origins of the word tsholnt as there are varieties of the food. Both the word and the food were introduced to Ashkenazi Jews in France around eight hundred years ago. From France, the dish traveled to Germany and later Eastern Europe, and immigrants from these areas, in turn, brought it with them to North America, Australia, South America, and anywhere else Ashkenazi Jews settled. Scholars agree, then, that the word tsholnt comes from Old French, though opinions differ greatly about its exact parsing. The most commonly accepted etymology comes from Max Weinreich's *History of the Yiddish Language*, in which he traces the word to "calentem" (that which is warm), the present participle of the Latin verb "calere" (to be warm). In Old French, the initial "c" was transformed to "ch," pronounced as the

HOW YIDDISH CHANGED AMERICA AND HOW AMERICA CHANGED YIDDISH

"tsh" in "tsholnt." Other theories include the French "chaud/lent," literally meaning "warm, slow," alluding to the cooking process (in French, the final "d" of "chaud" is not pronounced), and still others interpret the word pair as an abbreviation for "warm lentils" ("lentilles" in French), alluding to the ingredients.

Among the average tsholnt eaters, however, who may have been unfamiliar with the word's Romance origins, a number of folk etymologies were popular. In the United States, for example, the word was interpreted as coming from "shul ende," since the dish was eaten upon returning home from synagogue services (the end of shul). A less common notion holds that "tsholnt" comes from the Hebrew "she'lan," or "that which rested," referring to the stew's low-maintenance preparations.

Crisco Recipes for the Jewish Housewife

PROCTER & GAMBLE

When Procter & Gamble introduced Crisco in 1911, the company worked hard to convince American housewives that the new vegetable shortening (made from hydrogenated cottonseed oil) was a healthy alternative to butter and lard. Jews were targeted as early adopters because Crisco was pareve, a neutral fat that could be used in the preparation of either milk or meat dishes. In 1933, when Procter & Gamble published a seventy-seven-page pamphlet called Crisco Recipes for the Jewish Housewife, *it was an instant hit. Printed in Yiddish and English, the cookbook became a touchstone for a generation of assimilating Jews.*

קריסקא
רעסעפיעס

פאר
דער **אידישער**
באלעבאָסטע

BORSHT

2 pounds beets
1 quart cold water
Juice of 1 lemon
2 to 4 tablespoons sugar
Salt and pepper
4 egg yolks
Sour cream

Wash beets, grind them up fine, cover with the water. Cook until the beets are very tender and can be mashed up. Strain and use the beet pulp for beet kugelach. Cool the liquid and add the lemon juice, sugar, and seasonings. Beat the egg yolks and pour the partially cooled beet juice into the yolks, stirring constantly. Chill. When ready to serve, stir in sour cream.

MEAT KREPLACH

Makes about 24.

1 pound beef, veal, or lamb
1 egg
1 teaspoon salt
2/3 teaspoon pepper and nutmeg
1 small onion
1 tablespoon Crisco
1 recipe noodle dough

Grind the beef very fine, beat in the egg and seasoning. Fry the diced onion in Crisco and add to the chopped meat.

Cut the thinly rolled dough into 2-inch squares and place 1 tablespoon of the prepared meat in the center. Fold into triangles, pressing the edges together lightly. Fasten by moistening with water.

Drop into boiling water or salted water and boil for 20 minutes, or boil for 5 minutes, drain, and bake in a Criscoed dish for 20 minutes in a moderate oven (350F).

CARROT TSIMESS

1 pound fat brisket or beef
6 medium-sized carrots
Salt and pepper
2 tablespoons Crisco
1 tablespoons flour

Place the meat in a pot and cover with diced carrots. Season. Cover with boiling water. Cook for 3 hours over a slow fire, keeping well covered. Brown the flour in the Crisco and slowly add 1 cup of the carrot and meat liquor, stirring constantly. Add the carrots and cook uncovered until carrots become browned. Place the meat on a hot platter and surround with carrots.

EIER MIT KARTOFFELN (EGGS AND POTATOES)

Serves 4 to 5.

3 hard-boiled eggs
2 large cooked potatoes
1 cup hot sweet-sour sauce
Crisco
Bread crumbs
Salt and pepper

Slice the eggs and the potatoes. Rub a baking dish with Crisco. Put in a layer of the sauce. Add a layer of potatoes and a layer of eggs. Season. Continue until all potatoes and eggs are used. Sprinkle with bread crumbs. Dot with Crisco and pour the rest of the sauce over this. Bake until brown in a moderate oven (350F).

Holy Mole and Kamish!

ALISON SPARKS

Alison Sparks (b. 1958) is a developmental psychologist and a visiting scholar at Amherst College.

KAMISH BREAD

My great-grandmother, Anna Salzman Silverman, brought her recipe for Kamish Bread when she immigrated to the United States from Russia. My mother, Joan, taught her to speak and read in English and Anna taught her to make Kamish Bread. The name is a mystery to me. Most Jews call this Mandel Bread but we don't. Cookbook author Joan Nathan notes that this cookie comes from the Ukrainian Jewish community, yet my family has no known roots there. My Italian friends consider it a Jewish version of biscotti.

My mother and I always enjoyed making Kamish Bread during Chanukah. She often reminded me that her grandmother Anna used the same dough to make poppy-seed cookies, rolling it out and cutting perfect rounds with a glass, then topping them with a generous portion of poppy seeds before baking in the oven.

> *3 eggs*
> *1 cup sugar*
> *1 stick of butter*
> *1 teaspoon vanilla*
> *2–3 cups all-purpose unbleached flour*
> *1 teaspoon baking powder*
> *1/3 teaspoon salt*
> *Sugar and cinnamon*

Preheat oven to 350.

Cream butter and sugar. Beat the eggs and add to butter and sugar mixture. Sift dry ingredients and add to wet ingredients.

Roll the dough into 2 oval shaped loaves, about 8 inches in length and place on a baking sheet lined with parchment paper. Mix cinnamon and sugar and sprinkle over the top of the loaves. Bake for 25 minutes.

When cool, cut into ½-inch slices then return to a 250-degree oven to dry for an hour or so.

LATKES WITH MOLE

*I didn't just marry a wonderful man, I married into a rich and alluring cuisine.
I happen to have fallen in love with him and with mole on my first trip to his
home country. I remain smitten with both,* en serio. *I was inspired by the way
Mexicans put mole on most everything, over eggs in the morning, over enchiladas
in the evening. So why not over latkes at Chanukah? Although it is not something
I have observed in Mexico, it is the perfect expression of my family life.*

*I get questions about how many types of chile I use to make mole. The truth
is, I learned to make it with the premade base melted into chicken broth. That
is how I was taught by Ofelia, my mother-in-law. I tell myself that someday I
will learn to make one of the many other moles from Mexico's complex cuisine.
But for now, my Chanukah guests enjoy latkes with what they call "black gold."*

MOLE

2 tbsp. vegetable oil
1 onion, chopped
1 8-ounce jar mole base
2 cups chicken stock
1 to 2 quarts bittersweet chocolate

Make the mole: Heat the oil in a large saucepan over medium heat. Add
the onion and cook, stirring often, until soft and translucent.

Add a heaping tablespoon of the mole base to the saucepan, stirring to
combine with the onion. Add 1 cup of the chicken stock. Bring to a boil,
then lower heat and simmer, stirring regularly, until the mixture reaches
the consistency of a thick soup.

Alternate adding heaping tablespoons of mole base with cups of the
stock, keeping the mixture at a simmer and stirring regularly. This will
take about 20 minutes.

Continue cooking, stirring occasionally, until the mole reaches syrup-
like consistency. Then let it gently simmer for another 10 minutes, until

it becomes a thick, rich sauce. Add the chocolate to taste, stirring until it melts. Remove from heat and set aside while making the latkes.

Make the latkes: Follow the potato latkes recipe (below).

To serve, spoon mole over the latkes. Serve with sour cream and applesauce on the side. If desired, sprinkle lettuce over the top. Serve hot. Makes about 3 cups.

LATKES

2 pounds russet potatoes
1 onion
2 eggs, lightly beaten
2 tbsp. unbleached all-purpose flour
Salt and freshly grounded pepper to taste
Vegetable oil for frying
Shredded lettuce for topping (optional)

Preheat oven to 200 degrees. Peel and grate the potatoes. (This can be done in a food processor, but the texture is better if done by hand.) Place the grated potatoes in a colander with a plate beneath it. Sprinkle salt on the potatoes, cover them with a layer of paper towels, and then place a heavy object (such as a bowl or can) on top. Allow the potatoes to drain for 10 minutes.

While the potatoes are draining, peel the onion and grate it by hand. Set aside.

In a large bowl, combine the potatoes, onion, eggs, and flour and season generously with salt and pepper. Mix well.

In a large heavy skillet, add oil to a depth of about ¼ inch and heat over medium-high heat. Drop ¼ cup of potato mixture into the hot oil, flattening with a spatula. Fry the latkes until deep brown and crispy on both sides.

Drain the latkes on paper towels (pat them with the towels on both sides) and keep them warm in a single layer on a baking sheet in the oven until all of them have been made.

Hering mit pateytes

ISADORE LILLIAN

Isadore Lillian (1882–1960) was a prolific Galicia-born actor, playwright, and songwriter. Jane Peppler, a musician and author, researches and writes about Yiddish music and culture. On her website yiddishpennysongs.com, Peppler mentions two different recordings of this intentionally repetitive Yiddish vaudeville song from the Gaslight era: one from 1913 by Simon Paskal (Pascal) and a later one by Miriam Kressyn and Seymour Rechtzeit on their From Ellis Island to the East Side *LP.*

HERING MIT PATEYTES

In New York, if you want to make a living
Don't laugh at somebody who's peddling sausage
If you want to go into business, run, quickly,
Open a store, put up a sign, and start selling . . .

Herring with potatoes, herring with potatoes!
Don't bother with meat, steak,
Duck, sponge cake, and cheesecake
Chicken is a dog compared to this, it's understood!
The best dish for the belly is—herring with potatoes!

Eat what you want, it won't annoy me.
The Hungarian eats goulash, the Galitsyaner eats meat and sweets
Romanians eat corn pudding, the goyim eat crabs
The Germans eat sauerkraut. What do the Litvaks eat?

Herring with potatoes, herring with potatoes! . . .

Any of you have a bad stomach and can't chew?
Any of you suffer lack of appetite and can't digest?
Don't run to a doctor, your salvation doesn't lie there
It's I who have the best cure for a bad stomach. . . .

Herring with potatoes, herring with potatoes! . . .

Late at night a thief crept into a house
He'd soon opened the door and cracked the safe
When he opened the safe he almost lost his mind.
He thought there'd be gold lying there, but instead he found:

Herring with potatoes, herring with potatoes! . . .

My neighbor went to childbed, her shouts rose to the ceiling
A doctor said it positively was going to be twins
A second doctor soon swore it would be quadruplets
When she delivered, guess what she bore?

Herring with potatoes, herring with potatoes! . . .

In the Yiddish theater I've already seen a lot of shows
The names are sort of the same, I'm not going to forget them
"The Swarthy Jew," "The Pintele Yid," everybody knows those
Why shouldn't a writer make a show that will be called:

Herring with potatoes, herring with potatoes! . . .

An election is coming as you know, don't get involved in it
Democrats, Republicans, they'll have a pillow fight
Roosevelt, Taft, and Mr. Wilson, you shouldn't know from them
I hope in the next election they elect:

Herring with potatoes, herring with potatoes!

TRANSLATED BY JANE PEPPLER

PART IV

American
Commemoration

לאָזט מיר ניט דאָס ייִדישע וואָרט

אויף אַ רגע פֿאַרגעסן.

Lozt mir nit dos yidishe vort
af a rege fargesn.

Let me not forget for a moment
the Yiddish word.

—JACOB GLATSTEIN,
"THE JOY OF THE YIDDISH WORD"

WHEN THE NOVELIST David Bergelson surveyed the Yiddish literary scene in 1923, he perceived "three centers": Warsaw, Moscow, and New York. In the decades that followed, the fate of Yiddish literature in Warsaw and Moscow would be complex and tragic, and new centers would arise in places like Bueno Aires, Montreal, and Tel Aviv—but New York would continue to be one of the best places on earth to rub noses with a Yiddish writer. It still is.

Always connected to the work of Yiddish literary culture abroad, American Yiddish literature developed alongside and dynamically intertwined with American literary culture in English. In the 1910s, as Yiddish publishers pumped out popular books for an insatiable audience of Yiddish readers, Yiddish poets hung out with bohemians in Greenwich Village, publishing in their journals, and Yiddish playwrights saw their work performed in English by the most innovative American theater companies. When Sholem Aleichem died in 1916, tens of thousands of New Yorkers attended his funeral, and his will was read into the Congressional Record in Washington and printed in the *New York Times*. Yiddish novelists scored major bestsellers in translation with huge, ambitious novels—I. J. Singer's *The Brothers Ashkenazi* (1936) and Sholem Asch's *East River* (1946)—and in the postwar decades Isaac Bashevis Singer's stories, published weekly in the *Forverts*, became hot literary commodities in translation, in magazines such as *Playboy*, the *New Yorker*, and *Esquire* even before he was honored as the first (and so far, only) Yiddish writer to be awarded a Nobel Prize for Literature. Meanwhile, Yiddish poets of no less talent, but with less renown, were writing startling, intimate lyrics, and experimental writers were pushing the boundaries of what Yiddish prose could do.

The selection of American Yiddish literary works that follows is, by intention—and because it couldn't be otherwise—idiosyncratic and unpredictable. It aims to give readers a series of tastes, reflecting the variety and complexity of this extraordinary literary field.

FURTHER READING

John Felstiner, Jules Chametzky, Hilene Flanzbaum, Kathryn Hellerstein, eds. *Jewish American Literature: A Norton Anthology* (2000)

Benjamin and Barbara Harshav, eds., *American Yiddish Poetry: A Bilingual Anthology* (2007)

The Cafeteria

ISAAC BASHEVIS SINGER

Isaac Bashevis Singer (1904–1991) was awarded the Nobel Prize for Literature in 1978. An immigrant from Poland, he arrived in New York following the steps of his older brother, Israel Joshua Singer. He wrote essays, stories, and other writings for the Forverts, *at times under pseudonym. Saul Bellow translated his story "Gimpel the Fool," which heralded his talent for a young generation of American Jewish readers. For years he published his stories in* The New Yorker, *where he developed a distinct style. His numerous books include* Satan in Goray *(1935),* Gimpel the Fool and Other Stories *(1957),* The Magician of Lublin *(1960),* The Slave *(1962),* The Spinoza of Market Street *(1963),* A Friend of Kafka and Other Stories *(1970),* Enemies, a Love Story *(1972),* Old Love *(1979), and* Shadows on the Hudson *(1997). His work has been translated into dozens of languages. The following story, about the impact of memory on immigrants, appeared in* The New Yorker. *Dorothea Straus, who was married to Roger Straus, Jr. (co-founder and chairman of Farrar, Straus and Giroux), wrote about her relationship with Isaac Bashevis Singer in a memoir,* Under the Canopy *(1982).*

I

EVEN THOUGH I HAVE reached the point where a great part of my earnings is given away in taxes, I still have the habit of eating in cafeterias when I am by myself. I like to take a tray with a tin knife, fork, spoon, and paper napkin and to choose at the counter the food I enjoy. Besides, I meet there the landslayt from Poland, as well as all kinds of literary beginners and readers who know Yiddish. The moment I sit down at a table, they come over. "Hello, Aaron!" they greet me, and we talk about Yiddish literature, the Holocaust, the state of Israel, and often about acquaintances who were eating rice pudding or stewed prunes the last time I was here and are already in their graves. Since I seldom read a paper, I learn this news only later. Each time, I am startled, but at my age one has to be ready for such tidings. The food sticks in the throat; we look at one another in confusion, and our eyes ask mutely, Whose turn is next? Soon we begin to chew again. I am often reminded of a scene in a film about Africa. A lion attacks a herd of zebras and kills one. The frightened zebras run for a while and then they stop and start to graze again. Do they have a choice?

I cannot spend too long with these Yiddishists, because I am always busy. I am writing a novel, a story, an article. I have to lecture today or tomorrow; my datebook is crowded with all kinds of appointments for weeks and months in advance. It can happen that an hour after I leave the cafeteria I am on a train to Chicago or flying to California. But meanwhile we converse in the mother language and I hear of intrigues and pettiness about which, from a moral point of view, it would be better not to be informed. Everyone tries in his own way with all his means to grab as many honors and as much money and prestige as he can. None of us learns from all these deaths. Old age does not cleanse us. We don't repent at the gate of hell.

I have been moving around in this neighborhood for over thirty years— as long as I lived in Poland. I know each block, each house. There has been little building here on uptown Broadway in the last decades, and I have the illusion of having put down roots here. I have spoken in most of the synagogues. They know me in some of the stores and in the vegetarian restaurants. Women with whom I have had affairs live on the side streets. Even the pigeons know me; the moment I come out with a bag of feed, they begin to fly toward me from blocks away. It is an area that stretches from Ninety-sixth Street to Seventy-Second Street and from Central Park to Riverside Drive. Almost every day on my walk after lunch, I pass the funeral parlor that waits for us and all our ambitions and illusions. Sometimes I imagine that the funeral parlor is also a kind of cafeteria where one gets a quick eulogy or Kaddish on the way to eternity.

The cafeteria people I meet are mostly men: old bachelors like myself, would-be writers, retired teachers, some with dubious doctorate titles, a rabbi without a congregation, a painter of Jewish themes, a few translators—all immigrants from Poland or Russia. I seldom know their names. One of them disappears and I think he is already in the next world; suddenly he reappears and he tells me that he has tried to settle in Tel Aviv or Los Angeles. Again he eats his rice pudding, sweetens his coffee with saccharin. He has a few more wrinkles, but he tells the same stories and makes the same gestures. It may happen that he takes a paper from his pocket and reads me a poem he has written.

It was in the fifties that a woman appeared in the group who looked younger than the rest of us. She must have been in her early thirties; she was short, slim, with a girlish face, brown hair that she wore in a bun, a short nose, and dimples in her cheeks. Her eyes were hazel—actually, of an indefinite color. She dressed in a modest European way. She spoke Polish, Russian, and an idiomatic Yiddish. She always carried Yiddish newspapers and magazines. She had been in a prison camp in Russia and had spent some time in the camps in Germany before she obtained a visa for the United States. The men all hovered around her. They didn't let her pay the check. They gallantly brought her coffee and cheesecake. They listened to her talk and jokes. She had returned from the devastation still gay. She was introduced to me. Her name was Esther. I didn't know if she was unmarried, a widow, a divorcée. She told me she was working in a factory, where she sorted buttons. This fresh young woman did not fit into the group of elderly has-beens. It was also hard to understand why she couldn't find a better job than sorting buttons in New Jersey. But I didn't ask too many questions. She told me that she had read my writing while still in Poland, and later in the camps in Germany after the war. She said to me, and "You are my writer."

The moment she uttered those words I imagined I was in love with her. We were sitting alone (the other man at our table had gone to make a telephone call), and I said, "For such words I must kiss you."

"Well, what are you waiting for?"

She gave me both a kiss and a bite.

I said, "You are a ball of fire."

"Yes, fire from Gehenna."

A few days later, she invited me to her home. She lived on a street between Broadway and Riverside Drive with her father, who had no legs and sat in a wheelchair. His legs had been frozen in Siberia. He had tried to run away from one of Stalin's slave camps in the winter of 1944. He looked like a strong man, had a head of thick white hair, a ruddy face, and eyes full of energy. He spoke in a swaggering fashion, with boyish boastfulness and a cheerful laugh. In an hour, he told me his story. He was born in White Russia but he had lived long years in Warsaw, Lodz, and Vilna. In the beginning of the thirties, he became a Communist and soon afterward a functionary in the Party. In 1939 he escaped to Russia with his daughter. His wife and the other children remained in Nazi-occupied Warsaw. In Russia, somebody denounced him as a Trotskyite and he was sent to mine gold in the north. The G.P.U. sent people there to die. Even the strongest could not survive the cold and hunger for more than a year. They were exiled without a sentence. They died together: Zionists, Bundists, members of the Polish Socialist Party, Ukrainian Nationalists, and just refugees, all caught because of the labor shortage. They often died of scurvy or beriberi. Boris Merkin, Esther's father, spoke about this as if it were a big joke. He called the Stalinists outcasts, bandits, sycophants. He assured me that had it not been for the United States Hitler would have overrun all of Russia. He told how prisoners tricked the guards to get an extra piece of bread or a double portion of watery soup, and what methods were used in picking lice.

Esther called out, "Father, enough!"

"What's the matter—am I lying?"

"One can have enough even of *kreplach*."

"Daughter, you did it yourself."

When Esther went to the kitchen to make tea, I learned from her father that she had had a husband in Russia—a Polish Jew who had volunteered in the Red Army and perished in the war. Here in New York she was courted by a refugee, a former smuggler in Germany who had opened a bookbinding factory and become rich. "Persuade her to marry him," Boris Merkin said to me. "It would be good for me, too."

"Maybe she doesn't love him."

"There is no such thing as love. Give me a cigarette. In the camp, people climbed on one another like worms."

II

I had invited Esther to supper, but she called to say she had the grippe and must remain in bed. Then in a few days' time a situation arose that made me leave for Israel. On the way back, I stopped over in London and Paris. I wanted to write to Esther, but I had lost her address. When I returned to New York, I tried to call her, but there was no telephone listing for Boris Merkin or Esther Merkin—father and daughter must have been boarders in somebody else's apartment. Weeks passed and she did not show up in the cafeteria. I asked the group about her; nobody knew where she was. "She has most probably married that bookbinder," I said to myself. One evening, I went to the cafeteria with the premonition that I would find Esther there. I saw a black wall and boarded windows—the cafeteria had burned. The old bachelors were no doubt meeting in another cafeteria, or an Automat.

But where? To search is not in my nature. I had plenty of complications without Esther.

The summer passed; it was winter. Late one day, I walked by the cafeteria and again saw lights, a counter, guests. The owners had rebuilt. I entered, took a check, and saw Esther sitting alone at a table reading a Yiddish newspaper. She did not notice me, and I observed her for a while. She wore a man's fur fez and a jacket trimmed with a faded fur collar. She looked pale, as though recuperating from a sickness. Could that grippe have been the start of a serious illness? I went over to her table and asked, "What's new in buttons?"

She started and smiled. Then she called out, "Miracles do happen!"

"Where have you been?"

"Where did you disappear to?" she replied. "I thought you were still abroad."

"Where are our *cafeterianiks*?"

"They now go to the cafeteria on Fifty-Seventh Street and Eighth Avenue. They only reopened this place yesterday."

"May I bring you a cup of coffee?"

"I drink too much coffee. All right."

I went to get her coffee and a large egg cookie. While I stood at the counter, I turned my head and looked at her. Esther had taken off her mannish fur hat and smoothed her hair. She folded the newspaper, which meant that she was ready to talk. She got up and tilted the other chair against the table as a sign that the seat was taken. When I sat down, Esther said, "You left without saying goodbye, and there I was about to knock at the pearly gates of heaven."

"What happened?"

"Oh, the grippe became pneumonia. They gave me penicillin, and I am one of those who cannot take it. I got a rash all over my body. My father, too, is not well."

"What's the matter with your father?"

"High blood pressure. He had a kind of stroke and his mouth became all crooked."

"Oh, I'm sorry. Do you still work with buttons?"

"Yes, with buttons. At least I don't have to use my head, only my hands. I can think my own thoughts."

"What do you think about?"

"Whatnot. The other workers are all Puerto Ricans. They rattle away in Spanish from morning to night."

"Who takes care of your father?"

"Who? Nobody. I come home in the evening to make supper. He has one desire—to marry me off for my own good and, perhaps, for his comfort, but I can't marry a man I don't love."

"What is love?"

"You ask me! You write novels about it. But you're a man—I assume you really don't know what it is. A woman is a piece of merchandise to you. To me a man who talks nonsense or smiles like an idiot is repulsive. I would rather die than live with him. And a man who goes from one woman to another is not for me. I don't want to share with anybody."

"I'm afraid a time is coming when everybody will."

"That is not for me."

"What kind of person was your husband?"

"How did you know I had a husband? My father, I suppose. The minute I leave the room, he prattles. My husband believed in things and was ready to die for them. He was not exactly my type but I respected him and loved him, too. He wanted to die and he died like a hero. What else can I say?"

"And the others?"

"There were no others. Men were after me. The way people behaved in the war—you will never know. They lost all shame. On the bunks near me one time, a mother lay with one man and her daughter with another. People were like beasts—worse than beasts. In the middle of it all, I dreamed about love. Now I have even stopped dreaming. The men who come here are terrible bores. Most of them are half mad, too. One of them tried to read me a forty-page poem. I almost fainted."

"I wouldn't read you anything I'd written."

"I've been told how you behave—no!"

183

"No is no. Drink your coffee."

"You don't even try to persuade me. Most men around here plague you and you can't get rid of them. In Russia people suffered, but I have never met as many maniacs there as in New York City. The building where I live is a madhouse. My neighbors are lunatics. They accuse each other of all kinds of things. They sing, cry, break dishes. One of them jumped out of the window and killed herself. She was having an affair with a boy twenty years younger. In Russia the problem was to escape the lice; here you're surrounded by insanity."

We drank coffee and shared the egg cookie. Esther put down her cup. "I can't believe that I'm sitting with you at this table. I read all your articles under all your pen names. You tell so much about yourself I have the feeling I've known you for years. Still, you are a riddle to me."

"Men and women can never understand one another."

"No—I cannot understand my own father. Sometimes he is a complete stranger to me. He won't live long."

"Is he so sick?"

"It's everything together. He's lost the will to live. Why live without legs, without friends, without a family? They have all perished. He sits and reads the newspapers all day long. He acts as though he were interested in what's going on in the world. His ideals are gone, but he still hopes for a just revolution. How can a revolution help him? I myself never put my hopes in any movement or party. How can we hope when everything ends in death?"

"Hope in itself is a proof that there is no death."

"Yes, I know you often write about this. For me, death is the only comfort. What do the dead do? They continue to drink coffee and eat egg cookies? They still read newspapers? A life after death would be nothing but a joke."

III

Some of the *cafeterianiks* came back to the rebuilt cafeteria. New people appeared—all of them Europeans. They launched into long discussions in Yiddish, Polish, Russian, even Hebrew. Some of those who came from

Hungary mixed German, Hungarian, Yiddish-German—then all of a sudden they began to speak plain Galician Yiddish. They asked to have their coffee in glasses, and held lumps of sugar between their teeth when they drank. Many of them were my readers. They introduced themselves and reproached me for all kinds of literary errors: I contradicted myself, went too far in descriptions of sex, described Jews in such a way that anti-Semites could use it for propaganda. They told me their experiences in the ghettos, in the Nazi concentration camps, in Russia. They pointed out one another. "Do you see that fellow—in Russia he immediately became a Stalinist. He denounced his own friends. Here in America he has switched to anti-Bolshevism." The one who was spoken about seemed to sense that he was being maligned, because the moment my informant left he took his cup of coffee and his rice pudding, sat down at my table, and said, "Don't believe a word of what you are told. They invent all kinds of lies. What could you do in a country where the rope was always around your neck? You had to adjust yourself if you wanted to live and not die somewhere in Kazakhstan. To get a bowl of soup or a place to stay you had to sell your soul."

There was a table with a group of refugees who ignored me. They were not interested in literature and journalism but strictly in business. In Germany they had been smugglers. They seemed to be doing shady business here, too; they whispered to one another and winked, counted their money, wrote long lists of numbers. Somebody pointed out one of them. "He had a store in Auschwitz."

"What do you mean, a store?"

"God help us. He kept his merchandise in the straw where he slept—a rotten potato, sometimes a piece of soap, a tin spoon, a little fat. Still, he did business. Later, in Germany, he became such a big smuggler they once took forty thousand dollars away from him."

Sometimes months passed between my visits to the cafeteria. A year or two had gone by (perhaps three or four; I lost count), and Esther did not show up. I asked about her a few times. Someone said that she was going to the cafeteria on Forty-Second Street; another had heard that she was married. I learned that some of the cafeterianiks had died. They were beginning to settle down in the United States, had remarried, opened businesses, workshops, even had children again. Then came cancer or a heart attack. The result of the Hitler and Stalin years, it was said.

One day, I entered the cafeteria and saw Esther. She was sitting alone at a table. It was the same Esther. She was even wearing the same fur hat, but a strand of gray hair fell over her forehead. How strange—the fur hat, too, seemed to have grayed. The other *cafeterianiks* did not appear to be interested in her anymore, or they did not know her. Her face told of the time that had passed. There were shadows under her eyes. Her gaze was no longer so clear. Around her mouth was an expression that could be called bitterness, disenchantment. I greeted her. She smiled, but her smile immediately faded away. I asked, "What happened to you?"

"Oh, I'm still alive."

"May I sit down?"

"Please—certainly."

"May I bring you a cup of coffee?"

"No. Well, if you insist."

I noticed that she was smoking, and also that she was reading not the newspaper to which I contribute but a competition paper. She had gone over to the enemy. I brought her coffee and for myself stewed prunes—a remedy for constipation. I sat down. "Where were you all this time? I have asked for you."

"Really? Thank you."

"What happened?"

"Nothing good." She looked at me. I knew that she saw in me what I saw in her: the slow wilting of the flesh. She said, "You have no hair but you are white."

For a while we were silent. Then I said, "Your father—" and as I said it I knew that her father was not alive.

Esther said, "He has been dead for almost a year."

"Do you still sort buttons?"

"No, I became an operator in a dress shop."

"What happened to you personally, may I ask?"

"Oh nothing—absolutely nothing. You will not believe it, but I was sitting here thinking about you. I have fallen into some kind of trap. I don't know what to call it. I thought perhaps you could advise me. Do you still have the patience to listen to the troubles of little people like me? No, I didn't mean to insult you. I even doubted you would remember me. To make it short, I work but work is growing more difficult for me. I suffer from arthritis. I feel as if my bones would crack. I wake up in the morning and can't sit up. One doctor tells me that it's a disc in my back, others try to cure my nerves. One took X-rays and says that I have a tumor. He wanted me to go to the hospital for a few weeks, but I'm in no hurry for an operation. Suddenly a little lawyer showed up. He is a refugee himself and is connected with the German government. You know they're now giving reparation money. It's true that I escaped to Russia, but I'm a victim of the Nazis just the same. Besides, they don't know my biography so exactly. I could get a pension plus a few thousand dollars, but my dislocated disc is no good for the purpose because I got it later—after the camps. This lawyer says my only chance is to convince them that I am ruined psychically. It's the bitter truth, but how can you prove it? The German doctors, the neurologists, the psychiatrists require proof. Everything has to be according to the textbooks—just so and no different. The lawyer wants me to play insane. Naturally, he gets twenty percent of the reparation money—maybe more. Why he needs so much money I don't understand. He's already in his seventies, an old bachelor. He tried to make love to me and whatnot. He's half meshuga himself. But how can I play insane when actually I *am* insane? The whole thing revolts me and I'm afraid it will really drive me crazy. I hate swindle. But this shyster pursues me. I don't sleep. When the alarm rings in the morning, I wake up as shattered as I used to be in Russia when I had to walk to the forest and saw logs at four in the morning. Naturally, I take sleeping pills—if I didn't, I couldn't sleep at all. That is more or less the situation."

"Why don't you get married? You are still a good-looking woman."

"Well, the old question—there is nobody. It's too late. If you knew how I felt, you wouldn't ask such a question."

IV

A few weeks passed. Snow had been falling. After the snow came rain, then frost. I stood at my window and looked out at Broadway. The passersby half walked, half slipped. Cars moved slowly. The sky above the roofs shone violet, without a moon, without stars, and even though it was eight o'clock in the evening the light and the emptiness reminded me of dawn. The stores were deserted. For a moment, I had the feeling I was in Warsaw. The telephone rang and I rushed to answer it as I did ten, twenty, thirty years ago—still expecting the good tidings that a telephone call was about to bring me. I said hello, but there was no answer and I was seized by the fear that some evil power was trying to keep back the good news at the last minute. Then I heard a stammering. A woman's voice muttered my name.

"Yes, it is I."

"Excuse me for disturbing you. My name is Esther. We met a few weeks ago in the cafeteria—"

"Esther!" I exclaimed.

"I don't know how I got the courage to phone you. I need to talk to you about something. Naturally, if you have the time and—please forgive my presumption."

"No presumption. Would you like to come to my apartment?"

"If I will not be interrupting. It's difficult to talk in the cafeteria. It's noisy and there are eavesdroppers. What I want to tell you is a secret I wouldn't trust to anyone else."

"Please, come up."

I gave Esther directions. Then I tried to make order in my apartment, but I soon realized this was impossible. Letters, manuscripts lay around on tables and chairs. In the corners books and magazines were piled high. I opened the closets and threw inside whatever was under my hand: jackets, pants, shirts, shoes, slippers. I picked up an envelope and to my amazement saw that it had never been opened. I tore it open and found a check. "What's the matter with me—have I lost my mind?" I said out loud. I tried to read the letter that came with the check, but I had misplaced my glasses; my fountain pen was gone, too. Well—and where were my keys? I heard a bell ring and I didn't know whether it was the door or the telephone. I opened the door and saw Esther. It must have been snowing again, because her hat and the shoulders of her coat were trimmed with white. I asked her in, and my neighbor, the divorcée, who spied on me openly with no shame—and, God knows, with no sense of purpose—opened her door and stared at my guest.

Esther removed her boots and I took her coat and put it on the case of the *Encyclopedia Britannica*. I shoved a few manuscripts off the sofa so she could sit down. I said, "In my house there is sheer chaos."

"It doesn't matter."

I sat in an armchair strewn with socks and handkerchiefs. For a while we spoke about the weather, about the danger of being out in New York at night—even early in the evening. Then Esther said, "Do you remember the time I spoke to you about my lawyer—that I had to go to a psychiatrist because of the reparation money?"

"Yes, I remember."

"I didn't tell you everything. It was too wild. It still seems unbelievable, even to me. Don't interrupt me, I implore you. I'm not completely healthy— I may even say that I'm sick—but I know the difference between fact and illusion. I haven't slept for nights, and I kept wondering whether I should call you or not. I decided not to—but this evening it occurred to me that if I couldn't trust you with a thing like this, then there is no one I could talk to. I read you and I know that you have a sense of the great mysteries—" Esther said all this stammering and with pauses. For a moment her eyes smiled, and then they became sad and wavering.

I said, "You can tell me everything."

"I am afraid that you'll think me insane."

"I swear I will not."

Esther bit her lower lip. "I want you to know that I saw Hitler," she said.

Even though I was prepared for something unusual, my throat constricted. "When—where?"

189

"You see, you are frightened already. It happened three years ago—almost four. I saw him here on Broadway."

"On the street?"

"In the cafeteria."

I tried to swallow the lump in my throat. "Most probably someone resembling him," I said finally.

"I knew you would say that. But remember, you've promised to listen. You recall the fire in the cafeteria?"

"Yes, certainly."

"The fire has to do with it. Since you don't believe me anyhow, why draw it out? It happened this way. That night I didn't sleep. Usually when I can't sleep, I get up and make tea, or I try to read a book, but this time some power commanded me to get dressed and go out. I can't explain to you how I dared walk on Broadway at that late hour. It must have been two or three o'clock. I reached the cafeteria, thinking perhaps it stays open all night. I tried to look in, but the large window was covered by a curtain. There was a pale glow inside. I tried the revolving door and it turned. I went in and saw a scene I will not forget to the last day of my life. The tables were shoved together and around them sat men in white robes, like doctors or orderlies, all with swastikas on their sleeves. At the head sat Hitler. I beg you to hear me out—even a deranged person sometimes deserves to be listened to. They all spoke German. They didn't see me. They were busy with the Führer. It grew quiet and he started to talk. That abominable voice—I heard it many times on the radio. I didn't make out exactly what he said. I was too terrified to take it in. Suddenly one of his henchmen looked back at me and jumped up from his chair. How I came out alive I will never know. I ran with all my strength, and I was trembling all over. When I got home, I said to myself, 'Esther, you are not right in the head.' I still don't know how I lived through that night. The next morning, I didn't go straight to work but walked to the cafeteria to see if it was really there. Such an experience makes a person doubt his own senses. When I arrived, I found the place had burned down. When I saw this, I knew it had to do with what I had seen. Those who were there wanted all traces erased. These are the plain facts. I have no reason to fabricate such queer things."

We were both silent. Then I said, "You had a vision."

"What do you mean, a vision?"

"The past is not lost. An image from years ago remained present somewhere in the fourth dimension and it reached you just at that moment."

"As far as I know, Hitler never wore a long white robe."

"Perhaps he did."

"Why did the cafeteria burn down just that night?" Esther asked.

"It could be that the fire evoked the vision."

"There was no fire then. Somehow I foresaw that you would give me this kind of explanation. If this was a vision, my sitting here with you is also a vision."

"It couldn't have been anything else. Even if Hitler is living and is hiding out in the United States, he is not likely to meet his cronies at a cafeteria on Broadway. Besides, the cafeteria belongs to a Jew."

"I saw him as I am seeing you now."

"You had a glimpse back in time."

"Well, let it be so. But since then I have had no rest. I keep thinking about it. If I am destined to lose my mind, this will drive me to it."

The telephone rang and I jumped with a start. It was a wrong number. I sat down again. "What about the psychiatrist your lawyer sent you to? Tell it to him and you'll get full compensation."

Esther looked at me sidewise and unfriendly. "I know what you mean. I haven't fallen that low yet."

V

I was afraid that Esther would continue to call me. I even planned to change my telephone number. But weeks and months passed and I never heard from her or saw her. I didn't go to the cafeteria. But I often thought about her. How can the brain produce such nightmares? What goes on in that little marrow behind the skull? And what guarantee do I have that the same sort of thing will not happen to me? And how do we know that the human species will not end like this? I have played with the atom, the personality of *Homo sapiens* has been splitting. When it comes to technology, the brain still functions, but in everything else degeneration has begun. They are all insane: the Communists, the Fascists, the preachers of democracy, the writers, the painters, the clergy, the atheists. Soon technology, too, will disintegrate. Buildings will collapse, power plants will stop generating electricity. Generals will drop atomic bombs on their own populations. Mad revolutionaries will run in the streets, crying fantastic slogans. I have often thought that it would begin in New York. This metropolis has all the symptoms of a mind gone berserk.

But since insanity has not yet taken over altogether, one has to act as though there were still order—according to Vaihinger's principle of "as if." I continued with my scribbling. I delivered manuscripts to the publisher. I lectured. Four times a year, I sent checks to the federal government, the state. What was left after my expenses I put in the savings bank. A teller entered some numbers in my bankbook and this meant that I was provided for. Somebody printed a few lines in a magazine or newspaper, and this signified that my value as a writer had gone up. I saw with amazement that all my efforts turned into paper. My apartment was one big waste-paper basket. From day to day, all this paper was getting drier and more parched. I woke up at night fearful that it would ignite. There was not an hour when I did not hear the sirens of fire engines.

A year after I had last seen Esther, I was going to Toronto to read a paper about Yiddish in the second half of the nineteenth century. I put a few shirts in my valise as well as papers of all kinds, among them one that made me a citizen of the United States. I had enough paper money in my pocket to pay for a taxi to Grand Central. But the taxis seemed to be taken. Those that were not refused to stop. Didn't the drivers see me? Had I suddenly become one of those who see and are not seen? I decided to take the subway. On my way, I saw Esther. She was not alone but with someone I had known years ago, soon after I arrived in the United States. He was a frequenter of a cafeteria on East Broadway. He used to sit at a table, express opinions, criticize, grumble. He was a small man, with sunken cheeks the color of brick, and bulging eyes. He was angry at the new writers. He belittled the old ones. He rolled his own cigarettes and dropped ashes into the plates from which we ate. Almost two decades had passed since I had last seen him. Suddenly he appeared with Esther. He was even holding her arm. I had never seen Esther look so well. She was wearing a new coat, a new hat. She smiled at me and nodded. I wanted to stop her, but my watch showed that it was late. I barely managed to catch the train. In my bedroom, the bed was already made. I undressed and went to sleep.

In the middle of the night, I awoke. My car was being switched, and I almost fell out of bed. I could not sleep anymore and I tried to remember the name of the little man I had seen with Esther. But I was unable to. The thing I did remember was that even thirty years ago he had been far from young. He had come to the United States in 1905 after the revolution in Russia. In Europe, he had a reputation as a speaker and public figure. How old must he be now? According to my calculations, he had to be in the late eighties—perhaps even ninety. Is it possible that Esther could be intimate with such an old man? But this evening he had not looked old. The longer I brooded about it in the darkness, the stranger the encounter seemed to me. I even imagined that somewhere in a newspaper I had read that he had died. Do corpses walk around on Broadway? This would mean that Esther, too, was not living. I raised the window shade and sat up and looked out into the night—black, impenetrable, without a moon. A few stars ran along with the train for a while and then they disappeared. A lighted factory emerged; I saw machines but no operators. Then it was swallowed in the darkness and another group of stars began to follow the train. I was turning with the earth on its axis. I was circling with it around the sun and moving in the direction of a constellation whose name I had forgotten. Is there no death? Or is there no life?

I thought about what Esther had told me of seeing Hitler in the cafeteria. It had seemed utter nonsense, but now I began to reappraise the idea. If time and space are nothing more than forms of perception, as Kant argues, and quality, quantity, causality are only categories of thinking, why shouldn't Hitler confer with his Nazis in a cafeteria on Broadway? Esther didn't sound insane. She had seen a piece of reality that the heavenly censorship prohibits as a rule. She had caught a glimpse behind the curtain of the phenomena. I regretted that I had not asked for more details.

In Toronto, I had little time to ponder these matters, but when I returned to New York I went to the cafeteria for some private investigation. I met only one man I knew: a rabbi who had become an agnostic and given up his job. I asked him about Esther. He said, "The pretty little woman who used to come here?"

"Yes."

"I heard that she committed suicide."

"When—how?"

"I don't know. Perhaps we are not speaking about the same person."

No matter how many questions I asked and how much I described Esther, everything remained vague. Some young woman who used to come here had turned on the gas and made an end of herself—that was all the ex-rabbi could tell me.

I decided not to rest until I knew for certain what had happened to Esther and also to that half writer, half politician I remembered from East Broadway. But I grew busier from day to day. The cafeteria closed. The neighborhood changed. Years have passed and I have never seen Esther again. Yes, corpses do walk on Broadway. But why did Esther choose that particular corpse? She could have got a better bargain even in this world.

TRANSLATED BY DOROTHEA STRAUS

How Does It Feel to Be a Yiddish Writer in America?

ISAAC BASHEVIS SINGER

Singer was a frequent lecturer. He also released his memoirs in several volumes, including In My Father's Court *(1963),* A Little Boy in Search of God *(1976), and* Love and Exile *(1984). And he wrote children's books, book reviews, and essays, including the following one, published in the* Forverts *on May 23, 1965.*

I ONCE SAID that a Yiddish writer is like a ghost who can see but is not seen. Perhaps that is why I like to write "ghost" stories. The Yiddish writer not only belongs to a minority but he is a minority within a minority. He is a paradox to his own people. Theoretically, a Yiddish writer is dead. He moves around like one of my phantoms, a corpse who either ignores his own death or is not yet aware of it.

When I tell people what my occupation is, I expect them to shrug. And they do. I feel no insult when asked, "Does Yiddish still exist?" Or when I am solemnly informed that I am writing in a dead language. In truth I have written in two "dead" languages. Forty years ago, the Hebrew I was attempting to write in was considered dead. In heder I also studied Aramaic, another dead language. These dead tongues taught me one lesson: when it comes to language, the difference between life and death is negligible.

I have witnessed in my lifetime the resurrection of Hebrew. Yiddish too has grown almost overnight from a primitive tongue to a language immensely rich in idiom, imagery, and symbol. In my own time, Ukrainian, Belorussian, Lithuanian, Latvian, and many other tongues and dialects in Asia, Africa, and South America have sprung to life. We are living literally in an epoch of the resurrection of languages. The world forgets or pretends to forget that many languages today, which are the pride of those who speak them, were once looked down upon, as Yiddish is at present. They too were called vulgar tongues. In the early Middle Ages, Latin and Greek were the languages of the intellectual, and English, French, German, and Italian were a kind of Yiddish, spoken by peasants. As late as the nineteenth century, the nobles of Russia and Poland boasted of their children's ignorance of their mother tongues. French was the fashion then, even though this borrowed tongue failed miserably as a means of literary expression in the countries that had adopted it.

Many writers rose to greatness along with the languages that they helped to form. Pushkin, Dante, and Shakespeare did much to help create modern Russian, Italian, and English. Yiddish, although it was already spoken in those times, has been a few hundred years late in awakening. Modern Yiddish is only a few years older than I am. So rapidly have the changes come about that the language of books written in the beginning of this century are already somewhat obsolete. Even today, Yiddish still lacks a standardized spelling. The first Yiddish encyclopedia and a complete Yiddish dictionary are only now in the process of preparation.

This late maturing, however, carries with it some advantages. By writing in Yiddish, one is actually helping to establish the language. One chooses and polishes words extracted from an immense treasury of linguistic raw material. The Yiddish writer, I believe, is richer in topics and themes at his disposal than writers of any other modern tongue. Yiddish to him may be a literary Siberia, but one that is rich in virgin soil. It was not until the second half of the nineteenth century that the Jew began in earnest to develop a secular literature. The Jewish fiction writer has had no time to exploit the vast subject matter offered by our history. As a source for fiction, even Jewish contemporary life has barely been touched. Jewish life, whether in Russia, Poland, Israel, or anywhere in the world, because of its very dispersion and variety, is a literary mine of inexhaustible potentiality. To the humanist, Yiddish has the distinction of being perhaps the only language never spoken by men in power. There are few words in Yiddish for weapons, the paraphernalia of war, and even hunting.

Among the nations of the world, the life of the Jew was and remains a unique adventure. We are the only people who, after being driven from their land, have retained their identity for two thousand years. We are the only people to return to a land from which they were exiled two thousand years ago. We are the only group to retain its original culture over such a long period. The Jew's history is incredible. His very existence is an exception to the laws governing groups and cultures.

Since this article is not intended as a lesson in sociology or literature, I will now make a few remarks about myself. It may sound strange, but I happen to be an exception among the exceptions. The other exceptions refuse to accept my membership in their ranks.

Modern Hebrew and Yiddish literature, emerging simultaneously and created by practically the same writers, were nothing less than an adventure of the spirit, but those who created them were unconscious of their adventurous character. It may be that when, one day, the dead awake and emerge from their graves, they will not see their resurrection as unusual. They will as likely as not go about such practical tasks as finding their relatives and adjusting to the prevailing economy.

But in my case, I was born with the feeling that I am part of an unlikely adventure, something that couldn't have happened but happened just the same. The atmosphere of adventure permeated my home. My paternal grandfather was a Kabbalist, my maternal grandfather was a religious philosopher, my father was a Hasid, my mother an anti-Hasid, my sister suffered from hysterical seizures, my brother, I. J. Singer, tried rebelliously to become first a painter and then a writer. It was the entire household, not only I, who looked upon the worldly past, present, and future as one big adventure. My father always related the miracles of famous rabbis. My mother refuted them, but she was herself possessed by an unusual curiosity about the supernatural. My sister behaved as though possessed by a dybbuk. My brother, who was supposed to be the family rationalist, saw with uncanny clarity the bizarre unreality of Jewish life in Poland. The astonishment that came over me when I began to read Jewish history has not left me to this day. What astounds me more than anything else is seeing a Jew who is not baffled by his own existence. In a sense the whole human race should marvel and wonder. What is humanity but an incredible adventure on this earth, or perhaps in the cosmos?

For me, the function of literature in general, and particularly Yiddish literature, is to record this perplexity of the spirit. But to my regret, I have found little of this sense of wonderment in world literature and, alas, almost nothing of it in modern Yiddish literature. With few exceptions, modern Yiddish writing preaches a worldly positivism. It attaches itself to causes that seem to me both narrow and problematic. It is indifferent to the dark depths and strange undercurrents of Jewishness.

I know that our literature could not have been exactly as I would have wished it to be. A sea serpent, if it lives somewhere in the ocean, searches for its food just as any other creature does. It does not think of itself as a monster. Nor does it worry that according to the zoologist it is nothing more than a legend. It is not easy to speak a "freakish" language, to belong to an exceptional people, and to be part of a literature whose legitimacy is openly suspect. I sometimes dread the professor who, after examining me to detect what type of specimen I am, will pronounce me a prehistoric animal or one of evolution's embarrassing slips. I am often asked what I think about the future of Yiddish, and I hesitate to admit that I don't really care. There are at least two thousand languages and dialects in the world that are spoken by even fewer people than Yiddish. Many of them are in danger of being swallowed by the linguistic whales. There must be a number of good writers and exceptional talents who remain forever undiscovered to the large world because of the obscurity of their mediums. Even if adequate translation were possible, their chances of playing the role they deserve in literature would remain at best precarious.

Writers have never had any guarantees as to the number of their readers or the future of their languages. Nobody can tell what will happen to the words and phrases in use today or five hundred years from now. A new way of conveying ideas and images may be found that will make the written word, and perhaps even today's spoken word, completely superfluous. It is not the language that gives immortality to the writer. The very opposite is true: great writers do not let their languages become extinct.

I am amazed to see other nations go through ordeals comparable in some way to those the Jews had to undergo. I notice how many "new" languages are confronted with the problems Yiddish has faced and is still facing. Not only Yiddish but all languages are constantly in the throes of death and in the terrible effort of being reborn.

Because of the great demand for fiction on the part of the publisher and reader, and nature's small supply of genuine talent, producers of disguised journalism and pseudo-literature are taking over the artist's place almost everywhere and particularly in the large civilized countries. Fiction writing is becoming a forgotten art. The epoch of literary barbarism and deliberate literary amnesia has already begun.

In some eerie way the predicament of the Yiddish writer is becoming the predicament of the serious writer all over the world. The uncanny power of the cliché and mass production may drive all creative writers into a corner and may actually excommunicate the writer who refuses to adjust himself to the caprices of vast audiences and the economy of publishing. It has already happened in poetry. It is happening in drama. Serious fiction is next. Literature in America is already divided into a small number of bestsellers and books that remain in obscurity, or at best semi-obscurity. The lot of Yiddish today may be the lot of genuine fiction tomorrow. I personally don't look upon this as a misfortune. I have become accustomed to being a "ghost."

Literature, It's Like Orgasm!

JANET HADDA, KENNETH TURAN, ANITA NORICH, AARON LANSKY, ILAN STAVANS, RIVKA GALCHEN

Isaac Bashevis Singer's influence is enormous, not exclusively in Jewish literature but globally. These six brief reevaluations approach his standing from various perspectives. Janet Hadda (1945–2015) was a Yiddish professor of Germanic languages at UCLA, a psychoanalyst and a biographer. Among other books, she wrote Isaac Bashevis Singer: A Life *(1997). Kenneth Turan (b. 1947) is the film critic for* The Los Angeles Times *and the author, among other books, of* Free for All: Joe Papp, the Public, and the Greatest Theater Story Ever Told *(2009). Anita Norich (b. 1952) is an emerita professor of Yiddish at the University of Michigan. Her books include* The Homeless Imagination in the Fiction of Israel Joshua Singer *(1991). Aaron Lansky (b. 1955) is the founder and president of the Yiddish Book Center. He is the author of* Outwitting History: The Amazing Adventures of a Man Who Rescued a Million Yiddish Books *(2004). Ilan Stavans (b. 1961) is a Lewis-Sebring Professor of Humanities and Latin American and Latino Culture. His books include* On Borrowed Words: A Memoir of Language *(2001). Rivka Galchen is the award-winning author of a novel,* Atmospheric Disturbances *(FSG, 2008); a short-story collection,* American Innovations *(2014); an essay collection,* Little Labors *(2016); and a novel for young readers,* Rat Rule 79 *(Restless Books, 2019).*

JANET HADDA

In 1974, I was an assistant professor at UCLA. To my surprise, Bashevis filled Ackerman Ballroom, a huge space in the Student Union building. He gave a talk that was full of quips, one-liners, and bon mots. I was disgruntled, and my reaction soon turned to dismay. A member of the audience asked him to say something in Yiddish. "No one will understand me," he replied. "Yes, we will," a chorus chanted from the floor. "No one will understand me," Bashevis repeated. Then, from the back of the hall, came words in a clear galitsyaner dialect: "Why won't you talk Yiddish to us?" It was a student of mine, the daughter of immigrants. She spoke with the rich pronunciation of her parents, who had come from Galicia, an area north of the Eastern Carpathian Mountains. Traditionally, galitsyaner, Jews from Galicia, were considered less educated and less sophisticated than the Litvak counterparts (Jews from the area corresponding to Lithuania, Belorussia, and Latvia).

Bashevis knew that the members of his audience would recognize the galitsyaner-litvak stereotype, even if they were hazy about the geography. He replied in English, "I'll tell you a joke. Why doesn't God speak to us anymore? Why? Because He doesn't want us to know He's a Galitsyaner." The members of the audience howled with delight, not realizing, or not caring, that Bashevis had seduced them out of the desire to hear Yiddish. I was incensed, furious that my student had been the butt of a joke, and that no one understood the sly maneuver except for the perpetrator and me. I decided then and there that those in the Yiddish world who hated Bashevis had a point. He was manipulative, nasty, opportunistic, and cynical. Furthermore, he was a sellout; he had sacrificed his Yiddish soul for money and fame in America.

KENNETH TURAN

His penetrating blue eyes widened in disbelief. It was 1976, two years before his epochal Nobel Prize in Literature, and Isaac Bashevis Singer looked frankly skeptical when the young *Washington Post* reporter I was then hinted at his growing celebrity.

"I don't even think that I am famous now, but if you say so, who am I to say no," Singer said to me.

He punctuated this lilting, accentuated English with the most elegant of shrugs before adding the coup de grâce: "Today, to be famous, you have to be a Frank Sinatra."

ANITA NORICH

It was 1978, and I was a young grad student at Columbia who had recently found my way to Yiddish literature. Right after Singer won the Nobel Prize, I went to interview him. I'd met him at YIVO, at a talk he gave there, and I'd arranged to interview him for *Response*, a Jewish student magazine. It turned into what I later learned was the full Singer experience: we sat in his living room, Alma brought us tea, and we talked. And, of course, whereas I was nervous, he was relaxed and smiling impishly, as he used to do.

So I was interviewing him, and then at some point he turned the interview on me and asked what I was doing with Yiddish. I told him it was my mother tongue and I was learning more about it. I said I had been a double major in math and English in college, and I was getting a PhD in English literature because I wanted to teach, and because I loved it. He said that I seemed like a smart girl, and if I knew math, why was I wasting my time with literature? And I tried to explain that I really loved reading it and teaching it. And then, apropos of nothing, he said—and you've got to imagine him saying this in his thick Yiddish accent, "Literature, it's like orgasm!"

And of course I knew he wanted me to ask him exactly why literature was like orgasm! And so I sat there and just looked at him, thinking I would explode before I was going to ask him to explain that! And we had this staring contest for about thirty seconds, after which he said, "You vant I should tell you vy?" And so I finally said, "Sure, Mr. Singer, tell me why." And he said, "Literature, it's like orgasm, some things you can't teach!"

Well, I was not about to explain to Isaac Bashevis Singer that, in fact, you could teach both of those things! I just didn't think it was my place to do that!

AARON LANSKY

It was a cold day in November 1978. I was deep in research at Montreal's Jewish Public Library when a commotion broke out among the older Jews who gathered every afternoon to read the latest Yiddish newspapers from New York. The headline of that day's *Forverts* announced that Isaac Bashevis Singer had won the Nobel Prize in Literature. I assumed the older Jews would be thrilled by the news. After all, no Yiddish writer had won such an honor before, and this was a recognition, albeit a belated one, that Yiddish literature had arrived. I couldn't have been more wrong.

"*S'iz a shande far di goyim!* [It's a disgrace in the eyes of the non-Jews!]" one octogenarian proclaimed.

"*S'past nisht!* [It's unseemly!]" said another.

"*Tfu! Tfu! Tfu!*" spat a third.

I looked up from my work as they summarily rejected Bashevis (Singer's pen name in Yiddish) and began throwing out nominations of their own:

"Grade! They should have given it to Chaim Grade, better!"

"No, not Grade, Sutzkever!"

"And what's wrong with Sholem Aleichem?"

"Or I. J. Singer?"

"Or Rokhl Korn?"

The deliberations continued for what seemed like ten minutes before they finally reached a consensus: the 1978 Nobel Prize in Literature should have gone to I. L. Peretz, the "father" of modern Yiddish literature, who died in 1915. The head librarian, who had come over to restore order, patiently explained that the Swedish Academy could only award the prize to writers who were still alive. Whereupon an old man jumped to his feet and yelled, "*Akhhh, antisemitn!*"

ILAN STAVANS

I have been an Isaac Bashevis Singer reader since my adolescence. My Bobe Bela gave me a volume of his stories, *A Wedding in Brownsville*. I was mesmerized by the title story, which is about ghosts and is and isn't a Holocaust story. Years later, I found out Singer had been criticized for, among many other things, perverting the memory of the Shoah. For me, "A Wedding in Brownsville" does the opposite: it enhances it.

In my mid-fifties now, I think of Singer's books as my friends. He was a less capable novelist than his older brother, Israel Joshua. But he was a superb storyteller. He left us with more than three hundred short stories, where his talents are in abundant display. It is difficult to come up with my favorite. At the top of my list might be "Gimpel the Fool," in part because of the animosity between Singer and its translator, Saul Bellow. Calling it the most famous Yiddish story of all time would do a disservice to Sholem Aleichem, Yitskhok Leybush Peretz, Lamed Shapiro, and others, but I think it comes close. I also frequently return to "The Manuscript," "A Friend of Kafka," "The Cabbalist of East Broadway," "The Beard," "The Spinoza of Market Street," and even "Yentl, the Yeshiva Boy," which isn't a great story (and the musical based on it is worse), but it is extraordinarily thought-provoking. And I enjoy Singer's tales for children, especially those about the mythical town of Chelm.

All these stories continue to spark my own imagination. Singer once stated that good stories don't learn from one another. "What does *Madame Bovary* teach us?" he asked. "That a woman that was unfaithful to her husband commits suicide? We know that not all women who betray their husbands commit suicide or are killed. Many of them live to an old age. When Tolstoy wrote *Anna Karenina*, the story was the same. Anna also betrayed her husband and she also committed suicide. We learn actually from *Anna Karenina* nothing, for whatever we had to learn we could already have learned from *Madame Bovary*. But the story is beautiful anyhow."

I like that message: literature doesn't have a message. Yet it moves us deeply.

RIVKA GALCHEN

I have read Singer's short story "The Cafeteria" sixty or seventy times, and with each reading its luminescence only increases. A ghost story of sorts, Singer's tale is set in the kind of eatery that New York no longer has, populated by refugees and Holocaust survivors who are now mostly gone. Yet the tone of the story is cheerful, engaged, alive, still open to love and a wonder at darkness that leaves room for light. The narrator, a writer not unlike Singer, says of his meals at the cafeteria: "We talk about Yiddish literature, the Holocaust, the state of Israel and often about acquaintances who were eating rice pudding or stewed prunes the last time I was here and are already in their graves. . . . Each time, I am startled, but at my age one has to be ready for such tidings. The food sticks in the throat; we look at one another in confusion, and our eyes ask mutely, Whose turn is next? Soon we begin to chew again. I am often reminded of a scene in a film about Africa. A lion attacks a herd of zebra and kills one. The frightened zebras run for a while and then they stop and start to graze again. Do they have a choice?" Singer is a genius of the dark comedy of survival.

Poems

ANNA MARGOLIN

Rosa Harning Lebensboym (1887–1952) was born in present-day Belarus and settled in New York in 1913. She worked as an editor for the Yiddish newspaper Der Tog, *writing under her own name and several pseudonyms, including Anna Margolin. Under that name, she published a collection of poetry,* Lider (Poems), *in 1929. Shirley Kumove is a translator and the author of* Words Like Arrows: A Collection of Yiddish Folk Sayings *(1986) and* More Words, More Arrows: A Further Collection of Yiddish Folk Sayings *(1999). Maia Evrona is a writer and translator from Spanish and Yiddish who has received a fellowship from the National Endowment for the Arts.*

EPITAPH

She squandered her life
on rubbish, on nothing.

Perhaps she wanted it so, perhaps she desired
this misery, these seven knives of anguish
to spill this holy living wine
on rubbish, on nothing.

Now she lies with shattered face.
Her ravaged spirit has abandoned its cage.
Passerby, have pity, be silent—
Say nothing.

TRANSLATED BY SHIRLEY KUMOVE

MY HOME

Light gray houses swim and sway
along with damp fences, pale silver streets,
and people in doorways
bend, smile, fade away,
emerge and disappear,
through this rainbow of tears.

A girl sits by her window.
In the moonlight her hair streams like dark rain.
She searches with eyes stubborn and bright,
as if through a forest,
for her own distant figure.
Oh, child, why do you shiver
at my approach?

TRANSLATED BY MAIA EVRONA

GIRLS IN CROTONA PARK

Girls have woven themselves
into the autumn evening
as into a faded image.
Their eyes are cold, their smiles thin and wild.
Their clothes are lavender, apple green and old rose.
Through their veins dew flows.
They exchange words that are bright and empty.
In dreams they were loved by Botticelli.

TRANSLATED BY MAIA EVRONA

UNHAPPY

... And these people stare at me crookedly,
one might as well burst into tears. ...
I am unhappy with my furnished room,
I am unhappy with everything.

Swayed today on a strap on the el,
in rhythm with worn-down Jews.
The night was dark, like a slave's heart.
I am unhappy with these nights.

And the days are yellow and holy,
like verses in an old book of prayers,
perhaps I wouldn't feel so terrible,
if I didn't dream up poetry.

TRANSLATED BY MAIA EVRONA

Poems

CELIA DROPKIN

Celia Dropkin was born in 1888, in Babruysk, White Russia. She moved to Kiev to continue her studies and met there the famous Hebrew writer A. M. Gnessin. In 1909, she married Samuel Dropkin, a Bundist whose political activities forced him to leave Russia for America. She and their son joined him in New York City in 1912. They had six children. It was in New York that Dropkin began writing in Yiddish. She translated her Russian poems into Yiddish and made her literary debut in the States with an original Yiddish poem published in Naye velt *(New World magazine.) As she continued to be published, she became recognized by the two major Yiddish literary currents of the day: the Yunge and Inzikhistn movements. Dropkin was considered the leading woman writer of this movement. In 1925, Dropkin's poems were assembled and published by Vladek, the managing editor of the* Forverts, *under the title* In heysn vint *(In the Hot Wind). Years later, a complete collection of her work was published by Avram Lessin. Included were poems, children's rhymes, short stories, and reproductions of oil and watercolors painted in her later years. Dropkin died in 1956. Gene Zeiger (1943–2018) lived in Shelburne, Massachusetts. She published several collections of poetry, including* Sudden Dancing *(1988) and* Leaving Egypt *(1995), as well as a memoir,* How I Find Her: A Mother's Dying and a Daughter's Life *(2001). Maia Evrona has also translated the work of Anna Margolin, Abraham Sutzkever, and Malka Lee.*

I WILL RUN AWAY

I will run away from all of you
to my little boy—
I'll leave all of you—
you, with your thirsty, hot looks
you, with our cold stares,
I'll leave the faces of friends,
the faces of enemies and go
to his bright face.
I will rock him gently,
I will cover him softly,
I will awaken him by brushing his face
with kisses: "Mamma, Mamma . . . I'm your Mamma.
you alone may have me."
In the quiet circle of darkness beside my child's cradle,
I will be safe from all of you.

TRANSLATED BY GENF ZEIGER

YOU BEAM, I'M BEAMING

You beam, I'm beaming.
in us beams that divine being,
who makes of all a ruin
who knows nothing of the forbidden.

Hammer my hands,
hammer my feet to a cross;
set me aflame, aflame
to all my charms lay claim.

And leave me deep in shame,
drain me and throw me away,
and grow estranged, estranged,
along a different way.

TRANSLATED BY MAIA EVRONA

WHITE AS THE SNOW ON THE ALPS

White, as the snow on the Alps,
sharp, as the air at the peak,
with a spice, like ancient salves,
your beauty calls to me.

For you blind, like the untouched snow,
snatch away my breath, like air that is too thin.
And strangely, my head begins to spin
as if from a queer bewitching scent.

But you are just a boy from a small town
with a nose just a little too long,
you will adorn your wife with a ring
and grass will grow over me.

TRANSLATED BY MAIA EVRONA

Summoned Home

JACOB GLATSTEIN

Jacob Glatstein (1896–1971) was a leading exponent of Yiddish modernism in poetry and prose, and a distinguished literary critic. Born in Lublin, Poland, he arrived in New York in 1914, studied law at New York University, and published many collections of poetry and prose. The following is excerpted from a translation of his two autobiographical novels about an American's trip back to Poland in the 1930s, published as The Glatstein Chronicles (2010), *edited by Ruth R. Wisse. Maier Deshell (1928–2014) worked as an editor for* Commentary *and* The Jewish Publication Society *and turned to translating Yiddish literature after retiring.*

IN THE MORNING, informed by the ship's newspaper that Hitler had done away with his closest associates in the so-called Night of the Long Knives—apparently taking to heart Mussolini's advice never to share your rule with the fellow revolutionaries who aided your rise to power (by the same token, rather than pay back a debt owed to good friends, it might be easier to slaughter them)—I went looking for Jewish faces among the passengers.

The paper, an attractive miniature version of its counterparts on land, conveyed the news simply, without commentary, as if this were no more than a sensational tidbit, the severed heads of a dozen or so Nazi pederasts served up on a silver platter for the delectation of the passengers after their rich breakfast—yet another item on the ship's program to stave off boredom. The effort was wasted on the gentile passengers, who got no thrill from the news. They thumbed the scant pages, reading the jokes, the sports items, the announcements of afternoon activities, barely pausing over Hitler's bloody purge. When I tried to elicit some reaction from them about this report that had traveled from land to us at sea, many admitted that they hadn't seen the news at all, and those who had said things like "Hitler's a damn fool!" "Let them knock each other's brains out!" "Hmm . . . this is just the beginning!" My Scandinavian friend gave me a sharp lecture on Marxism, exclaiming, "By God, the Danes hate the Germans! It's high time Roosevelt said something about this."

None of these responses cheered me, lacking as they were in Jewish understanding and feeling. I realized that to the gentiles, Hitler meant something altogether different than he did to me. My non-Jewish fellow passengers, whether provoked to anger or not, regarded Hitler as merely Germany's dictator. To me, to 600,000 German Jews, and indeed to all seventeen million Jews worldwide, Hitler was the embodiment of the dreaded historical hatemonger, latest in a long line of persecutors that stretched from Haman, Torquemada, and Chmielnicki, to Krushevan and

Józef Haller, a beast with a murderous paw, wielding a bloody pen that was writing a dreadful new chapter of Jewish history.

The casual reaction of my gentile fellow passengers to the Hitler news was the first slap in the face I had received as a Jew on this floating international paradise. I felt isolated, even offended that news of such importance to me should fall on such indifferent ears. I longed for a "warm Jewish heart" to share my emotion. The boxer had complained about the "bastards" trying to pass for *goyim*, but I began to discern a few Jewish faces. Perhaps under the impact of the Hitler-news, they were coming out of hiding and also looking for company.

My first such discovery was a dignified gentleman in house slippers, a prosperous-looking man with a trimmed beard, sitting on a bench, poring over a sacred text, soundlessly mouthing the words. He was altogether an exemplar of Jewish aristocratic bearing. His beautiful, delicate hands hesitated before turning the page he had just studied, as though he were sorry to leave a passage still so full of immeasurable wisdom. He had sought out the quietest corner of the deck, apparently unwilling to let even his whispers reach the ears of an alien, hostile world, not, God forbid, because he feared that world but because of its undying hatred of Jews. "The whole world is our enemy," he declared, when I buttonholed him for his reaction to the Hitler news. The Nazi bloodbath was no special concern of his. With fine Jewish humor he explained that such events were family squabbles, as at a wedding to which we Jews were not invited either by the groom's side or the bride's. The moral of the Hitler purge was that they all hated us. How this followed from the massacre of Nazis slaying one another he didn't say, but he assured me that all the enemies of Israel could be made to disappear by studying a sacred Jewish text.

The man looked to be about seventy, on the cusp of the Bible's allotted span of years. He radiated a serenity that could not be bought for a king's treasure. The rabbinic dictum "The day is short and the task great" didn't seem to concern him. In leisurely fashion he studied the sacred texts for the sheer intellectual pleasure this gave him, engaging in the holy activity for its own sake. He considered the reward of the world to come beside the point, and besides, the world to come was still far off. It was refreshing to find an American Jew who fit Lao Tse's aphoristic descriptions of wisdom, in sharp contrast to the more general type of American Jew, who didn't question the average life span cited in actuarial tables positing that one would drop dead like an exhausted horse in one's fifties, and who consequently thought it necessary to speed things up, discharge one's responsibilities with dispatch, and gulp down the bit of pleasure that life affords. This type did not believe in getting too wrapped up in children, either: What was the point of forming close relationships with them, if you would be a father for only—twenty years?

This slipper-clad Jew emitted the same aura of Sabbath calm that descended over our house like a secret when Mother and Father would shut their bedroom door for a nap following the Sabbath-afternoon meal, a stillness that would prevail until darkness fell and the time came for Father to take down the iron bolts and bars from his shop. The smell of the rusted metal, the clanking of the frozen keys, and the appearance of the first customer of the new week—these were the signals that the God of Abraham had rekindled all the lamps, marking the end of the holy Sabbath and the start of another care-filled week. Suddenly, this gentle Jew studying his holy texts on the ship's deck seemed a bridge linking my first seventeen, eighteen years at home with the present journey back to it—a return voyage to see my dying mother. "Her ears are as yellow as wax," my aunt had written. "Pack your things and come immediately, and may God help us all and bring you here in time to find her still alive."

The ship seemed to be carrying me back to childhood, as though it were sailing backward in time. The two decades I had passed in America crumbled to dust between my fingers. Suddenly, all that mattered were the first years of my life, now straining to link up with the home that was awaiting me, like the two parts of a toy that need to be joined. I was awash in memories. Hitherto I had strongly resisted the temptation to submit my early years to the scalpel. I thought I should wait another twenty years and postpone any autobiographical exercise until I was sixty, by which time the fortunes of Yiddish letters would probably have sunk so low as to preclude any interest in serious literature and left nothing for a writer but to become a purveyor of old gossip, satisfying people's curiosity about other people's lives. Now here I was, making some concession to the evil impulse and beginning to root around in my memories in a way that I hadn't done since I had left home.

Imagine a place with no dragons, no scorpions, no buffalo or bison, no lions or leopards, not even a ram or deer. Who can fathom the misery of a child in a town devoid of such fauna? Elsewhere the wide world holds many such blessings, but not Lublin, which contains nothing but a town clock and a fire warden who, every quarter-hour, sounds the hours until midnight, when everything slumbers but the flitting shadows around the synagogue. My Lublin didn't appear on small maps, and on the larger ones was only a faint, barely legible marking. Really big maps, however, showed not only Lublin but also a tiny squiggle indicating the Bystrzyca rivulet (known to us by its Yiddish equivalent, the Bistshitse), a minor tributary of the Vistula River that flowed through Warsaw, home of the big-city branch of our family.

Long before I was conceived, there was a paternal great-grandfather with the German-sounding name of Enzl, and a grandfather called Yosl Enzls, neither of whom I knew. Enzl was just a name to me, and it sounded more like a nickname. The family archivists—that is to say, my older uncles and aunts—described him as a soft-spoken, sweet-tempered man, who earned his meager living as a sexton and who was reputed to be one of the thirty-six secret saints by whose grace the world is sustained. Grandfather Yosl Enzls was a more fleshed-out figure in my consciousness. He ran a workshop that sewed ladies' garments for well-to-do customers—the high-born daughters of the gentry and of the governor, as well as wealthy women in general. A softhearted exploiter of the working class, he employed thirty or so girls, who ate and slept on tables in the shop, where they also warbled their love songs and collected their dowries, courtesy of the employer, when they left to get married.

This grandfather was no great scholar, but he scrupulously observed all the Jewish laws and attended daily prayer services. He prayed with even greater fervor when he knew that there were carriages pulled up outside the shop with customers waiting for him to return and personally fit them for wedding dresses—and wait they would, he was sure. Those who knew about such matters claimed that he wasn't much of a craftsman, just an ordinary tailor, who got by on personal charm and his winning ways with people. He left behind seven sons, sturdy as oaks, and no inheritance, unless you count poverty a bequest. When he died of a stroke—brought on by the grief of seeing my father, his sixth son, go off to serve in the czar's army—all that remained was an empty, decrepit workshop.

My mother's side boasted a line of small-town Polish rabbis, and a great-grandmother Drezl, also the wife of a rabbi, who was widowed young. Drezl was six weeks pregnant when her husband died. Since this might have led to ugly gossip, she announced her condition before the open grave, to forestall any dirty rumors that might be spread about her—God forbid! For added insurance, she named the daughter born to her, Bine, after her late husband, Binyomin.

As a respected rabbi's widow, my great-grandmother was given an important community appointment, attendant at the mikvah, the women's ritual bath. I have clear memories of the meticulous way she would go about fulfilling her duties. My mother must have regarded my prepubescent masculinity as of no moment when she took me along to the mikvah and sat me down on a wet bench while the women, young and old, splashed in the water, performing their ritual ablutions under my great-grandmother's stern and competent supervision. During a break from her duties, she would press a coin into my hand, with the wish that my little heart be as open to Torah as was God's Holy Temple.

When she died at the age of one hundred, her son, my grandfather, poor soul, was left an orphan at seventy. Grandfather Avrom was a widower, who lived with us for as long as I can remember, as much a fixture of the household as my father, mother, and brothers. He had a beautiful white beard that had become slightly stained from all the snuff he had pushed up his nose, and he owned a number of snuff boxes, all of them plain, proletarian ones, made of wood or bone, not silver, let alone gold. It took Grandfather longer than a prima donna to perform his toilette. Before going out, he would polish his boots, comb out his beard, and look himself over in the mirror. When he was already standing in the doorway, he would call me over for a final inspection, to make sure that no bit of feather still clung to him. Every Friday afternoon he went to the bathhouse, returning home with time to spare for a nap, before going to usher in the Sabbath at his Hasidic rebbe's synagogue. It was our custom never to touch the braided Sabbath loaf, the challah, until Grandfather had come home to recite the *kiddush* blessing over the wine.

Grandfather was a goldsmith. He had all sorts of strange tools, the strangest being a bellows used in the melting of gold that left a coating of soot over the whole house. He made his services available, gratis, to all in the family, repairing and cleaning their rings, earrings, and brooches—the only exception being Mother, who had to hound him for weeks before he would attend to her jewelry. Sometimes, he would set out with his tools to nearby villages, returning with a deficit that took several glasses of brandy and a hearty meal to overcome. After such indulgence, his cheeks turned red as beets, his blue, carefree eyes started to blink, and soon he would be stretched out on his bed, snoring rhythmically into his lower lip, his beard rising and falling on his chest. The children of the house were ordered to walk on tiptoe, because, as Mother loudly declared, as much to provoke him as to command our attention, "Grandfather, the great breadwinner, has returned from afar and is taking a nap."

The ship was barely rocking. The slipper-clad Jew had dozed off. The air grew sharper and a wondrously cool fragrance rose from the sea, of saltwater long warmed by the sun.

TRANSLATED BY MAIER DESHELL

Madame

MOYSHE-LEYB HALPERN

Moyshe-Leyb Halpern (1886–1932) was a beloved and sometimes controversial American Yiddish poet. Born in Zlotshev [Zolochiv], Galicia, he studied art in Vienna and immigrated to the US in 1908. His collections included In New York *(1919) and* The Golden Peacock *(1924). Aaron Rubinstein is the University and Digital Archivist at the University of Massachusetts, Amherst.*

MADAME

How fine your touch against your skin!
Yes, madame, you are a woman,
And you are wise and you are fair;
Oh, just to follow tremblingly,
Observing your every move
Just as a slave before your door
Kneeling before you every day. . . .
But, unfortunate me, madame, I cannot be a slave.

It's true, madame, you plague my sleep,
You pull me in as if bewitched,
And when your hand near touches me
A wonderland bursts into bloom,
A wonderland of woven light,
And as it were a floating dove
My love takes off into the land. . . .
If only the way to you, madame,
Were just a little closer.

Oh yes, madame! I'm telling you:
You pull the heart out of my chest.
Your beauty is extravagant:
Just like the gorgeous evening skies
Which burn in distant Orient;
Your beauty fully dazzles me,
Dazzles and like wine besots. . . .
It's a shame, madame, because It cannot last forever.
Forgive me, madame, my fresh mouth,
I know this is a waste of breath. . . .
I am a fool who has to pay
For, after all, I'm wild and young,

So go ahead, cut out my tongue
It really is quite unrefined. . . .
So go and murder me, madame,
I can't be someone else.

TRANSLATED BY AARON RUBINSTEIN

from Across America

PERETZ HIRSCHBEIN

Peretz Hirschbein (1880–1948), acclaimed novelist and playwright, had a passion for traveling. Across America *is his 1918 chronicle of train travel that took him to big cities, small coal-mining towns, and fishing villages. This excerpt describes his impressions of New York. Jessica Kirzane, a lecturer in Yiddish at the University of Chicago, is also the translator of Miriam Karpilov's* Diary of a Lonely Girl, or the Battle Against Free Love *(2019), among other works.*

THE FIRST CITY that most of our immigrants see when they arrive in America, and from which most of them build their first impressions of America—the city where long-held hopes are wiped away in an instant and where, after many trying days and nights, the hope begins to grow anew, appearing as though from under a gray veil—this is the city that is called New York.

I am familiar with many great cities across this wide world, but none of them can compare with New York.

New York is built by two hands that live in enmity with one another: one hand builds, and the other destroys. One erects brick walls, the other tears down that building and gathers stone and steel to build its illustrious ten-story successor. And this goes almost entirely unnoticed. You walk down a street day after day and you don't notice how little houses are demolished and taller buildings have grown in their place. New York builds itself over and over again in stone and rock. Day in and day out they tear the ground apart with dynamite. One day it's out your window and the next day the bedrock under your own home is torn apart until you are flung from your bed with the force of it. But you still don't notice. It doesn't bother you, as though you yourself have already been turned into stone. And these changes come with such speed, with such a wild gallop, that often before your eyes a little wooden house becomes a two-story building, the building becomes a church, the church becomes a theater, the theater becomes a Yiddish school, the Yiddish school becomes a stable for horses and automobiles, the stable becomes a poor little skyscraper, which looks up submissively to the tops of the "real" skyscrapers.

Impermanence peeks out from all corners. Energetic people who can't keep still come here from faraway places, stop for a short while, and during that time whole mountains of stone and steel are formed. A house is erected and it starts to feel small, so it is torn down and a larger one is built. The trains are let loose one after the other over everyone's head: four pillars, crisscrossing iron bars, and over them rails, and the train races along and deafens everyone, numbs their feelings, tears away at their nerves. You hardly know when it happened; you didn't even have time to look around. It's as if it appeared overnight. And although the train up there was meant to be for the convenience of the millions of people below, it turns out that most of them still find themselves underneath it, on the ground. When the train rushes over their heads, all they can do is pull down their hats over their ears and think quietly to themselves, "How in God's name can I get away from here?"

New York is not a model of building but rather a model of destruction.

TRANSLATED BY JESSICA KIRZANE

Oedipus in Brooklyn

BLUME LEMPEL

Blume Lempel (1907–99) was born in Khorostkov, Ukraine, and spent almost ten years in Paris before the outbreak of the Second World War. After immigrating to New York in 1939, she began to publish fiction in Yiddish newspapers and magazines, including a serialized novel, which appeared as Storm Over Paris *(1954). A selection of her stories in English was published as* Oedipus in Brooklyn and Other Stories by Blume Lempel *(2016), translated by Ellen Cassedy and Yermiyahu Ahron Taub. Cassedy is the author of* We Are Here: Memories of the Lithuanian Holocaust *(2012) and the translator of* On the Landing: Stories by Yenta Mash *(2018). Taub is the author of the short-story collection,* Prodigal Children in the House of G-d *(2018) and six books of poetry, including* A moyz tsvishn vakldike volkn-kratsers: geklibene Yidishe lider/A Mouse Among Tottering Skyscrapers: Selected Yiddish Poems *(2017).*

SYLVIA WAS NO JOCASTA. She'd never even heard of the Greek tragedies. But fate led her into a narrow strait with no way out. For a while she struggled; then she surrendered to the inevitable. Eyes closed, lips sealed, she yielded to the whims of fortune and said "yes" to the burning "no" inscribed by the ancients in the holy books.

She was twenty-nine years old when she became a widow. One fine Sunday morning, as she busied herself with the housework, her husband took their only child for a ride in his new car. He wanted to demonstrate how rapidly his Chrysler swallowed the miles, how easily it climbed mountains and overtook Cadillacs with the flick of a finger. He was brought home dead. Their nine-year-old son was hospitalized for months and emerged from the operations totally blind.

Sylvia sank into a deep depression. For days she lay in bed with the door closed and shades drawn. She saw no one, spoke to no one, wanted only to die. But the responsibility of caring for her blind son and the benefits issued by the insurance company slowly drew her out of her lethargy. With the help of psychoanalysis, she began to see that suicide would not solve her problem. She had eyes; she could find a way to adapt and understand. She was an adult; the problem was not herself but her son. It was up to her to find a way to see for them both—to be his guide, the cane in his hand, the stubborn sunbeam that cracked the concrete and drew the green sprout up from the deep, the lone drop of water that nourished the root in the desert. She had no choice: she was a mother. Providence had so ordained.

Like a wild animal caught in a trap with no hope of escape, Sylvia began to adjust to her new circumstances. Even in a dungeon, she told herself, life went on. Even a prisoner on death row found reasons for optimism.

Sylvia was no stranger to misfortune. In the space of a few months, she had lost both her parents. Her father's death was as violent and sudden as her husband's. He was pumping soda water when a man came into the candy store, asked for an ice cream soda, then ordered him to open the register and hand over all the cash. When her father refused, the robber shot him dead.

Sylvia's mother could not bear the blow. Within a year she was lying beside her husband. By this time Sylvia was engaged. The marriage took place soon after the tragedy with her parents. The young couple sold the candy store, left the Bronx, and moved to Brooklyn. They rented an apartment near Prospect Park—new neighbors, a new world. Here, no one knew about her painful past, and Sylvia was not inclined to speak of it. She devoted herself to caring for her husband and later to raising their son. With motherly pride she pushed the stroller along the worn paths in the park. Sitting together on the benches, she and the other young mothers imagined their children's future as they played on the grass.

Ten years passed, and then misfortune struck. Now Sylvia understood how her mother had felt. She too wanted to follow her husband to the grave. But fate denied her that luxury. She had to stay alive for the sake of her son. Danny became the driving force in her life, the electric current that kept her going. She took pleasure in his joys, trembled with his fears, aspired to his hopes, dreamed his dreams, experienced all his childish emotions.

Every morning mother and son went to school together. She sat in a corner and watched the blind children learn to see the world through their fingers. She too began to touch things, to feel with her fingers every obstacle in her path. She even counted the steps between one room and the next. In the evening she refrained from turning on the lights. She set the table, ate dinner, and washed the dishes in the dark. Then mother and son would pass the time with special games: chess for the blind, checkers for the blind. When she got into bed, she would turn on her bedside lamp and lose herself in someone else's life within the pages of a novel.

Danny himself was a voracious reader in Braille. Everything interested him. He still remembered what things had looked like before the light was extinguished, and now he ordered his mother to illuminate the dim fog of his new world, to feed his love of colors and bring them back more vividly than ever. She was to paint for him all the subtle hues in the park as the sun slipped behind the clouds. Hungry for color, he demanded the impossible.

Sylvia struggled to find the required words. Never before had she clothed the world in colors. Now color became the bridge that bound the two of them together.

The boy's sense of smell also intensified. He could predict a change in the weather by sniffing the air, sense the rain hanging in the wind. He could recognize people by the smell of their clothing and even sought to discern their character with his nose.

Danny would stand in front of the mirror and bore into the glass with his sightless eyes. He brushed his hair, patted his face, adjusted his dark glasses. He felt for the crease in his trousers, tried to guess the color of his shoes and socks. Everything had to match—shirt with sweater, sweater with jacket.

When Danny turned thirteen, he tired of the color game. He stopped asking, grew silent and despondent. He couldn't bear conversation and avoided people. Even his mother's voice irritated him; he wanted only quiet. He liked the sound of leaves rustling in the wind. Every day they walked in the park and listened to the cries of the animals at the zoo. Behind the guard's back, they threw peanuts to the monkeys in their cage. Of all the hungry mouths in the park, Danny was especially devoted to the lively squirrels. They waited for him near the Lincoln statue, not far from the kiosk where nuts were sold, and as soon as they picked up his scent they came down from the trees and surrounded him, perched on his shoulders, and emptied his bag.

"They must think I'm a god," Danny remarked one day.

The sudden observation surprised Sylvia and frightened her. She looked at her son with alarm. How had he come up with such an idea? When a blizzard came, Danny insisted on going to the park. He needed to, he said; the squirrels were expecting him.

"In this weather? Let's wait until morning. The snow will have stopped by then."

"If you won't take me, I'll go alone," he insisted.

"Is it so important?"

"Very important. The squirrels mustn't find out that their god is blind."

Danny grew taller and heavier, his muscles covered with a thick layer of fat. The doctor recommended exercises and swimming. "I gather you have no close relatives nearby," he said. "Why not move to a milder climate? Pick a place near the water where your son can burn off some energy."

Sylvia took the doctor's advice. She left Brooklyn, Prospect Park, and the shops and storekeepers of Flatbush Avenue, and moved down to Florida.

Danny fell in love with the sea. He swam for hours in the mild, clear turquoise waters of the South Atlantic, drowning his frustrations in the soft arms of the waves. In the evenings he strummed his guitar, expressing the moodiness that had lately overtaken him.

Sylvia sensed danger in his strumming, in his ripe muscles, in the awakening masculinity of his body. She felt it in his silence, his sigh, his casual touch, and never more than when they lay side by side on the sand in the hot sun. Every time they touched, his body trembled. She opened her eyes and saw his muscles straining as he absentmindedly sifted the hot sand between his fingers.

What Danny was thinking behind his dark glasses, she couldn't see—or didn't want to see. As for her own thoughts, the more she tried to sweep them under the rug or hide them under her pillow, the more insistent they became. They winked at her from the foaming waves and from the transistor radio that never stopped yammering, stirring her blood with its songs of love, luck, and sorrow.

When Danny turned sixteen, his mother was thirty-six years old. Men were attracted to her plump, shapely limbs. They showered her with compliments, propositions, promises of paradise on earth. But Danny stood in the way. The local doctor in whom Sylvia confided suggested that she enroll her son in an institution. She must not sacrifice her own life on Danny's account, he said. And Danny himself would benefit. The schools were competent; they would provide him with an opportunity to learn a trade. He would become productive, even independent. He would meet young women in similar circumstances, and in time he would marry and live out his destiny.

Danny rejected the idea out of hand. Every time Sylvia tried to bring it up he became agitated. "I don't want their schools!" he shouted. "I don't want to adjust to their world! Let the world adjust to me!"

Passive by nature, accustomed to bending with the wind, Sylvia did not fight back. The two continued with their daily routine. They delighted in their little house by the sea and enjoyed tending the flowers and shrubs in the garden. Danny's lifetime pension relieved them of worry about the future. Every day they walked into town to buy whatever they needed. Then they bathed in the sea, lay on the beach, and baked in the sun. But this good life quickly became monotonous. Tomorrow was the same as yesterday, yesterday just like today. Time stood still, as if the flora and fauna, the fish of the sea and the birds of the air were imprisoned inside a bubble, man and beast alike forced to take part in the age-old game that Adam and Eve had dreamed up in the Garden of Eden.

All day and all night, fiery instincts seethed within them. Mother and son hid their feelings, concealed their thoughts behind the study of the exotic birds, plants, and ecological characteristics of the semitropical region. Sylvia strove to recreate the strange landscape in Danny's imagination. She painted for him the splendor of the blue heron with its spreading wings, the delicate beauty of the white egret, the ibis with its bill like a spoon. She described the southern mangrove trees whose roots braided whole islands populated by crocodiles, alligators warming themselves in the sun, pink flamingos watching for fish. The entire area was teeming with life.

"I never heard of these birds," Danny said. "All these plants and animals are too strange. I don't want to hear about them."

Every day Danny became more phlegmatic, unkempt, and preoccupied. For him it was enough to swim and to bake in the sun in silence.

Often some stranger would attach himself to them. Danny couldn't bear the company of these men or the sound of his mother's laughter. Real and imaginary ailments overtook him: a headache, a stomachache, even a nervous case of the hiccups provided an excuse to leave.

On the way home, Danny would insist that they make a detour or lose themselves within the crowd in a shop before heading back to the house.

"You have eyes," he argued. "I have to make sure no one is following us. You might be giving a signal so you can run off with him. Maybe you want to get rid of me."

It wasn't only jealousy that tormented Danny. He was truly afraid of strangers. He didn't trust the sighted world. After each such encounter he would walk around the house sniffing the air for unfamiliar scents. Nor did sleep bring peace to his jangled nerves. He cried out and woke himself with his screams.

During one such night of troubled sleep, Danny opened the door to his mother's room, felt his way to her side, and patted the blanket. He had dreamed that a man was in bed with her.

Frightened, Sylvia encircled him with her bare arms and tried to soothe him. He was trembling. She moved over in the bed to make room for him. He nestled into her arms and buried his head in her soft bosom. The silky folds of her nightgown cooled his face. He breathed in the scent of the lotion she had rubbed into her skin. Under cover of night, intoxicated with her rich femininity, his body became aroused, hot and demanding. The rhythm in his blood sought and found the narrow route to the open sea. Without words, without caresses, as mute and urgent as a magic incantation, he took her.

Sylvia did not resist the stormy rhythm. Deep within the river of her femininity she remembered other rhythms, other embraces in which she'd engaged as an active partner with her husband. She remembered words that had stirred her blood, penetrated to the depths of her being. Now she pressed her ear to her son's mouth, but no words came—only the hot, mute plea of a thirsty man in the desert.

Sylvia did not muster the power or will to repel this desperate assault. She persuaded herself that she was lying not with her son but with the specter of her husband. A power stronger than death had broken through the barrier between this world and that, and in the form of her son had come to demand the debt she owed to his unlived life.

That summer the heat was intense. A blinding haze hung in the air like carbon fumes. The earth was scorched, the waterways dried up, the white egrets disappeared. The roots of the mangrove trees, naked and greedy, waited for a drop of water. Creeping insects of all kinds eked out their slithery existence, leaving behind silver threads of slime on the desiccated waterbed.

Only the sea in its stoic indifference did not cease its endless song.

The brief tropical rains failed to cool the atmosphere. Buckets of rain would fall, and a moment later the sun would come out, dry up the puddles, and thicken the heavy air. The heat weighed on the spirit and muddled common sense. Nor did the sea soothe the spirit; its salts and minerals scalded the skin and drove people from the water.

Sylvia and Danny hid from the sun. In the house, the air conditioner cooled their parched bodies. Mute, without words, without tenderness, without promise, without hope, they coupled day and night—on the floor, and after sunset on the hot sand.

Under the press of the tropical sun, their ingrained Jewish modesty evaporated. All that remained was the naked kernel of lust. In the thick mist of that summer, even instinct veered off course. Nature played tricks with her own taboo—and Sylvia discovered that she was pregnant. She did not tell her son. She didn't even try to think about the tragedy of her situation. She knew she could have an abortion. The doctor would ask no questions. For a few hundred dollars he would sharpen his scissors and poke at her womb and the nightmare would trickle out. But Sylvia did nothing. She relied on nature in its wisdom to take its course. The same power that had led her into the mire would lead her out again.

Once while Sylvia and Danny were walking along the shore, he grew suddenly loquacious.

"Have you ever read the Bible?" he asked.

"No," Sylvia replied.

"You must have heard of Adam and Eve," he said. "Why do you think Cain murdered his brother Abel? I'll tell you: it was jealousy, pure and simple. The two brothers both wanted their mother, and they both gave her presents. Cain, the farmer, brought her the sweetest fruit of the earth, and Abel, the shepherd, gave his youngest and fattest sheep. And when Cain found out that Eve liked Abel's gift better than his, he picked up a scythe and murdered his brother."

"How do you know all this?"

"I know a lot of things," Danny said, "more than you think. You think I'm just a blind cripple. But actually my blindness helps me see better, much better. Sometimes I feel like my own creator, even my own god. I can feel a cosmic power running through, pushing me to create my own world, to go looking for the secret of all secrets. You can't possibly understand—you don't want to. Maybe I don't even understand myself, but I have a feeling I'm on the right path, and that's all that matters."

Sylvia could not grasp what Danny was saying, nor did she try. The world of rock and roll had hypnotized her. The barbaric rhythm afforded her a secret passage to no-man's land, far removed from the problems of the real world. The pictures conjured by the music called to her spirit and filled every cell in her body with restless longing. Just as the tropical rain did not cool the air, so was Sylvia unable to still her boiling blood. She began to feel like a burden on Danny. Often he would take the dog and slip out of the house, leaving her alone until late at night.

At times like this Sylvia would lie still, staring at the wall and waiting. She closed her eyes and imagined that she, too, was blind: she neither saw nor knew what was required of her. She lay as motionless as a mite in the sand, inhaling her own stale aroma and the perfume of her hair that spilled across the pillow like golden apple cider.

The jungle beat of the rock and roll music pounded on. Over and over, it happened: two bodies joined together, sensing each other's demands like telephone antennae and yielding without a word. Maybe they remained silent for fear of awakening reality, as if some magical spirit would be roused and vanish into nothing with a snap of the fingers, like the prince in the fairy tale.

Both of them wanted to prolong the moment. Perhaps they wanted to trick the laws of nature into standing still—unaware that nature does not allow anything to remain static. Even the riverbed changes its course, mountains erupt, and tiny particles of coral rise out of the abyss to form new continents.

Perhaps Danny did not know his mother was pregnant. Or perhaps he was waiting for her to tell him. Sylvia said nothing as she felt the rising life wriggling within her, knocking on the wall of her being, demanding its right to exist.

When the first pains impinged on her consciousness, Sylvia opened her eyes and looked around in surprise, as if she had no idea what could be causing them.

It was the middle of the night. The house was pitch black. She rose from her bed. Barefoot, wearing only her nightgown, she went out into the street.

A low sky hung over the sea. The Milky Way parted the darkness in two. From time to time a star slipped and fell into the ocean. The sea accepted everything. In the same stoical manner as always, it continued to sing its intrinsic song, just as it had day in and day out, year in and year out, all through the ages.

Sylvia walked far out along the water's edge toward the seawall where she and Danny had often sat. She liked to dabble her feet in the cool water and watch the sea crabs hurrying in and out of nooks and crannies.

Once she had picked up one of these crabs and laid it in Danny's hand. Danny had played with the crab, had asked how many feet it had and what it looked like. Was it a male or a female?

"Hard to know," Sylvia answered.

"Maybe it doesn't know either," Danny said. "Why should it? It's only a pawn on the evolutionary chessboard. We are, too—toys in the hands of fortune, nature's experiment with something new. I know, Sylvia, I can feel it, I can see what other people can't. Look at this crab; it's as blind as I am, but blindness tells it where to go. It never gets lost. It never has doubts. It knows what's a dream and what's reality."

"What is reality?" Sylvia asked.

Danny didn't answer right away. He took off his dark glasses and polished them with care. Only when they were perched on his nose once again did he reply with a flourish.

"You want to know what is real? Why do you need to? Do you think if you know you'll be worth more than a crab? Well, you're wrong."

"A crab doesn't have to pay for its sins," Sylvia interrupted him. "A person does."

Danny's face reddened with anger. "What's the matter with you? How do you think you've sinned? Anyway, there's no such thing as sin. Only Man suffers from such a disease. When it comes time to pay, I'll get in line ahead of you. And I'll have some questions, too—if there's anyone to ask."

Now Sylvia ran to the seawall where they often sat. The pains resumed, sharper and more frequent than before. She ran along the white foam at the water's edge and tried to scramble up onto the rock where she had once scratched her name. But her bare feet slipped and she stumbled and fell headfirst into the water. For a while she struggled against the morning tide. She tried to cry out, but the incoming water filled her mouth. A high wave rushed in. It lifted up her velvet-smooth body, battered it from side to side, threw it on its back and pulled it deeper into the sea. The wave rocked her back and forth, toying with her. It lifted her nightgown, loosened her hair. Another wave rushed in and slammed her back onto the beach. Her protruding belly jabbed against a sharp stone.

The morning sun found Sylvia lying face up beside the stone wall. A flock of pelicans with baggy throats pecked avidly at her open belly. Exotic seaweed transported from distant lands tangled in her apple-cider hair. Nimble sea creatures explored her silky body. Up above, gray-white vultures searching for carrion circled with raucous cries. Not quite ready to claim their prey, they settled onto the sun-splashed stone bridge and patiently awaited their turn.

TRANSLATED BY ELLEN CASSEDY
AND YERMIYAHU AHRON TAUB

The New House

ROKHL KORN

Rokhl Korn (1898–1982) was born and raised in Galicia and began publishing Yiddish poetry and fiction in 1919 in the leading Polish and international Yiddish journals. After surviving the Second World War and losing most of her family, she moved to Montreal in 1949 with her daughter, and became one of the central figures in Montreal's Yiddish literary scene. Seymour Levitan's translations of Yiddish poems and stories are included in numerous anthologies, and he has edited and translated volumes of poetry by Rukhl Fishman and Rokhl Korn.

MY FATHER BROUGHT his young wife to a very old house. Who knows how many generations grew up there, regardless of the winter wind that tore in through the cracks around the windows as if it were the real master of the house.

My mother was too considerate to show how disappointed she was with this place ("the other side of nowhere," she called it). It was the place where I was born, the farming estate "Sukha Gura," which means Dry Mountain. She couldn't get accustomed to the old house or the coarse Jews of the surrounding villages, though she tried not to let my father see how she felt. He realized it without her saying so, but it took almost six years till the new house was begun.

First they felled the oldest oaks in our woods. Our oak grove, the *dubnik*, as the peasants called it, was admittedly thinner because of this, but the house would be much stronger and warmer than a brick house. Oak is as strong as iron, maybe even stronger, they said. It doesn't rot in the wet, it just gets stronger. Even the sheathing for underwater telephone wires was made of oak. The only wood that compares to oak in strength is beech—in strength, but not in durability.

They set up sawhorses in the farmyard and dragged the huge tree trunks onto them and began to cut the beams. The air smelled of sawdust, the bite of fresh-cut wood, and the secret expectation of the great unknown wonder, the new house. The workmen ruled lines in the earth and measured the posts and boards. The man they call Panye Mayster went around all day long with a meter stick in his boot top and a fat pencil behind his ear. He had a piece of wood with a long thin string wound around it. He'd pull a blackened ember out from under the oven, unwind the string, and rub it on the ember till it was black. Then he would go to the posts and boards, lay the meter stick on them, and flick his fingers against the tightened string. The black marks that remained on the brown wood were the measurements for walls, doors, windows.

Large pots of food had to be cooked for the workers. We had to unyoke the horses from the plow or harrow and go into town to buy longer nails or order window frames and whatnot. It didn't bother me at all that the running of the farm was disturbed, that the fields wouldn't be sown in time this year. All day long I was busy picking up the smoothest bits and chunks of wood. I was looking forward with feverish expectation to what would come out of the lumber that was piling up. And as a matter of fact there was something new every day. The house grew larger, taller. I had huge respect for these uneducated gentile workmen who fit the boards together so that they held even without nails. I was amazed at their calloused hands, so expert at matching posts and boards of different kinds of wood from trees that would never have had anything to do with each other.

I was forever underfoot; I was everywhere. I mustn't miss any of the house building that was going on. My mother lived in constant fear that a board would hit me or an unsecured beam would fall, and she tried to trick me into the house.

Finally, they set up the rafters in the latest kind of triangular framework, and at the very peak of it they put a little pine tree as a sign that the house was finished. The workmen were given glasses of spirits, there was the tossing back of vodka, good wishes in honor of the new house, and immediately they packed up their tools in their sacks, tucked their axes and saws under their arms, and left. And all at once it was quiet and lonely without the hammering and sawing and the yells of *"Podavay!"* ("Hand it to me!"). A little while later, the masons and the carpenters came. They poured a hill of sand mixed with water and lime, which they kneaded and slapped over the walls. But this didn't really have the holiday feeling you get while the house is being built. Until—until one fine day a few young Jewish men came up from the town of Moshtsisk with brushes and pails of paint. They immediately made themselves at home, whistled, sang, and kidded with the gentile serving girls in a free and easy way. They asked for a lot of milk and mixed it with various colors. They called for milk nearly every half hour, and to this day I'm not sure if they really needed it or just wanted the opportunity to pinch Marishka, who couldn't protect herself while holding a jug full of milk in both hands. Finally the painting began. They held a strip of paper cut in one of various patterns against the wall, ran the brush over it, and when they lifted it, there were colored stripes on the walls, or leaves, or dots of color. Then they laid another strip of paper over the same spot, brushed it with another color, and there were flowers. I was amazed that they were able to fit each strip of paper exactly in the place where it was supposed to be without ever making a mistake. And when they painted the ceiling of the largest room, these singing workers, whom my mother considered a bit too bold, impressed me even more. In the corners of the room, using finer brushes now and without the help of patterned paper, they drew lines of three different colors that looped into the forms of leaves facing in different directions. In the center of the ceiling the form was repeated but larger and spread out like a nest for the ceiling lamp, which for the time being was still packed in its box.

When it came to the oven, made not from brick but from small stones that hold the heat longer, the chief painter, the one who whistled more and joked more than any of them, went up to it, stood looking at it, taking in the size and shape of the slim triangular oven. When he spit decisively, it was clear he knew how to manage my mother's special wish that the oven should be "really remarkable," as if the rest of the house were only an addition to the oven, as if all her thoughts and dreams would warm themselves there.

And once again I didn't step away for a moment. What would come of those red brushstrokes?

But no matter how much I begged them to, the painters wouldn't reveal the secret. It was to be a surprise for my mother. Finally, after working half the day, the chief painter wiped his brush on a piece of stiffened linen and proudly called in my mother to contemplate his masterwork. My mother wiped her hands on her apron, looked at it from one side and the other, went up close, and finally asked, "What exactly is it?" The painter just stood there, downcast and stunned. "What? Don't you recognize it? Can't you see that it's a doe?—which is what you'd expect for a woman who owns an estate." When you looked closely you could actually see a leaping doe, but my mother still wasn't pleased. The more passionately the painter defended his artwork, the more quietly and firmly my mother answered. This wasn't what she had in mind. This was the first time I saw my mother insist on having her way. She was always willing to give way, not wanting to cause pain, and when a worker botched a job, she'd say nothing about it; in fact she would comfort him.

In the end, the painter had to give in and painted out the doe. First the tips of her horns disappeared, then her neck, and soon the doe was just one big brown smudge, as if she were swallowed up by an abyss. I was sad about that, because I'd begun to get used to her. She had already become a friend for me to talk to when no one was there. This time the painter's brush didn't fly so quickly. It paused thoughtfully, stopping from time to time as if resisting a temptation that would lead it astray exactly where it mustn't go.

When the painter finished his work, everyone without exception was struck by the picture on the oven, and my mother paid the workers more than they'd asked for. On a twig with pink blossoms sat a bird of a kind that we never saw in our region. Its feet held the twig so firmly that you could see the nails on every claw. Its head was thrown back, its beak half open, its neck and yellow breast puffed out, and you not only saw that the bird was singing, you could practically hear the sound that poured out of its straining throat.

The new house was ready. A large kitchen with two windows to the south, a large bedroom with one window to the south, the other to the east, another room set aside for my father's mother, bobe Chaye. My bobe Chaye had four married daughters, but she lived with her youngest child, her only son. She decided to do her own cooking in the new house, so a separate stove was built for her in her room. Then there was also a room we called the "office," probably because my father's bookcase was there, along with a table and chairs. When the tablecloth was removed after eating, my father would sit there and read his Viennese newspapers, *Die Neue Freie Press* and *Neues Wiener Journal*. In the midmorning my father would sit over his books. Often he would write something, and when Volf and Yantsie, the sons of his oldest sister, came up from the village, he would read them what he had written. It was from them I learned years later that my father wrote essays and philosophical studies in Hebrew and German. The manuscripts were tied together and stored in a large chest. I wasn't fated to read what my father wrote. During the First World War, when my mother fled to Vienna with her three children, the house was robbed, most of our things were taken, and apparently my father's manuscripts were destroyed.

The office opened onto a small, oblong room with a high window. This little room was called the "entry." It was to serve as the front hall for guests so they wouldn't have to enter through the kitchen. In it was a shrage, which in our region is what we called an open wardrobe for hanging up outer garments. In addition to the office door and the front door to the house with its four steps, there was a third door off the entry, the door to the largest room with its three windows, the salon, which the servants called "the parlor." It was never completed. My father, who had been sick for a long time, began to get weaker and weaker. He had long coughing fits and spit the phlegm into a little bottle, which he corked up and kept in his pocket. At first he would travel to his doctor in the city, but now more and more frequently we had to hitch the horses to the buggy to bring Dr. Lebedovitch up to us. So "the parlor" was left to be finished some other year. The windows were already installed, the walls plastered; we only needed to lay the floor and paint the walls.

In the meantime, we kept the big mangle there, with three heavy stones on it so that laundry that passed through the two rollers would be flattened by the weight and be that much easier to press. On the walls we hung hitching hoops for wagons, reins, halters, and blinders for horses. And in the middle we placed the newly bought machine for separating milk and cream. It was proud of itself not just for its special appearance but for its foreign-sounding name, "Alpha Separator." People came from the whole village to look at this wonder. They just couldn't comprehend how the machine had the sense to separate the milk from the cream. Like a spoiled rich child, the meager stream of honored cream flowed out of a narrow tube, while the common thin milk, its essence taken from it, gushed out of the larger tube in a rush.

This salon, with its three large windows, one to the north, two to the west, our room for receiving important visitors, was never finished. It came down in the world before it managed to shine, even just once, with a carpet, velvet furniture, and a crystal chandelier.

TRANSLATED BY SEYMOUR LEVITAN

Woe Is Me that My City Is Now Only a Memory

CHAIM GRADE

Chaim Grade (1910–1982) was a leading Yiddish novelist, poet, and memoirist. Born in Vilnius, Lithuania, he received an intense religious education and began to write secular poetry in his early twenties. He lost many family members in the Second World War, and immigrated to the US in 1948, where his works were published in Yiddish and, increasingly, in English translation, including The Agunah *(1974),* The Yeshiva *(2 vols. 1967–68), and* Synagogue and Street *(1974). The following poem is included in volume 3 of Emanuel S. Goldsmith's anthology* Yiddish Literature in America 1870–2000 *(2015). Zumoff, an endocrinologist by profession and a Yiddish translator and activist, is president emeritus of the Workmen's Circle/Arbeiter Ring.*

Woe is me that my city is now only a memory.
Home, which I can find only in native eyes—
also in the clouds you reveal yourself like a flaming chariot—
you are constantly at the back of my heart and mind.
But where you stood, you exist no longer,
O Princess Vilna, distinguished one, renowned the world over.
It is precisely in the crown city of the Temple that I hear your lament,
destroyed courtyard of the great marble synagogue;
it is precisely in the city for which our lips constantly fever
for it to be restored forever and ever
that I think of you, whose road ended suddenly
in a forest at Ponar, my royal tombs.

Sons of Israel, the prickly Sabras,
speak with rage about my destroyed home:
"Your rifles were toy rifles!"
and I answer with enraged words.
You smile sadly, Vilna, my Queen Esther,
Jewish duchess with eyes of black onyx.
The truth is that on Sabbath night, on a bluish chaise longue,
rifle-shaped spice boxes refreshed you.
You were as full of crosses as Jerusalem,
golden Catholic and Orthodox crosses,
but the baptized river could not flood
your back alleys, full of the Torah of Yavne.

You sat in your poor little shop,
and for your pennies, earned by honest hard work,
you would buy a candle in the synagogue and a roll for a student,
just as sparrows fly to the sky from crumbs.
You greeted each guest with a smile,

but you have no home in the New York Babylon.
You also have no temple yet on holy ground—
there's no headstone on your grave.
Over my head hangs a prayer shawl—your glow and shadow
to hide my tear-filled eyes from people.
No matter how much I wail within myself,
I haven't yet succeeded in sufficiently lamenting
your smashed holy thresholds.

Where I live, the red Indian summer can still substitute
for your autumn gold, my charming city,
but what can take the place for me
of the autumnally silent loneliness
of your wept-from-the-heart *yom kippurs*?
My winter approaches and covers my eyebrows with snow;
frost penetrates me like a bare, naked tree trunk.
Shine for me, my Light of Exile,
as long as I can derive pure gold
from your remaining glowing coals.
All of us will pass away, but the sun continues to shine.
God is the unceasing Creator forever—
God alone knows, my holy Vilna,
whether there are heirs left to say *kaddish* for you.

TRANSLATED BY BARNETT ZUMOFF

Coney Island

VICTOR PACKER

Victor Packer (1897–1958) was a producer, writer, and performer for American Yiddish radio and theater. In the late 1930s, working for the Brooklyn station WLTH, he filled up to four hours a day with a wide variety of audio programs. "Coney Island" is one of many "rhythmic recitation" poems he wrote and performed on air during those years. An award-winning author, record and radio producer, and performer, Henry Sapoznik is director of the Mayrent Institute for Yiddish Culture at the University of Wisconsin–Madison.

CONEY ISLAND

Sand and people.
People and sand.
On the sand a world of people.
On the people a sea of sand.
People dipped in sand.
People laid in sand.
People mixed in sand.
People soaked in sand.
Who is damp and
Who is dry
Who's still wet fresh from the sea
Who's all covered in mud
And who's just dirty as can be
There's no room, you'll have to stand
And forget lying down
A mattress in the sand
A world stretches out there
Whole peoples
Whole races
Whole castes
Whole tribes
There are mountains of people
All thrown together
An entire "Internationale"
Spread in every direction
And everyone lies together
With no distinctions

Mixed in the muck and mire
A man and wife wallow
Scattered among the whole stockyard

Flesh and skin
Hands and feet and feet and hands
Hips, backs, loins atop the sands
Knees and thighs and hips
Rouged cheeks
Red lips
Everything is pressed together
Everything is squeezed together
There are limbs with limbs
There are limbs near limbs
There are limbs under limbs
There are limbs on limbs
It's a clearinghouse of bones
A limb exchange

A hand gets to know a foot
While a foot ends up on a head.
An arm dukes it out with a knee
And a knee puts its foot down.
A neck kisses a stomach
And the stomach gets comfy with a rib.
A cheek meets a lip
And they make a trade.
A hand strays over a heart
And a heaaaaaaaaaart
Finally finds some skin.
A mouth plants itself on an ear
But the ear is deaf to it.
An elbow surrounded
A neck like a rope
So eyes threw the elbow
A stolen glance
And eyes look

Eyes twinkle
Eyes glance
Eyes glimmer
Eyes burn
Eyes devour man and wife
Hands lay entwined
Hands lay enshrined
Around bodies
Around hips
Around limbs
Around skins

There are couples
There are groups
And lovers
And brothers
But mostly strangers lie
With others
But this one and the other
And that one and the other
One winks at the other
And they peep at each other
It's a display of bodies
A concourse of feet
Eyes appraise as they measure
Who's a dish
And who's a dog
Who leaves you wanting more
Who's a nauseating bore
There, ugliness
And charm
Have all assembled by the shore

Beauty and crudity
Go hand in hand and
Launch a united front
Right there on the sand
Lithe young women lying
Sinuous and snaky
Just beside half-ton
Bountiful ladies
Bodies hued all red and brown
Singed by the sun
While their neighbors are
Swollen like a balloon
It's an easy breezy world
Where clothes are mostly shed
Where skin is just barely covered
By a tiny piece of thread
So here lies temptation
And there, ostentation
Yet everything
Is dirt-encrusted,
Scattered, and slathered
Just try and unwind
You can literally drown
In the waves of rind from
Oranges
And bananas
And apples
Eggs
Pears
You trudge through their wrappers
And fall into disrepair

Near everyone is a sack
Filled to bursting and more
And everyone eats a portion
Or someone eats for four
Mouths work wonders, let me tell you
As they binge to beat the band
And inhale what's at hand
Sandwiches filled
With sand

Oy! do the people
Have fun and
Oy! life on the sand is fun and
Long live Coney Island!
Everything is appetizing
Nothing is forbidden
It's all easy, fine, and free
Those who want to meet someone
That'll happen one, two, three
You sidle yourself over
Reaching with your hands
Suddenly, you're good friends
There's no reason to
Be alone
No one needs to be
Forced
No one needs to be
Coerced
One thing leads to another
And everyone's nicely tanned
And laid out together
You don't even need to talk
The eyes do all the talking

But if someone's eyes make
You want to roam
All you need to do is move
From the sand into the foam

The ocean is a pleasure
You can cavort
And laugh, too
The sea is so friendly to Jews
It isn't bothered by what you do
You go from the sand into the sea
Lively, happy and glad
At first still half-above
Then your whole body dunks under
Whole breakers
Whole waves
Soaking ribs
Soaking hips
And the water strokes, surrounds them
Like a lover his beloved
He whispers to her and splashes her
And flings her upside down
There are those who swim slowly, smoothly
And then break into a gallop
And those who swim on their back
Or on their side or belly, and there
Are those who go in headfirst with
Their feet up in the air
Those who splash and make a tumult
Those who swim all quiet and still
And the sea with its tricks
Does just what it will

There's a couple in the water
Swimming together as a pair
Then a wave gives chase
Drives them off and splits them
And now one swims alone
Thrown far out beyond the tide
A wave drags him under and places
A bathing beauty at his side
He is old and she is young
He could be her dad
But the ocean keeps to itself
And pretends it doesn't care
It throws them and it heaves them
And propels them as a pair
While waves beating
Hunting
Running
Accompanying everyone everywhere
Rhythmic, rhythmic
There are bodies
In the watery rips
Rhythmic, rhythmic
The cadences of hands
And feet and hips
Blustery lips and mouths
Gulp for air
And gasp there
With a very strange sigh:

EHHHHHHH . . . FRRRRRRRRRRRRRRRR
EHHHHHHH . . . FRRRRRRRRRRRRRRRR
EHHHHHHH . . . FRRRRRRRRRRRRRRRR
EHHHHHHH . . . FRRRRRRRRRRRRRRRR

EHHHHHHH . . . Ahhhhhhhhh
EHHHHHHH . . . Ahhhhhhhhh
EHHHHHHH . . . Ahhhhhhhhh
EHHHHHHH . . . Ahhhhhhhhh
Oh the water, dear old water
You're so clear and you're so blue
Oh the water, dear old water
Like a woman's caressing you
OY!
OY!!
OY!!!
OYYYYYYYYY!
Suddenly all loud and clear
The sound of an old Jew way out there
Splashing himself from top to toe
OY!
OY!!
OY!!!
OYYYYYYYYY!
Leaning and preening
In the water
He splashes his head
OY!
OY!!
OY!!!
OYYYYYYYYY!
He moans and he groans
And rinses in a rush
And dunks and plunks himself
Like in a mikvah
As he makes the Sabbath
For himself
OY!

OY!!
OY!!!
OYYYYYYYYY!
When he gulps and he gurgles
And he makes a holy racket
BRRRIT'SCOLD
BRRRIT'SCOLD
BRRRIT'SCOLD
BRRRIT'SCOLD
He turns this way and that
And again till he's sore
VAVAVAVAVAVAVVVO!
No more strength, no more.

TRANSLATED BY HENRY SAPOZNIK

from **Messiah in America**

MOYSHE NADIR

Isaac Reiss (1885–1943) was better known by his pseudonym, Moyshe Nadir. A satirist and writer, he published widely in American Yiddish newspapers and magazines, and was popular in the early 1920s in Greenwich Village bohemian circles. The following is a portion of Act I from Nadir's satirical five-act play, Meshiakh in Amerike (Messiah in America, 1932), *which was first performed by the celebrated Artef theatrical company in New York in 1933. The play takes place in the New York of the early 1930s. Targeting American capitalism, the plot is about a Broadway theater producer, Menachem Josef, who comes up with the idea of bringing the Messiah "with seven shows a week plus matinees on Shabbos and Sundays and redemption on an installment plan." It turns out he has competition from a young Coney Island producer, Scoundrel Johnnie: a messiah who can play football and dance the Black Bottom. Michael Shapiro has been by turns a street beggar, a taxi driver, a piano tuner, a research mathematician, and a bioinformatician. He currently resides in London.*

The curtain goes up. Menakhem-Yoysef sits at the table with his secretary Jackie Bluffer, a healthy, loud-mouthed boy with more balls than brains. Wears large, black-framed glasses.

MENAKHEM-YOYSEF: (*Has a large handsome graying head, a sick, restless, feverish, energetic face. He spits continuously as if he had something stuck to his lip.*) It's gotta be new! It should make a racket! We haven't done anything new in a long time.

JACKIE: I had new business cards printed up for you Mr. Menakhem-Yoysef. You're really gonna like them. Here. (*Holds up a calling card.*) It's got a motto: (*reads from the card*) Menakhem-Yoysef, Theatrical Producer, Number 32 Broadway, New York. (*To Menakhem-Yoysef*) That's nothing. Read the motto.

BOTH: (*Almost a duet*) You can curse my mother, just remember my name.

JACKIE: So, do you like it?

MENAKHEM-YOYSEF: It's good. It's good. Bravo! (*Slaps Jackie on the back.*) The main thing, y'unerstan me, it's gotta make a racket. It's gotta go beyond. You get it? You think I need the money? I don't have enough money? (*Sad.*) I have so little money. If that Scoundrel Johnnie has eighty-five thousand dollars, I've gotta have at least ninety thousand. Just to spite him, y'unerstan?

JACKIE: Of course I understand. My brains haven't shriveled. (*Flatteringly.*) Otherwise, how could I be your secretary? (*kissing ass*) A fellow needs his head on screwed on to be your secretary.

MENAKHEM-YOYSEF: My wife always nags me. I work too much. I don't watch my health. What do you think? You don't think she's right, my wife? But it's not about living, it's about outliving the other guy. Y'unerstan? If Scoundrel Johnnie lives to be sixty, I've gotta live to sixty-one. And if he lives to 102, I've gotta live to 103. (*Remembers.*) Listen, what happened with that Swedish ballet, Jackie?

JACKIE: Nothing happened. They wanted too much money.

MENAKHEM-YOYSEF: There's no such thing as too much money in show business. The more money an artist gets, the greater he is. That's what the (*rolls his eyes*) discerning audience thinks. Ha ha! The great, aristocratic audience—They like to be swindled. Remember when I put on *The Golden Peacock*? At first, nobody came. Remember, Jack? Tickets were cheap. And nobody came. And the musicians and the choir cost us a pile of money. So what did I do? I got rid of half the musicians, fired half the choir, doubled the price and they started coming. (*Differently.*) The Swedish Ballet—how much did they want?

JACKIE: Thirty-two hundred a week and a guaranteed sixteen weeks.

MENAKHEM-YOYSEF: That's too much. Not worth it. Anyway, they're probably too good. American audiences won't like it. Whaddaya say? Maybe a woman that killed a few people? Or maybe a pretty girl who jumped from the twenty-first floor and didn't die.

JACKIE: There was a woman like that.

MENAKHEM-YOYSEF: (*Perks up.*) What did she do?

JACKIE: She swallowed her own teeth. Three times already. The papers were full of it.

MENAKHEM-YOYSEF: Good. Bring her here. We'll put her name up in lights. Can she sing?

JACKIE: No.

MENAKHEM-YOYSEF: Can she dance?

JACKIE: No.

MENAKHEM-YOYSEF: Can she play an instrument?

JACKIE: Not that either.

MENAKHEM-YOYSEF: Can she walk a tightrope? Can she crochet a sock with her feet?

JACKIE: No.

MENAKHEM-YOYSEF: Is she pretty?

JACKIE: No. (*Unhappy*) She can't do anything except swallow her teeth.

MENAKHEM-YOYSEF: In that case she'll be good for later in the season. Right now, early winter, we need something better. It's gotta grab 'em. It's gotta make a racket. Y'unerstan?

JACKIE: (*Thinking.*) I've got it!

MENAKHEM-YOYSEF: What?

JACKIE: A spitter!

MENAKHEM-YOYSEF: A spitter! What do you mean, a spitter?

JACKIE: It's something new. It's a guy who can spit further than anyone. His record is six meters.

MENAKHEM-YOYSEF: Six meters is no big deal. I think somebody's already spit further. He's been out-spit.

JACKIE: (*Hurt.*) What are you saying Mr. Menakhem-Yoysef? Nobody's spit six meters. Except the Philadelphia Spitter. And that guy's dead.

MENAKHEM-YOYSEF: (*Earnest, philosophical.*) That's how it is. The best in the land are all dying out. (*Pause.*) How much does he want?

JACKIE: The spitter? He charges 450 dollars a show. I think it's an honest living.

MENAKHEM-YOYSEF: If that's what he makes, that's what he earns, of course. There's no question. But for me, it's too much. I'm not in it for some cause here. It's not like I'm trying to bring the Messiah.

JACKIE: (*Brought up sharp by the last word. Something's just occurred to him.*) What did you say? Messiah? And why not bring the Messiah? If you can make a dollar, why not? How is the Messiah any worse than a Spitter?

MENAKHEM-YOYSEF: Is that just talk or do you mean business?

JACKIE: I mean business. (*Draws closer. Becomes fervent, eloquent.*) You see, it's like this: In America, we have a lot of Jews. In New York alone, we have God knows how many Jews. Am I right, or not?

MENAKHEM-YOYSEF: Right.

JACKIE: So. Good. Figure like this. Every Jew is waiting for the Messiah. And every Jew that's waiting for the Messiah can afford, let's say, a dollar seventy-five for a ticket. Am I right, or not?

MENAKHEM-YOYSEF: Right!

JACKIE: Figure like this. Two thousand people a night at a dollar seventy-five, we gross three thousand five hundred dollars a night. Am I right, or not?

MENAKHEM-YOYSEF: Right!

JACKIE: Figure like this: Seven shows a week, plus two matinees, Shabbos and Sunday, we have nine shows a week. At $3,500 a show. That makes. . . .

MENAKHEM-YOYSEF: (*Cool and cautious.*) Wait. Let's shut the door. (*Does it, looking around to see if anyone's listening.*) All in all, I like it. Let's do it. But where are we going to get a Messiah?

JACKIE: Hang on. We'll get to that. Meanwhile, figure like this. (*Picks up a piece of paper. Computes, writes, erases, crumples up the used paper, throws it away.*) Besides the $3,500 a show we can also have private redemptions, too. Every Jew who wants to be redeemed has to pay thirty-five dollars. Even better: We'll start a Joint Share Redemption Society in Messiah's name. What's his name anyway, this Jewish Messiah?

MENAKHEM-YOYSEF: God only knows!

JACKIE: Well, it doesn't matter. We'll call the society simply "The First Messiah Redemption Society." Five dollars a share, and when you have fifteen shares, you're redeemed.

MENAKHEM-YOYSEF: (*Forgets himself for a moment.*) From what?

JACKIE: The hell should I know. What difference does it make? Jews want someone to redeem them. Good. We'll redeem them. The main thing is, it'll make a buck. Ha! What do you say, Mr. Menakhem-Yoysef? A good idea, or what?

MENAKHEM-YOYSEF: Yes. An excellent idea. Most of all, I like it because it's democratic. With us, there's no aristocrats, no fat cats. Pay your five dollars and you're redeemed. No second-class redemption for the poor. They can be redeemed bit by bit.

JACKIE: You can be redeemed on the installment plan, as a special for the poor. Sort of a Third Class Redemption. How does this sound: you pay in fifty cents a day, in ten days you get a coupon. And in around 150 days, you're a redeemed man.

MENAKHEM-YOYSEF: (*Thinks and thinks.*) On the whole, the more I think about it, the more I like it. I like it better than the Spitter. I mean, the Spitter isn't bad either. Don't get me wrong. But he wants too much. If we make money on the Messiah, then later we can get the Spitter, too. But the thing is: where are we gonna get a Messiah?

JACKIE: I've been thinking about that. Where exactly can you get a Messiah? Hmmm . . . I have it! I have an uncle. He's a greenhorn— fresh off the boat. Been here for two weeks. From Galicia. Still wears a big velvet hat and *peyes*. It's like this: If we can persuade him. Hang on I'll just call him up. (*Into the telephone.*) Hello, Jackson 4031. Yes. Hello. Uncle! Uncle Simcha! This is Jack. Yankel. Yes, Yaahnkel. Listen. Uncle. I have some business for you. Come over here. Take the train to 43rd Street. It's close by. But come right away. We'll wait. Ha! What? Well of course. You think it's free? OK. fine. But don't delay; we're waiting. Goodbye. Goodbye. (*Hangs up the telephone.*) He'll be here soon. You'll get a look at this bird. If this guy isn't the Messiah, I don't know who is. The main thing is, we can get him cheap because he's out of work. He's also sickly, so he can't do heavy work. And he can't spend too long on his feet. Also, he has a . . . you know, a . . . (*whispers in his ear*) hernia.

MENAKHEM-YOYSEF: It doesn't matter. On the contrary, it's even better. A Jewish Messiah should have a hernia. We should start thinking about a poster. Something like. . . . It should just scream! With a portrait of Messiah and endorsements by rabbis and priests and all that stuff. The main thing, it should make a racket. (*The black phone rings.*) Who's speaking? Hah? The man from the furniture company? (*Angry. Disguises his voice.*) No. Menakhem-Yoysef isn't in. Ha? What? Yes. He's out of town. Out of town? Ha? How long? For a year. (*Curt.*) Goodbye! (*Before he's hung up the little phone rings. He holds it and cradles it lovingly while saying goodbye into the other phone. Now he speaks gently and lyrically.*) Ha? Anna? How are you, my love? Yes. All's well. Jack and I are just setting up a great deal. Scoundrel Johnnie is going to look like a seven-month runt next to us. Ha? No, I can't talk about it on the phone. Yes, my dearest. Thank you. What would I like to say to you? What? Yes, of course

I do. . . . Good. Goodbye, sweetheart, goodbye. Goodbye. (*The big phone rings again. He gives the phone a dirty look. The transformation from nice to nasty should be agile.*) Ha? What? Who's speaking? The man from the electric company? (*Suddenly very mild to Jack while covering the mouthpiece.*) Do you know who that was? That was Anna, the *Daytshke* from the circus. (*To the telephone.*) Ha? Mr. Menakhem-Yoysef isn't here. (*Again to Jackie, gestures for him to take the phone.*)

JACKIE: *To the phone, like Menakhem-Yoysef.*) Ha? What? No. Not here. Mr. Menakhem-Yoysef is away. Where? Argentina. Yes. Goodbye!

MENAKHEM-YOYSEF: (*Irritated*) Money. Give them money. Anything like money, but give them money. (*Different. Practical. Takes a pencil in hand.*) So. That makes: $3,500 a show, nine shows a week. We gross . . . , take away rent . . . and, uh . . . and uh . . . eighty-five . . . 644 . . . take away nineteen . . . leaves 18,000. Six eighths minus thirty-one and a sixth, we have 921 times 811 . . . carry seven, take away sixteen . . . leaves a total of . . .

(*Entrance of Messiah. We hear a knock on the door.*)

JACKIE: That must be him, my uncle. We've gotta put on our hats. (*To Menakhem-Yoysef.*) Put on your hat. He's a greenie, my uncle, fresh off the boat, and a fanatic. If he sees us sitting around bareheaded he might not deal with us at all. (*They put on hats.*)

(*Enter Messiah.*)

MESSIAH: (*An old, simpleminded Jew with a beard like a broom, big curly peyes, wears a big velvet hat. A fanatical, disapproving, laconic Jew who "suddenly finds himself in the American wasteland." His Galitsyaner accent should be clear, not overdone. He substitutes "P" for "B".*)

JACKIE: Sholem aleykhem, uncle. (*Offers his hand.*) Sit down.

MESSIAH: (*Sits.*) You needed me? (*Puffs on a pipe.*)

JACKIE: This is my boss, Mr. Menakhem-Yoysef.

MENAKHEM-YOYSEF: Sholem aleykhem. (*Offers his hand, sizes him up. Winks to Jack, "This is good."*)

MESSIAH: And . . . Well . . . ? What can I do for you?

JACKIE: (*Pokes Menakhem-Yoysef, he should take things in hand.*)

MENAKHEM-YOYSEF: (*Getting excited.*) It's like this, Reb Uncle. What was your name again?

MESSIAH: My name? They call me Simcha. Why?

JACKIE: (*In uncle's ear.*) Mr. Menakhem-Yoysef is a great man. He has a heart of gold.

MESSIAH: (*Slow, reticent.*) Mmh. . . . Heart? Fine, but what do you want from me?

MENAKHEM-YOYSEF: (*Almost bursts out, but quickly stops himself.*) All we want from you is just. . . . (*different*) Have you ever been in a theater, Reb, uh, Reb Simcha?

MESSIAH: I was in a theater, once. In Lemberg. And so?

JACKIE: It doesn't matter. Mr. Menakhem-Yoysef is just asking.

MESSIAH: Just asking?

MENAKHEM-YOYSEF: (*Trying to draw him out.*) And how did you like it, the theater?

MESSIAH: How did I like? My daughter left me in the lobby. I looked in and saw it was dark. I didn't want to go in. Why should I sit in the dark? When the lights came on, I went in. What it's all about, I couldn't see. Ten cents an apple. Fifteen cents for a bottle of soda water. The lights went out again, so I went back to the lobby and waited around. What would I do in the dark? Then I went in again. Still ten cents an apple, fifteen cents for soda water. So then I know. This is nothing with more nothing.

MENAKHEM-YOYSEF: (*All the while exploding in little bursts of suppressed laughter. Holds himself back. Scratches his head. Is lost in thought.*)

JACKIE: (*Slaps him on the back.*) Don't worry, uncle. With us, you'll learn a thing or two. And make a buck. And we'll give you an easy job, too.

MESSIAH: But heaven forbid, I won't have to work on Shabbos, will I?

JACKIE: What are you saying? That—Heaven forbid—we're not Jews?

MESSIAH: How would I know? In America, they say even the stones are treyf.

JACKIE: Don't believe it, uncle. In America there are a lot of pious Jews that pray and say the blessings and wash before eating and go to the bathhouse and even believe in the Messiah.

MESSIAH: (*Hears the word "Messiah" and lets out a long high-pitched sigh.*)

MENAKHEM-YOYSEF: It's like this. We'll give you thirty-five dollars a week to start.

MESSIAH: (*Hesitant*) You'll give me thirty-five dollars a week? For what?

MENAKHEM-YOYSEF: For nothing. Just because I like your beard. (*Admires his beard.*) You have a very beautiful beard.

MESSIAH: (*A little bit proud.*) I have—praises be—a beautiful beard. Why not?

JACKIE: I'll say. A Jew with such a beard—*keyneynore*—in America!

MENAKHEM-YOYSEF: (*Proceeding as if on ice.*) It's ... uh ... why shouldn't you, let's say ... so to speak, that is ... Is there a Messiah on Earth, do you believe?

MESSIAH: (*Plainly.*) What else? God forbid I shouldn't believe.

JACKIE: (*Picks up the thread.*) That's what I say. As soon as we all believe (*winks to Menakhem-Yoysef*) then he must come. But why shouldn't he come a little sooner?

MENAKHEM-YOYSEF: (*Blurts out.*) And if he should come, why not directly to our firm? We've brought the greatest. Last year, we had Jack Dempsey and Kid McCoy. Two years ago we had the guy who ate nails.

MESSIAH: Nails?

JACKIE: Nails, dear uncle, this big! (*Shows the length with his finger.*) He ate them.

MENAKHEM-YOYSEF: And the woman with three legs? Who brought her?

JACKIE: We did. We did.

MENAKHEM-YOYSEF: So. It's like this. Just sign this piece of paper. (*Writes something quickly on a piece of paper and hands it to him to sign.*)

JACKIE: Sign, Uncle. Luck like this, you meet once in a hundred years. Just think, thirty-five dollars a week. For a greenie.

MENAKHEM-YOYSEF: It's a lot of money, but I'm doing it because of your nephew Jack. And because . . . I like your beard. You have a beautiful beard.

MESSIAH: (*Proud.*) We all have beautiful beards in our family. A livelihood, maybe not. . . .

JACKIE: You'll make a living too. As long as you're healthy. Sign.

MESSIAH: In Yiddish?

MENAKHEM-YOYSEF: In Yiddish. Of course in Yiddish. Do you think in America everything's *goyish*?

MESSIAH: I don't know. But I've already made a splotch. Should I blot it?

MENAKHEM-YOYSEF: No. It'll dry soon.

JACKIE: Leave it. It's good luck. (*Shakes his hand.*)

MENAKHEM-YOYSEF: Carry yourself like a man. You'll eat bread and butter with us.

JACKIE: Of course my uncle will do as he's told. What is he? Some kid who doesn't know about work?

MENAKHEM-YOYSEF: Later, when business is good, we'll give you, not thirty-five dollars a week, but forty-five dollars a week.

JACKIE: And maybe even fifty. (*To his uncle, softly.*) Do you know what that means? In your money, that's five-hundred zlotys a week. You'll be a big shot.

MESSIAH: Let me see. You gives me thirty-five dollars a week, forty dollars a week, fifty dollars a week. But what I should do, you don't say.

JACKIE: You don't have to do anything, Uncle. What should you do?

MESSIAH: Well, what should I do?

MENAKHEM-YOYSEF: Do? How shall I put it . . . Carry yourself like a man. Pious. Holy. Like a great rabbi. The main thing is the beard and the *peyes*. Don't—God forbid—cut them off.

MESSIAH: What are you saying? (*Grabs his beard and* peyes *as if to shield them from harm.*) Heaven forbid! (*Smiles graciously.*) It's for the beard and *peyes* you're paying me thirty-five dollars a week?

JACKIE: What do you think, Uncle? In America, do we know how to value Yiddishkeit, or what?

269

MESSIAH: Of course, it sounds wonderful. May God smile on you. Well then, I'll go home.

MENAKHEM-YOYSEF: Wait. We need to photograph you.

MESSIAH: What for?

JACKIE: Don't worry, Uncle, we need this for . . . business.

MESSIAH: What business?

MENAKHEM-YOYSEF: We need to show the world that there are still real Jews in America.

JACKIE: Do it, Uncle. What are worrying about? Moishe Montefiore had his picture taken, and you, not?

MESSIAH: I dunno. Fine. (*Gives himself over.*)

JACKIE: (*Calls into the next room.*) Hey Jim! Bring out the camera!

(*Enter Jim.*)

JIM: (*Jim is an Irishman with a red face. Chews and spits continually. Sleeves rolled up, white cap with the logo of a flour company, "Hekersey Flour", that the company gives away free for advertising. He brings out the camera.*) Who?

JACKIE: That guy.

JIM: Full length or just the head? (*Spits.*)

JACKIE: (*To Menakhem-Yoysef*) What do you think? I think just the head is good.

MENAKHEM-YOYSEF: (*Joking*) Just the head is already too much. If you could just take the beard.

MESSIAH: (*Grabs his beard.*) What are you saying?

JACKIE: Don't be scared, Uncle. Mr. Menakhem-Yoysef just means take a *picture* of the beard.

MESSIAH: I see . . . ! I thought you meant. . . .

(*Scene: The photographer, a bit of a joker, sets up the camera like a machine gun. Messiah keeps backing away. Jim goes after him with the camera. They keep circling in one direction. Finally goes under the black cloth and waves his hands.*)

JIM: Stop moving.

MESSIAH: (*To Jack*) I don't like this. Why's this goy hiding his face? Tell him not to hurt me.

JACKIE: Don't be afraid, Uncle. He won't hurt you.

MESSIAH: If he's not going to hurt me, why's he hiding?

JACKIE: He has to.

MESSIAH: (*Gives in.*) Well, so be it. If he must, he must. It won't hurt, will it, Yankel?

JACKIE: It won't hurt, Uncle. Why should it hurt?

MESSIAH: How should I know? This is America.

JIM: (*Loads the camera, frightening Messiah.*) Smile a little, please.

MESSIAH: Why should I smile? (*To Jack*) Do I have to smile, Yankel?

JACKIE: You have to, Uncle.

MESSIAH: So be it. You gotta do what you gotta do. (*Weak.*) Wait a minute. Get me some water. I don't feel good.

JIM: (*Brings him water. He drinks like one about to faint.*)

JIM: (*Impatient.*) So. Smile! (*Angry*) Smile already, Goddammit!

MESSIAH: (*Smiles like someone who's had his throat cut. There's a pop from the flash, which frightens him. He falls off his chair.*)

JIM: (*Leaves smiling. Looks at Messiah like a wild man.*)

MESSIAH: (*Groans.*) It's not so easy to earn a little bread.

JACK: (*Helps him.*)

MESSIAH: Mhh. . . . Thank God it's over. Can I go now?

(*All the while, Menakhem-Yoysef has been talking with Jack.*)

MENAKHEM-YOYSEF: (*Smoking a cigar.*) To tell you the truth, I'd rather have you start right away. (*To Jack.*) We have to work the press. We have to call the reporters, get them over here at once. (*Remembers.*) We've got to let the editors know before they go to press. Maybe we can break the story today. (*To Jack.*) Meanwhile, take this bird of yours to the next room.

JACKIE: (*To Messiah.*) Come, Uncle, we'll go in here for a bit.

MESSIAH: What for?

JACKIE: We have to, Uncle, we have to.

MESSIAH: Well. You gotta do what you've gotta do. (*Jack and Messiah off.*)

TRANSLATED BY MICHAEL SHAPIRO

Pour Out Thy Wrath

LAMED SHAPIRO

Lamed Shapiro (1878–1948) was born in Ukraine. Before he immigrated to New York in 1906, he was conscripted into the Imperial Russian Army and witnessed a pogrom. The experience impacted him dearly. His story "The Kiss," which takes place in one, is about the revenge of a victim against his victimizer. Other famous stories are "White Challah" and "The Jewish State." Shapiro worked for Forverts *and other periodicals. In 1921, he moved to Los Angeles and was active in the Communist Party. He died poor from alcoholism. This story is part of the book* The Jewish State and Other Stories *(1971), which was translated by Curt Leviant, portions of which were originally published in Yiddish as* Di yidishe melukhe un andere zakhn *(1919). His work in English also includes* The Cross and Other Jewish Stories *(2007). This is a new translation by Heather Valencia, a teacher, researcher, and translator of modern Yiddish language and literatures based in Scotland, whose books include a translation of Esther Kreitman's novel* Diamonds *(2009).*

TRUE, IT HAD BEEN A TERRIBLE STORM. Yet when you are nine years old you quickly forget even the most violent tempest. And Meyerl had turned nine a few weeks before Passover. However, it was also true that winds were always blowing through their house: biting, icy gusts which cut into him and reminded him of that storm. In fact, Meyerl spent more time in the wild streets of New York than in the house. Tartilov—and then New York. New York had flooded over Tartilov and washed it out of his memory. The only thing he still remembered was a dream from that time. And besides, when you are nine years old you quickly forget any storm. But even if it was just a dream it was still terrifying!

At that time, they had been studying in heder. They were really just going through the motions, because at the end of term, on the Days of Repentance leading up to Rosh Hashanah, the rebbe relaxed a little. So while they were sitting learning, suddenly from the street came the sound of doors banging, and through the windows of the heder they saw Jews running around as if they had gone mad. They were jerking and spinning about, just like leaves in a whirlwind, when a witch rises up from the earth in a pillar of dust and spins through the street, so swift and unexpected that a shiver goes through your body. Seeing the people running around in the street, the rebbe collapsed onto his chair, as white as a corpse, his lower lip trembling uncontrollably.

Meyerl never saw him again. Afterward people said that the rebbe had been murdered. Meyerl was not pleased to hear this even though the rebbe used to beat the pupils brutally. But he also wasn't sorry about it either. He just didn't really understand what had happened. What did that mean: "murdered"? And so the whole puzzling question completely disappeared from his mind, together with the rebbe.

It was only then that the real terror began. For two days, together with some older people, he and some boys hid in the bathhouse without food, drink, or parents. The adults wouldn't allow him to go home, and once, when he started screaming, they almost smothered him. He carried on sobbing and shaking, unable to stop crying immediately. A few times he dozed off, and when he woke with a start, nothing had changed. In the midst of all the horror, he only heard one word—"goyim"—which conjured up in his mind an image of something really terrible. The rest of it was very confused. In fact, he did not actually witness anything directly. Later, when it was all over, no one came to look for him, and he was taken to his home by a stranger. Neither his father nor his mother said anything to him, but acted as if he had just come back from heder as usual.

Everything in the house was smashed. His father's arm had been dislocated and his face beaten up. His mother was lying on the bed with her blonde hair tousled, her eyes puffy as if she had overslept, her face pale and dirty. Her whole body looked untidy, like a heavy, crumpled bedspread. Meyerl's father silently paced about the house, not looking at anyone, his bandaged arm hanging in a white sling around his neck. Meyerl suddenly sensed some kind of hidden horror and burst out sobbing. His father merely looked at him with a bleak, morose expression and continued pacing about the room without saying a word.

Three weeks later they sailed for America. During the voyage the sea was very rough, and Meyerl's mother lay below on her bunk, the whole time vomiting violently. Meyerl was fine. His father however kept on pacing backward and forward on the deck, even in the heaviest rain, until one of the ship's crew came and drove him below deck.

Meyerl didn't know exactly what happened, but at one point a goy on board annoyed his father—laughing at him, or something like that—and his father drew himself up and gave him a look. It was only a look, but the goy was frightened. He retreated and started crossing himself while spitting and muttering inaudibly. When Meyerl saw the way his father twisted up his mouth and ground his teeth, with his eyes protruding out of their sockets, he was also scared. Meyerl had never seen him looking like that. But soon his father started pacing the deck again with his head buried in the collar of his coat, his hands in his sleeves, and his back hunched.

When they landed in New York, Meyerl's head began to spin, and pretty soon Tartilov had turned into a dream.

2

It was the beginning of winter, and soon masses of fresh, white snow began to fall. Meyerl had become a real American boy. Like all boys, he went to school, he learned to throw snowballs, fly on skates, and light fires in the middle of the street and no one was upset. Like all boys, he lived mostly on the streets and would only come home to grab some food or sleep.

Cold biting drafts penetrated the house, making it seem strange and eerie. Meyerl's father, a thin, large-boned man with a dark-skinned face and a black beard, had always been quiet and only rarely did one hear him say things to his wife like: "Listen to me, Tsipe. . . ." Now he was completely silent and it was really frightening. Mother, on the other hand, had always been lively and talkative, constantly bustling around with her "Shloyme" this and "Shloyme" that, and telling lots of stories. But now all this had changed completely. Father constantly paced around the room while Mother followed him with her eyes like a child, as if she was desperate to say something but did not dare to. And there was something different about her expression. What was it, exactly? It was something that reminded Meyerl of the eyes of the dog Mishka that he loved to play with back there, in the shtetl that had become a dream.

Sometimes, waking up suddenly in the middle of the night, Meyerl heard his mother sobbing. At those times his father, in the other bed, would be smoking his cigar, drawing on it fiercely. It was frightening to see the glow flaring up each time in the darkness as if of its own accord, hovering just over where his father's dark head must be lying. As sleep overcame Meyerl, his mother, the glowing cigar, and the whole room would jumble together in his head and then fade away. Twice that winter his mother was ill. The first time it lasted for two days and the second time for four, but both times it seemed very serious. Her face was fiery-red, and she bit her lower lip so hard with her sharp white teeth that it bled. Despite this, terrible wild groans came from her revealing her dreadful pain. She vomited frequently as she had during the sea voyage. The vomiting was so violent that it seemed as if her intestines were going to come up.

At these times she did not look at Meyerl's father pleadingly. No, this was something different . . . this was like . . . what was it like? . . . Oh yes! It was like the time when Mishka had a sharp thorn stuck deep in his paw, and he squealed and howled with furious rage while chewing his paw as if to devour it and the thorn together.

Father also was different during those periods. He didn't just pace but ran about the room with the smoking cigar crackling ceaselessly between his teeth. Instead of the one cloud that perpetually hovered motionless over his brow, now cloud after cloud chased each other, twisting into the deep broad furrows. From time to time it was as if flashes of lightning passed over and then were immediately extinguished again. He did not look at his wife, and neither of them paid any attention to Meyerl, who felt altogether lost and lonely.

It was strange, but it was at those times that Meyerl felt drawn to stay at home. In the street everything was just as usual, whereas at home. . . . There, it was rather like the atmosphere of the synagogue during the Days of Awe when the shofar was blown as tall fathers with prayer shawls over their heads stood holding their breath, and from far away the note of the *tkiye* reverberated over the congregation—a solitary, powerful, long-drawn-out sound: to-to-u-uuuuuuuuu!

Both times after his mother recovered a dark shadow would descend on the house. Father became even gloomier than before, and Mother's expression, as she followed him with her eyes, was more submissive and dejected than ever. Meyerl in turn would run out of the house and into the noisy street.

3

The white snows had become less frequent and soon they departed altogether like birds leaving the nest. It felt as if something new was in the air. What it actually was, Meyerl couldn't really say. But in any case, it must be something good, something very good, because all the people in the street were very happy about it. You could see that in their brighter and friendlier faces.

On the morning of the Eve of Passover the sky also cleared a little at home. It was as if the outdoors and the indoors were clasping hands through the window, which had been opened for the first time. This friendliness made Meyerl feel happier.

Father and Mother made preparations for Passover. They were, however, meager preparations: there was no festive, noisy matzo-bakery so they instead bought a package of old, cold, ready-baked matzos. There was no barrel of borsht for Passover standing in the corner covered with coarse unbleached linen. There were no dusty Passover dishes to get down from the attic where they had been kept for years. Instead, Father bought cheap unmatched odds and ends of crockery from a street peddler. But all the same, there was still a slightly festive atmosphere that warmed the heart. Once or twice, back in Tartilov, Meyerl had lain in bed at night with his eyes open, his heart petrified with fear, listening to the dark stillness. It seemed as if the whole world—his whole family—had died. But the sudden simple crowing of a rooster was enough to fill his heart again with a warm stream of joy and homely comfort.

Father's face brightened up a little. When he was wiping the glasses for Passover, although his eyes still stared rather distractedly, his lips looked as if they might just break into a smile at any moment. Mother looked almost cheerful as she bustled around in the kitchen, preparing the first of the matzo-pancakes, which were sizzling and chattering in the pan, when a neighbor came in to borrow a pot. Meyerl was standing beside his mother. The neighbor took her pot, and the women started exchanging a few words about the forthcoming festival. Then the neighbor said: "And there'll soon be something else to celebrate in your house, won't there?" pointing at Mother with a smile and a wink. It was then that Meyerl suddenly noticed for the first time that his mother's figure had become round and full. But he had no time to think about it, for he heard the crash of breaking glasses from the other room. His mother stood as if she had been struck dumb, and his father appeared in the doorway.

"Get out!"

His voice made the windowpanes rattle, as though a heavy wagon was riding over the cobblestones.

With a clumsy movement, the terrified neighbor turned around and left.

4

Father and Mother looked awkward in their festive clothes, with their faces like mourners at a funeral. In fact, the whole "seder" seemed awkward. The atmosphere was more like the last evening meal before the fast of Tisha B'av. When Meyerl began chanting the Four Questions in an expressionless voice, like someone hired for the job, he felt his heart aching; around him all was strangely silent, like in the synagogue when an orphan is reciting his first kaddish. . . .

Mother's lips were moving without any sound at all. From time to time she wet her finger and turned over the pages, one after the other, and a large, heavy, shining teardrop slowly rolled down her beautiful but unhappy face, falling on the siddur, on the white tablecloth, or on her clothes. Father did not look at her. Did he see her weeping? And how strangely he recited the Haggadah! He chanted a little bit of it with a melody, with long-drawn-out tones, and then suddenly his voice would break down with a choking sound, as if a hand was squeezing his throat. Then he would look at the Haggadah again, or his unfocused eyes would stray around the room. He would start to recite again, until his voice broke down once more. . . .

They hardly ate anything and each of them said the grace privately and silently. Suddenly Father said: "Meyer, open the door."

Rather nervously, full of vague fear of the Prophet Elijah, Meyerl pulled the door open.

"*Shfoykh khamoskho el hagoyim, asher loy yedoukho*—Pour out Thy wrath upon the nations that know Thee not!"

A slight shudder ran down Meyerl's spine. A voice that was completely strange to him resounded from one corner of the room to the other, shot up to the ceiling, flung itself downwards again and began to ricochet off the four walls, like a caged bird going berserk. Meyerl turned to look at his father and his hair stood on end with terror. A wild figure in a long snow-white robe, as straight as a taut violin string, with a black beard and a thin, dark-skinned face stood by the table. Its eyes were burning with a dark, eerie fire. It grated its teeth and its voice turned into the wild howling of an animal roaring for quivering flesh and warm blood. Mother sprang out of her chair, shaking in every limb. She looked at Father for an instant and then threw herself down at his feet, clutching the hem of his long white robe with both hands and letting out a wail.

"Shloyme, Shloyme. Kill me, Shloyme! Put an end to me! Oh, the agony, the agony!"

Meyerl felt all his insides turning over, as if a large hand with long talons had dug into and twisted them with one tearing movement. His mouth opened wide, and the scream of a terrified child burst out of his throat. Tartilov suddenly whirled in front of his eyes. Terrified Jews were rushing about in the street like leaves in a storm. The pale rebbe was sitting on his chair, his lower lip trembling. Mother was lying on the bed, all screwed up like a crumpled bedspread. Meyerl sensed as clearly as if it had been written there in front of his eyes that all that was not over, that it was just beginning, that the real, enormous calamity was just coming, was just about to fall on their house, on their heads, like a thunderclap. Once again a scream of wild helpless terror burst out of his throat.

A few Italian neighbors were standing in the corridor, staring at this incomprehensible scene and whispering fearfully to each other. In the room the terrible curse still resounded; one instant ringing out in strong steel-like tones, and in the next, in the rasping, persistent death rattle of a slaughtered man:

Mighty God! Pour out
Thy great wrath upon the nations
Who have no God in their hearts!
Thy great wrath upon the kingdoms,
That know not thy name!
My body they have devoured, devoured
My house they have laid waste, laid waste!
Let Thy wrathful anger pursue them!
Pursue them—and overtake them,
Overtake them—and destroy them utterly
From under the heavens!

TRANSLATED BY HEATHER VALENCIA

Mr. Friedkin and Shoshana

JOSEPH OPATOSHU

The novel Hibru *by Joseph Opatoshu (1886–1954) portrays the professional and personal lives of teachers, young immigrant men from Eastern Europe who wander like lost souls in the land of opportunity, seeking a livelihood, meaning, and love. It is set on the Lower East Side of New York in the 1910s. The title refers to Hebrew schools, supplementary schools that boys attended in the afternoon after public school. The schools provided students with a Jewish education and prepared them for their bar mitzvahs. This selection is Chapter 13, with a new title provided by the translator. It opens with Mr. Friedkin—the novel's protagonist and the principal of a Hebrew school—in a state of agitation precipitated by his colleague Ziskind's declaration of belief in Jesus. Born in Poland, Opatoshu immigrated to America in 1907. His novels include* The Last Revolt *(1952) and* Bar-Kokhba *(1953). Shulamith Z. Berger is the curator of special collections and Hebraica-Judaica at the Mendel Gottesman Library of Yeshiva University.*

FRIEDKIN WANDERED AROUND lost in thought for several days after the scene at Ziskind's. He realized that until now he'd never let life touch him; life had passed by him like a shallow stream flowing between high shores, never jostling nor leaving a trace on him. He was sorry that he had frittered away more than half his life on nothing more than the pursuit of creature comforts. The children in school exchanged puzzled glances. They couldn't understand the change in Friedkin. He treated them politely, like adults, and the children responded and sat calmly. For the first time in years he didn't feel worn out when he dismissed the class. He walked down the steps briskly, cheerfully exchanged greetings with the teachers, and thought he was on his way to a new life.

Friedkin got ahold of a New Testament, stayed up late at night, and read it diligently. This went on for a few days. Very often, poring over the New Testament, he recited the words mechanically, without understanding the meaning, and perverse thoughts crept into his head about a Jewish Pope, Jewish cardinals, and about the missionary, Ziskind. He fantasized himself sitting on the Pope's golden throne. He knew it was impossible, yet he imagined receiving Jewish deputations regarding blood libels and issuing papal bulls to all the nations decreeing that blood libels are ugly, false accusations of ritual murder leveled against the Jews. Every time he thought about blood libels, it brought to mind the scholar Daniel Chwolson, a convert from Judaism but a great advocate for his people. Friedkin then transformed himself from a Pope to that professor in the czar's court, determined to demonstrate the greatness of the Jews to the world. He soon grew sick and tired of the New Testament.

On top of that, Shoshana came over almost every evening, leaving him little time to think of much else. He gradually forgot about the incident with Ziskind. Shoshana's visits also grew distasteful, and he thought about how to distance himself from her. Just then the secretary of the school handed him a letter of dismissal, notifying him that he must look for another position at the end of the term. The news thoroughly

283

unnerved him. It drove everything else out of his head, and all Friedkin could concentrate on was finding a concrete solution. He curried favor with the secretary of the school, hinted that he'd marry his daughter at any time, and wrote poison pen letters about a teacher, Green, accusing him of violating Shabbos—nothing helped. As the time for him to vacate his position grew closer, he became more despondent. He realized he had no one to pour his heart out to, that he was still a stranger in New York; he might as well have just gotten off the boat yesterday.

And here stood Shoshana with wide-open arms, desiring him just the way he was, and he grew warmer at the thought. He told himself that she was a seamstress, she could open her own place, and if it were successful he'd be set for life. Every time he contemplated breaking up with Shoshana, convinced he'd soon find a better match, she would, as if just to spite him for the thought, visit him in progressively lighter, see-through clothing. She wouldn't leave him alone, toying with him like a cat with a ball of yarn. The more she tempted him, the more he wanted to escape, but all he could manage to do in the few hours before she visited was to parade around his room all dressed up.

Shoshana came in and didn't greet him. She sat with her hat on, and like a person with something to hide, she looked down at the floor helplessly, without saying a thing.

"What's wrong, Shoshana?" Friedkin asked.

She looked at him with watery eyes, her lips trembling as though she were about to burst into tears. She bit her lower lip with her white teeth and stayed in the same position.

"Shoshana, say something, what is it?" Friedkin went to her and touched her gently on her shoulder. "Did someone hurt you?"

"Nothing; leave me alone." She twisted as though she wanted to shake off his hand and wept quietly.

"What's going on, Shoshana?" Friedkin implored her. "Why are you crying? You've got to tell me; I'm not a stranger. Did someone offend you? Why aren't you saying anything?"

She looked up, wiped her eyes, opened her mouth, and sobbed even more fiercely. Friedkin began kissing her hands, not even knowing what he was saying: "Shoshana, why are you crying? Please, tell me! Nu, Shoshana?"

"I can't," she said in a low voice.

"You've got to tell me!" Friedkin kept kissing her. "You mustn't be ashamed in front of me! What, am I a stranger?"

Shoshana gasped and clutched at her heart. Her head bobbed as though she were about to faint.

"Some water?" Friedkin jumped up. She nodded. Friedkin brought a glass of water, sprinkled her face, poured a bit into her mouth, and stretched her out on the bed. She came to, motioned for him to sit next to her, and asked him to loosen her corset. Friedkin unbuttoned her corset, put another pillow under her head, and begged her to calm down. All of a sudden Shoshana got off the bed, sat down on the rocking chair, and without looking at Friedkin, just barely got out the words: "I'm pregnant."

"What?" Friedkin opened his eyes, like a calf being led to the slaughter.

"Exactly what you heard." Shoshana started crying again.

"How can you be so sure?" Friedkin drew closer.

She didn't answer, hid her face in her hands, and burst into sobs.

This time, Friedkin clenched his lips, stiffened his chin, didn't say anything, and started to pace across the room. Thousands of thoughts ran through his head in that one minute. None of the thoughts stayed with him; they flew in all directions and he suddenly felt drained. He lowered himself onto the bed, looked at her awhile with dazed eyes as though he had just woken up, and again asked, now with a smile, "You're really pregnant?"

"You don't believe me!" Her nostrils quivered and tears flowed from her eyes. "Where should I go, then? What would you have me do?"

"I don't know why you're crying." He suddenly went over to her. "It's from me, you say?"

"Who else?"

She stood wild-eyed, like a mother defending her cubs.

"I believe you, I believe you," Friedkin stammered in fear. "Why are you crying? It's my child, you say. Good! Good!"

Shoshana took a few steps toward Friedkin, looked at him as though she were thinking of saying something, put her hands dejectedly on his shoulders, laid her head on his chest, and wept quietly. Friedkin led her to the bed, sat down next to her, and tried to comfort her. "I beg you, Shoshana, please calm down! Crying won't help at all! Nu, Shoshana?"

She started to wipe her eyes, leaned against Friedkin's shoulder, avoided looking at him, and was silent.

Friedkin sat forlorn. He had often daydreamed about getting married, but now the prospect felt like a rope thrust around his neck by a hidden hand, poised to suffocate him at any moment. He observed Shoshana's profile, with the delicate dark hairs on her cheek, so thin they almost curled; he felt the hot breath from her nostrils, and he shuddered. He couldn't comprehend what she wanted from him. He felt everything around him constrict and couldn't breathe, wishing he could be free from her.

"Why are you quiet?" Shoshana instinctively interrupted the silence and snuggled up to him.

"What am I supposed to say?" Friedkin shrugged his shoulders helplessly.

"I see you're suffering." She ran her fingers through his thin hair, wrinkling her forehead a bit as though contemplating what to say. "You know, a man suffers more beautifully than a woman, quietly; it's truly tragic. With a woman, it's melodramatic. You know, I despise self-satisfied men with fat faces. . . . A man who chases women, a 'ladies' man,' I don't like that, that's not a man. . . . I don't mean a man ought to be indifferent to women, but a man whose mission is to enjoy women and who wastes days and nights for the sake of a kiss is, in my opinion, worse than a man who is a gambler! And I promise you," Shoshana hugged Friedkin with her bare arms, "we'll have a comfortable home and the main thing is, whatever you earn will be fine! If you'll make ten dollars a week, we'll live on ten. Do you get more?"

"Of course," Friedkin answered, feeling that now they had switched roles. "My salary from the school alone is sixteen dollars a week. With private lessons, bar mitzvahs, I can make twenty-five!"

"So we can truly save." Shoshana's spirits lifted. "That'll be useful . . . I've also laid away a few dollars. . . . "

They looked at each other and laughed. Shoshana kissed his eyes, brushed his ear with her lips, and whispered softly, "Tomorrow we'll go look for rooms, all right? You'll see how clean I'll keep everything; every corner will be spick-and-span! Do you know how good a cook I am? I bake, too! We won't make an official wedding; why waste money? It would be a pity! We'll go to a rabbi and have a Jewish ceremony, with a chuppah. What do you say?" she cajoled him.

"All right," Friedkin answered, feeling the rope being pulled tighter around his neck, and for the last time he tried to free himself. "Shoshana, how are you so sure? I mean, how do you know that—"

"That what?"

"I mean," Friedkin stammered, "how do you know that. . . . Did you ask a doctor? I mean, are you really sure you're pregnant?"

"What am I, a little girl?" Shoshana was offended. "You're talking, please forgive me, like a. . . . Why wouldn't I know? And I'll tell you the truth: the first minute I felt miserable; now I'm happy. When a woman loves a man, she wants to have his child!"

Friedkin didn't respond, just leaned his elbows on his knees, set his head in his hands in despair as though he'd suffered a tragedy, and stared into space.

Shoshana took his hand, stroked it, and clung to him, instinctively understanding that she mustn't be lighthearted now; the mildest flirt would distress him even more. She didn't say anything, letting the mood grow more serious. Then she sighed deeply and began: "You know, it's an ugly world! When I think about it, I haven't had a minute of happiness in my life!" She looked at him for a few moments, took his hand, held it to her right cheek, then the left, let go, and became even more earnest.

"I was never a child! When I was five, after my mother died, I had to raise my two little sisters. I washed them, combed their hair, took care of the house, and whenever one of my sisters fell and hurt herself, my father would slap me. My father was a fierce man, an angry man. I never heard a good word from him. I remember it as though it happened yesterday." Shoshana again took Friedkin's hand. "I was seven years old. I got a new dress for Pesach, and the first day I wore it outside, it got caught on a nail and ripped terribly. Did my father ever beat me! Oy, did I hate him then. Later I survived a pogrom, hiding in a garret for over a day and a night. What do you know from that? Then the journey to the Land of Israel, with a group of orphans. . . . I've been through a lot!"

"Oh, that's right, you're from Kishinev. . . . " Friedkin said.

"Yes, I lived through the first Kishinev pogrom." Shoshana's eyes flashed like lightning. It seemed as though she had told the story many times before, knowing it always impressed. "I lay in an attic, didn't make a sound, and sucked on my finger. And when I got even hungrier, I took that finger out of my mouth and chewed on another. You'll laugh, but every time I switched fingers, I felt better. My father sat in a bundle of straw. Every once in a while he stuck out his head to see how I was doing. He comforted me by saying that soon someone would send us something to eat. Strange, whenever I think of my father, I remember what his eyes looked like then—huge, terrified, like a crazy person's. It bothered me that he discussed matters with me as though I had grown up overnight and actually become a mother. Every time he moved around the attic, I was terrified, as though the bundle of straw were walking, not my father. And every time, I called out to him, as if to convince myself we were safe at home, that this really was my father."

She grew silent, wiped away her tears, and was sunk in thought.

"And what happened in the end?" Friedkin had grown curious.

"What do you think!" She heaved a sigh. "At dawn, just when we decided to go down, a few hooligans came up to the attic, scattered everything, and one shoved his hand in the bundle of straw as he passed it and pulled my father out.

"I'll never forget how he looked then. His beard had become so thin that you could count each and every hair. He avoided looking at me, ashamed, and with wide-open eyes he threw himself at the feet of the goyim, embraced their ankles, kissed them, and cried with a peculiar, piercing voice that shot needles through my entire body.

"I covered myself up more, squeezed my eyes closed, and was suddenly filled with hatred—why didn't I attack the goyim, bite off one of their fingers? I think I pressed my eyes shut, but I still saw the goyim search him and take everything he had. A young *sheygets* punched him in the face and he fell on his knees, covered with blood. I felt like everything was exploding inside me, I so badly wanted to attack the *sheygets*. I bit my fingers and pinched my skin—how can I let a *sheygets* attack my father? I was sure that as soon as I'd stand up, someone would hit me over the head with a crowbar.

"They kept beating my father. They ripped off his clothes, wanted to know where he hid money, but he only groaned and begged them to stop. He kissed the hands that beat him, kissed the feet that trampled him, and suddenly cried out, 'Reyzele! Reyzele! They're killing me! My daughter, they're going to murder your father.'

"For the first time, I heard my father, who'd always terrified me, crying and pleading for me, his eight-year-old daughter, to save him. I swallowed hot tears and bit my right hand until I drew blood, asking myself why didn't I get up from my spot. But the fear that I'd be beaten over my head with a crowbar stopped me dead in my tracks, and I didn't move a muscle.

"Meanwhile, a young peasant grabbed my father by his scrawny beard and started to lead him away from the attic. My father was bloody, with these wide-open eyes, and he looked so pathetic that I shrieked. I forgot that I could be killed. I couldn't bear to watch them hurt my father; I flung myself at him in one leap, twisted my arms and legs around him, and screamed, '*Tate*, don't go! Father!'

"I felt a pair of strong hands seize me, lift me up, and as I flew down to the stone floor I saw sparks in front of my eyes. . . . "

As Shoshana told the story, Friedkin gazed into her eyes, carried away by her experience, and sensed that she was gradually gaining stature in his eyes. He forgot all the issues married life entailed and wondered why he had always been so afraid of getting married. Everything looked rosy. He didn't want to think. He knew that others supported wives and children on even less money than he earned.

Friedkin's mood brightened. He complimented Shoshana and laughed. Even though he didn't want to think about anything, he pictured the meals she'd cook for him and the furniture she'd buy. He didn't quite believe that he was going to become a father so easily! What was the difference between yesterday, when he was still just a bachelor, and today? He used to lie awake in bed at night fantasizing about his wedding, and now, suddenly, a woman confided in him that he's already as good as married, that soon he'll be a father. He looked at Shoshana, noticed her tousled hair, her black eyes, and wanted to find something similar to himself in her. Although there was no resemblance, he found some part of himself mirrored in her face when he looked into her eyes for a long time.

Late at night he escorted her home. He was happy and planned to go looking for an apartment the next day and stand under a chuppah the day after.

When Shoshana entered her building, Friedkin remained outside. He listened to her walk up the steps, rest on every floor with a sigh, then close the door and lock it. And suddenly everything was still. He was tired and just stood there a while, envious that Shoshana could go to bed right away. Then he shlepped himself home.

The silent streets and the people who were hunched over scurrying here and there, disappearing into dark buildings, affected Friedkin, and his good mood gradually disappeared.

Someone came toward him from a side street. This very tall stranger walked quickly and flapped his arms like wings. Friedkin instinctively wanted to play it safe by crossing the street, but he reminded himself that he was getting married and would soon need to protect his wife. He gathered his courage, went toward the stranger, and trembled. He took another few steps, couldn't endure the tension, and started to step off the sidewalk when suddenly he became calm and his fear melted—the stranger was wearing glasses.

TRANSLATED BY SHULAMITH BERGER

God of Mercy

DAVID FRISCHMANN

The following are excerpts from a short parody of Sholem Asch's famous play by the prolific Polish writer David Frischmann (1859–1922), who wrote in both Hebrew and Yiddish. The spoof first appeared in a Warsaw journal called Teatervelt *(Theater World, 1908). In* God of Vengeance, *Yankl the brothel-owner struggled to keep his daughter pure by buying a Torah scroll; in Frischmann's parody, Yankl is an assimilated, successful businessman who hires a nubile "nanny" for his son to distract him from the temptations of Talmudic study. Binyomin (Benjamin) Weiner is a writer, scholar of Yiddish and Irish literature, musician and homesteader, and the spiritual leader of the Jewish Community of Amherst, in Amherst, Massachusetts.*

ACT ONE

Soreh and Ruvendl (Ruvendl is Soreh's son, a pain in the butt, who is drawn, as if by tongs, to the idlers and young men in the study house, and thereby fouls his father's aristocratic airs.)

SOREH: What are you stumbling around here for, so bent and hunch-backed and useless? Your face, it's covered with boils and sores, and your nose, it looks like pure Rashiscript! You look like a lamed-vovnik! What are you looking for?

RUVENDL: I'm getting my tfiln-zak, my talis-kotn, my Khok l'Yisroel, my prayer book, my Gemore, my Yisod v'Shoyresh ho-Avoyde, my Miseles Yeshorim, and my Layv Ivri, and I'm going down to the study house, Mommy.

SOREH: *(Horrified.)* Such misfortune has befallen me! When your father sees you, he'll have an apoplectic fit! He'll yell and moan and carry on, and give you such a scolding! Think, my son, about all that Daddy has done to steer you down the right path. Even just now, he is [. . .] bringing home for you a nanny, a beautiful, young, alluring maiden, and with God's help this young maiden will serve you as a good-luck charm, to help rid you of your idleness and teach you what life is really about, teach you how to be lively, just as Father wants. Having a nanny, dear son, is like, pardon the comparison, having a Torah scroll in the house.[. . .] Soon all the rich men's children will come to you because of her, and they will be your new friends, darling boy. Soon we'll have to make you a whole new suit for lawn tennis, and you'll have to take dance lessons. Shh, Daddy's coming! For God's sake, don't look so sickly—act like you have some life in you!

YANKL: Ruvendl, throw away that tfiln-zak and that prayer book, and take that yarmulke off your head.

(Ruvendl remains stoop-shouldered and silent.)

292

Come over here, to Daddy. Don't be afraid. I won't do you any harm. *(Takes him by the hand.)* Daddy loves you very much. Daddy's getting you a present. Blood and milk. [. . .] Cost me a lot of money, I tell you. . . .

RUVENDL: *(Remains silent.)*

YANKL: She'll be waiting for you in your room. I'll give her a little cot in your bedroom, so she'll always be there to rid you of angry, foolish memories. Slowly but surely she'll make a man of you. Before long, not one bit of your idleness will remain. [. . .] You must understand, my son: A maiden in your room is very much like, pardon the comparison, a Torah scroll in a drama. Her shirt is like the curtain over the ark. Her body is like the sacred parchment; holding the yad is like kissing; her head is like the Torah crown. . . .

RUVENDL: *(Lost in dreams, whispering, barely audible.)* Oh, downstairs, the study house, the holy ark, taking out and putting away the Torah, raising it up and wrapping it. . . .

YANKL: *(Stamping his foot)* This is your rightful place, you brat! Here's where you'll have your putting away the Torah, here's where you'll do your raising and wrapping!

ACT TWO

In the Study House.

ZALMAN: Time to go to bed. Turn off the lamp, and we'll sleep. *(The room is semi-darkened.)*

RITCHE: They say that Napoleon once said, "Wherever it itches, that's where you should scratch."

PITCHE: They say that Rothschild, may his memory be blessed, once said, "When you lie down with dogs, you get up with fleas."

RITCHE: I remember once in our little village: I was just a little kid then. I lay on a bench, a hard one, like right now, and in the holes of that wall there were some kind of little living creatures crawling, like right now. One of them crawled out of the wall and onto the bench.

And from the bench onto my father, and from my father onto me, like right now. Suddenly, it was winter. . . .

ZALMAN: If I had enough money, I'd run away to the Lumzher Yeshiva.

MENACHEM: Yes, yes, away. If Ruvendl would come too, then we could all run away. [. . .] His father's money would be enough for all of us. . . .

RUVENDL: *(Sticking his head through the door.)* Quiet, speak softly! Everyone's asleep at my house, so I stole away and came over here. Where's Menachem? I was drawn to him! [. . .] I'm afraid that my father will find out, and give me a beating. If my father catches me here in the study house, he'll lay me dead in the earth.

MENACHEM: *(Whispering.)* Come, Ruvendl, it's so warm over here, the air smells so nice, come.

RUVENDL: Quiet, quiet, I'm afraid. He hid the key under the nanny's pillow. So that I would have to come to her. And I stole away from my bed, to come here, nearly naked. I l went over to where she was, on the little bed. She was lying there, half-uncovered. We must remain covered! I nearly touched the devil's hand! She nearly touched me as I reached my hand under her head, to get the key. In what kind of a black year would I have anything to do with such a girl? I was drawn away to you! Oh, this is the stuff that tragedies are made of!

MENACHEM: But you are cold, Ruvendl. Calm yourself, soothe yourself with me. . . . Let's lie down here on the bench. [. . .] This way the wrinkles grow deeper, and the hunchback more crooked, and the neck bends further. Oh, how sweet! Just like blades of grass waving on the meadow in a drama. . . . Rest your nose in the hunch of my back. I'm embracing you with my sidelocks, my curling sidelocks. It's so cool, just as if there were water flowing between us like in a drama. I want to embrace you like a maiden-bride. Do you want that?

RUVENDL: Yes, yes. . . .

MENACHEM: We will sleep in one bed, every night. Your father will never come near us, we'll be far away from him. Will you run away with me, far, far away? Yes, yes. Come, let's run away, run away to a distant yeshiva.

(Menachem grabs Ruvendl, and voilà, off they go. They disappear into the distance—just like in a drama. A gruff voice is heard all of a sudden—just like in a drama. Yankl appears, his hair disheveled and his eyes wild, dressed in a sleeping robe, a burning candle in his hand, just like—pardon the comparison—in a piece of teater-shtik.)

YANKL: Ruvendl, Ruvendl, where are you?

(Pause. Teater-shtik.)

Ruvendl, is Ruvendl here?

IDLERS: What. . . . We don't know!

YANKL: You don't know?! *(He runs out in a fit of madness. He returns a minute later, dragging his wife, Soreh, by the locks of her hair. A pause befitting a great tragedy.)* Where is your son? Your son!

(Everyone begins to tremble, except the curtain. The curtain falls silently.)

TRANSLATED BY BINYOMIN WEINER

Torture

MALKA HEIFETZ-TUSSMAN

Born in 1896 and raised in Volyn, Russia, at the age of sixteen Malka Heifetz-Tussman left for America, where she lived in Milwaukee and attended the University of Wisconsin. She then moved to California, where she was to spend most of her life working as a teacher. After her first book appeared in 1949 she was a presence in the Yiddish literary community, publishing essays, stories, and poems in European and American Yiddish journals, as well as translating such poets as Dylan Thomas and Anna Akhmatova into Yiddish. Her books, which include Leaves Do Not Fall *and* Now is Ever, *present poems, both tragic and musical, that engage the most difficult troubles with a light and knowing compassion. When she died in 1987 at the age of ninety-one, she left behind a large and varied body of work, but one that always struggled with the basic questions of humanity and responsibility. Jack Hirschman is a prolific poet and social activist, former Poet Laureate of San Francisco, and the author of dozens of books.*

TORTURE

Loving
drained me pale, I
became quiet,
thin, weightless,
Flesh pushed me over, I
got swollen,
becoming flabby, becoming
heavy with lust.
(God
where are you
not: in the sharpest torture,
even in the dirty fire of hell
I see the shadow of your lashes)
And flesh is a dummy with eyes,
and when it cries it's
such a, such
a desolate pity

TRANSLATED BY JACK HIRSCHMAN

PART V
Oy, the Children!

דער מענטש טראַכט און גאָט לאַכט.

Der mentsh trakht un got lakht.

Man plans and God laughs.

WHILE THE YIDDISH LANGUAGE has been passed down lovingly in some American families, in many others the possibility that a younger generation would grow up to speak and read in *mame-loshn* was simply never given much thought. Even the great Yiddish writer Sholem Aleichem understood that his descendants probably wouldn't read his work in the original. When he died in 1916, his will requested that on his *yortsayt*, the anniversary of his death, his children and their children gather and "select one of my stories, one of the really joyous ones, and read it aloud *in whatever language they understand best*." Sholem Aleichem himself had mostly spoken to his children in Russian. Many other Yiddish writers, and a vast number of everyday Yiddish speakers, likewise understood that their American-born children would have at best a complicated relationship to the language, having heard it in hushed tones when the elders didn't want the children to hear, or in exuberant outbursts when English couldn't quite do the job.

But a complex relationship isn't the same thing as no relationship. In fact, generations of children and even grandchildren who grew up hearing Yiddish at home often developed powerful feelings about the language, seeing it as a unique link to their childhood, to their parents and grandparents, and to earlier times and places. Many of them have gone on to phenomenal success in American culture as prizewinning writers, musicians, professors, and even Hollywood stars. Some brought Yiddish with them, in one form or another, finding ways to use their chosen field—sometimes poetry, film, or comic books, among others— to reflect on the language, and the culture of those who spoke it. By no means always reverent, and sometimes furious or confused, the results have in some cases become touchstones in American culture. The selections gathered in this part offer a relatively small and eclectic survey of this output.

FURTHER READING

J. Hoberman and Jeffrey Shandler, *Entertaining America: Jews, Movies, and Broadcasting* (2003)

Paul Buhle, *From the Lower East Side to Hollywood: Jews in American Popular Culture* (2004)

Goodbye and Good Luck

GRACE PALEY

Aside from writing stories, essays, and poetry, Grace Paley (1922–2007) was active in left-wing political causes, most prominently against the Vietnam War. Her literary style is simple, straightforward, and conversational. She taught at Sarah Lawrence College, among other places. Her books include The Little Disturbances of Man *(1959),* Enormous Changes at the Last Minute *(1974),* Later the Same Day *(1985), and* Just as I Thought *(1998). Her* Collected Stories *was released in 1994.*

I WAS POPULAR IN CERTAIN CIRCLES, says Aunt Rose. I wasn't no thinner then, only more stationary in the flesh. In time to come, Lillie, don't be surprised—change is a fact of God. From this no one is excused. Only a person like your mama stands on one foot, she don't notice how big her behind is getting and sings in the canary's ear for thirty years. Who's listening? Papa's in the shop. You and Seymour, thinking about yourself. So she waits in a spotless kitchen for a kind word and thinks—poor Rosie. . . .

Poor Rosie! If there was more life in my little sister, she would know my heart is a regular college of feelings and there is such information between my corset and me that her whole married life is a kindergarten.

Nowadays you could find me any time in a hotel, uptown or downtown. Who needs an apartment to live like a maid with a dustrag in the hand, sneezing? I'm in very good with the busboys, it's more interesting than home, all kinds of people, everybody with a reason. . . .

And my reason, Lillie, is a long time ago I said to the forelady, "Missus, if I can't sit by the window, I can't sit." "If you can't sit, girlie," she says pointedly, "go stand on the street corner." And that's how I got unemployed in novelty wear.

For my next job I answered an ad which said: "Refined young lady, medium salary, cultural organization." I went by trolley to the address, the Russian Art Theater of Second Avenue, where they played only the best Yiddish plays. They needed a ticket seller, someone like me, who likes the public but is very sharp on crooks: The man who interviewed me was the manager, a certain type.

Immediately he said: "Rosie Lieber, you surely got a build on you!"

"It takes all kinds, Mr. Krimberg."

"Don't misunderstand me, little girl," he said. "I appreciate, I appreciate. A young lady lacking fore and aft, her blood is so busy warming the toes and the fingertips, it don't have time to circulate where it's most required."

Everybody likes kindness. I said to him: "Only don't be Mr. Krimberg, and we'll make a good bargain." We did: Nine dollars a week, a glass of tea every night, a free ticket once a week for Mama, and I could go watch rehearsals any time I wanted.

My first nine dollars was in the grocer's hands ready to move on already, when Krimberg said to me, "Rosie, here's a great gentleman, a member of this remarkable theater, wants to meet you, impressed no doubt by your big brown eyes."

And who was it, Lillie? Listen to me, before my very eyes was Volodya Vlashkin, called by the people of those days the Valentino of Second Avenue. I took one look, and I said to myself: Where did a Jewish boy grow up so big? "Just outside Kiev," he told me.

How? "My mama nursed me till I was six. I was the only boy in the village to have such health."

"My goodness, Vlashkin, six years old! She must have had shredded wheat there, not breasts, poor woman."

"My mother was beautiful," he said. "She had eyes like stars."

He had such a way of expressing himself, it brought tears.

To Krimberg, Vlashkin said after this introduction: "Who is responsible for hiding this wonderful young person in a cage?"

"That is where the ticket seller sells."

"So, David, go in there and sell tickets for a half hour. I have something in mind in regards to the future of this girl and this company. Go, David, be a good boy. And you, Miss Lieber, please, I suggest Feinberg's for a glass of tea. The rehearsals are long. I enjoy a quiet interlude with a friendly person."

So he took me there, Feinberg's, then around the corner, a place so full of Hungarians, it was deafening. In the back room was a table of honor for him. On the tablecloth embroidered by the lady of the house was Here Vlashkin Eats. We finished one glass of tea in quietness, out of thirst, when I finally made up my mind what to say.

"Mr. Vlashkin, I saw you a couple weeks ago, even before I started working here, in *The Seagull*. Believe me, if I was that girl, I wouldn't look even for a minute on the young bourgeois fellow. He could fall out of the play altogether. How Chekhov could put him in the same play as you, I can't understand."

"You liked me?" he asked, taking my hand and kindly patting it. "Well, well, young people still like me . . . so, and you like the theater too? Good. And you, Rose, you know you have such a nice hand, so warm to the touch, such a fine skin, tell me, why do you wear a scarf around your neck? You only hide your young, young throat. These are not olden times, my child, to live in shame."

"Who's ashamed?" I said, taking off the kerchief, but my hand right away went to the kerchief's place, because the truth is, it really was olden times, and I was still of a nature to melt with shame.

"Have some more tea, my dear."

"No, thank you, I am a samovar already."

"Dorfmann!" he hollered like a king. "Bring this child a seltzer with fresh ice!"

In weeks to follow I had the privilege to know him better and better as a person—also the opportunity to see him in his profession. The time was autumn; the theater full of coming and going. Rehearsing without end. After *The Seagull* flopped, *The Salesman from Istanbul* played, a great success.

Here the ladies went crazy. On the opening night, in the middle of the first scene, one missus—a widow or her husband worked too long hours—began to clap and sing out, "Oi, oi, Vlashkin." Soon there was such a tumult, the actors had to stop acting. Vlashkin stepped forward. Only not Vlashkin to the eyes . . . a younger man with pitch-black hair, lively on restless feet, his mouth clever. A half a century later at the end of the play he came out again, a gray philosopher, a student of life from only reading books, his hands as smooth as silk. . . . I cried to think who I was—nothing—and such a man could look at me with interest.

Then I got a small raise, due to he kindly put in a good word for me, and also for fifty cents a night I was the pleasure together with cousins, in-laws, and plain stage-struck kids to be part of a crowd scene and to see like he saw every single night the hundreds of pale faces waiting for his feelings to make them laugh or bend down their heads in sorrow.

The sad day came, I kissed my mama goodbye. Vlashkin helped me to get a reasonable room near the theater to be more free. Also my outstanding friend would have a place to recline away from the noise of the dressing rooms. She cried and she cried. "This is a way of living, Mama," I said. "Besides, I am driven by love."

"You! You, a nothing, a rotten hole in a piece of cheese, are you telling me what is life?" she screamed.

Very insulted, I went away from her. But I am good-natured—you know fat people are like that—kind, and I thought to myself, poor Mama . . . it is true she got more of an idea of life than me. She married who she didn't like, a sick man, his spirit already swallowed up by God. He never washed. He had an unhappy smell. His teeth fell out, his hair disappeared, he got smaller, shriveled up little by little, till goodbye and good luck he was gone and only came to Mama's mind when she went to the mailbox: under the stairs to get the electric bill. In memory of him and out of respect for mankind, I decided to live for love.

Don't laugh, you ignorant girl.

Do you think it was easy for me? I had to give Mama a little something. Ruthie was saving up with your papa for linens, a couple knives and forks. In the morning I had to do piecework if I wanted to keep by myself. So I made flowers. Before lunchtime every day a whole garden grew on my table.

This was my independence, Lillie dear, blooming, but it didn't have no roots and its face was paper. Meanwhile Krimberg went after me too. No doubt observing the success of Vlashkin, he thought, "Aha, open sesame. . . . " Others in the company similar. After me in those years were the following: Krimberg I mentioned. Carl Zimmer, played innocent young fellows with a wig. Charlie Peel, a Christian who fell in the soup by accident, a creator of beautiful sets. "Color is his middle name," says Vlashkin, always to the point.

I put this in to show you your fat old aunt was not crazy out of loneliness. In those noisy years I had friends among interesting people who admired me for reasons of youth and that I was a first-class listener.

The actresses—Raisele, Marya, Esther Leopold—were only interested in tomorrow. After them was the rich men, producers, the whole garment center; their past is a pincushion, future the eye of a needle.

Finally the day came, I no longer could keep my tact in my mouth. I said: "Vlashkin, I hear by carrier pigeon you have a wife, children, the whole combination."

"True, I don't tell stories. I make no pretense."

"That isn't the question. What is this lady like? It hurts me to ask, but tell me, Vlashkin . . . a man's life is something I don't clearly see."

"Little girl, I have told you a hundred times, this small room is the convent of my troubled spirit. Here I come to your innocent shelter to refresh myself in the midst of an agonized life."

"Ach, Vlashkin, serious, serious, who is this lady?"

"Rosie, she is a fine woman of the middle classes, a good mother to my children, three in number, girls all, a good cook, in her youth handsome, now no longer young. You see, could I be more frank? I entrust you, dear, with my soul."

It was some few months later at the New Year's ball of the Russian Artists Club, I met Mrs. Vlashkin, a woman with black hair in a low bun, straight and too proud. She sat at a small table speaking in a deep voice to whoever stopped a moment to converse. Her Yiddish was perfect, each word cut like a special jewel. I looked at her. She noticed me like she noticed everybody, cold like Christmas morning. Then she got tired. Vlashkin called a taxi and I never saw her again. Poor woman, she did not know I was on the same stage with her. The poison I was to her role, she did not know.

Later on that night in front of my door I said to Vlashkin, "No more. This isn't for me. I am sick from it all. I am no home breaker."

"Girlie," he said, "don't be foolish."

"No, no, goodbye, good luck," I said. "I am sincere."

So I went and stayed with Mama for a week's vacation and cleaned up all the closets and scrubbed the walls till the paint came off. She was very grateful, all the same her hard life made her say, "Now we see the end. If you live like a bum, you are finally a lunatic."

After this few days I came back to my life. When we met, me and Vlashkin, we said only hello and goodbye, and then for a few sad years, with the head we nodded as if to say, "Yes, yes, I know who you are."

Meanwhile in the field was a whole new strategy. Your mama and your grandmama brought around—boys. Your own father had a brother, you never even seen him. Ruben. A serious fellow, his idealism was his hat and his coat. "Rosie, I offer you a big new free happy unusual life." How? "With me, we will raise up the sands of Palestine to make a nation. That is the land of tomorrow for us Jews." "Ha-ha, Ruben, I'll go tomorrow then." "Rosie!" says Ruben. "We need strong women like you, mothers and farmers." "You don't fool me, Ruben, what you need is dray horses. But for that you need more money." "I don't like your attitude, Rose." "In that case, go and multiply. Goodbye."

Another fellow: Yonkel Gurstein, a regular sport, dressed to kill, with such an excitable nature. In those days—it looks to me like yesterday—the youngest girls wore undergarments like Battle Creek, Michigan. To him it was a matter of seconds. Where did he practice, a Jewish boy? Nowadays I suppose it is easier, Lillie? My goodness. I ain't asking you nothing—touchy, touchy. . . .

Well, by now you must know yourself, honey, whatever you do, life don't stop. It only sits a minute and dreams a dream.

While I was saying to all these silly youngsters "no, no, no," Vlashkin went to Europe and toured a few seasons . . . Moscow, Prague, London, even Berlin—already a pessimistic place. When he came back he wrote a book you can get from the library even today, *The Jewish Actor Abroad*. If someday you're interested enough in my lonesome years, you could read it. You could absorb the flavor of the man from the book. No, no, I am not mentioned. After all, who am I? When the book came out I stopped him in the street to say congratulations. But I am not a liar, so I pointed out, too, the egotism of many parts—even the critics said something along such lines.

"Talk is cheap," Vlashkin answered me. "But who are the critics? Tell me, do they create? Not to mention," he continues, "there is a line in

Shakespeare in one of the plays from the great history of England. It says, 'Self-loving is not so vile a sin, my liege, as self-neglecting.' This idea also appears in modern times in the moralistic followers of Freud. . . . Rosie, are you listening? You asked a question. By the way, you look very well. How come no wedding ring?"

I walked away from this conversation in tears. But this talking in the street opened the happy road up for more discussions. In regard to many things. . . . For instance, the management—very narrow-minded—wouldn't give him any more certain young men's parts. Fools. What youngest man knew enough about life to be as young as him?

"Rosie, Rosie," he said to me one day. "I see by the clock on your rosy, rosy face you must be thirty."

"The hands are slow, Vlashkin. On a week before Thursday I was thirty-four."

"Is that so? Rosie, I worry about you. It has been on my mind to talk to you. You are losing your time. Do you understand it? A woman should not lose her time."

"Oi, Vlashkin, if you are my friend, what is time?"

For this he had no answer, only looked at me surprised. We went instead, full of interest but not with our former speed, up to my new place on Ninety-Fourth Street. The same pictures on the wall, all of Vlashkin, only now everything painted red and black, which was stylish, and new upholstery.

A few years ago there was a book by another member of that fine company, an actress, the one that learned English very good and went uptown—Marya Kavkaz, in which she says certain things regarding Vlashkin. Such as, he was her lover for eleven years, she's not ashamed to write this down. Without respect for him, his wife, and children, or even others who also may have feelings in the matter.

Now, Lillie, don't be surprised. This is called a fact of life. An actor's soul must be like a diamond. The more faces it got the more shining is his name. Honey, you will no doubt love and marry one man and have a couple kids and be happy forever till you die tired. More than that, a person like us don't have to know. But a great artist like Volodya Vlashkin . . . in order to make a job on the stage, he's got to practice. I understand it now, to him life is like a rehearsal.

Myself, when I saw him in *The Father-in-Law*—an older man in love with a darling young girl, his son's wife, played by Raisele Maisel—I cried. What he said to this girl, how he whispered such sweetness, how all his hot feelings were on his face. . . . Lillie, all this experience he had with me. The very words were the same. You can imagine how proud I was.

So the story creeps to an end.

I noticed it first on my mother's face, the rotten handwriting of time, scribbled up and down her cheeks, across her forehead back and forth—a child could read—it said old, old, old. But it troubled my heart most to see these realities scratched on Vlashkin's wonderful expression.

First the company fell apart. The theater ended. Esther Leopold died from being very aged. Krimberg had a heart attack. Many went to Broadway. Also Raisele changed her name to Roslyn and was a comical hit in the movies. Vlashkin himself, no place to go, retired. It said in the paper, "An actor without peer, he will write his memoirs and spend his last years in the bosom of his family among his thriving grandchildren, the apple of his wife's doting eye."

This is journalism.

We made for him a great dinner of honor. At this dinner I said to him, for the last time, I thought, "Goodbye, dear friend, topic of my life, now we part." And to myself I said further: Finished. This is your lonesome bed. A lady what they call fat and fifty. You made it personally. From this lonesome bed you will finally fall to a bed not so lonesome, only crowded with a million bones.

And now comes? Lillie, guess.

Last week, washing my underwear in the basin, I get a buzz on the phone. "Excuse me, is this the Rose Lieber formerly connected with the Russian Art Theater?"

"It is."

"Well, well, how do you do, Rose? This is Vlashkin."

"Vlashkin! Volodya Vlashkin?"

"In fact. How are you, Rose?"

"Living, Vlashkin, thank you."

"You are all right? Really, Rose? Your health is good? You are working?"

"My health, considering the weight it must carry, is first class. I am back for some years now where I started, in novelty wear."

"Very interesting."

"Listen, Vlashkin, tell me the truth, what's on your mind?"

"My mind? Rosie, I am looking up an old friend, an old warmhearted companion of more joyful days. My circumstances, by the way, are changed. I am retired, as you know. Also I am a free man."

"What? What do you mean?"

"Mrs. Vlashkin is divorcing me."

"What came over her? Did you start drinking or something from melancholy?"

"She is divorcing me for adultery."

"But, Vlashkin, you should excuse me, don't be insulted, but you got maybe seventeen, eighteen years on me, and even me, all this nonsense—this daydreams and nightmares—is mostly for the pleasure of conversation alone."

"I pointed all this out to her. My dear, I said, my time is past, my blood is as dry as my bones. The truth is, Rose, she isn't accustomed to have a man around all day, reading out loud from the papers the interesting events of our time, waiting for breakfast, waiting for lunch. So all day she gets madder and madder. By nighttime a furious old lady gives me my supper. She has information from the last fifty years to pepper my soup. Surely there was a Judas in that theater, saying every day, 'Vlashkin, Vlashkin, Vlashkin . . .' and while my heart was circulating with his smiles he was on the wire passing the dope to my wife."

"Such a foolish end, Volodya, to such a lively story. What are your plans?"

"First, could I ask you for dinner and the theater—uptown, of course? After this . . . we are old friends. I have money to burn. What your heart desires. Others are like grass, the north wind of time has cut out their heart. Of you, Rosie, I recreate only kindness. What a woman should be to a man, you were to me. Do you think, Rosie, a couple of old pals like us could have a few good times among the material things of this world?"

My answer, Lillie, in a minute was altogether. "Yes, yes, come up," I said. "Ask the room by the switchboard, let us talk."

So he came that night and every night in the week, we talked of his long life. Even at the end of time, a fascinating man. And like men are, too, till time's end, trying to get away in one piece.

"Listen, Rosie," he explains the other day. "I was married to my wife, do you realize, nearly half a century. What good was it? Look at the bitterness. The more I think of it, the more I think we would be fools to marry."

"Volodya Vlashkin," I told him straight, "when I was young I warmed your cold back many a night, no questions asked. You admit it, I didn't make no demands. I was softhearted. I didn't want to be called Rosie Lieber, a breaker up of homes. But now, Vlashkin, you are a free man. How could you ask me to go with you on trains to stay in strange hotels, among Americans, not your wife? Be ashamed."

So now, darling Lillie, tell this story to your mama from your young mouth. She don't listen to a word from me. She only screams, "I'll faint, I'll faint." Tell her after all I'll have a husband, which, as everybody knows, a woman should have at least one before the end of that story.

My goodness, I am already late. Give me a kiss. After all, I watched you grow from a plain seed. So give me a couple wishes on my wedding day. A long and happy life. Many years of love. Hug Mama, tell her from Aunt Rose, goodbye and good luck.

Sholem Aleichem's Revolution

CYNTHIA OZICK

A daughter of immigrants, Cynthia Ozick (b. 1928) was born in New York City. Her essays and stories tackle a wide range of literary topics. Her story "Envy: or, Yiddish in America" (1968) reflects on the impact of Isaac Bashevis Singer's contribution to Yiddish literature. Ozick is the author of numerous books, including The Pagan Rabbi and Other Stories *(1971),* Art & Ardor *(1983),* The Shawl *(1989),* Metaphor & Memory *(1989),* The Puttermesser Papers *(1997), and* Foreign Bodies *(2010). The following essay appeared in* The New Yorker *on March 20, 1988.*

YIDDISH IS A DIRECT, spirited, and spiritually alert language that is almost a thousand years old—centuries older than Chaucerian English, but, like the robust speech of Chaucer's pilgrims, expressively rooted in the quotidian lives of ordinary folk. It is hard to be pretentious or elevated in Yiddish, and easy to poke fun. Yiddish is especially handy for satire, cynicism, familiarity, abuse, sentimentality, and resignation, for a sense of high irony, and for putting people in their place and events in bitter perspective: all the defensive verbal baggage an involuntarily migratory nation is likely to need en route to the next temporary refuge. In its tenderer mien, Yiddish is capable of a touching conversational intimacy with a consoling and accessible God. If Yiddish lacks cathedral grandeur, there is the compensation of coziness, of smallness, of a lovingly close, empathic, and embracing Creator, who can be appealed to in the diminutive. Yiddish is a household tongue, and God, like other members of the family, is sweetly informal in it.

Starting in the early medieval period, the Jews of Europe were rarely allowed a chance to feel at home. Consequently, Yiddish developed on the move, evolving out of a fusion of various tenth-century urban German dialects (not exclusively Middle High German, a linguistic misapprehension that has been superseded by recent scholarship), and strengthened in its idiosyncrasies by contributions from French, Italian, Slavic, Hebrew, and Aramaic (the language of the Talmud and of Jesus). Until the end of the eighteenth century, Yiddish was overwhelmingly the vernacular of European Jewish communities from Amsterdam to Smolensk, from the Baltic to the Balkans, and as far south as Italy. Driven relentlessly eastward by the international brutality of the Crusaders and by the localized brutality of periodic pogroms, the language suffered successive uprootings and took on new morphological influences. In 1492, when Columbus sailed the ocean blue and Ferdinand and Isabella issued their anti-Jewish edict of expulsion, the language of the Spanish Jews—called Judezmo or Ladino—began to undergo upheavals of its own, fleeing the depredations of the Inquisition to Holland, Italy, Turkey, and North Africa, and even the New World.

And all the while Yiddish remained a language without a name, or almost. "Yiddish" means "Jewish," or what Jews speak, but this term became current only toward the close of the nineteenth century. Previously, the everyday speech of Ashkenazi Jews (that is, Jews without Spanish- or Arabic-language connections) was designated "Judeo-German," which essentially misrepresented it, since it was steadfastly a language in its own right, with its own regionalisms and dialects. To think of Yiddish (as many speakers of German tend to) as merely a fossilized or corrupted old German dialect would oblige us, similarly, to think of French as a deformed and slurred vestige of an outlying Latin patois deposited on the Rhône by a defunct Roman colony. But "Judeo-German" at least implied a modicum of dignity; at any rate, it was a scholar's word. The name that the Jews themselves—intellectuals in particular—habitually clapped on Yiddish was not a name at all. It was, until the miraculous year 1888, a term of opprobrium—*zhargon*. Gibberish; prattle; a sub-tongue; something less than a respectably cultivated language. Yiddish was "jargon" to the intellectuals despite its then eleven million speakers (before the Nazi decimations), despite the profusion of its press, its theatre, its secular educational systems, and its religious and political movements, and despite its long (though questionable) history of literary productivity.

In 1888—effectively overnight—this contemptuous view of Yiddish was reversed, and by a single powerful pen writing in Yiddish. The pen had a pen name: Sholem Aleichem, a Hebrew salutation that literally means "Peace to you" (the familiar Arabic cognate is *"salaam alaykum"*), and conveys a vigorously affectionate delight in encountering a friend, or someone who can immediately become a friend, if not a confidant. Almost no phrase is more common in Yiddish—as common as a handshake. The pseudonym itself declared a revolutionary intention: Yiddish as a literary vehicle was at last to be welcomed, respected, celebrated. The name, like the writer, looked to a program, and Sholem Aleichem was already a prolific author of short stories and feuilletons when, in 1888, at the age of twenty-nine, he founded a seminal Yiddish literary annual, *Di yidishe folksbibliotek* (*The Popular Jewish Library*). The money ran out in a couple of years, and the new periodical vanished. But the revisionist ardor of its first issue alone—an electrifying burst of promulgation and demonstration—permanently changed the fortunes of Yiddish. The despised *zhargon* was all at once removed from scorn and placed in a pantheon of high literary art, complete with a tradition, precursors, genres, a sense of historical development, and uncompromising critical goals—a conscious patrimony that, only the day before, no one had dreamed was there.

It had not been there. The aesthetics of literary self-awareness, a preoccupation with generational classifications, issues of precedent and continuity—all these were fictions, deliberate inventions of Sholem Aleichem himself. It was Sholem Aleichem who, invoking Gogol and Turgenev as models, established the genres and identified a radical precursor—the novelist and critic Sholem Yankev Abramovitsh, who used the nom de plume Mendele Moykher Sforim (Mendele the Book Peddler). In the very hour when Sholem Aleichem was naming him the "grandfather" of Yiddish literature, Mendele was no more than fifty-two years old—in mid-career. Dan Miron, of Columbia, a leading scholar of Yiddish letters (who reveals all these marvels in his enchanting study "A Traveler Disguised"), writes, "What was unimaginable in 1885 was taken for granted in 1895. In 1880 Yiddish writers did not suspect that they had a history; by the early 1890s they already had produced one 'classic' writer; before the century ended *The History of Yiddish Literature in the Nineteenth Century* was written in English for American readers by a Harvard instructor." It was, in short, a process of historical mythmaking so rapid and extreme that the historians themselves swallowed it whole in no time at all. And Sholem Aleichem was the premier mythmaker and founder of that process.

But why was Yiddish so disreputable that it needed a Sholem Aleichem to fabricate a grand intellectual pedigree for it? Like any other language, it did have a genuine history, after all: a living Jewish civilization had eaten, slept, wept, laughed, borne babies, and earned its bread or failed to, and had, in fact, written and read stories in Yiddish for nearly five centuries. Contempt for Yiddish, moreover, was simultaneously internal and external—Gentiles of every class as well as Jewish intellectuals habitually derided it. The Gentile world despised Yiddish as a marginal tongue because it was spoken by a people deemed marginal by Christendom; that was simple enough. And, while it is true that the prejudices of the majority can sometimes manage to leave an unsavory mark on a minority's view of itself, Gentile scorn for Yiddish had almost nothing to do with the contumely that Jewish social and intellectual standards reserved for it. From the Jewish standpoint, the trouble with Yiddish was that it wasn't Hebrew. Yiddish was the language of exile—temporary, make-do. It belonged to an unfortunate phase of history—an ephemeral, if oppressive, nightmare lightened only by the unquenchable hope of national restoration. Yiddish was uncultivated, an empty vessel, useless for significant expression and high experience. It was the instrument of women and the ignorant, categories that frequently overlapped.

Hebrew, by contrast, was regarded as synonymous with Jewish reality. Besides being the language of Scripture, of the liturgy, of daily prayer, it was the sole medium of serious life, which could mean one thing only: serious learning. In a society where fundamental literacy was expected of everyone without exception, including women, and where the scholar was situated at the apex of communal distinction, "ignorant" signified insufficient mastery of Hebrew. Everyone, including women—who could recite from the Hebrew prayer book—had some degree of access to Hebrew. A young boy's basic education began with the Pentateuch; if he never acquired much of anything else, he still had that, along with the daily prayer book, the Passover Haggadah, and a smattering of commentary. And, of course, Yiddish itself, written in the Hebrew alphabet, is peppered with liturgical and biblical allusions and with homelier matter in Hebrew as well—which is why, though a knowledge of Yiddish may assure an understanding of a sentence in German, the reverse is not so likely. From the time of the destruction of the Second Temple, in the year 70, Hebrew remained a living language, in everyday reading and writing use.

It may have suffered severe popular contraction—practically no one *spoke* it—but it never became moribund. My father, for example, wrote a rather formal, Victorian-style English, but when he wanted to address a letter to a person of learning—a rabbi he respected, perhaps, or the headmaster of a yeshiva—he never considered writing in English or Yiddish; in the world he was reared in (he was born in White Russia in 1892), Hebrew was the only appropriate vehicle for a civilized pen. It took—and gave—the measure of a mind. You might tie your shoelaces in Yiddish, but Hebrew was the avenue of thought and, certainly, of civility.

When Enlightenment ideas finally spread to the isolated Yiddish-speaking communities of Eastern Europe, arriving a century late, they turned out to have a somewhat different character. Like the Gentile Enlightenment, Haskalah—the name for the Enlightenment movement among Jews—fostered secularization and an optimistic program for the improvement of the common people. At first view, it might seem that Hebrew would have been left behind in the turmoil of the new liberalization, that the language of the Bible would, at the least, attenuate in an atmosphere where the claims of piety were thinning out—just as Latin, after the decline of the authority of Christian scholasticism, was gradually compelled to give way to a diversity of vernaculars. In Jewish society, exactly the opposite happened: the progress of Haskalah only intensified the superior status of Hebrew and accelerated its secular use. As the temporal more and more replaced the theological (though these phrases don't quite fit the way in which Jewish spiritual traditions and this-worldliness are intertwined), Hebrew pressed more urgently than ever toward the forefront of intellectual life. Hebrew belles-lettres began to be taken seriously by temperaments that had formerly regarded stories and novels as a species of levity, fit only for women and the ignorant—and therefore written exclusively in Yiddish. The first Hebrew novel—*The Love of Zion*, by Abraham Mapu—appeared in 1853 and was followed by wave after explosive wave of literary forms: fiction, essays, poetry. Hebrew composition, which over the last millennium or so had been employed chiefly in scholarly responsa on ethical and juridical issues, was suddenly converted into high imaginative art. Not that original Hebrew literature had never before burst out in the European Jewish experience: the majestic poets of medieval Spain had astounded their little historical span with lyrical masterpieces to vie with the Song of Songs, and the experimental poets of Renaissance Italy had echoed Petrarch and Dante in Hebrew stanzas.

But the influence of Hebrew on nineteenth-century Eastern European Jews was so dominant that it was presumed the literary stigma attached to Yiddish would never be effaced. And at the same time a noisy rush of activism, expressed in competing currents of cultural and political idealism, was beginning to awaken a harassed community to the potential of change and renewal. The most ancient of these currents, faithfully reiterated three times a day in the prayer book, refreshed in every season by religious festivals geared to biblical agricultural cycles, was the spirit of national return to Jerusalem. Under the influence of Haskalah, the renascence of literary Hebrew nourished and was nourished by this irreducible grain of religio-national aspiration immemorially incorporated in the traditional Jewish sensibility. The more secularized Hebrew became, and the more dedicated to belles-lettres, the more it found itself, by virtue of *being* Hebrew, harking back to the old emotional sources—sometimes even while manifestly repudiating them. The Hebrew belletrists might appear to be focusing on modernist issues of craft and style—particularly at the expense of Yiddish, which the Hebraists declared lacked any possibility of style—but the prestige of Hebrew was also the prestige of national consciousness.

This was the cultural situation into which Sholem Aleichem thrust his manifesto for the equal status of Yiddish.

He was born Sholem Rabinovitsh in a town in the Ukraine in 1859—only three years after the abolition of a czarist conscription scheme for the assimilation of Jewish children, whereby boys were seized at age twelve and subjected to thirty-one years of military confinement. He died in New York in 1916—three months after the death of Henry James—having been driven here two years before by the upheavals of war and revolution; but he had fled Russia nearly a decade before that, after living through the ferocious government-sponsored pogroms of 1905. No version or variety of political or social malevolence failed to touch the Jews of Russia, and Sholem Aleichem—whose fame was that of a sprightly comic artist—omitted few of these brutalities from his tales. The comparison with Mark Twain that emerged in Sholem Aleichem's own lifetime was apt: both men kept people laughing even as they probed the darkness—though Sholem Aleichem, for whom cruelty had an explicit habitation and a name, never fell prey to a generalized misanthropy of the "Pudd'nhead Wilson" sort.

As a boy, Sholem Aleichem had Pickwickian propensities, and entertained his family with mimicry and comic skits. His writer's gift, reflecting the normal bilingualism of Jewish life, rapidly turned up in both Yiddish and Hebrew. Soon, though, he acquired a third literary language. After a conventional cheder training (Bible and Talmud in a one-room school), he managed to gain admission to a Russian secondary school; the university education that would ordinarily follow was mainly closed to Jews. But his exposure to Russian studies enabled him to get a job as a Russian tutor in a Russified Jewish family of means—he eventually married his young pupil, Olga Loyev—and emphatically opened Russian to him as a literary instrument. Though his earliest serious literary venture of any kind was a novel in imitation of Mapu, called *The Daughter of Zion* and written in Hebrew, his first published articles appeared in Russian, Hebrew, and Yiddish.

When he ultimately settled on Yiddish, he disappointed no one more than his father, a struggling innkeeper who was an enthusiastic disciple of Haskalah and had hoped his son would develop into an exclusively Hebrew writer. And, much later, after Sholem Aleichem had become virtually an institution, and was celebrated as the soul of Jewish self-understanding wherever Yiddish was spoken, the language that prevailed as the mother tongue of his household was not Yiddish but Russian; he raised his children in it. If this suggests itself as a paradox, it also reminds us of Isaac Babel, born thirty-five years after Sholem Aleichem, and arrested and silenced by the Soviets in 1939. Babel, too, wrote a handful of stories that might be described as revealing the soul of Jewish self-understanding. (One of them, "Shabbos Nachamu," with its Hebrew-Yiddish title, could readily pass for a romping fable of Sholem Aleichem's, except for the Chekhovian cadence of its last syllables.) Whether because he chose to write in Russian, or for some other reason, Babel is not usually counted as a Jewish writer. This leads one to imagine what the consequences might have been if Sholem Aleichem, like Babel, had committed himself wholly to Russian: it is highly probable that Russian literature would have been augmented by still another dazzling writer. What is certain is that there would have been no Sholem Aleichem. To produce a Sholem Aleichem, Yiddish was a sine qua non.

That may appear to be an unremarkable statement. One might just as well say that to produce a Guy de Maupassant, French is a sine qua non, or that to produce a Selma Lagerlöf, Swedish is indispensable. For these writers, though, there was no difference between the legacy of the literary mainstream and the daily language, which seemed no more a matter of choice than breathing; for them, literature was conducted in the vernacular. But Sholem Aleichem was faced with a cultural redundancy—internal bilingualism—known almost nowhere else in Europe (Ireland, with important differences, comes to mind). Yiddish was the common language of breathing, the people's language, and Hebrew was the language of the elitist literary center. In these circumstances, to choose Yiddish—to insist that it be taken seriously—was a mettlesome and revolutionary act.

In a way, a version of this revolution—a revolution in favor of Yiddish—had occurred a century before, with the advent of the Hasidic movement: romantic, populist, anti-establishment, increasingly cultlike in its attachment to charismatic teachers. The Hasidic leaders, resenting the stringently rationalist intellectualism that dominated Jewish communal life, enlisted the Yiddish-speaking masses against the authority of the learned (where "learned" always meant "learned in Hebrew"), and offered instead the lively consolations of an emotional pietism. The movement caught on despite—or maybe because of—the fact that scholarliness was unstintingly prized, far above earning power: a scholar-husband was a great catch, and the bride's father would gladly support him if he could; so, often, would the bride. (My Russian grandmother, for instance, the mother of eight, ran a dry goods shop while my grandfather typically spent all his waking hours in study.) The corollary of this, not unexpectedly, was that simple people deficient in learning were looked down on. At its inception, Hasidism was a popular rebellion against this sort of intellectual elitism; it threw off rigor and lavished dance, song, legend, story, merriment, and mysticism (the last too frequently fading into superstitious practice) on ordinary mortals, whose psalms and prayers were in Hebrew but whose grammar was at best lame.

While there lurked in Hasidism a kind of precedent for an unashamed turn to the Yiddish tale—including at least one fabulist of Kafka-like artistry—Sholem Aleichem's revolution had another source. Like the belletristic passions of the Hebraists, it belonged to the Enlightenment. For the Hasidim, stories told in Yiddish were appurtenances of a fervent piety; for Sholem Aleichem, they were vessels of a conscious literary art. What he had in common with the Hasidic impulse was a tenderness toward plain folk and the ambition to address the human heart unassumingly and directly, in its everyday tongue. And he had, through the refinements of Haskalah, all the complexities of high literary seriousness and what we nowadays call the strategies of the text. This combination of irreconcilables—the popular broad leniency of Hasidism and the elevated channeled pointedness of Haskalah—may be what fashioned him into the master of irony we know as Sholem Aleichem.

Of course, we do not really know him—not in English, anyhow. And, with the passing of the decades since the Nazi extirpation of Yiddish-speaking European civilization, fewer and fewer native readers of literary Yiddish are left. For Americans, Sholem Aleichem has always been no more than a rumor, or two or three rumors, all of them misleading. First, there is the rumor of permanent inaccessibility because of the "special flavor" of Yiddish itself—its unfamiliar cultural premises and idiomatic uniqueness. But every language is in precisely that sense untranslatable; Robert Frost's mot—poetry is what gets lost in translation—is famous,

323

and the Hebrew poet Bialik compared translation to kissing through a handkerchief. Yiddish is as amenable to translation as any other language—though that may mean, despite certain glorious exceptions, not very. As for the historical and cultural idiosyncrasies inherent in Yiddish, they are not especially difficult or esoteric; for the most part, they require about as much background as, say, managing to figure out what a name day is in Chekhov. Saturated in allusiveness as he is, Sholem Aleichem is a thousand times closer to Dickens and Mark Twain and Will Rogers than he can possibly be to more encumbered figures; he was a popular presence, and stupendously so. His lectures and readings were mobbed; he was a household friend; he was cherished as a family valuable. His fiftieth birthday was a public event, and at his death hundreds of thousands filled the streets as his cortège wound through the Bronx and Harlem, down to the lower East Side and into Brooklyn for the burial.

And still he was not what another rumor makes him out to be: simpleminded, sentimental, peasantlike, old-countryish, naive, premodern—the occasion of nostalgia for a sweeter time, pogroms notwithstanding. It would be easy to blame *Fiddler on the Roof* for these distortions, but the Broadway musical—to which all those adjectives do apply, plus slickness—didn't arrive until 1964, and Sholem Aleichem had been misrepresented in this way long, long before. In fact, these well-established misconceptions may have been the inspiration for the emptied-out, prettified, romantic vulgarization (the Yiddish word for it is *shund*) typified by the musical's book and lyrics: exactly the sort of *shund* that Sholem Aleichem, in seeking new literary standards for Yiddish, had battled against from the start. Whatever the success of *Fiddler on the Roof*, its chief nontheatrical accomplishment has been to reduce the reputation of a literary master to the very thing he repudiated.

That the sophisticated chronicler of a society in transition should be misconstrued as a genial rustic is something worse than a literary embarrassment. Dickens is not interchangeable with Sam Weller, or Mark Twain with Aunt Polly, or Sholem Aleichem with Tevye (and even the Tevye we think we know isn't the Tevye on the page). This quandary of misperceived reputation may possibly stem from the garbled attitudes of some of the Yiddish-speaking immigrants' descendants, who inherited a culture—failed to inherit it, rather—only in its most debilitated hour, when it was about to give up the ghost. The process of attenuation through competing influences had already begun in the Jewish villages of Eastern Europe (and was to become Sholem Aleichem's great subject). In the rush to Americanization, the immigrants, zealously setting out to shake off the village ways they had brought with them, ended by encouraging amnesia of the central motifs and texts of their civilization. A certain text orientation remained, to be sure, and their American-born successors would learn to bring it to bear on Whitman and James and Emerson and Faulkner, not to mention Bloomsbury; but the more intrinsic themes of Jewish conceptual life came to be understood only feebly, vestigially, at a time when they were either substantially diluted by the new culture or were disappearing altogether. Among the immigrants' children and grandchildren, the mis-shapen shard was mainly taken for the original cup. And generations that in the old country had been vividly and characteristically distinct from the surrounding peasant society were themselves dismissed as peasants by their "modern" offspring—university-educated, perhaps, but tone-deaf to their own history.

Now, toward the end of the twentieth century—with a startling abundance that seems close to mysterious—we are witnessing a conscientious push toward a kind of restitution. There is that which wants us finally to see—to see fairly, accurately, richly—into the substance of Yiddish prose and poetry, even if necessarily through the diminishments of translation. The buzz of anthologists hopeful of gaining attention for Yiddish has always been with us, but a worshipful air of do-goodism, whether hearty or wistful or polemical, has frequently trailed these votary efforts. A serious critical focus was inaugurated more than thirty years ago by Irving Howe and his collaborator, the late Yiddish poet Eliezer Greenberg, with their thick pair of *Treasuries*—collections of Yiddish stories and poems enhanced by first-rate introductions. These were succeeded, in 1972, by the Howe-Greenberg *Voices from the Yiddish*, a compilation of

325

literary and historical essays, memoirs, and diaries, and, in 1974, by selections from the tales of I. L. Peretz, one of the three classic writers of the Yiddish narrative (Mendele and Sholem Aleichem are the others). The last two or three years, however, have brought about an eruption—if this word is too strong, "efflorescence" is not nearly strong enough—of dedicated translation: *My Mother's Sabbath Days*, a memoir by Chaim Grade, translated by Channa Kleinerman Goldstein and Inna Hecker Grade; the extant parts of *The Family Mashber*, an extraordinary work long quiescent in the Soviet Union, by Der Nister (The Hidden One, the pen name of Pinkhas Kahanovitsh, who died in a Soviet prison in 1950), translated by Leonard Wolf; *American Yiddish Poetry*, the first of a series of scholarly anthologies projected by Benjamin and Barbara Harshav and designed to support the thesis that poetry written in Yiddish on American soil and expressive of American experience counts significantly as American poetry; the splendid new *Penguin Book of Modern Yiddish Verse*, a landmark volume, brilliantly edited and introduced by Irving Howe, Ruth R. Wisse, of McGill University, and Khone Shmeruk, of the Hebrew University in Jerusalem; *In the Storm* and *The Nightingale*, novels by Sholem Aleichem, lucidly translated by Aliza Shevrin; Richard J. Fein's devoted rendering of the poetry of Jacob Glatstein; and others, doubtless, which have escaped me. One result of all this publishing activity is that Isaac Bashevis Singer, the sole Yiddish-language Nobel winner and the only Yiddish writer familiar in any significant degree to American readers, can finally be seen as one figure among a multitude in a diverse, complex, and turbulent community of letters. Too often, Singer, lacking an appropriate cultural horizon and seemingly without an ancestry, has had the look in English of a hermit of language fallen out of a silent congregation and standing strangely apart. The current stir of industry among translators begins at last to hint at the range and amplitude of modern Yiddish literature.

All these freshly revealed novelists and poets are, in one respect or another, the heirs of Sholem Aleichem, and if there is a single work among those now emerging in English which is the herald and signature of the rest, it is, unsurprisingly, Sholem Aleichem's *Tevye the Dairyman and the Railroad Stories* (Schocken, 1987), issued under the auspices of the newly organized Library of Yiddish Classics, of which Professor Wisse is the series editor. The eight Tevye stories are without doubt the nucleus of any understanding of how Yiddish leaped into world literature a hundred years ago (even though world literature may not have taken note of it, then or since). Professor Miron speaks of "the homiletic-sentimental streak" in Yiddish fiction before Mendele and Sholem Aleichem: "definitely anti-artistic, inimical to irony, to conscious structural artistry, to the idea of literary technique, to stylistic perfection, and favorable to moralistic ser-monizing, to unbridled emotionalism, and to stylistic sloppiness." Tevye stands for everything antithetical to such a catalog. What one notices first is not the comedy—because the comedy is what Sholem Aleichem is famous for, the comedy is what is expected—but the shock of darkness. Poverty and persecution: while not even Sholem Aleichem can make these funny, he can satirize their reasons for being, or else he can set against them the standard and example of Tevye (as Mark Twain does with Huck Finn). Tevye is not any sort of scholar—that goes without saying. He is a *milkhiker*, meaning that he owns a cow; "dairyman" is too exalted a word for the owner of a cow, a horse, and a wagon. But he is not a fool, he is certainly not a peasant, and he is by no means the malaprop he is reputed to be. Tevye is intelligent; more, he is loving, witty, virtuous, generous, open, unwilling to sacrifice human feeling to grandiose aims—and all without a grain of heroism or sentimentality. His voice is monologic, partly out of deepest intimacy—a sense of tête-à-tête with God or the reader—and partly out of verbal ingenuity, theatricality, even the sweep of aria. Tevye is never optimistic—he is too much at home with the worst that can happen. And he is never wiped out by despair—he is too much at home with Scripture and with the knowledge of frailty, mutability, mortality. When his wife, Golde, dies, he quotes from the morning prayer "What are we and what is our life?" and from Ecclesiastes, "Let us hear the conclusion of the whole matter: fear God and keep His commandments, for that is the whole of man."

Tevye's play with sources, biblical and liturgical, is the enchantment—and brevity—of his wit. (A glossary ensures that nearly all of it is gratifyingly at our fingertips.) Though his citations are mostly designed for comical juxtaposition—"And it came to pass," he will chant, with biblical sonorousness, about an ordinary wagon ride from Yehupetz to Boiberik—occasionally a passage is straightforwardly approached, and then the glancingness of Tevye's brushstroke only abets the resonance of the verse. That sentence from Ecclesiastes, for instance: Tevye doesn't recite it in its entirety. What he actually says is *"ki zeh koyl ha'odem"* ("for that is the whole of man"), and the six scant Hebrew syllables instantly call up, for Tevye and his readers, the full quotation, the tremor of memory aroused by its ancestral uses, the tone and heft of the surrounding passages. Again, it is worth keeping in mind that Tevye is not to be regarded as an educated man: he is a peddler of milk and cheese. And still he has a mastery of a plenitude of texts that enables him to send them aloft like experimental kites, twisting their lines as they sail. By contrast, it would be unimaginable for a rustic in a novel by Thomas Hardy (Sholem Aleichem's contemporary, who outlived him by more than a decade) to have memorized a representative handful of Shakespeare's plays from earliest childhood, and to have the habit of liberally quoting from one or another of these dozens and dozens of times, not only accurately and aptly but stingingly, pointedly, absurdly, and always to an immediate purpose; we would reject such a character as madly idiosyncratic, if not wholly implausible. And yet Tevye is a vivacious, persuasive creature, warm with the blood of reality. In his world, it is not only plausible, it is not unusual, for a milkman or a carpenter to know the Pentateuch and the Psalms inside out, and considerable other scriptural and rabbinic territory as well, and to have mastered the daily and holiday prayer books—no slender volumes, these—backward and forward. Tevye's cosmos is verbal. Biblical phrases are as palpable to him as his old horse. When he wants to remark that he has no secrets, he tosses in a fragment from Genesis: "And the Lord said, Shall I hide from Abraham that thing which I do?" When his only cow dies, he invokes a Psalm: "The sorrows of death compassed me, and the pains of hell got hold upon me: I found trouble and sorrow." When his daughter Shprintze is being courted by an unsuitable young man, he draws from the Song of Songs: "a lily among thorns." Chaffing a utopian socialist, he turns to a rabbinic tractate, "The Ethics of the Fathers," for its illumination of a type of artlessness: "What's mine is yours and what's yours is mine." It is all done with feather-light economy; he drops in only two or three words of the verse in question—an elegant minimal-ism—confident that his audience will recognize the source and fill in the rest. Or perhaps sometimes not so confident. In a superbly clarifying historical introduction, Hillel Halkin, the translator, remarks that Tevye's quotations, "depending on the situation and the person he is talking to, can serve any conceivable purpose: to impress, to inform, to amuse, to intimidate, to comfort, to scold, to ridicule, to show off, to avoid, to put down, to stake a claim of equality or create a mood of intimacy." And he is not above "deliberately inventing, confusing, or misattributing a quote," Halkin continues, "in order to mock an ignoramus who will never know the difference, thus scoring a little private triumph of which he himself is the sole witness."

These virtuoso dartings of language—the prestidigitator's flash from biblical eloquence to its mundane applicability—have a cavorting bril-liance reminiscent of the tricks and coruscations of *Finnegans Wake*, where sentences are also put under the pressure of multiple reverberations. Or think of Harold Bloom's thesis of "misprision," whereby an influential resource is usurped for purposeful "misinterpretation," engendering new life in a new text. While these macaronic comparisons—Tevye in the company of James Joyce and Harold Bloom—may have the same farcical impact as Tevye's own juxtapositions, they serve the point, which is that Sholem Aleichem's Tevye is about as far from the mind, tone, tempera-ment, and language of either folk art or *Fiddler*-type showbiz as Boiberik is from Patagonia. Tevye is the stylistic invention of a self-conscious verbal artist, and if he stands for, and speaks for, the folk, that is the consequence of the artist's power. Tevye's manner emerges from the wit and genius of Sholem Aleichem.

Tevye's matter, however—his good and bad luck, his daily travail and occasional victory, the events in his family and in his village and in the next village—belongs unalloyedly to the folk. What happens to Tevye is what is happening to all Jews in the Russian Pale of Settlement; his tales are as political as they are individual, and it is entirely pertinent that Halkin provides a list of government-instigated depredations against Russian Jews from 1881 to 1904, including numbers of pogroms, blood-libel charges, restrictions, expulsions, closed towns and cities, special taxes, identity passes, quotas, and other oppressive and humiliating measures. Tevye's life is assaulted by them all (as are the lives of the characters in *The Railroad Stories*).

Tevye starts off, in the first of the eight tales, gently enough, with a generous ladling of burlesque. Ten years ago, he recounts in "Tevye Strikes It Rich," "I was such a miserable beggar that rags were too good for me." Unexpectedly, he and his nag stumble into an act of slapstick kindness, he is rewarded with a cow, and his career as a *milkhiker* is launched. In the second story, "Tevye Blows a Small Fortune," he is taken in by a con man, a Jew even poorer than he is; when he catches up with the swindler, who by then has lost everything and looks like it, Tevye ends by forgiving him and blaming himself. "The Lord giveth and the Lord taketh away," he quotes from Job. But with the third story, "Today's Children," and the remaining five, social and cultural disintegrations begin to rule the narrative. Against the stiff precedents of arranged marriage, Tevye's daughter Tsaytl and a poor young tailor decide to marry for love. Tevye accedes, but he is discontent on three strong counts: custom has been violated and the world turned upside down; Tsaytl has rejected an older widower of some means, a butcher, in whose household there will always be enough to eat; and, foremost, Tevye himself is a textual snob with aristocratic aspirations, who would like to claim a learned son-in-law. Neither the butcher nor the tailor is capable of the nuanced study of "*di kleyne pintelekh*" ("the fine points"). Still, Tevye defends his daughter's autonomy for the sake of her happiness, despite his certainty that she will go hungry. "What do you have against her that you want to marry her?" he teases the young tailor.

In "Hodl," a story that extends the theme of social decomposition, Tevye's daughter of that name also makes her own marital choice—a student revolutionary, a socialist intellectual, who is arrested and sent to Siberia. Hodl insists on following him into exile, and when Tevye has driven her in his wagon to the railroad station he closes the tale in sardonic melancholy: "Let's talk about something more cheerful. Have you heard any news of the cholera in Odessa?"

But the truly unthinkable is yet to come: in "Chava," Tevye's most rebellious daughter elopes with Chvedka, an educated Gentile village boy (a social rarity in himself). Tevye is torn by anguish and terror. Not only has Chava cut the thread of religious and historic continuity, but she has also joined up with the persecutors. The village priest takes charge of her, because, he says, "we Christians have your good in mind," and Tevye responds, "It would have been kinder to poison me or put a bullet in my head. If you're really such a good friend of mine, do me one favor: leave my daughter alone!" In Tevye's universe, the loss of a daughter to Christianity—which for him has never revealed anything but a murderous face—is the ultimate tragedy; he sobs for her as for a kidnapped child. (*Fiddler on the Roof* conspicuously Americanizes these perceptions. When a pogrom is threatened, Chava reappears, with her suitably liberal and pluralist-minded husband, who announces, in solidarity, "We cannot stay among people who can do such things to others," and even throws in a post-Holocaust declaration against Gentile "silence." But Sholem Aleichem's Chava returns "to her father and her God," chastened, remorseful, and without Chvedka.) In "Shprintze," the daughter of the sixth tale—her name, by the way, is more decorous than it sounds, deriving from the Italian *speranza*—is jilted by a well-off young rattlebrain who is fond of horses, and drowns herself. Beilke, the daughter of "Tevye Leaves for the Land of Israel," marries a coarse parvenu who, ashamed of a "cheesemonger" father-in-law, wants to pay Tevye off to get him out of the way, even offering him the fulfillment of a dream—a ticket to Palestine. Shprintze and Beilke are the center of "class" stories: as traditional influences lose their hold, position based on material possessions begins to outweigh the authority of intellectual accomplishment, marking a growing leniency toward Gentile ways (typified by Shprintze's feckless suitor's preoccupation with "horses, fishing, and bicycles"). The aristocracy of learning—the essential principle and pillar of shtetl life—is breaking down; the mores of the outer society are creeping, even streaming, in.

In the final narrative, "Lekh-lekho" (the opening words of God's command to Abraham, "Get thee out of thy country"), everything has come apart. Tevye's wife, the pragmatic foil for his idealism, is dead. Beilke and her husband have lost their money and are laboring in the sweatshops of America. Tsaytl's husband, the young tailor, is struck down by consumption, and the hope of Palestine vanishes for Tevye as he takes in his impoverished daughter and her children. On top of all this, it is the time of the Beilis blood-libel trial—a Jew accused, as late as 1911, of killing a Christian child for its blood. (This grisly anti-Semitic fantasy turns up as far back as Chaucer's "Prioress's Tale.") Tevye's Gentile neighbors, after a meeting of the village council, are preparing for a pogrom. "Since you Jews have been beaten up everywhere, why let you get away with it here?" argues Ivan Paparilo, the village elder. "We just aren't certain what kind of pogrom to have. Should we just smash your windows, should we tear up your pillows and blankets and scatter all the feathers, or should we also burn down your house and barn with everything in them?" To which Tevye replies, "If that's what you've decided, who am I to object? You must have good reasons for thinking that Tevye deserves to see his life go up in smoke. . . . You do know there's a God above, don't you? Mind you, I'm not talking about my God or your God—I'm talking about the God of us all. . . . It may very well be that He wants you to punish me for being guilty of nothing at all. But the opposite may also be true." Tevye finally manages to talk the villagers out of the pogrom—they want it, they explain, only to save face with the towns that have had one. Instead, all the Jews in the village—among them Tevye's family, including the returned Chava—are expelled by order of the provincial governor; and there the Tevye tales end. "Anyone can be a goy," Tevye concludes, "but a Jew must be born one. . . . It's a lucky thing

I was, then, because otherwise how would I ever know what it's like to be homeless and wander all over the world without resting my head on the same pillow two nights running?"

Thus the somber matter of Sholem Aleichem's comedy. Tevye's dicta run all through it: what he thinks about God ("Why doesn't He do something? Why doesn't He say something?"), about wickedness ("My problem was men. Why did they have to be so bad when they could just as well have been good?"), about the goals of life ("to do a little good in His world before you die—to give a bit of money to charity, to take someone needy under your wing, even to sit down with educated Jews and study some Torah"), about the situation in Russia ("pogroms in Kishinev, riots, troubles, the new Constantution [Constitution] . . . God wanted to do us Jews a favor and so He sent us a new catastrophe, a Constantution"), about education ("I'd sooner eat a buttered pig than sit down to a meal with an illiterate. A Jew who can't read a Jewish book is a hundred times worse than a sinner"), about reserve ("Secretive people annoy me"), about opportunity ("A cow can sooner jump over a roof than a Jew get into a Russian university! . . . They guard their schools from us like a bowl of cream from a cat"), about faith and resignation ("A Jew has to hope. So what if things couldn't be worse? That's why there are Jews in the world!"), about what to do with money if one ever got any ("Make a contribution to charity that would be the envy of any rich Jew"), about ignorance, love, decency, poverty, misery, anti-Semitism, and the tardiness of the Messiah.

"The Railroad Stories," the second half of the Halkin volume, are similar in their use of a monologic narrator, and certainly in their cheerless subject matter. The storyteller of "Baranovich Station" sums up what Jews traveling by train—men scrambling for a living—talk about: "From the Revolution we passed to the Constitution, and from the Constitution it was but a short step to the pogroms, the massacres of Jews, the new anti-Semitic legislation, the expulsion from the villages, the mass flight to America, and all the other trials and tribulations that you hear about these fine days: bankruptcies, expropriations, military emergencies, executions, starvation, cholera, Purishkevich [V. N. Purishkevich was the founder of an anti-Semitic movement called the Black Hundreds] . . . " If we didn't absolutely grasp it before, we can profoundly recognize it now: Sholem Aleichem's is a literature of crisis.

And yet "The Railroad Stories," in their slightness and vitality and scattershot abundance—there are twenty of them—strike with a comic sharpness that to my mind exceeds even the effervescent artistry of the Tevye tales. Tevye's voice is elastic, simultaneously innocent and knowing, never short on acuteness or energy or observation or ironic fervor; but "The Railroad Stories," perhaps because they are largely unfamiliar to us and have never been contaminated by reductiveness, yield the plain shock of their form. Their form is all plotless trajectory: one doesn't apprehend the mark until after the mark has been hit. To come on these stories with no previous inkling of their existence (I imagine this will be the experience of numbers of readers) is to understand what it is to marvel at form—or formlessness—in the hands of literary genius. There are pronounced resemblances to early Chekhov and to Babel and Gorky, as well as a recognizable source—the casual sketch that is the outgrowth of the feuilleton, here strengthened and darkened by denser resonances. Nevertheless, the landscape is for the most part uniquely Sholem Aleichem's, a Russia not easily duplicated even by the sympathetic Chekhov, who in his letters could now and then toss off an anti-Semitic crack as lightly as a shrug. The most Chekhovian of these stories, "Eighteen from Pereshchepena"—a vignette of comic misunderstanding that, when untangled, is seen to be tragic—appears at first to be about the quota system in schools but actually turns on the dread of forced military service: the eighteen Jewish youths "taken" from the town of Pereshchepena are revealed to be unlucky conscripts, not lucky students. "The Wedding That Came Without Its Band" lustily caricatures a pogrom that doesn't come off: a trainload of hooligans "in full battle gear, too, with clubs, and tar," get so drunk—"the conductor and the stoker and even the policeman"—that they are left behind by the locomotive intended to carry them to their prey. In "The Miracle of Hoshana Rabbah," a venturesome Jew named Berl and an anti-Semitic

334

priest find themselves, improbably but perilously, alone together aboard a runaway locomotive. The priest, exasperated with Berl, threatens to push him off. "Just look at the difference, Father, between you and me," says Berl as the engine hurtles wildly on. "I'm doing my best to stop this locomotive, because I'm trying to save us both, and all you can think of is throwing me out of it—in other words, of murdering your fellow man!" An antic moral fable, wherein the priest is shamed and tamed. But there are plenty of Jewish rascals, too—con men and cardsharps and thieves, a pimp and a cowardly apostate, and even an insurance arsonist. And there are any number of desolate Jews—a teenage suicide, a desperate father who pursues a Gentile "professor of medicine" to beg him to tend his dying boy, Jews without residence permits who risk arrest by sneaking into town to see a doctor.

All these characters, whether avoiding or perpetrating pogroms, whether hostile or farcical or pathetic or paradoxical, are flushed with the rosiness of comedy. Comedy, the product of ridicule, is too brittle a mode in the absence of compassion and too soppy a mode in the absence of briskness. Sholem Aleichem is always brisk and always ready to display just enough (sparing) kindliness to keep the tone on the far side of soppiness. Here, in "Third Class," he is matter-of-fact without coldness, satiric without meanness, loving without mawkishness:

> When you go third class and wake up in the morning to discover that you've left your tefillin and your prayer shawl at home, there isn't any cause for alarm—you only need to ask and you'll be given someone else's, along with whatever else you require. All that's expected of you in return, once you're done praying, is to open your suitcase and display your own wares. Vodka, cake, a hard-boiled egg, a drumstick, a piece of fish—it's all grist for the mill. Perhaps you have an apple, an orange, a piece of strudel? Out with it, no need to be ashamed! Everyone will be glad to share it with you, no one stands on ceremony here . . . Before long each of us not only knows all about the others' troubles, he knows about every trial and

tribulation that ever befell a Jew anywhere. It's enough to warm the cockles of your heart!

The close-knittedness—or huddling, or nestling—of frequently threatened poor Jews, collectively and individually powerless, who bloom in the fond and comradely safety of fellow Jews on a train; the caustic notion of adversity as one's oldest intimate; trials and tribulations that nevertheless warm the cockles: all this is Sholem Aleichem defining, so to speak, the connotations of his nom de plume.

That these ironies can rise so pungently from a page in English testifies to how clear and broad an opening the translator has bored into the original, where psychological sighs and skeptical gestures are more slender than a hair, or else are hidden—a grain here, a grain there—in the crannies of language. Halkin, an Israeli born and reared in the United States, is an accomplished translator from Hebrew who is here tackling Yiddish for the first time. His able text empowers the reader to come away confident of having been given a reasonable measure of access. Now and then, he achieves much more than the merely reasonable—a true bridge between languages. Happy moments like this: "Menachem Mendl was his name: a wheeler, a dealer, a schemer, a dreamer, a bag of hot air." Or this: "He called him a scoundrel, a degenerate, a know-nothing, a leech, a bloodsucker, a fiend, a traitor, a disgrace to the Jewish people." Such jubilant and exuberant flights let us know without question that we have been catapulted right inside what Maurice Samuel once called "the world of Sholem Aleichem."

But even where there is generous overall access there can be problems and irritations. Especially with Sholem Aleichem, tone is everything. Halkin's work, stemming, perhaps, from his frank belief in "untranslatabilities," is too often jarred by sudden clangs that do violence to both tongues and result in startling distractions in the English while derailing our expectations of the Yiddish. Either we are in Sholem Aleichem's milieu or we are not—that is the crux. To transmute Sholem Aleichem's easy, idiomatic language into familiar slang is not necessarily a bad or inept solution; it requires of the translator a facile and supple ear, alert to the equation of idioms in two cultures. And it isn't that Hillel Halkin lacks such an ear—just the opposite. What he lacks, I am afraid, is an instinct for what is apropos. American street talk is preposterous in the mouths of people in a forest outside Yehupetz on the way to Boiberik, and the more skillfully and lavishly these relaxed Americanisms are deployed, the more preposterous they seem. "He looks at me like the dumb bunny he is," "I blew in this morning," "It drives me up the wall," "Holy suffering catfish!"—absurd locutions for poor Jews in a Russian railway carriage at the turn of the century, especially in the company of the occasional British "Quite" and a stilted "A black plague take them all" (a stock imprecation that in Yiddish stings without sounding rococo). And what are we to do with a Tevye who is "bushed," who downs his brandy with "Cheers!" (even *Fiddler* stuck by "*l'chaim!*"), who tells someone "You're off your trolley"? With ripe improbability, the Jews on the train say "the gospel truth," "a federal case," "Doesn't that beat all for low-downness," "Tried to pin such a bum rap on me," "You're all bollixed up," "Some meatball he was," and, painfully, for dancing, "Everyone cut the rug up." Somewhere there is an agonizing 1940s "swell." Under such an assault, tone collapses and imagination dies.

But these are phrases snatched out of context. Here is a bit of dialogue between Tevye and his daughter Chava concerning Chvedka, the young Gentile she will eventually run off with:

"Well, then," I say, "what sort of person is he? Perhaps you could enlighten me."

"Even if I told you," she says, "you wouldn't understand. Chvedka is a second Gorky."

"A second Gorky?" I say. "And who, pray tell, was the first?"

"Gorky," she says, "is only just about the most important man alive."

"Is he?" I say. "And just where does he live, this Mr. Important of yours? What's his act and what makes him such a big deal?"

In the Yiddish, Tevye's bitterness is less elaborately spoken, and is effectively more cutting. Instead of "Perhaps you could enlighten me," Tevye comes back with a curt "Let's hear," all the more biting for its brevity. "Pray tell," absent in the original, is too fancy; Tevye grunts out his sardonic helplessness in a single fricative, a *zhe* attached to the sentence's opening word. This *zhe*, in no way portable into English, is nonetheless rawly expressive, and deserves better than the tinkle of Halkin's "Pray tell." But the real blow to Tevye's language (and his moral cosmos) is struck in the last line, which, in the light of the Yiddish original, is insupportably charmless and hollow—lingo far too carelessly parochial to reflect Tevye's sufferings in a Pharaonic Russia. Agreed, the original is intimidating: "*Vu zitst er, der tane dayner, vos iz zayn gesheft un vos far a droshe hot er gedarshnt?*"—literally, "Where does he sit, that *tane* of yours, how does he get his living, and what kind of a *droshe* has he preached?" A *tane* is one of the classical scholastics known as *tannaim*, whose hermeneutics appear in the Mishna, a collection of sixty-three tractates of law and ethics that constitute the foundation of the Talmud; a *droshe* is a commentary, often formidably allusive, prepared by a serious student of homiletics. For Tevye to compare a Russian peasant boy, whose father he judges to be a swineherd and a drunk, with the most influential sages of antiquity is bruising sarcasm—and not only because Chvedka's family outlook is so remote from the impassioned patrimony of Jewish learning.

More appositely, Tevye is making the point that the Gorky he has never heard of stands as a mote in relation to that patrimony. From Tevye's perspective—and his perspective always includes historical memory, with its emphasis on survival and continuity—Chava, in pursuing Chvedka, is venturing into the transgressions of spiritual self-erasure; Tevye is altogether untouched by that cosmopolitan Western liberalism which will overwhelmingly claim his deracinated descendants. In half a moment, the dialogue has moved from the joke of "a second Gorky" to the outcry of a crumbling tradition wherein a secular Russian author is starting to assume major cultural authority for Jews. However difficult it may be for a translator to convey all this—so complex and hurtful a knot of social and emotional attitudes ingeniously trapped in a few Yiddish syllables—it is certain that Halkin's "this Mr. Important of yours," with its echoes of old radio programs (Molly Goldberg, Fred Allen's Mrs. Nussbaum), does not nearly achieve a solution.

Even so, given its strengths, Halkin's work is likely to serve as the indispensable Sholem Aleichem for some time to come.

Prisoner on the Hell Planet: A Case History

from The Complete Maus: A Survivor's Tale

ART SPIEGELMAN

Art Spiegelman (née Itzhak Avraham ben Zeev, 1948) is the Pulitzer Prize-winning cartoonist of Maus *(1991), a path-opening graphic novel serialized in* Raw *(1980–91) about Spiegelman's father's experience as a Polish Jew in Auschwitz. A comics advocate, his other books include* In the Shadow of No Towers *(2004), about the September 11, 2001 terrorist attack. The following four pages, inspired by German Expressionism, are part of* Maus *and were drawn in 1972. They are about Spiegelman's mother's suicide and his way to tackle the pain it generated.*

THE NEXT WEEK WE SPENT IN MOURNING... MY FATHER'S FRIENDS ALL OFFERED ME HOSTILITY MIXED IN WITH THEIR CONDO-LENCES....

ARTHUR—WE'RE *SO* SORRY...

IT'S HIS FAULT— THE PUNK *!*

THEY THINK IT'S MY FAULT *!!*

...BUT, FOR THE MOST PART, I WAS LEFT ALONE WITH MY THOUGHTS...

MENOPAUSAL DEPRESSION

HITLER DID IT!

MOMMY!

BITCH

...*I* REMEMBERED THE LAST TIME I SAW HER...

...ARTIE...

SHE CAME INTO MY ROOM... IT WAS LATE AT NIGHT....

...ARTIE... YOU... STILL... LOVE... ME.... DON'T YOU? ....

...I TURNED AWAY, RESENTFUL OF THE WAY SHE TIGHTENED THE UMBILICAL CORD...

SURE, MA!

...SHE WALKED OUT AND CLOSED THE DOOR!

CLIK!

AGH!

WELL, MOM, IF YOU'RE LISTENING...

CONGRATULATIONS!... YOU'VE COMMITTED THE PERFECT CRIME ....

...YOU PUT ME HERE .... SHORTED ALL MY CIR-CUITS... CUT MY NERVE ENDINGS ... AND CROSSED MY WIRES!....

...YOU *MURDERED* ME, MOMMY, AND YOU LEFT ME HERE TO TAKE THE RAP *!!!*

PIPE DOWN, MAC! SOME OF US ARE TRYING TO SLEEP!

© art spiegelman, 1972

To Aunt Rose

ALLEN GINSBERG

Allen Ginsberg (1926–97) was a leading voice in the Beat generation of writers during the sixties, which includes Jack Kerouac and William S. Burroughs. A political activist, he pushed poetry into new frontiers, experimenting with style as well as altered states of consciousness to explore new sounds and imagery. He is most famous for his books Howl and Other Poems *(1956) and* Kaddish and Other Poems *(1961). The following poem comes from* Kaddish.

TO AUNT ROSE

Aunt Rose—now—might I see you
with your thin face and buck tooth smile and pain
           of rheumatism—and a long black heavy shoe
                 for your bony left leg
       limping down the long hall in Newark on the running carpet
                 past the black grand piano
                     in the day room
                         where the parties were
             and I sang Spanish loyalist songs
             in a high squeaky voice
                     (hysterical) the committee listening
             while you limped around the room
                 collected the money—
Aunt Honey, Uncle Sam, a stranger with a cloth arm
           in his pocket
                 and huge young bald head
                     of Abraham Lincoln Brigade

—your long sad face
           your tears of sexual frustration
                 (what smothered sobs and bony hips
                     under the pillows of Osborne Terrace)
—the time I stood on the toilet seat naked
             and you powdered my thighs with calamine
                 against the poison ivy—my tender
                     and shamed first black curled hairs
what were you thinking in secret heart then
                 knowing me a man already—
and I an ignorant girl of family silence on the thin pedestal
             of my legs in the bathroom—Museum of Newark.

346

Aunt Rose
Hitler is dead, Hitler is in Eternity; Hitler is with
        Tamburlaine and Emily Brontë

Though I see you walking still, a ghost on Osborne Terrace
            down the long dark hall to the front door
        limping a little with a pinched smile
        in what must have been a silken
                flower dress
welcoming my father, the Poet, on his visit to Newark
            —see you arriving in the living room
                dancing on your crippled leg
            and clapping hands his book
                had been accepted by Liveright

Hitler is dead and Liveright's gone out of business
The Attic of the Past and *Everlasting Minute* are out of print
                Uncle Harry sold his last silk stocking
            Claire quit interpretive dancing school
                Buba sits a wrinkled monument in Old
                Ladies Home blinking at new babies

last time I saw you was the hospital
            pale skull protruding under ashen skin
                blue veined unconscious girl
                    in an oxygen tent
            the war in Spain has ended long ago
                Aunt Rose

On Maurice Sendak's *Vilde khayes!*

ILAN STAVANS

The Yiddish influence in America manifests itself visibly in the explosion of Jewish picture books, an industry tracing its roots to the medieval Passover Haggadah. Jews have played an essential role in expanding this industry, including most prominently Maurice Sendak (1928–2012), author of Where the Wild Things Are *(1963),* In the Night Kitchen *(1970),* Seven Little Monsters *(1977), and* Outside Over There *(1981).*

MAURICE SENDAK'S famous children's book *Where the Wild Things Are* is an astonishing exploration of otherness that resonates far beyond its intended audience. Sendak, who published it in 1963 at the age of thirty-five (although he started it several years before), once said, "You cannot write for children. They're much too complicated. You can only write books that are of interest to them."

The theme of *Where the Wild Things Are* is difficult to summarize. Is it the search for individual freedom? The fright that comes with internalizing one's ghosts? The longing for comfort and a good hot meal after a temper tantrum? Conversely, the arithmetic of the volume is easy to grasp: thirty-seven unnumbered pages, eighteen color illustrations (excluding the cover and title page), 338 words, and ten full sentences—not much for a picture book whose influence has proved immeasurable.

Narrated in the past tense, the plot is about an imaginative little boy named Max who one night makes mischief dressed up as a wolf. In the first section Max hangs a rope, constructs a tent, climbs on books, and scares his dog. Exasperated, Max's mother calls him "WILD THING!" (The dialogue between Max and his mother, sparse and pointed, is always in capital letters.) He retorts, "I'LL EAT YOU UP," and she sends him to his room without dinner. The setting for the adventures that follow is Max's empty stomach.

From here on the action takes place in Max's room, which transmogrifies before his eyes. Upset by his punishment, Max perceives a forest (looking very much like a theatrical set) growing around him, and he giggles at the sight until "the walls became the world all around." An ocean appears and Max, on his private boat, sails through time and space for several weeks, almost a year, until he reaches the place where the wild things are.

This place may well be Sendak's most stunning creation: a dreamlike but threatening land where creatures "roared their terrible roars and gnashed their terrible teeth and rolled their terrible eyes and showed their terrible claws." But Max doesn't fall prey to these creatures. Instead, he commands: "BE STILL!" and by staring at their yellow eyes without blinking tames them. Max has magical powers.

Sendak presents monsters and wild things as synonymous. The distinctive creatures look somewhat endearing, their features juxtaposing elements from diverse species. Several display recognizable human hands and feet. One has a bull head, another a bizarre rooster's head. A third displays a chest that appears to be indelibly wearing pajamas. The unifying characteristic of all the monsters is their upright position and their big yellow eyes. Soon the wild things make Max their king and he presides over them with a golden crown and a scepter. But although he becomes their ruler, he isn't a tyrant. He plays with them: they all bow to the moon, swing on tree branches, and carry Max on their backs. The monsters honor him by calling him "the most wild thing of all."

In a move that echoes the early section of the book, Max eventually gets tired of the rumpus and sends the monsters off to bed without supper. Then the little boy becomes lonely. He smells good things to eat and feels hungry. He wants to be where "someone loves him best of all"; as a result, he gives up being king.

The monsters don't want him to go, so they threaten to eat him up, just as Max threatened his mother earlier in the plot. Confusing destruction with devotion, they warn that they'll eat him because "We love you so much!" Max refuses to stay and the monsters again exhibit their terrible roars, teeth, and claws. But the boy perseveres. He sails back through time and space until he finds himself in his own room, looking just as it always did. And, of course, his supper is waiting for him, still hot. The ending of the book asserts a mother's triumphant love.

Sendak was born in Brooklyn to Polish immigrants. His father was a tailor who told his children biblical stories in dramatically embellished form. His mother was psychologically unstable. His parents, the experience of watching Walt Disney's *Fantasia* at an early age, and the presence, visible and invisible, of relatives whose lives had been touched by the Holocaust defined the young Sendak's world view. The parents spoke

Yiddish to him. They often sent him to his room. And his mother called him *vilde khaye*, wild beast.

Some read *Where the Wild Things Are* as a tale about innocence and courage, manliness, or even the rite of passage of a child seeking to define his limits in a world he doesn't yet understand. Others seek a psychoanalytic explanation, looking at the disparity between the authority of the outside world and Max's subconscious desires. A third interpretation, tangentially inspired by Shakespeare's *The Tempest*, approaches the plot through the prism of colonialism and abandonment. Like Prospero the magician, Max is exiled in a distant land surrounded by the sea. He becomes the ruler of the natives, subduing them, until he decides to leave them behind. Whatever interpretation one chooses (to me, they all seem forced), the book's memorable title invites us to understand Max's otherness at home and abroad.

The volume forms a triptych with Sendak's *In the Night Kitchen* and *Outside Over There*. *Where the Wild Things Are* has been adapted for opera and recast as a musical as well as a film (with a screenplay by Dave Eggers and Spike Jonze, and directed by Jonze). None of these variations comes remotely close to the power of the original.

Apparently, the first draft of *Where the Wild Things Are* featured horses instead of monsters. Sendak's editor at Harper & Row, Ursula Nordstrom, realizing that the author couldn't draw horses very well (the original title was *Where the Wild Horses Are*), asked him to change the characters into creatures he could ably depict. Sendak opted for lovable monsters that, in his own words, resembled the immigrant aunts, uncles, and cousins who visited his childhood home in Brooklyn and for whom he felt both affection and disdain. He saw them as rowdy and impolite: they "could eat you up." In the opera, these monsters have names: Tzippy, Moishe, Aaron, Emile, and Bernard.

In the realm of children's literature, Sendak's method is revolutionary. He shows only what Max experiences and refrains from moralizing or reflecting on the events. Jewishness is implied: although no reference is explicitly made to it, the entire book is permeated with Jewish sensibility.

Max inhabits his own universe; he resists outside authority; he arrives in alien lands but assimilates the inhabitants' culture so well that he becomes a leader. Most of all, he longs for a return to his origins, the only place he feels truly at home.

Upon publication, *Where the Wild Things Are* received negative reviews and was considered inappropriate for young readers. Librarians often put it out of children's reach. Parents objected to Max's mother as mean, and disapproved of the way he defied her. But Sendak knows that we are all beasts inside. In children's literature he found a humble, modest genre and made it explode. In a 2004 interview, Sendak said, "People often ask, 'What happens to Max?' It's such a coy question. 'Well, he's in therapy forever,' I reply, 'and has to wear a straitjacket.'"

Mama Goes Where Papa Goes

SOPHIE TUCKER

Sophie Tucker (1886–1966) was a world-famous comedian and singer, one of the most popular American performers of the first half of the twentieth century. Born in present-day Ukraine, she arrived in the US as a baby, and debuted on the American vaudeville stage in 1907. Her greatest hits included "Some of These Days" and "My Yiddishe Momme." Even as her international fame grew—she performed for the British royal family in 1926—she would occasionally perform in Yiddish for Jewish audiences, as she did with her song "Mama Goes Where Papa Goes." What follows is an English translation of the Yiddish version of that song. Adah Hetko is a musician.

MAMA GOES WHERE PAPA GOES

Listen up, my man
I have something to say
It is no kind of plan
To mistreat me this way

You come along home
And you eat 'til you're stuffed
Leave me behind
and go out looking for "fun"
What you do ain't okay,
From now on, your ways must change

The mama goes where the papa goes
The papa shan't go out alone
Mama goes, because she gets it:
It's not to *kheyder* that you're headin'

When I see how you shave your face and you dress yourself up
I already know Torah's not what you're thinking of

The mama goes where the papa goes
You shan't go out alone at night
You hear me, Shmerl?
You shan't go out alone at night

You've already had your supper
Was it enough for you?
You don't look at me, you just read the news,

Say, what are you lacking?
Be a clever kid
You've got a wife here who can give you everything
It won't help you at all that you talk a lot,
I know you'll be running to your *shikselekh*

Listen up, Shmerl
Let that open door be,
Before you go out shaking shimmies, you can shake here with me

You can't fill yourself up here with *koshere* steak,
Then go out spending money with your *shikselekh*, eating *treyfe* cake,
So you'd better stop with the "monkey business"
Or you might just catch some kinda terrible sickness

I'm telling you,
The mama goes, where the papa goes
[thank you. . . .]
The papa shan't go out alone

TRANSLATED BY ADAH HETKO

On Being Indecent

PAULA VOGEL AND VICTORIA MYERS

Paula Vogel (b. 1951) is the Pulitzer Prize–winning playwright of The Oldest Profession *(1981),* The Baltimore Waltz *(1992),* Hot 'N' Throbbing *(1994),* How I Learned to Drive *(1997), and* Desdemona: A Play about a Handkerchief *(1993). For years, Vogel taught at Brown, before moving to Yale.* Indecent, *about Sholem Asch's* God of Vengeance, *premiered on Broadway in 2017. Victoria Myers is the editor-in-chief of* The Interval, *where she interviews numerous Tony Award and Pulitzer Prize winners and nominees. The following is a fragment of an interview about* Indecent.

VICTORIA MYERS: *Indecent* is obviously in relationship to *God of Vengeance*, but do you also see it as being in relation to other plays and other works of art?

PAULA VOGEL: Absolutely, there's always a homage in everything that I write, usually in every scene. I never have the time to write hand-written notes, so instead I write plays, and I tuck in little valentines within the scenes. Definitely there is a valentine to an astonishing Polish director, by the name of Tadeusz Kantor, who used his childhood in Poland during the Second World War to create theatrical sculptures about his memory of getting through the war as a child. An astonishing play called *Wielopole, Wielopole*. And he did a play called *The Dead Class*, where he remembered his elementary school classmates in this tiny village, but they were basically like Siamese twins, two mannequins of their childhood selves played by their adult selves, and they were all dead, and they come back to life in this classroom. I've never seen anything like that. When I told Rebecca that, she came up with the amazing visuals that begin and end the play. There's a big valentine in this to him. Thornton Wilder, I think I write almost every play with a valentine to Thornton Wilder. The third act of *Our Town*, with the members of the cemetery sitting in chairs in the rain, is a huge part of it, and the stage manager, Lemml, is absolutely a valentine to the stage manager of *Our Town*. And there are many, many more valentines in this. We have an astonishing choreographer, and he's making valentines to the dancers and the dance makers he loves. Lisa Gutkind and Aaron Halva are writing original music looking over their shoulders.

MYERS: One of the things I found really interesting about the piece is it's an ensemble piece, but there's also this way where you have men looking at and writing about women, not just in the character of Sholem Asch, but also Lemml. What was your thought process for using the male gaze within the structure of the piece?

357

VOGEL: There were a couple of initial impulses that I had. One was that I wanted us all, at the end of the play, to feel that we were native speakers of Yiddish, and that we were in that last audience [of *God of Vengeance*]. But the second thing was that I wanted us all to recognize how amazing and beautiful female desire is in worlds in which the agency was given to men. The fact that the first scene in the salon, it's men who are performing the women. I wanted the challenge of, how do I float women through this play and make them concrete and specific with material bodies, but also show men kind of creating a repository of their imagination and their desire?

I'm hoping the fact that women artists have created it makes that somewhat clear. It's true of every play I write. If I write *Baltimore Waltz*, for example, I want every man and woman in the audience to think how beautiful the male body is. How could you not be in love with men? That's a beautiful, beautiful thing. In this play, I'm asking the audience to look at the women in the way perhaps Sholem Asch looked at the women, which was revolutionary in how beautiful women are. The difference is that we've changed the characters in the original *God of Vengeance*, so that it's not a passive younger woman with an older, more aggressive, experienced woman, but rather that the younger woman is acting on her desires. And that's a fairly significant shift. How did these women become the agents of their desire, rather than get passively caught in the desire? It's a beautiful play written by a young married man in 1906 with an astonishing love scene. But I do think it plays differently now, and I think we're in the twenty-first century, and I think in order for *God of Vengeance* to come back into the canon, we have to look at female desire differently, particularly in this country. What's terrifying is that we are, once again, in risk of policing women and the desire of women, both through things like cutting rights of abortion, control over our bodies, and policing sexuality. That's where we are.

So in many, many ways, I feel like I'm on just the flip side of the coin that Sholem Asch was showing at a time when the policing was alive and well and extremely dangerous within the Jewish community. And I think of him—he's a very brave and honest writer for his time. And I'm using him in the present tense because I think of him in the present tense; I don't think of writers as dead. I don't think of actors as dead. That's very much a part of this play. I think the art continues their life force long after they're gone.

MYERS: The specter of the Holocaust hangs over the events of the play. How did you work with the fact that you have the audience coming in with a prior knowledge of what was going to happen? When did you want to tap into that, and when did you maybe want to give them the opportunity to forget and think, "Oh, maybe going back to Poland will be okay"?

VOGEL: That's one of the primary challenges. Our paradigm shifted in the world after 9/11, our paradigm shifted after HIV. You can never go back, and our paradigm certainly shifted after 1938 and the Holocaust. How can we forget that? That was sort of our aim. So one of the aims is to create characters and cast members who don't know what their future holds, and to present them in such a way that we're kind of empathizing and caught up in them—through the music, through the dance, through the fact that we're spending time in struggles that were very real conflicts: Do you cut out the lovemaking with two women in love, and make it sexual instead? Do you get fired from a production because your Yiddish accent is too strong and you're going to be replaced, and your lover happens to be your scene partner, right? How do you deal with that? All of that. It's the struggles we have right now. We don't know in the next [few] years how our paradigm is shifting. Our paradigm has shifted since November [2016]. We're on the brink of a paradigm shift. We have to remember the innocence that we have in the moment before the paradigm shifts. That's my hope. To me, drama is not about what is going to happen, it's about how did it happen. Can we re-remember?

Can we forget what we know, so that we can re-remember what we know in a new light and think, "I didn't know that. I didn't realize that impact of it"? So it's more a reinterpretation.

The other thing I want to say is that what I think is extraordinary right now is this remarkable generation of twenty-first-century audience members and artists and writers and actors, and I love them. I think this is an extraordinary time of theater. It's time to retell the story so that I can hear how it's happening for a new generation. We're at this point in time when the members in our families, in our society, who remembered the actual events are dying and are no longer with us. We can't forget. We have to re-witness. We have to reanimate, we have to relive it, and I think this is an important time to do it. So that it's not thought of as history. It's a real danger if we think of what happened in 1938 in Germany and Poland and all through Europe as history. It allows us not to notice how we've restricted immigration for Syrian refugees. There was a real shudder down our backs with the recent chemical attacks by Assad. If we forget this, we are doomed to repeat it. I think this is a good time to remember. So I don't think of it as history, and I don't think of it as past at all.

MYERS: Does that feel like a greater responsibility?

VOGEL: Not to mention the fact that as I have said, in this moment in time we have to say we are all Muslim. We have to say we are all Latino/Latina. In terms of the hate and the rhetoric: we are all lesbians, we are all transgender. This play said in 1907, "We are all Jewish. We are all women." Because Sholem Asch really looked at the plight of domestic violence and women. Yes, we feel the responsibility. Responsibility, though, also means how do we live with that knowledge and with some joy and lightness in our hearts, so that we have some resiliency to face what's happening politically every day? You can't do it simply by accepting responsibility. You have to think of how to come together and rejoice and celebrate all of the things that are good in our communities. So it may sound strange to be combining those two artistic principles of witnessing and responsibility with celebration and commemoration, but that's what we're trying to do as a troupe.

MYERS: I wanted to talk a little bit about the music in the play, particularly one specific choice. Toward the end of the play, you have the music cue of "Oklahoma."

VOGEL: Yes. That's totally mine.

MYERS: I wanted to ask if you'd talk a little bit about that, especially because it's this meta moment, since theater and the entertainment industry were a way in which Jews became a part of American society, and if you go to the Museum of Jewish Heritage, you get to the end of the exhibit, and it basically ends with Rodgers and Hammerstein and Barbra Streisand.

VOGEL: Exactly. In a way, I want us to remember that there was a time in this country in which Jews were not seen as white people. We were not seen as Americans. Nor were Italians or Irish people. There was a moment in time in which we were seen as invaders, foreigners, aliens. When I first wrote that, we went through robust questioning about it, and I kept saying, "I can't quite articulate why." I can now. We watch the troupe, and then they're no more. They're no longer with us. We decided that that was going to be the end of live music at that moment. But I also want to say the community lives forward. And we tied it in with, "Very few write in Yiddish anymore," as we're listening to "Oklahoma." That we become what is very much considered part of the mainstream, and what it is to be American. So, it's very important for me. The fact that two Jewish boys from New York could be writing a musical about middle America, the heartland of Oklahoma, and it's perfectly accepted and celebrated and becomes the most successful long-running musical, I think it's important. I did want to do that. I wanted it to be recorded song. It's no longer live. So, it is a moment of history in which whatever the story brings us to, the Jewish impact on American culture is alive and well and continues.

361

MYERS: The characters in *Indecent* are almost all Jewish. Do you feel like there's anything about the play that is intrinsically Jewish in form?

VOGEL: I feel the process is not just Jewish, it was in the nineteenth century that we became a repertory troupe that traveled together, and we worked on it together, and we went from town to town. We developed a shorthand the way the Yiddish troupes did as they traveled through Europe. We thought about that a lot when we tried to set up a process and get theaters to co-produce together. Do I think there's anything Jewish [about the form]? This is an interesting thing: I can't see my fingerprints. I can't see the fingerprints on the play because I'm in it and I'm too close. It's the same way that people say, "Oh, your sense of humor." I can't see my sense of humor. A lot of people say, "This is a very Jewish sense of humor." I accept that as a great compliment because we're not going to survive unless we have a sense of humor, right? But that's nothing I have control over. I'm kind of really eager to read about what people see when they come to see it. I hope it makes Jews feel really great and proud as a community. I hope my former students feel all of the valentines that I'm writing to them, and trying to think about, "What is this legacy in the twenty-first century?" They've kept me writing for a very long time, because I'm answering back to what they're writing.

Yiddish Hollywood

FYVUSH FINKEL, WALTER MATTHAU, ALAN ALDA, ELLIOTT GOULD, ALAN KING, JERRY STILLER, JOAN MICKLIN SILVER, LEONARD NIMOY

Fyvush Finkel (1922–2016) was an Emmy-winning actor known for roles in Fiddler on the Roof *(1971),* Little Shop of Horrors *(1986), and the TV show* Picket Fences *(1992–96). Walter Matthau (1920–2000) was a theater and film actor and comedian in movies such as* The Fortune Cookie *(1966),* The Odd Couple *(1968), and* Grumpy Old Men *(1993). Alan Alda (1936–) is an award-winning actor known for his roles on* M*A*S*H *(1972–83),* Crimes and Misdemeanors *(1989), and others. Elliott Gould (1938–) is an actor known for roles in* Bob & Carol & Ted & Alice *(1969), the* Ocean's 11 *franchise, and dozens of TV and film projects. Alan King (1927–2004), comedian and actor, was a regular guest host of Johnny Carson's* The Tonight Show *and host of the 1972 Academy Awards. Jerry Stiller (1927–) is an actor known for his role as Frank Costanza on the TV show* Seinfeld, *among many other roles. Joan Micklin Silver (1935–) is the director of* Hester Street *(1975),* Crossing Delancey *(1988), and other films. Leonard Nimoy (1931–2015), was an actor and artist known for his role as Spock on the TV show* Star Trek *(1966–69) and other roles.*

FYVUSH FINKEL

"My goodness, when I was a kid in Brownsville Yiddish was all we spoke until we went to school," said Fyvush Finkel, star of TV's *Picket Fences.* "My mother was from Minsk, my father from Warsaw, which was quite a combination, like a Northerner marrying a Southerner."

Finkel's Yiddish theater ventures began when he was nine years old in 1931. "Every show had a wedding, and every wedding had a boy that stopped the show singing 'Oh Promise Me.' I got a dollar a performance, which was considered pretty good."

When he grew older, Finkel joined a traveling Yiddish troupe that sometimes had a rough time filling empty seats—especially in Pittsburgh. "'You don't understand the audiences we have here in Pittsburgh,' the theater manager told me. 'They just want to see how long an actor can live without eating.'"

Returning to New York, Finkel found that an actor's responsibilities included "running to the *Forward* and arguing with the critics. It isn't like the American theater, where [a bad review] hurts but you don't do anything. In the Yiddish theater, don't ask how they used to run after each other and yell in the Garden Cafeteria. 'What do you know from talent?' the actors would scream. 'You're not a critic, you're nothing.'"

During one of his visits to the Yiddish press, Finkel met Abraham Reisen. "He seemed a fine gentlemen, a very learned man. Once he was given, as a present, a checking account with $1,000 on deposit; but he didn't understand, he thought he could use every check in the book and write them for any amount he wanted. He had a talented pen, but he never knew anything about money.

WALTER MATTHAU

In 1936 as a young man of sixteen, Walter Matthau spent a great deal of his time in New York's Second Avenue Theater "right across the street from Moskowitz and Lupowitz's Romanian Broiler." But, at least at first, he came to Yiddish theater not as an actor but a peddler.

"The only thought I gave was to selling ice cream and cherry drinks, any other thought didn't quite enter my mind," he says. "The three-flavor bricks I was selling cost fifteen cents, an awful lot of money for a small brick, and in order to make it sound very official, I used to holler as loud as I could, 'Get your Federal Ice Cream here!'"

Matthau's vocal strength caught the attention of the management, which was presenting Herman Yablokoff's *The Dishwasher* at the time. "They said, 'Let's get those two tall kids, Matthau and Bummie Tresser, they can play the immigration police.' I also got to be the first fake cellist in a symphony orchestra because I could imitate a real cellist better than anyone else. I hammed it up like Itzhak Perlman."

Though Yiddish was only occasionally heard in his home, Matthau soon progressed to minor speaking parts in the theater. "In *Sgt. Naftula*, starring Leo Fuchs, I was one of three soldiers playing pinochle in a foxhole. Fuchs bids 300, someone else bids 350, I say '400' and then the whole trench explodes, we're all dead. Fuchs, all tattered and bloody, just manages to pick up his head, looks at my cards and says, 'He wouldn't have made it.'"

ALAN ALDA

Though not Jewish, Alan Alda has had considerable acquaintance with Yiddish and its literature, starting with his father, the actor Robert Alda: "He learned it in the Catskills when he started out; it's the unofficial language of show business."

Alda and his wife Arlene used to entertain themselves by reading Sholem Aleichem stories aloud and attending Howard Da Silva's public readings of Yiddish stories. "There was one story about two workers who finally get a chance to go to the opera, and one says, 'I wonder how it goes with the plumbing in this building?' Those writers wrote with a pungency; Arlene and I still use that phrase when we're in strange surroundings."

To Alda, stories like that are "an expression of the character of the Jewish people. They have an acute sense of humor which they're able to express even in the midst of their deepest suffering."

As an example, Alda says, "I'll never forget sitting next to Simon Wiesenthal at a fundraising dinner. He was in the middle of telling a joke when a man came up to the table and said, 'Remember me?'

"It turned out to be a man he hadn't seen since they'd been in the camps together. They spoke and then Wiesenthal turned back to me and, with tears still on his face, finished the joke. To me, that was the essence of Jewish humor: not to hide from the truth but to use it to tell the truth. And the feeling that there is something about laughter that is, in itself, valuable."

ELLIOTT GOULD

When Elliott Gould hears Yiddish spoken, "It evokes warmth, like hearing a part of myself before I was conscious. It represents a life to me, bridging major gaps in my existence."

As a child, Gould says, "the Yiddish phrase I remember most was 'Loz im,' 'Leave him alone.' Occasionally I was taken to Yiddish drama on Second Avenue and, though everybody seemed to know what was going on, I didn't understand a word.

"Historically, culturally, and traditionally, Yiddish was more than a language to me. I sensed and felt that, even though I didn't understand any of the words. It was hard enough for me to understand the actions of people in English, let alone in a language that didn't seem to be a language. I felt without a doubt that I was related to it and it to me, but I didn't understand those words."

One of the stories Gould reads for the Center's radio series is Philip Roth's "The Conversion of the Jews," and the actor finds a certain symmetry in that. "I tested for the film of Roth's *Goodbye, Columbus* and didn't get the part, but what's bashert is bashert—that's one of my favorite words. I'm grateful to have the opportunity to do this work now. It's something that has been buried here, in my bones and marrow forever, and I want to be able to share it."

ALAN KING

Like many children of immigrants, Alan King learned Yiddish because "my parents spoke it when they didn't want us to hear. But once we understood that, they went on to Russian and then to Polish. And that's how we became linguists."

Despite the presence of all these languages, King said, "my father insisted on English. He was a Zionist and a socialist, but he wanted us all to be Yankee Doodle Dandies. He was a cutter by trade; in our house David Dubinsky [a prominent labor leader] was revered. And it was always 'Dubinsky,' just one word, like 'Sinatra' or 'Hildegard.'"

An actor by trade, King spoke Yiddish with some of the masters. "Jimmy Cagney, he was raised in Hell's Kitchen, he knew Yiddish. Paul Muni was the king of Yiddish theater, we always used to talk it. Edward G. Robinson spoke Yiddish fluently, he spoke it as good as my mother. And Zero Mostel, could he speak Yiddish! He was crazy, the wildest, most wonderful man."

Always ready to make a joke ("My daughter is living on a mountain in Flagstaff, Arizona, learning to speak Hopi Yiddish"), King's feeling for the language came in part from his grandfather. "He was an itinerant rabbi in one of those downstairs shuls where you had to be the rabbi, the shammes, the gabbai, everything,"

As to the language's future, King saw no reason not to be hopeful. "If we survived the bad times, why wouldn't we survive the good?" he asked. "If you think of what happened during the five or six or seven hundred years when Yiddish was spoken, hopefully the worst is over."

JERRY STILLER

Jerry Stiller did not exactly come from a small family. "My mother was the youngest of ten children, so I had a lot of aunts and uncles and cousins. When they came over from Europe, they all moved into the same building, at 61 Columbia Street on the Lower East Side. My parents used Yiddish only when they fought: It was 'You greenhorn, only the worst things should happen to you.' When things really got nasty, they switched to Polish."

Stiller's family came from a town in Poland called Frampol, which figures prominently in some stories by Isaac Bashevis Singer. "I used to see Singer in a restaurant on 86th Street and Broadway in New York, eating shredded wheat and skim milk after he'd won the Nobel Prize. On Sundays he'd line up at the corner for the *New York Times*. He'd just won the Prize, I wanted to give him one free."

When he was an eighteen-year-old G.I. stationed in Italy, Stiller met a Jewish family during holiday services at a Naples synagogue. Two years later he was riding a bus in New York when someone got on and asked for directions in Yiddish. It was the father of the family he'd met in Naples, and now he lived at 61 Columbia Street, Stiller's old address. "When that happens, you have to ask yourself, what is going on?"

Stiller learned much of his Yiddish through a course at New York's 92nd Street Y. "The man who taught it began by singing a song called 'Bulbes.' 'When you hear this,' he said, 'You'll know how beautiful the language is.' And once he sang the song, you learned it. It connected you to something you didn't know you knew."

JOAN MICKLIN SILVER

Though she had made a number of prizewinning shorts, director Joan Micklin Silver was "having a terrible time finding work in features" in the early 1970s. Her husband, Ray, offered to help put together the financing for a theatrical picture, and the search for a subject began.

Since Silver thought "this might be the only one I ever do, I wanted to make one that really counted for my family." Already familiar with Abraham Cahan's short story "Yekl," she decided to adapt it. "It might not have been exactly the right film to choose for my first one, but as my mother used to say, 'God looks after children and fools.'"

The result was *Hester Street*—probably the only film with substantial Yiddish dialogue ever nominated for an Academy Award (for star Carol

Kane as Best Actress). Most of the principals learned their Yiddish pho-netically, and had the advantage of performing in the company of Yiddish theater veterans like Zvee Scooler and Leib Lensky.

Born and raised in Omaha, Silver's parents were Yiddish speakers from Russia. "They often told wonderful jokes in Yiddish, but when it came to telling them to us in English they'd say, 'It doesn't quite translate, it doesn't quite work.'" The director's only regret is that her father never saw *Hester Street*. "He was the kind of man who belonged to an orthodox, a conservative and a reform synagogue; he thought it was important to support them all. I'm very sorry he didn't live to see this."

LEONARD NIMOY

"Yiddish is a long story with me, it goes way back," said Leonard Nimoy. "And in some wonderful way it's been burgeoning in the last couple of years."

He grew up in an apartment in Boston his family shared with his grandparents. "Yiddish was not a secret language, it was necessary for communication. My connection with my grandfather was extremely deep. He was the guy who walked out of Europe first, and he always had the loose dollar in his pocket to hand you so you could do the thing your parents said you couldn't because there was no money."

When Nimoy moved to Los Angeles as a young actor, he found that his command of *mame-loshn* meant he could pick up $35 playing juveniles in Yiddish theater productions that had brought only the stars with them from New York. And, in 1952 and 1953, he found himself acting, albeit in English, with the great Maurice Schwartz.

"We did Jacob Gordin's *God, Man and Satan* and Sholem Aleichem's *It's Hard to Be a Jew*. Schwartz was a great actor, there was a theatricality about him, he could play everything from a lightweight fop tripping across the stage to a gigantic tragedian weighing 1,000 pounds. He considered him-self a serious theater man and his frustration was that he never achieved the great success in the English language he was always hoping for."

His Yiddish getting rusty, Nimoy was asked to participate in a joint fundraiser for YIVO and the Circle in the Square Theater in New York. He went back and studied with UCLA professor Janet Hadda and said the language has become "such a deep-rooted, living thing to me, I've found myself dreaming in Yiddish. That's how much it means."

from A Bintel Brief: Love and Longing in Old New York

LIANA FINCK

The original Forverts *column "Bintel Brief" was the brainchild of editor-in-chief Abraham Cahan. It responded to letters from these mostly poor and variably educated Jewish immigrants in New York and became one of the most popular features in the newspaper. Liana Finck (b. 1986), a contributor to* The New Yorker *and a granddaughter of immigrants whose parents grew up Orthodox in Brooklyn and Queens, turned segments of the column into the graphic novel* A Bintel Brief: Love and Longing in Old New York *(2014). She is also the author of* Passing for Human *(2018).*

a great deal in my life. My father died before I was born, and when I was three weeks old my mother died, too. My grandmother gave me away to a poor tailor and his wife. I got so used to them—

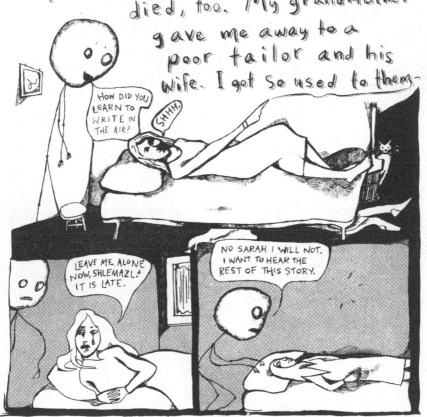

In time one of the tailor's appren-
tices fell in love with me, and I
didn't reject his love. He was a
fine, honest, quiet young man
and we became one body and
soul. When I turned seventeen
my bridegroom came to me
with a plan, that we should go to America,
and I agreed. It was hard for me to
take leave of the tailor's good family,
who had kept me as their own child,
and oceans of tears were shed when
we parted.

AT LAST YOU REACHED YOUR FINGER DOWN AND YOU TOUCHED MY BELOVED, AND TOOK HIM FROM ME. BUT HE STILL LIVES IN ME. THAT IS WHY I CAN DO THIS:

When we came to America my bride-groom immediately began to work and he supported me. I'll give you an example of his loyalty: Once, during the summer in terrible heat, I slept on the roof. But it started to rain and I was soaked through. I got very sick and had to be taken to the hospital. The doctor said I could be saved only by a blood transfusion. My bridegroom said immediately that he was ready to give me his blood. And so, thanks to him, I survived. In time I went to work in the "famous" Triangle shop. Later my bridegroom also got a job there. Even at work, he wanted to be with me. He told me then, "We will both work hard for a while and then we'll get married. We will save every cent so we'll be able to set up a home and you'll never have to work in a shop again." Thus my good bridegroom mused about the golden future. Then there was that terrible fire that took one hundred and forty-seven young blossoming lives.

ZAP!

After this I lay in the hospital for five weeks, and came home shattered. This is the fourth year that I am alone and I still see before me the horrible scenes of the fire. I see the good face of my bridegroom, also the burnt, blackened face in the morgue. The angel of death, also, is always before my eyes. I am weak and nervous, yet there is now a young man who wishes to marry me. I know that I can never love him. But this man doesn't want to leave me, and my friends try to persuade me to marry him. I decided to write to you, because I want to hear your advice.

Respectfully,
a faithful reader

It is senseless for this girl to sacrifice her life in memory of her faithful bridegroom, since this would not bring him back to life. What the earth covers must be forgotten. She has suffered enough in her life already and is advised to take herself in hand and begin her life anew.

Singer: A Purim Parody

ANONYMOUS

A handwritten letter written in Yiddish by Isaac Bashevis Singer to Magdalena Salazar, his Mexican maid of seven years in the Upper West Side apartment he shared with his wife, Alma, offers insight into a previously unknown romantic liaison by the Nobel Prize winner. Stuck to a Zabar's grocery list that had a late reworking of Singer's "Gimpel the Fool" scribbled on it, the letter was found during Digitize Yiddish Week at the Harry Ransom Humanities Center, in Austin, Texas. Singer refers to Abraham Cahan as "Ab." Mrs. Salazar, who stopped working for the Singers in 1964, wasn't mentioned in Singer's will in 1991, the year of his death. The translation, by Jeremy Fuchs, was published in The Jewish Daily Forward *on February 10, 2010.*

Dear Shmilke,

I've asked my publisher to deposit $150 a month from the royalties into the bank account I set up for you. Alma doesn't need to know about it, and I've made sure she won't find out. The lawyer and I have already gone over the details. But please make sure you don't leave any bank receipts around the house. Alma's a terrible snoop.

How long ago did I give you the Spanish/Yiddish dictionary? I got it from a friend in Buenos Aires; I told him I wanted to sprinkle some Spanish in something I'm finishing. And now look! You must be the first Indian ever to speak *dos mame-loshn* so fluently. Even Alma didn't know the word for "vacuum cleaner" until she heard it from you. Of course, when she and I were born, there was no such thing as a vacuum cleaner. It truly is a new age!

It will be a pleasure to meet your niece in February, when she returns from Puebla. I don't know what chipotle is but I'm always ready to learn new things. How old is she? Your description of her made me think of a girlfriend I had in Warsaw, who died in the war.

I gave you my brother's memoir, *Of a World That Is No More*, because I thought it would add to your understanding of my past. Many people say my brother was a better novelist than I am. It isn't true, but I thought I'd give you a chance to compare for yourself. Oh, and keep in mind that the stories I tell in *In My Father's Court* aren't always accurate. In fact, I made up most of it while recovering from a serious Purim bender in the spring of 1931. Ab. Cahan and I would often laugh about those half-truths while out drinking after klaberjass tournaments. I miss Ab. He could be a pain in the ass sometimes, but he was a hell of an editor.

I was wondering if you could give me a quick summary of the note you left under my pillow last Tuesday, and which I can't seem to find. I know: the last time you gave me a piece of writing, I misplaced that one, too. I'm absentminded. But you're wrong: I do care! And I do think you have talent. The sense [*three illegible words follow*] is a miracle of poetic compression and I'm the first to recognize it. Maybe you can help me translate one of my stories. I think my stories would really appeal to the Mexican literary sensibility. Did you know there's a pretty good-sized Yiddish-speaking population in Mexico City? It's true. They love me there.

I will stay in Florida with Alma for another eight weeks. I dream of your plump kneydlekh; don't share them with anyone. They are mine! I also look forward to caressing your sweet breasts.

—TU YITZJOK GALÁN

Dedications to **Bashert**

IRENA KLEPFISZ

Irina Klepfisz (1941–) is a poet and teacher. Born in the Warsaw Ghetto, she survived the war in hiding and arrived in New York with her mother in 1949. A graduate of City College of New York and the University of Chicago, she has taught at Barnard College and other universities, and has published several collections of poetry, including A Few Words in the Mother Tongue: Poems Selected and New, 1971–1990 *(1990). The following are the dedications to her poem "Bashert." The Yiddish word "bashert" means inevitable, (pre)destined.*

These words are dedicated to those who died

These words are dedicated to those who died
because they had no love and felt alone in the world
because they were afraid to be alone and tried to stick it out
because they could not ask
because they were shunned
because they were sick and their bodies could not resist the disease
because they played it safe
because they had no connections
because they had no faith
because they felt they did not belong and wanted to die

These words are dedicated to those who died
because they were loners and liked it
because they acquired friends and drew others to them
because they took risks
because they were stubborn and refused to give up
because they asked for too much

These words are dedicated to those who died
because a card was lost and a number was skipped
because a bed was denied
because a place was filled and no other place was left

These words are dedicated to those who died
because someone did not follow through
because someone was overworked and forgot
because someone left everything to God
because someone was late
because someone did not arrive at all
because someone told them to wait and they just couldn't any longer

These words are dedicated to those who died
because death is a punishment
because death is a reward
because death is the final rest
because death is eternal rage

These words are dedicated to those who died

Bashert

These words are dedicated to those who survived

These words are dedicated to those who survived
because their second grade teacher gave them books
because they did not draw attention to themselves and got lost
in the shuffle
because they knew someone who knew someone else who could
help them and bumped them into a corner on a Thursday
afternoon
because they played it safe
because they were lucky

These words are dedicated to those who survived
because they knew how to cut corners
because they drew attention to themselves and always got picked
because they took risks
because they had no principles and were hard

These words are dedicated to those who survived
because they refused to give up and defied statistics
because they had faith and trusted in God
because they expected the worst and were always prepared
because they were angry
because they could ask
because they mooched off others and saved their strength
because they endured humiliation
because they turned the other cheek
because they looked the other way

These words are dedicated to those who survived
because life is a wilderness and they were savage
because life is an awakening and they were alert

because life is a flowering and they blossomed
because life is a struggle and they struggled
because life is a gift and they were free to accept it

These words are dedicated to those who survived

Bashert

from The Yiddish Policemen's Union

MICHAEL CHABON

A native of Washington, DC, Michael Chabon (b. 1963) is the author of sixteen books, including the Pulitzer Prize–winning novel The Amazing Adventures of Kavalier & Clay *(2000),* Telegraph Avenue *(2012), and* Moonglow *(2016). The following is Chapter 3 from* The Yiddish Policemen's Union *(2007), a detective novel set in an imaginary, post-Second World War Yiddish-speaking Alaska.*

IN THE STREET THE WIND shakes rain from the flaps of its overcoat. Landsman tucks himself into the hotel doorway. Two men, one with a cello case strapped to his back, the other cradling a violin or viola, struggle against the weather toward the door of Pearl of Manila across the street. The symphony hall is ten blocks and a world away from this end of Max Nordau Street, but the craving of a Jew for pork, in particular when it has been deep-fried, is a force greater than night or distance or a cold blast off the Gulf of Alaska. Landsman himself is fighting the urge to return to room 505, and his bottle of slivovitz, and his World's Fair souvenir glass.

Instead, he lights a papiros. After a decade of abstinence, Landsman took up smoking again not quite three years ago. His then-wife was pregnant at the time. It was a much-discussed and in some quarters a long-desired pregnancy—her first—but not a planned one. As with many pregnancies that are discussed too long there was a history of ambivalence in the prospective father. At seventeen weeks and a day— the day Landsman bought his first package of Broadways in ten years— they got a bad result. Some but not all of the cells that made up the fetus, code-named Django, had an extra chromosome on the twentieth pair. A mosaicism, it was called. It might cause grave abnormalities. It might have no effect at all. In the available literature, a faithful person could find encouragement, and a faithless one ample reason to despond. Landsman's view of things—ambivalent, despondent, and with no faith in anything—prevailed. A doctor with half a dozen laminaria dilators broke the seal on the life of Django Landsman. Three months later, Landsman and his cigarettes moved out of the house on Tshernovits Island that he and Bina had shared for nearly all the fifteen years of their marriage. It was not that he couldn't live with the guilt. He just couldn't live with it and Bina, too.

An old man, pushing himself like a rickety handcart, weaves a course toward the door of the hotel. A short man, under five feet, dragging a large valise. Landsman observes the long white coat, worn open over a white suit with a waistcoat, and the wide-brimmed white hat pulled down over his ears. A white beard and sidelocks, wispy and thick at the same time. The valise an ancient chimera of stained brocade and scratched hide. The whole right side of the man's body sags five degrees lower than the left, where the suitcase, which must contain the old boy's entire collection of lead ingots, weighs it down. The man stops and raises a finger, as if he has a question to pose of Landsman. The wind toys with the man's whiskers and with the brim of his hat. From his beard, armpits, breath, and skin, the wind plucks a rich smell of stale tobacco and wet flannel and the sweat of a man who lives in the street. Landsman notes the color of the man's antiquated boots, yellowish ivory, like his beard, with sharp toes and buttons running up the sides.

Landsman recalls that he used to see this nut a lot, back when he was arresting Tenenboym for petty theft and possession. The yid was no younger then and is no older now. People used to call him Elijah, because he turned up in all kinds of unlikely spots, with his pushke box and his indefinable air of having something important to say.

"Darling," he says to Landsman now: "This is the Hotel Zamenhof, no?"

His Yiddish sounds a bit exotic to Landsman, flavored with Dutch maybe. He is bent and frail, but his face, apart from crow's feet around the blue eyes, looks youthful and unlined. The eyes themselves hold a match flame of eagerness that puzzles Landsman. The prospect of a night at the Zamenhof does not often give rise to such anticipation.

"That's right." Landsman offers Elijah the Prophet a Broadway, and the little man takes two and tucks one into the reliquary of his breast pocket. "Hot and cold water. Licensed shammes right on the premises."

"Are you the manager, sweetness?"

Landsman can't help smiling at that. He steps aside, gesturing toward the door. "The manager's inside," he says.

But the little man just stands there getting rained on, his beard fluttering like a flag of truce. He gazes up at the faceless face of the Zamenhof, gray in the murky streetlight. A narrow pile of dirty white brick and slit windows, three or four blocks off the tawdriest stretch of Monastir

Street, the place has all the allure of a dehumidifier. Its neon sign blinks on and off, tormenting the dreams of the losers across the street at the Blackpool.

"The Zamenhof," the old man says, echoing the intermittent letters on the neon sign. "Not the Zamenhof. The Zamenhof."

Now the latke, a rookie named Netsky, comes jogging up, holding on to his round, flat, wide-brimmed patrolman's hat.

"Detective," the latke says, out of breath, and then gives the old man a squint and a nod. "Evening, Grandpa. Right, uh, Detective, sorry, I just got the call, I was hung up for a minute there." Netsky has coffee on his breath and powdered sugar on the right cuff of his blue coat. "Where's the dead yid?"

"In two-oh-eight," Landsman says, opening the door for the latke, then turning back to the old man. "Coming in, Grandpa?"

"No," Elijah says, with a hint of mild emotion that Landsman can't quite read. It might be regret, or relief, or the grim satisfaction of a man with a taste for disappointment. The flicker trapped in the old man's eyes has given way to a film of tears. "I was only curious. Thank you, Officer Landsman."

"It's Detective now," Landsman says, startled that the old man has retrieved his name. "You *remember* me, Grandpa?"

"I remember everything, darling." Elijah reaches into a hip pocket of his bleach yellow coat and takes out his pushke, a wooden casket, about the size of a box meant for index cards, painted black. On the front of the box, Hebrew words are painted: L'ERETZ YISROEL. Cut into the top of the box is a narrow slit for coins or a folded dollar bill. "A small donation?" Elijah says.

The Holy Land has never seemed more remote or unattainable than it does to a Jew of Sitka. It is on the far side of the planet, a wretched place ruled by men united only in their resolve to keep out all but a worn fistful of small-change Jews. For half a century, Arab strongmen and Muslim partisans, Persians and Egyptians, socialists and nationalists and monarchists, pan-Arabists and pan-Islamists, traditionalists and the Party of

Ali, have all sunk their teeth into Eretz Yisroel and worried it down to bone and gristle. Jerusalem is a city of blood and slogans painted on the wall, severed heads on telephone poles. Observant Jews around the world have not abandoned their hope to dwell one day in the land of Zion. But Jews have been tossed out of the joint three times now—in 586 BCE, in 70 CE, and with savage finality in 1948. It's hard even for the faithful not to feel a sense of discouragement about their chances of once again getting a foot in the door.

Landsman gets out his wallet and pokes a folded twenty into Elijah's pushke. "Lots of luck," he says.

The little man hoists his heavy valise and starts to shuffle away. Landsman reaches out and pulls at Elijah's sleeve, a question formulating in his heart, a child's question about the old wish of his people for a home. Elijah turns with a look of practiced wariness. Maybe Landsman is some kind of troublemaker. Landsman feels the question ebb away like the nicotine in his bloodstream.

"What you got in the bag, Grandpa?" Landsman says. "Looks heavy."

"It's a book."

"One book?"

"It's very big."

"Long story?"

"Very long."

"What about?"

"It's about Messiah," Elijah says. "Now please take your hand off me."

Landsman lets go. The old man straightens his back and raises his head. The clouds on his eyes blow over, and he looks angry, disdainful, and not in the least old.

"Messiah is coming," he says. It isn't quite a warning and yet somehow as a promise of redemption, it lacks a certain warmth.

"That works out well," Landsman says, jerking his thumb toward the hotel lobby. "As of tonight we have a vacancy."

Elijah looks hurt, or maybe just disgusted. He opens the black box and looks inside. He takes out the twenty-dollar bill that Landsman gave him and hands it back. Then he picks up his suitcase, settles his floppy white hat down over his head, and trudges off into the rain.

Landsman crumples the twenty and drops it into his hip pocket. He grinds his papiros under his shoe and goes into the hotel.

"Who's the nut?" Netsky says.

"They call him Elijah. He's harmless," says Tenenboym from behind the steel mesh of the reception window. "You used to see him around sometimes. Always pimping for Messiah." Tenenboym clacks a gold toothpick against his molars. "Listen, Detective, I'm not supposed to say anything. But I might as well tell you. Management is sending out a letter tomorrow."

"I can't wait to hear this," Landsman says.

"The owners sold out to a Kansas City concern."

"They're tossing us."

"Maybe," Tenenboym says. "Maybe not. Nobody's status is clear. But it's not out of the question that you might have to move out."

"Is that what it's going to say in the letter?"

Tenenboym shrugs. "The letter's all written in lawyer."

Landsman puts Netsky the latke on the front door. "Don't tell them what they heard or saw," he reminds him. "And don't give them a hard time, even if they look like they could use one."

Menashe Shpringer, the criminalist working the graveyard shift, blows into the lobby in a black coat and fur hat, with a rattling of rain. In one hand Shpringer carries a dripping umbrella. With the other he tows a chrome caddy to which his black vinyl toolbox and a plastic bin, with holes for handles, are strapped with bungee cord. Shpringer is a fireplug, his bowed legs and simian arms affixed to his neck without apparent benefit of shoulders. His face is mostly jowl and his ridged forehead looks like one of those domed beehives you see representing Industry in medieval woodcuts. The bin is blazoned with the single word EVIDENCE in blue letters.

"Are you leaving town?" Shpringer says. It's not an uncommon greeting these days. A lot of people have left town in the past couple of years, fled the District for the short roster of places that will welcome them, or that have tired of hearing about pogroms secondhand and are hoping to throw one for themselves. Landsman says that as far as he knows, he is not going anywhere. Most of the places that will take Jews require that you have a near relative living there. All of Landsman's nearest relatives are dead or facing Reversion themselves.

"Then let me say goodbye to you now, forever," Shpringer says. "Tomorrow night at this time I will be basking in the warm Saskatchewan sun."

"Saskatoon?" Landsman guesses.

"Thirty below they had today," Shpringer says. "That was the high."

"Look at it this way," Landsman says. "You could be living in this dump."

"The Zamenhof." In his memory, Shpringer pulls Landsman's file, and frowns at its contents. "That's right. Home sweet home, eh?"

"It suits me in my current style of life."

Shpringer smiles a thin smile from which almost every trace of pity has been erased.

"Which way to the dead man?" he says.

Between Vilna and Dixie

STEVE STERN AND ANDREW FURMAN

Steve Stern (b. 1947) is the author of many short-story collections and novels, including Lazar Malkin Enters Heaven *(1986) and* The Frozen Rabbi *(2010). Andrew Furman is a literary scholar and novelist whose books include* Contemporary Jewish-American Writers and the Multicultural Dilemma *(2000) and* Bitten: My Unexpected Love Affair with Florida *(2014). The following fragment of a conversation took place in 2001.*

ANDREW FURMAN: You grew up in Memphis, Tennessee, perhaps not the likeliest place for a budding Jewish-American writer to be raised. Can you describe what it was like to grow up Jewish in Memphis? Did you have a religious upbringing?

STEVE STERN: Growing up, the synagogue I attended was so divested of tradition, so progressive, that the joke was they closed on the High Holidays. No kidding, the rabbi wore ecclesiastical robes, there was an enormous pipe organ, a choir, the barest smattering of Hebrew in the liturgy. I thought I was a Methodist.

FURMAN: So it was a Reform congregation.

STERN: Extremely. Reform in the days when the idea was to actively erase any conspicuous vestiges of an old-country Jewish heritage. That's probably unfair, an exaggeration, but not much of an exaggeration. In hindsight, I suspect the impulse was to render the Southern Jews virtually invisible. If you go back to the same congregation now in its new location on the city's affluent perimeter you'll find that they've revived bar mitzvah in place of confirmation; they now have optional kippas and tallits; and the rabbi carries the Torah up and down the aisles. All these nods to tradition. I think that when the Reform movement in the South had finished doing its hatchet job on the heritage, the congregation had a kind of existential vertigo and lobbied for a return to an observance that could reinforce their identity as Jews.

FURMAN: What about the role of literature in your home when you were growing up? Were there many books, Jewish and otherwise?

STERN: We had a set of Reader's Digest condensed novels on a shelf. . . . Seriously, the house was a bit of a cultural wasteland—no literature, no music, no art.

FURMAN: I find that surprising, not about the books so much, but no music? No art?

STERN: Well, we had a television in almost every room. My father had a grocery store and got them as premiums. He'd sell so many boxes

397

of soap flakes, and they'd give him a blender, a rifle, a TV. We had TVs out the wazoo—compulsory television watching. I'd want to read a book, but they wouldn't let me. "Sit down, *The Price Is Right* is on!" "But I want to read *Anna Karenina*!"

FURMAN: Speaking of Tolstoy, how did you develop a literary consciousness growing up in this environment? How did you come to read *Anna Karenina*?

STERN: I came to books via a pretty circuitous route. I use the same analogy with regard to the way I arrived at a kind of Jewish consciousness: it was similar to how Richard Dreyfuss makes his way to that mesa in the desert in *Close Encounters of the Third Kind*. You find yourself somehow obsessed with things you've formerly had no particular relation to. I've learned to be content with irrational explanations. I feel that I was bushwhacked by literature, especially Jewish literature, "struck down on the road to Damascus." There was nothing in my upbringing that should have pointed me in that direction.

FURMAN: I asked you about your growing literary consciousness and you answered by speaking primarily to the development of your Jewish consciousness, which makes me wonder about the connection between your evolving Jewish and literary sensibilities.

STERN: Obviously there's no hard distinction between the two. I came to an appreciation of Jewishness, a term I'm more comfortable with than Judaism, since I'm not observant through books. Truthfully, I come to almost everything through books, which sometimes become for me their own primary experience. When I was a kid, I used to "lift" weights. But rather than actually lift them, I read books about weightlifting, then looked at the weights and looked in the mirror, wondering where are the washboard abs? The melon deltoids? The world led me through mysterious means to books, but the books, containing worlds, didn't always send me back to the realm of first-hand experience. How Jewish is that?

FURMAN: Which writers would you say had the most profound influence on your developing consciousness as a reader and a writer?

STERN: My literary awakening really began with the moderns—Joyce, Kafka, Woolf. Joyce's *Portrait of the Artist as a Young Man* was probably the book most responsible for prompting me to begin writing fiction. I had been writing poetry for years, mostly frivolous, semi-nonsensical stuff intended more to amuse than anything else. Then a few misguided friends began taking my doggerel seriously, a thing I'd been afraid to do myself. From there, it seemed such a small (albeit perilous) step to taking myself seriously—and that was the beginning of the awful end of innocence.

I must have been seventeen. I visited my freshman roommate's sister's boyfriend, a scholarly graduate student with an impressive library. I'd never known anyone with a personal library. Browsing, I took down a copy of *Portrait* quite by chance, and read the first page. The moo cow came down the road, and the language seemed to be evolving in grace and complexity before my very eyes. It was like a repetition of what had been happening . . . what I'd like to believe had been happening . . . in my mind for the past few years—the naive affection for language assuming a certain self-consciousness in its effort to extract significance from raw experience. Something like that. Also there was a lyrical quality that I didn't know was allowed in prose. I didn't know you could do these things—create a narrative with a language so supple and fluid. So I began by reading that book and I never looked back.

FURMAN: Some readers of your work have noted certain affinities with the great Yiddish master I. B. Singer and the Jewish-American writer Bernard Malamud. Do you recognize their influence on your work?

STERN: Certainly no writer of so-called Jewish fiction can avoid the formative influences of Singer and Malamud, try as he might. But for me it was Isaac Babel—he's the one who first beckoned me toward distinctly Jewish subjects and materials.

FURMAN: What was it about Babel's work that inspired you? When I think of, say, the stories in *Red Cavalry*, I don't immediately think of your work.

STERN: Not so much that book, which recounted Babel's great dramatic departure from his Jewish origins. More the Odessa stories, which were written later and involve a return. There I encountered the kind of compression and lyricism and the occasional violation of the normative bounds of reality that I loved most, attached to a Jewish milieu. I first read Babel on a hippie commune in Arkansas, and from where I sat—in the scrub woods lousy with scorpions and copperheads—even grinding poverty and pogroms looked good. Seriously, I found myself envying his dangerously colorful childhood—which, but for the remove of a couple of generations, might have been mine.

FURMAN: So did you feel disenfranchised, Steve, that you didn't have that horrible experience?

STERN: Of course. I thought, God, I've had to abuse myself all those years, and here's a kid who gets persecution and the nightmare of history dumped in his lap. But then he also gets community and a collective experience that gives him an automatic sense of identity, of the type that we assimilated Jews long for in our bones. Sometimes the bones long for what the mind rejects.

FURMAN: So what is your sense of your identity as a writer or as a Jew, or both?

STERN: It's tenuous. I'm always aspiring to an authenticity that can never really be mine. My subjects and materials are mostly gleaned from second- and third-hand experience, from poaching sources that only first-hand witnesses have an inherent right to. I'm always afraid that readers will sense an inauthentic impersonation.

FURMAN: Did winning the National Jewish Book Award for *The Wedding Jester* in 1999 help relieve some of your anxiety on this front?

STERN: I suppose I'll never entirely get over the sense that I've been pulling the wool over everyone's eyes. I went reluctantly to the National Jewish Book Award ceremony, half-suspecting that the whole thing was a set-up: I'd been lured there to be publicly unmasked as a fraud. I'd be asked to pay reparations.

FURMAN: The world that you write about, as you note, is by and large not the contemporary Jewish world, but the world three or four generations removed. How do you find your specific characters and their world?

STERN: I'd written a couple of books in my early thirties that surprised me by their insistence on Jewish protagonists and themes—themes that from this vantage seem only superficially explored. Meanwhile, after the obligatory years of wayward Bohemianism, I'd come back to my native Memphis. I'd been teaching English as an adjunct, when one banner afternoon I got a call from the school saying that enrollment was down, and my services would no longer be needed. About three minutes later, as these things are so often diabolically orchestrated, my agent phoned to tell me that she was getting luke-warm responses to my two books and, truth be known, she wasn't too keen on them herself. . . .

So, I'm thirty-four years old, thinking that life has essentially bottomed out, and I should now find something suitably desperate to do. So I went to the Center for Southern Folklore, run by a child-hood friend, Judy Peiser, and asked for a job. Folklore was, after all, a poor relation to literature, so maybe I could attach myself to it in some special way. Judy assigned me the tedious task of transcribing oral history interviews with the survivors of Beale Street, which was the Main Street of Black America for many years. Having grown up in suburban Memphis with no sense of or interest in the city's past, I found myself spellbound. I'm listening to stories of honky-tonks and brothels, gamblers and minstrels and riverboat roustabouts, realizing that not only did Memphis have a history, but that its history was a treasure trove—and, wouldn't you know it, there was also a Jewish component.

It seemed that romantic old Beale Street had also had a Jewish mercantile district consisting primarily of pawn shops, and between the Blacks and the Jewish shopkeepers a unique interaction had transpired. So I'm listening and growing more excited as I listen, greedy for information; because not only was my heretofore ignored Southern heritage coming alive, but that heritage had a distinctly Jewish dimension. I felt as if I'd fallen down a rabbit hole, but into Aladdin's cave. So I'm vocal in my celebration, and the Folklore Center people think: he's local, he's Jewish, he works cheap; so they made me the Ethnic Heritage Director for a project they called Lox and Grits. I was supposed to compile an archive of oral history testimonies about the Southern Jewish experience, and I began with the old pawnbrokers from Beale Street.

Of course the shops had gone the way of the rest of the street, destroyed by "urban renewal," but I located several brokers in their retirement. They kept referring to a place called the Pinch, where they had grown up. They described it as sort of an East European ghetto community plunked down on the bluff along North Main Street, intact from around the time of the great wave of immigration in the 1880s and 1890s up until about the Second World War. I'd never heard of the place while growing up, nor would I have been especially interested. But now, primed with a newfound nostalgia bordering on the rabid, I couldn't hear enough.

FURMAN: So immediately you started translating the work you were doing on the Folklore project into your own fiction?

STERN: No. In fact, I don't think I had any ambition to perform that kind of translation. I was too busy consuming information to worry about what to do with it. I was running around unearthing informants, the children of immigrants, all of them advanced in years. I was hounding them for memories, while they complained that it was too long ago: the Pinch was anyway a squalid place better left to the blight and rubble it had since become. Then the memories would start to trickle forth, and in a while the floodgates would open. Soon North Main Street began to reconstitute itself in my mind, a ghost community imposing its substance over the empty lots and boarded-up buildings. I had the sense of raising a lost city from the sea.

FURMAN: You mention how the Pinch became real for you upon con-
ducting these oral histories. I'm wondering what role you believe
your fiction now plays in making this place real, in retrieving or
re-creating the Pinch?

STERN: Clearly, I'd been looking for a home for my fiction, shopping for
a tradition. I'm aware of the irony. So many of the Jewish-American
writers of the generation before me couldn't rid themselves of
tradition fast enough. Circumscribed by their parents' Old World
values, they imbibed the heady freedom of America and asserted
their independence with a vengeance. But in some ways, I think
they threw out the baby with the bath water. With independence
came all the alienation and existential dread that had become the
(by now) hackneyed themes of the second half of the twentieth
century. In discovering the Pinch and acquainting myself with
its ghosts, I thought I saw the possibility of striking a synthesis
between past and present. Just as North Main Street embodied the
tensions between Vilna and Dixie, so could my writing combine
the flavor of Yiddishkeit with a modern sensibility. It was worth
a try. So I wrote a book of stories set on North Main Street called
Lazar Malkin Enters Heaven [1986], and the rest is (largely forgotten) history.

FURMAN: I'm wondering about ways that particular audiences have
responded to your work. People in the publishing industry—agents,
editors, reviewers. Also, let's say, Jewish readers and gentile readers.
Have you noticed any trends?

STERN: My fear is that dwelling as much with ghosts as I do can be self-
defeating. You might find that you're writing for ghosts as well, that
your audience is a kind of Jewish version of a zombie jamboree.

FURMAN: You imply that your work is largely overlooked by mainstream
readers, but I'm wondering if there's reason to be more sanguine. I
hear a lot these days about the resurgence of Yiddishkeit in America,
and I'm wondering if you feel that we are in the midst of such a
resurgence, and if your work is part of this resurgence.

STERN: I hear these rumors too. I live in the hinterlands and always have, far from any Jewish community, literary or otherwise. Maybe it's important for me to reserve the right to think of myself as an outsider—it's a romantic attitude that I cling to in my advancing senescence. Of course, I'm aware that Yiddish programs are turning up in the oddest places, a veritable epidemic, but still I'm not sanguine. I've visited the Yiddish Book Center in Amherst, several times in fact, and I'm very grateful that it exists. But when I walk into its beautiful new compound and look over into the atrium where a million Yiddish books have been gathered, I get a sinking feeling as if I were looking into an archaeological dig. To me (and I hope I'm wrong), the resurgence of Yiddish is a temporary aberration. I spoke before of the Reform Jews of the South, who got a nosebleed from their lack of Jewish identity and so began to restore the accessories of tradition. I think there's a similar impulse among the generation that's attempting quixotically, and with the best of intentions, to resurrect Yiddish. Cynthia Ozick once chastised me for my own halting study of the Yiddish language, suggesting that the very act of studying it was a measure of its moribundity. I'm afraid I'm inclined to agree.

FURMAN: I'd like to talk about some of your recurrent themes. Many of your stories seem to dramatize escape or flight. I'm thinking of stories like "The Tale of a Kite" or "Swan Song" in *The Wedding Jester* or the stunning novella, "Hyman the Magnificent," in *A Plague of Dreamers* [1994], and for that matter, "Zelik Rifkin and the Tree of Dreams" in the same book. What is it about this theme that inspires you?

STERN: I think I have a literary answer here (which is partly a cop-out) and also a more complex personal answer. Clearly, the theme of escape, of Exodus, of the flight toward redemption, is fundamentally Jewish. The biblical examples are manifold. But in the secular sphere we also have a number of models, such as the rabbi's son, Harry Houdini, the inspiration behind my story "Hyman the Magnificent." I'd argue it was no coincidence that the escape artist's popularity coincided with the great wave of immigration, in particular Jewish immigration, to this country. Here was one of the great mass exoduses in Jewish history, on a scale for which there was no precedent, with each individual involved performing his or her own personal flight to salvation. What's interesting, and powerfully ironic, is that a Jewish escape artist, performing his diverse releases from bondage, the physical corollary of a spiritual release from the material plane should have become such a universal symbol.

FURMAN: You also mentioned a personal explanation.

STERN: That one's harder to address. I suppose that for myself—and in this I think I'm far from alone—the impulse to write comes in large part from being uncomfortable in the confinement to my own skin. My peculiar discomfort fueled a yearning for escape or transcendence, and it's no secret that writing fiction is often an attempt to mythologize one's deepest yearnings. What was a turning point for me—as much of a revelation as the discovery of the Pinch—was finding that the mythologies I was fabricating had echoes in Jewish lore.

FURMAN: Can you elaborate on these parallels?

STERN: I'm kind of an armchair mystic. I read a lot about Kabbalah, mostly through the works of Gershom Scholem and his successors. Kabbalah is full of characters attempting, through various mystical disciplines, to scale the Tree of Life, to ascend from the terrestrial to the celestial. They're forever trying to draw Heaven down to Earth or raise Earth up to Heaven, to preside over the marriage of the two spheres. Witness the tale of Rabbi Akiva and his cronies storming Paradise, or Isaac Luria's beautiful theory of gathering the scattered sparks of divinity and returning them to their source. One of my first North Main Street stories was called "Lazar Malkin Enters Heaven." It is about a character who refuses to die; so the Angel of Death packs him up in a burlap sack and carries him off to Paradise alive. In my ignorance, I thought myself very clever; then I discovered that tales of characters entering Heaven alive were practically a Kabbalistic standard. In Genesis, you've got a couple of lines about Enoch: "He walked with God and was not." And that's about it, the only reference to Enoch. But that was all the Kabbalists needed. They use the Bible like a trampoline. They evolved a whole literature about Enoch, a cobbler who stitches Heaven to Earth as he sews his shoes. For his piety he's transported to Heaven alive and transformed into the archangel Metatron, the recording angel who sits at God's right side. Then there's Elijah, who never died but continues to commute between Heaven and Earth to guide lost souls. And so on. It seems to me that my stories have echoes that grow louder as they reverberate back through time, that they're much larger than me, in fact, which is a kind of vindication, a way of validating my own meshugas.

FURMAN: If we can switch gears, I want to talk about your current position as a creative writing instructor at Skidmore College. Do you feel too removed from your subject living in the pastoral environs of upstate New York? And how does the teaching of writing influence your career as a writer?

STERN: Since it hasn't existed materially for some time, the Pinch has always been a pretty portable milieu. Its location has always been mostly in my head. Truth is, after three books set there, I'd like to think I've kicked the dust of North Main Street off my heels. Now I write stories set on the Lower East Side of New York or in some Ukrainian shtetl; I blink, and they revert back to the Pinch.

FURMAN: And your teaching? How do you balance the energy that it takes to teach writing and the energy that it takes to write imaginative fiction?

STERN: I don't balance it very well. I have a good job, I like my colleagues, and the other writers at Skidmore are my family. But I love to make up stories. I've been doing it for years. I've never had a great deal of faith in myself as a writer. I've had to evade myself in order to touch the material. But when I enter a story . . . that is where I want to live. I think that's the case for every writer. And at the risk of sounding ungrateful, I confess I've always been ambivalent about the teaching of creative writing. I've never been able to take the nourishment from teaching writing that so many writers talk about, that symbiosis between the desk and the classroom. You use the same energy to teach that you do to write, and I've always feared that that energy is finite. I work hard when I teach, and I'm proud that I do it well, but I can't help resenting that the energy I expend in the endeavor is not better used in making stories.

FURMAN: What are you working on now?

STERN: I recently spent a scant three and a half years writing a novel set in the immigrant ghetto of the Lower East Side of New York. It was a book in which the Yiddish theater met the Jewish underworld, and while I was excited by the material, I never managed to breathe real life into the thing. When I tried to revise it, the book turned into something else. I'm a little reluctant to talk about work in progress, but I'll tell you that the new book was inspired by a story by I. L. Peretz called, appropriately, "Stories." In it a young man captivates a woman by spinning an exotic tale in installments. She has only contempt for him but is helplessly fascinated by the tale, which keeps her returning for more. Using Peretz's story as a trigger for my own gave me a vehicle (to mix a metaphor) for exploring the tensions between the real and the imaginary, and so forth. I like working on the book, despite my suspicion that God doesn't want me to write novels.

Stan Mack's Chronicles of Circumcision

STAN MACK

For twenty years, Stan Mack (b. 1939) published a cartoon series in The Village Voice *called "Stan Mack's Real Life Funnies," which later mutated into "True Tales." His books include* Heartbreak and Roses *(1994), with Janet Bode. For children, he has done* Where's My Cheese? *(1977) and* Ten Bears in My Bed *(1974). He is also the author and illustrator of* Janet and Me: An Illustrated Story of Love and Loss *(2004), about his relationship with his partner Janet Bode. Mack wrote and illustrated* The Story of the Jews: A 4,000-Year Adventure *(2001). The following cartoon was first published in* The American Bystander *(2018).*

PART VI

The Other Americas

די גאנצע וועלט איז איין שטאָט.

Di gantse velt iz eyn shtot.

The whole world is one town.

AMERICA IS A LOADED WORD. It refers not only to the United States, but first and foremost to two entire continents that stretch from the Arctic to the Patagonia. That the United States has appropriated the title for itself often generates discomfort elsewhere on this side of the Atlantic.

The vagaries of immigration in the nineteenth and early twentieth centuries, and a drastic, xenophobic reduction of opportunities to enter the US for European Jewish immigrants after 1924 meant that many Yiddish-speaking Jews wound up elsewhere on the continent. Vibrant Yiddish communities developed particularly in Argentina and Canada. Buenos Aires, for example, was the home of one of the most ambitious Yiddish publishing projects of all time: *Dos poylishe yidntum* [*Polish Jewry*], a 175-volume series of literary classics and original works, standard in size and bound in colorful boards, which included the first version of the book by Elie Wiesel that would become known around the world as *Night* (1956). In Montreal, meanwhile, the remarkable Jewish Public Library hosted the greatest Yiddish literary and cultural figures from around the world for spirited readings and Q&A sessions, all in the original.

Yiddish life thrived in other countries, too, including Cuba, Mexico, Brazil, Peru, Chile, Uruguay, and Colombia. This section features memoirs, essays, and stories by and about these Yiddish speakers who found homes for themselves in Canada, Mexico, and South America, and which reflect the ways in which the fate of Yiddish in the new world was tied to the different opportunities offered throughout the continent.

FURTHER READING

Alan Astro, ed., *Yiddish South of the Border: An Anthology of Latin American Yiddish Writing* (2003)

Rebecca Margolis, *Jewish Roots, Canadian Soil: Yiddish Culture in Montreal, 1905–1945* (2011)

A Room Named Ruth

RUTH BEHAR

Born in Cuba, Ruth Behar (b. 1956) is a cultural anthropologist who teaches at the University of Michigan. Her family, part Sephardic, part Ashkenazic, left the island after Fidel Castro took power. Behar has returned countless times, helping to foster Cuban–American relations. Her books include Translated Woman: Crossing the Border with Esperanza's Story *(1993),* The Vulnerable Observer: Anthropology that Breaks Your Heart *(1996),* An Island Called Home: Returning to Jewish Cuba *(2007),* Traveling Heavy: A Memory in between Journeys *(2013), and* Lucky Broken Girl *(2017). She lives in Ann Arbor, Michigan. This essay was published in 2007.*

SINCE THE TIME of Columbus's first voyage, Jewish "conversos" were present in Cuba. "Conversos" were Jews who had converted to Catholicism rather than choose expulsion from Spain in 1492. They were viewed with suspicion, because many were secret Jews who wore a Catholic mask to ward off persecution by the Inquisition. Luis de Torres, a Jewish "converso," traveled with Columbus to Cuba as a translator just in case any of the natives happened to speak Hebrew, Aramaic, or Arabic.

But the history of the Jews in Cuba as openly practicing Jews begins much later, when three distinct Jewish groups took form: American Jewish expatriates who settled in Cuba after the War of 1898, as Spanish colonial rule ended and American postcolonial domination took root; Sephardic Jews who arrived in Cuba from Turkey as early as 1904 and continued in greater numbers following the dissolution of the Ottoman Empire; and Ashkenazi Jews, largely from Poland, who came after the 1924 Immigration and Nationality Act, which imposed a quota on their immigration to the United States. Polish Jews settled in Cuba in such large numbers that Cubans assumed all Jews on the island came from Poland. The term "polaco," or Pole, became interchangeable with the word "Jew." It is the term still used in Cuba today to refer to a Jewish person, even someone of Sephardic background, or any native-born Cuban with Jewish ancestry.

The American Jews maintained American schools and hired English-speaking rabbis for their synagogue. In contrast, the Sephardic and Ashkenazi Jews from Europe came penniless. Initially many thought of Cuba as a transitory location, as "Hotel Cuba," but when it became clear that the island wasn't an easy stepping-stone to reach the United States, they began to aspire to be Cuban and viewed Cuba as their promised land. In the early years these immigrants worked as peddlers. They took their wares not only to cities, but also to towns and villages and sugar mills in the countryside, establishing a Jewish presence even in remote corners of the island.

Over time, the immigrants prospered. By 1950, about 15 percent had become wealthy merchants who owned large stores and wholesale enterprises. But the majority ran small mom-and-pop shops in Old Havana and provincial cities and towns. In a little more than three decades, the immigrants and their first-generation offspring created an impressive range of educational, social, and cultural institutions. They founded Jewish schools and Jewish newspapers, in which every ideological and religious position was represented from Zionist to Communist. Five synagogues existed in Havana. The oldest was the Chevet Ahim, built by Sephardic Jews in 1914, on a street that couldn't have been more ironically named: The Street of the Inquisitor. The larger part of the Jewish community was in Havana, but there were synagogues in Santa Clara, Camaguey, and Santiago de Cuba, and Jewish associations across the island.

In Havana, Jews were so convinced they'd landed in a safe haven, they expected to stay forever. In the mid to late 1950s, on the eve of the Revolution, they publicly displayed their desire for a permanent place on Cuban soil by building three enormous new synagogues: Adath Israel, an Orthodox synagogue, the Patronato, a Jewish community center, and the Centro Sefaradi, a Sephardic temple, completed as members uttered their last goodbyes.

When the Revolution began in 1959, most of the Jews supported Fidel Castro. My mother said that she and my father, who'd married young and become parents to me and my brother in their early twenties, were thrilled to receive a reduction in their rent. But she also recalled that her Uncle Moises, who owned real estate in Havana as well as a thriving machine supply store, wasn't happy with the revolutionary reforms. He, like other Jews with a stake in capitalist ventures, kept a nervous eye on the changes, but hung on, hoping the reforms wouldn't hit too close to his investments.

But by 1961, as more and more businesses, including mom-and-pop shops, were seized by government militia, their Jewish owners didn't hesitate any longer; they took the first plane out, many on the very day they lost their stores. The dissolution of the Jewish community in Cuba was swift, intense, like a lit candle snuffed by the wind. Of the fifteen to twenty thousand Jews who'd been in Cuba, only about two thousand chose to remain: a tenth of the Jewish community.

Suddenly it was all over: the tropical paradise was no more. Everything had to be abandoned, the dead left in their graves, the Torahs left in their synagogues, the schools, and the stores, and the homes, and everything in them, forsaken.

Although I was only a child, I was part of the mass exodus of the Jews who left Cuba after the Revolution and settled in the United States. Many went to New York and New Jersey, but most of the community landed in Miami with the other Cuban exiles, where the tropical climate made them feel more at home. Living through an unexpectedly hurried double uprooting led Jewish Cubans to think of their time in Cuba as even more enchanted than it had been. Frozen prematurely in time, they had to remake their identity as "Jubans" living in both the Jewish and the Cuban diaspora in the United States. To console themselves for their lost island, they worked doubly hard, and many achieved a level of success and wealth that would have been impossible to attain even under the best conditions in Cuba.

Very few Jewish Cubans left family behind on the island. Most left through a pattern of chain migration. As a result, the predominant attitude was not to look back. The focus was on building new lives in the United States, on striving for the prosperity of the American dream. The Cuban chapter of our diasporic wandering was over. If you looked back, like Lot's wife, you might turn into a pillar of salt.

As I grew older, I sought an outlet for my nomadic longings in the field of cultural anthropology. At first I traveled to Spain and Mexico, but I always knew that I needed to go back to Cuba and see what had become of my lost Jewish home.

When I returned to the island in 1991, it was the beginning of the "special period," a time of existential uncertainty, scarcity, and hunger. The collapse of the former Soviet Union left Cuba stranded. Soviet subsidies had supported a social welfare system that gave Cubans access to inexpensive rationed food, material goods, education, and health care. As this safety net unraveled, material conditions worsened. The Castro government started investing heavily in tourism. Luxurious tourist reserves were soon occupied by foreigners, but closed to Cubans on the island, who felt the sting of hypocrisy at how the Revolution's leaders had contradicted their goal of building an equitable society.

The economic crisis brought on such a profound moral crisis that the government felt it had no choice but to allow God and the saints to return to Cuba. In 1991 the Cuban Communist Party decreed that Party members could have religious affiliations. A year later, it was written into the Cuban constitution that the state would be secular rather than atheist. Cubans were suddenly at liberty to mix and match Jesus Christ, Karl Marx, independence leader José Martí, and Fidel Castro into their spiritual pantheon.

The door to religious freedom swung open and increasing numbers of Cubans turned to Catholicism, Protestantism, Pentecostal faiths, Masonic rituals, Judaism, and the Afro-Cuban religions of Santeria and palo monte (known as a form of ancestor worship). Religion offered Cubans another way of thinking about power and human destiny at a time of cognitive dissonance. They could carve out an alternative space to pursue new social networks and explore fresh ideas about faith and community that filled the void left by state rhetoric and policies.

To facilitate the flow of hard currency, in the summer of 1993 the US dollar, the currency of the imperialist enemy, was declared a legal currency in Cuba, to exist side by side with the Cuban peso. New hotels sprang up in tourist resorts like Varadero, and Eusebio Leal Spengler, the official historian of the city, began the project of restoring Havana, a city so fascinatingly in ruins that it has continually been likened by outside observers to Pompeii.

With the return to Cuba of both the US dollar and God, the island became safe again for Americans and soon they were arriving in droves, the curators looking for art, Ry Cooder looking for Cuban music, the undergrads looking for revolutionary hipness, the grad students looking for dissertation topics.

American Jews also started to go to Cuba in record numbers, and the island is now a favorite site for Jewish American philanthropy. Numerous "mitzvah projects" have been bestowed upon the Jews of Cuba, making it possible for members of the community to learn Hebrew and Jewish history, to undergo conversion to Judaism, to be circumcised, to celebrate bar and bat mitzvahs and Jewish weddings, to travel on all-expenses-paid group vacations to resort areas in Cuba, and to eat chicken dinners after Friday and Saturday Jewish services, which for many are the main substantive meals of the week.

Going to Cuba to see the Jews who remain there has become a touristic—anthropological—Jewish solidarity mission. Jews from around the world, but especially from the United States, want to know them, study them, photograph them, film them, interview them, help them, uplift them, share with them, dream with them, own a piece of their story, give them medicine, heal them. The very idea that Jews have survived under Communist rule in Cuba seems incredible, even miraculous.

What began for me as an intensely personal search for a lost Jewish home soon changed as I watched with admiration, but also some trepidation, as the island's Jewish community was revitalized before my eyes through the charitable support of American Jews. I wasn't alone in my quest to learn about Jewish life in Cuba. I became the anthropologist more than I wanted to be—for I was in the position of being "in the between." I was the ultimate insider and the ultimate outsider.

Caught between the old family photographs that gave me my first glimpse of a lost Cuba I couldn't remember and the anthropological obsession with seeing real people in real places, I came to feel that the best way to tell the story of the Jews of Cuba was through storytelling in words and pictures. In collaboration with the Havana-based photographer Humberto Mayol, I traveled all over Cuba searching for Jews, Humberto with his camera and I with my pen.

The Jews of Cuba, I discovered, represent Jews in extremis, Jews in an outpost of civilization, Jews who should have perished but didn't, Jews flourishing in the last of the Communist lands, Jews who still breathe the revolutionary air of Che Guevara.

These Jews on the island have little in common with the immigrant Jewish Cuban community in the United States. Jews in Cuba are largely converts, Jews by choice. Most have converted because they are Jewish on their paternal rather than maternal side (being born from a Jewish womb is a traditional requirement for being a Jew) or because they have married a person of Jewish descent. They are mixed racially and a great deal poorer than Jewish Cubans in the United States. Like all Cubans on the island, they have limited access to information, few opportunities to travel, and little hope of economic mobility.

And yet, even with scarce resources, the responsibility of the Jews who remain in Cuba is to guard the Jewish legacy and keep it from disappearing.

It is the Jews on the island today who chant from the Torahs brought eighty years ago from Poland and Turkey.

Upon them has fallen the burden of preserving the scattered bits and pieces of Jewish life, the archaeological relics that have survived: wine cups, mezuzes, a ketubah, family photographs, a tattered shirt from Auschwitz. Ida Gutstadt holding the prison shirt that belonged to her father, a Holocaust survivor.

I learn that Jews in Cuba carry with them their old photographs and passports, letters, and postcards, as if at any moment they might be asked to prove their Jewishness.

On my first visits to Cuba in the early 1990s, I'd huddle on the Sabbath in the Patronato with a handful of other congregants as pigeons flew in and out of the torn roof. By 2002, Hollywood director Steven Spielberg had visited the Jews of Cuba. While in Havana for a film festival, he asked to be shown the Jewish cemetery and the Patronato, by then newly renovated with support from the Jewish Cuban community in Miami and complete with air conditioning, a computer room, and a video screening room. It was an emotional visit for Spielberg, and before leaving he thanked the Jews of Cuba for their labor of cultural preservation.

From pigeons in the synagogue to Spielberg in the synagogue—that defines the dramatic arc of transformations I have witnessed as a traveler to Jewish Cuba.

Maybe irony must inevitably accompany any nostalgic search for home. I found more irony than I could have imagined at the Hotel Raquel, which opened its doors for business in May 2003. Located in the heart of the Spanish colonial center in Old Havana, near the cathedral, the hotel is aptly situated on Calle Amargura, Bitterness Street.

This is a prime real estate area in the emerging Cuba of the twenty-first century. Old Havana has been slated for tourist development by the industrious Eusebio Leal Spengler, who works with the state-owned company Habaguanex to reinvest tourist profits in new and unusual restoration projects. Ever since UNESCO declared Old Havana a world heritage site in 1982, providing seed money for the initial restoration of the crumbling buildings in the area, Leal has overseen the transformation of the colonial center.

According to Leal, the Hotel Raquel was built with a unique purpose: to offer a welcoming home away from home for the Jewish traveler. In particular, the aim is to attract American Jewish visitors. They have been traveling in large numbers to Cuba over the last decade and their presence has not gone unnoticed by the Cuban government.

No luxury has been spared at the Hotel Raquel, Leal tells me. The lobby has marble columns and an original nineteenth-century Italian marble statue. The dining room is set off from the rest of the lobby with dark wooden dividers topped with menorahs and Stars of David encrusted into stained-glass panels. The Garden of Eden restaurant serves potato latkes, vegetable kugel, gefilte fish, Moroccan turkey, Hungarian goulash, borsht, and matzo ball soup.

An intimate hotel with twenty-five rooms, each room is named after a biblical character or biblical place: Abraham, Sarah, Isaac, Rebecca, Esther . . . Samuel, David, Solomon . . . Sinai and Jordan. And then there is room 206, the room named Ruth.

I stay at the Hotel Raquel after it opens, when I travel to Cuba on an all-expenses-paid trip as a study leader with a group of scholars and writers. The room I occupy, of course, is the Ruth room. But I feel strange going in and out of "my room." I have to walk past rooms named for my parents, grandparents, and great-grandparents, even cousins and a great-uncle. It is simply surreal, seeing the names of family members, living and dead, posted on these hotel rooms in Havana. It's as if I've landed in a stage set for a Jewish Cuban Diasporaland.

I come to feel, and to fear, that I must give up all hope of ever recovering my lost home in Cuba. What's left for people like me, people like Lot's wife who are always looking back, is an air-conditioned room so cold I shiver each night getting into bed. A room that bears my name at the Jewish-themed hotel in Havana. A room that is mine if I am willing to pay the price. But a hotel room in Havana named Ruth wasn't my idea of the home I hoped to reclaim.

After staying in the Ruth room I learn that many women in Cuba who marry men of Jewish background and convert to Judaism take the name Ruth as their Hebrew name. I ask the Ruth in Santa Clara, the Ruth in Guantánamo, and the Ruth in Havana why they chose the name Ruth and they tell me Ruth was the first woman to convert to Judaism and they identify with her. None of these women could stay in the Ruth room, even if they could pay for it. The Cuban government doesn't allow Cuban nationals to stay in hotels built for foreign tourists. That is how irony works: I have a hotel room and the privilege of being able to come and go as I please; they have a home in Cuba, but can't go anywhere else. Mine is a strange comfort, to know that Ruth isn't just the name of a hotel room on Bitterness Street, but the name of real women who choose to live as Jews in Cuba.

After decades of minimal information and maximum disinformation about Cuba, there is now available an outpouring of material in English on every facet of Cuban life from architecture and music to politics and religion. Tourist guidebooks about Cuba can be found in the travel section of every American bookstore. Until the recent tightening of the embargo, there was a story about Cuba in the *New York Times* at least once a week. But news of Cuba continues to be in constant demand. Everyone wants to know what will happen after Fidel Castro passes on.

The numbers of Americans who will travel to Cuba in coming years are expected to grow dramatically. It has been predicted that a million American tourists will visit Cuba during the first year after the embargo is lifted. As many as five million will visit annually within five years (and the population of Cuba is only eleven million). Training courses are underway to prepare American travel agents for the anticipated stampede once US policy changes.

I have a feeling that when that time comes, even if I decide I want the Ruth room, it's going to be booked.

Flies and Little People (From a Trip to the West)

JOSEPH GOODMAN

Joseph Goodman was born in Russia in the 1860s, immigrated to the US in the 1880s, and wrote for Yiddish newspapers and magazines in the US and Canada. This essay comes from Collected Writings *(1919). Hannah Berliner Fischthal is a scholar and translator of Yiddish literature.*

I'M IN PORTAL. It is the main entrance through which Americans come into western Canada to settle on the fertile fields of Saskatchewan and Alberta—the "El Dorado" of wheat and corn.

I have been in the border town a week. The work is quite easy. I need to examine the immigrants. I understand what I have to do. What Jew does not know how to ask questions? The job would be quite pleasant if I had to examine bricks and classify pieces of wood instead of examining people with feelings. It is my duty to decide which of the many immigrants are desirable to have as future Canadian citizens and which ones should be sent back. I simply need to follow certain criteria and obey the laws. I comprehend, perhaps for the first time, that the law is not always right. It seems impossible to harness duty with feelings, law with compassion, to tie them together so that they may harmoniously pull the wagon of society . . . !

And I, a "bureaucrat," am in Portal almost a week. There are clouds on my heart and despair in my soul. I am staying in the town's only hotel. It is called a hotel, but it is simply a two-story building, cold as the North Pole in winter and hot as the upper bench in a Russian sweat bath in the summer. It is like the hell of New York in the summer, when the roguish icemen are on strike. . . .

When I left Winnipeg, it was still very cold. I thought there would be no summer. Here, however, I am roasting and burning as though I were on fire. . . . Apparently they wanted to give me quite a heated reception . . . and I got it.

The stationmaster approaches. After the usual greetings, he gives me the news that it is 106 degrees in the shade.

I answer him bluntly: "If it is too hot for you, get out of the shade!"

I could not enter the hotel because of the flies. There were flies of all kinds. In my heated fantasy, I imagined that all the assorted flies were holding a convention in Portal.

I begin to classify them, "every fly to its species." A fly is circling my ear. I cannot shoo it away. It tickles my ear; I cannot get rid of it. I drive it

425

away, but it comes back again. I conclude that it must be from the species "Agitator," a creature that annoys for no reason, a nudnik. The housefly that is always in the kitchen is obviously a female, for she is a transformation of my next-door neighbor. She goes to all the pots, smells the pudding, tastes the compote, takes a lick from all the dishes, and sticks her nose into every corner.

I consider with some respect the large fat-bellied fly, which cannot fly high because it is so heavy and stuffed. It crawls around with chutzpah, inspecting all the crumbs of food that are found on the table, and does not allow the smaller flies to get near. It doesn't give them a chance. I recognize the species "Corporation Fly," from a trust magnate. . . .

And here is a young fly, light, moving with pretty wings, with a little red curious mouth. It wants to fly. It becomes interested in a piece of flypaper. It is curious; it wants to learn. It slowly steals over to the paper, and it licks the edge, which is pleasing and sweet. It creeps a little farther, but it still stands on the edge of the paper, out of danger. Curiosity, or perhaps the desire for adventure, inspires it to go a little farther. It gets glued to the paper. No more flying. It is caught in the trap. . . .

Poor, innocent little fly. . . . For very little enjoyment, it suffered such a terrible fate. . . .

And I leave off the fly classification before I get flies on the brain. I remain sitting, waiting for the train, which should be bringing more immigrants. That will perhaps drive away the laziness that has overcome me, and perhaps also the loneliness and the boredom.

An hour later, a train from St. Paul comes and brings the usual number of immigrants, businesspeople, workers searching for a new market for their products, and also tourists searching for sensations in foreign lands.

The tourists are rich vagabonds who have no home, who shlep themselves around the world in Pullman cars or in first-class cabins of a steamship. They are an international class of people who do nothing. They used to meet often in Europe, but with the start of the war, they were forced to remain on this continent. The number of tourists on the Canadian railways has grown enormously.

I enter the observation car and contemplate the passengers. After one glance at them, I do not need to ask who they are or what they are. I classify them as easily as the flies in the hotel. . . . There is a mishmash of nationalities. Immigrants arrive from Africa, Australia, New Zealand, America, France, Russia, and England. There are young and old widows. There are married women who wait impatiently to become widows, longing to wear stylish black dresses. There is an actress who wants to marry a millionaire, and there is a millionaire's young wife who hotly desires to become an actress. There are several persons from the underworld. Those women look modest next to the half-naked, décolleté married ladies. And their men—it may be that they were just released from prison, but the other men should actually be locked up there, if justice were not so blind. . . .

There are flies, little people, more flies, Goldbugs, Silverbugs, a writer of checks, and writers of love notes. There are beauties that were bought by old men, and there are old men who were sold by pretty women.

Fie on them! Flies, flies!

Thank God that the stationmaster cannot read this. He would surely say that I am "crazy from the heat". . . .

TRANSLATED BY HANNAH BERLINER FISCHTHAL

Popocatépetl

ISAAC BERLINER

Isaac Berliner (1899–1957) emigrated from Poland to Mexico. He was a peddler and wrote for Yiddish-language newspapers. Along with Moshe Glikovsky and Yankev (aka Jacobo) Glantz, Berliner was one of the country's three most distinguished Yiddish intellectuals. He wrote Shtot fun palatsn (City of Palaces, 1936), *an expressionistic collection of poetry that was illustrated by famous muralist Diego Rivera. The following poem, about one of the volcanoes surrounding Mexico City, is part of it.*

POPOCATÉPETL

Popo—
laying stolid with a plumage of stone,
crying from your body, with a quiet scream,
are thousands of years.

in the bluish dawn of rose,
the sun hides its whitish head
with rainbow stripes,
like a hairband.

Winds—
hidden monsters in the gallop,
throwing themselves onto you, yelling as they pillage,
humming songs and whistling
from unknown lands.

what secrets,
stored in the passing of generations,
are hidden inside you?

what scars,
stapled in blood,
are engraved in individual stones?

Carry me inside your body, Popo,
stone-like,
conveying
your mysteries in my silence.

Popo—
furtive hoary giant,
the sun throws you a ray
in the darkening moments of dusk,
enlightening you fully.

I see in you now
ancient generations gone,
their blood spilled
from your vertebral column.

What plethora of travelers wandered on your silvery skin?
Have you counted their steps?

At your knees
death announces its journey,
and on your back,
this frigid, whitish inscrutability
pours . . .

TRANSLATED BY ILAN STAVANS

Bontshe Shvayg in Lethbridge

GOLDIE MORGENTALER

Goldie Morgentaler is Professor of English literature at the University of Lethbridge. She is the daughter of Chava Rosenfarb (1923–2011), a Polish Holocaust survivor who published poetry, prose, and drama in both English and Yiddish. Morgentaler has translated Rosenfarb's oeuvre with the author herself, including The Tree of Life: A Trilogy of Life in the Lodz Ghetto (2006) and Survivors: Seven Short Stories (2004).

I TEACH JEWISH LITERATURE to non-Jews. That statement may not seem very remarkable; after all, I also teach Victorian literature to non-Victorians and nineteenth-century literature to students born in the late twentieth century. From a pedagogical point of view, how much difference is there?

Let me try to answer this in a roundabout way, beginning with two histories: my own and that of Lethbridge, Alberta. Lethbridge is a small city of 80,000, spectacularly located within sight of the Rockies in the southern part of what has been, until the recent economic downturn, the richest province in Canada. I came to Lethbridge in 1997, armed with a PhD on Dickens, to teach nineteenth-century British and American literature. I also had an MA in Jewish studies and had taught Yiddish and published on Yiddish literature, but my background in Jewish studies seemed to have no relevance to my work at the University of Lethbridge. My courses focused solely on canonical British and American literature, never anything Jewish.

This was my fault. I was afraid.

In eastern Canada, Albertans are often stereotyped as rednecks, partly perhaps out of jealousy at their oil wealth and partly because agriculture—especially cattle farming—is the major source, next to oil, of the province's wealth. Alberta is also by far the most conservative Canadian province, as well as the most religious. And southern Alberta is the Canadian Bible Belt, home to a large variety of denominations and sects: the Hutterites, the Mennonites, the Seventh-Day Adventists. The Catholic Church and the Dutch Reformed Church are strong presences in Lethbridge, and even stronger is the Mormon Church. The University of Lethbridge began life as a Mormon institution.

I am a Montrealer. My understanding of Alberta had been shaped by the province's election of several Social Credit governments in the 1970s and by the Keegstra case of the 1980s. Social Credit was a political and economic movement that was ideologically hostile to Jews; the Keegstra case concerned Jim Keegstra, a high school teacher in Eckville, Alberta, who was convicted of a hate crime after teaching, among other things, that the Holocaust was a fabrication. The case caused an uproar and left eastern Canadian Jews like me with the impression that Alberta was a rural no-man's land of anti-Jewish hostility.

So when I arrived in Lethbridge in the late 1990s I was convinced that Jewish culture was unwelcome, or at best not of great interest, to the vast majority of Albertans, and hence to the majority of students at the University of Lethbridge. This conviction was reinforced by the small number of Jews in Lethbridge itself: even in the university, the Jewish professors could be counted on the fingers of one hand. Lethbridge has, in fact, been my first experience of living in a community where there are hardly any Jews.

It was not always so. Lethbridge was once home to quite a large Jewish community. Michael Wex, the best-selling author of several books on Yiddish, grew up in Lethbridge and wrote about the experience in a book called *Shlepping the Exile*. But from the 1970s on the Jewish community declined precipitously, leaving the city with a minuscule Jewish presence and a synagogue that barely has a congregation.

For all these reasons, I thought a full-term course on Jewish literature would not draw students or would draw the wrong kind of students. Still, I was tempted.

I tested the waters by teaching I. L. Peretz's classic story "Bontshe Shvayg" to my first-year introductory literature class. Set in the nineteenth century during czarist times, "Bontshe Shvayg" is the story of a man whose life is one long narrative of suffering and injustice, from the moment the moyel's hand slips during his circumcision to the day that he dies unknown and unmourned in the workhouse and is buried in an unmarked pauper's grave. Bontshe's work as a porter carrying heavy loads often goes unpaid. His only child dies, his wife runs off with another man. Spat upon and despised, he suffers endless injury, humiliation, and injustice—yet he never complains, never raises his voice against God or man. On Earth nobody notices his passing. But in Heaven there is a joyful to-do when Bontshe's soul ascends after his death, because here is

433

that rare thing: a genuinely saintly soul. During the obligatory trial to see if he should be allowed into Heaven, the prosecuting angel has nothing to say against Bontshe; not even the smallest sin can be laid to his account. Therefore, the voice of God decrees that Bontshe's soul should have whatever it desires; he has only to ask and it will be given. With all the vast resources of Heaven his for the asking, what is Bontshe's request? Nothing but a roll with butter every morning. The story ends with the heavenly prosecutor laughing.

The students understood the story well enough, but many understood it in Christian terms. Certainly the story is a kind of parable, and a number of interpretations are possible. But what is not open to interpretation is the fact that Bontshe is Jewish. The story mentions his circumcision, his bar mitzvah, and the fact that he is forced by anti-Semitic regulations to walk in the gutter while carrying his loads rather than on the sidewalks. Yet time and again when I have given students this story to read, some have told me that Bontshe is literally the figure of Jesus, or that he is a symbol of Christ. One student even decided that Bontshe Shvayg is simply a Russian version of the name Jesus Christ.

The connection between submission and sanctity, which is at the heart of this story, also caused dissent and confusion among my students. Peretz's story clearly questions the religious assumption that a life lived without complaint will be rewarded in Heaven. This concept is common to both Judaism and Christianity. But if I suggested to my students that there is a saintly aspect to Bontshe's passivity they resisted the notion, because in Christianity saintliness is often attached to performing miracles and Bontshe performs none. Even the term "Christian" caused problems, because, as I quickly learned, certain branches of Protestantism do not recognize Catholics as Christians.

These kinds of confusions and misapprehensions—my own and my students'—gave me pause. If I taught an entire course on this material, I would have to start from scratch, explaining the most basic differences between Judaism and Christianity. When, in 2006, I finally decided to give it a try—first having to persuade the curriculum committee to allow

Yiddish literature in translation to be taught in the English department, given that no one in any other department had the expertise—compiling the syllabus proved far more complex than preparing a Victorian literature course.

How does one teach Yiddish literature without teaching something about the history of the countries in which it was created—mainly Poland, Ukraine, Russia—and the history of the Jews in those countries? How does one teach Jewish literature of the nineteenth and twentieth centuries without teaching about anti-Semitism, which was pervasive throughout this region at this time and sanctioned by the government? How many references to the persecution of the Jews in Eastern Europe are too many references? There is no way to avoid the topic of suffering. But how much gloom is too much gloom? How many pogrom stories should one teach? How many novels about the Holocaust?

Yiddish literature is permeated by unexplained references to Jewish practices and rituals, to biblical liturgy, and to Ashkenazic folk beliefs, references that are never explained because the authors assumed that their readers knew what they meant. Thus Bontshe Shvayg is never directly identified as Jewish: references to circumcision and bar mitzvah make his nationality and religion clear, but only if a reader knows that these are Jewish practices. Similarly, in Lamed Shapiro's pogrom story "The Cross," it is crucially important that the female protagonist, Minna, is not Jewish, but the text never overtly states that she is a Russian gentile. To Yiddish readers, Minna's blue eyes and light-colored hair would have given this fact away. Also, Minna's father is a commissar in the tsarist government, and in an anti-Semitic society like prerevolutionary Russia no Jew would ever have held so high a position. But in order to know this, one would need to know the history of the Jews in Russia.

When I finally did start teaching the class, I was in for a few surprises. Not only had most of my students never heard the word "pogrom," they were also unaware of the long history of Jewish persecution in Europe. Most of them thought that anti-Semitism began and ended with the Holocaust. My assumption that this history was widely known—gleaned from my

435

early years as a student at the Jewish People's School in Montreal and from having lived much of my life in large Jewish communities—proved to be totally unfounded. Most non-Jews, I have come to realize—and not just my young Albertan students—know little about the history of the Jews. Nor are they necessarily aware of anti-Semitism's roots in Christianity. From Sholem Aleichem to Peretz and beyond, canonical Yiddish literature does not mince words when it comes to identifying the tormentors of Jews as Christians.

I began the course with the Tevye stories by Sholem Aleichem, hoping that the students would be familiar with them from the musical *Fiddler on the Roof*. Some of the problems I had anticipated solved themselves. I had worried that the many biblical and Hebraic allusions in the text might put off the students and that I would have to spend most of the class time explaining these. To my delight, Sholem Aleichem and Tevye proved that good literature is good literature: despite being unsure of the meaning of certain words and customs, the students related well to the stories' generational conflicts. The most interesting snag revolved around an issue of cultural specificity.

Sholem Aleichem's Tevye stories are set in Ukraine during tsarist times. Each one of Tevye's three eldest daughters rebels against her father in a different way, and all the rebellions revolve around marriage. The rebellion of the first two daughters is relatively mild, and Tevye forgives them with only minor qualms. But the third daughter, Chava, marries a gentile. In order to do this, she is forced by Russian law to convert to Christianity. This Tevye cannot forgive.

The fact that he cannot forgive her, that in accordance with Jewish law he pronounces her dead and forbids his wife and children to mention her name again, goes against the grain of every modern liberal impulse. Why should Chava not marry the man she loves? Why must she sacrifice her father's love and the love of her family in order to do so? When I ask my students if Tevye is right not to forgive Chava, they invariably say no. In arguing with her father, Chava in fact makes a very strong case for loving someone without regard to their ethnic or religious origin. It is hard not to agree with her, especially from the perspective of tolerant, liberal-minded, multiracial, twenty-first-century Canada.

But in tsarist Russia, marrying outside the faith meant literally throwing in your lot with the oppressor. The American-Jewish writers who transmuted Sholem Aleichem's Tevye stories into *Fiddler on the Roof* changed the plot in order to make the Christians in this episode more sympathetic: Chava's gentile husband accompanies her and her family into exile. But in Sholem Aleichem's original, Chava leaves her husband when her family is thrown out of their home, choosing to follow her family into exile rather than stay in her marriage. Only then does her father forgive her. The implication is clear: intermarriage, in a setting in which Jews are persecuted, constitutes betrayal.

Even without the complication of anti-Semitism, Chava's story raises troubling questions for a minority group that worries constantly about the dangers posed by assimilation. How does a minority culture maintain itself if it tolerates intermarriage? Will intermarriage with members of the dominant culture lead to the eventual extinction of the group as a whole? Are both the religion and the culture more secure, ironically, in countries where Jews are persecuted or isolated, because there they are less likely to merge with the mainstream?

What makes Jewish literature universal is the fact that these kinds of questions can be generalized to non-Jewish minority literatures as well. Studying what is specific to one culture is often the first step toward understanding many cultures. And that, finally, is the best reason, I think, for studying literature altogether.

The first time I taught the Jewish literature course was at the second-year level and it drew fourteen students, not one of whom was Jewish. I soon realized that the course needed to be taught at a more advanced level and offered it as a third-year course. To my great surprise and delight, it drew thirty students—again, not one was Jewish. Both times the students were curious and wished to expand their horizons rather than simply fulfill their credit requirements. Some were seeking to supplement their Religious Studies classes at the university and had a little previous knowledge. Some came from strongly Christian backgrounds and were not confused by references in the texts to biblical figures; others had no religious education whatsoever. I only once had a student who seemed to enjoy baiting me with anti-Jewish remarks, but he seldom came to class and eventually dropped out. For the most part, all the students seemed interested and engaged, with the result that these became my favorite classes to teach.

I did occasionally get strange comments and questions. For instance: if a man is already circumcised and he wants to convert to Judaism, must he be circumcised a little more? One student wrote in a paper that in Judaism death is an unknown part of the religion. Another, writing on I. B. Singer's "Yentl the Yeshiva Boy," formulated the plot complication this way: "Unfortunately, Yentl's sex prevents her from openly studying the sacred texts with trained professionals." The term "trained professionals" for learned rabbis and yeshiva scholars seems very funny to me, although, of course, the statement is not inaccurate.

But these kinds of bloopers and misunderstandings are common to undergraduates of all backgrounds. I don't think it mattered that my students were not Jewish. Yes, I did spend a great deal of class time explaining details I might have been tempted to pass over with Jewish students. And I occasionally passed over things I should have explained because I assumed they were widely known—such as what matzo is. Yet I was constantly impressed that many of my advanced students knew more than I expected.

In the end it does not matter whether students are Jewish or not Jewish. What matters is that they be sympathetic to another point of view, that they be open to a reality radically different from their own. And it is the function of literature—and of teaching—to bridge the gap between realities.

The Yiddish Terrorist

CLAUDIA MIRELSTEIN

Claudia Mirelstein (b. 1974) is a journalist, novelist, and teacher. She teaches at the Universidad de Los Andes. Her books include Dioses sin seguidores (Gods without Followers, 2011), Amor y paz (Love and Peace, 2015), *and* Las tormentas del corazón (The Heart's Torments, 2017). *Bernard Levinson is a translator living in Brooklyn. He has rendered into English books by Piedad Bonnett, Orietta Lozano, and Lucy Bonifaz.*

Ministry of Foreign Affairs
Interrogation Dossier #79436-AF12
Name: Ina Betancourt Palacio
Place and Date of Birth: Bogotá, December 25, 1961
Citizenship: Colombian and French.
Partial account recorded on July 15, 2008 with emphasis to FARC terrorist
    Jardiel Poncela:*

MY NAME IS Ina Betancourt Palacio. In total, I was in bondage for over six years: I was kidnapped on February 18, 2002; my release took place on July 2, 2008. In response to your question, yes, I speak Yiddish to my son Jorge Tata Poncela Betancourt.

Though I don't say it in public because I feel regretful, I come from the Colombian upper class. My mother was gorgeous; this explains why she was a beauty queen. But the family wasn't into distractions; it was involved in politics. My father was Foreign Minister and my mother a congresswoman who worked in shelters. When Luis Carlos Galán, the candidate for Colombia's president, was assassinated in 1989, she was right behind him.

Since I was little, I was involved in environmental issues. Unlike my mother, I knew the biggest challenge facing Colombia was the decimation of its natural resources. I studied political science at the Sorbonne. In 1983, I married a French citizen, Fabrice Debayle. We lived in Paris for years. Our two children, Laurent and Margaret, were born there. Debayle and I divorced in 1994, which is when I returned to Colombia. For a while, I worked for the Ministry of Finance.

I was a senator and anti-corruption activist before I ran as a presidential candidate in 2002 with the Partido Verde Oxígeno, also known as *Green*. My autobiography appeared the year prior. It is called *Las turbulencias del corazón* (in English, *Green Is the Color of Hope* [2004]).

---

* [. . .] denotes redacted segment.

I was scheduled to visit the demilitarized zone in a campaign stint. There were a number of roadblocks. My campaign manager suggested I take a helicopter. I agreed but there were rumors the FARC (Revolutionary Armed Forces of Colombia) had taken over the airport from where copters took off and landed. I chose to go on a van from Florencia to San Vicente del Caguán. I was kidnapped about one hour into the trip.

The FARC blindfolded me, my driver, and two other people in the van. They put us in a school bus. We drove for many hours. I know we arrived in the jungle because of the humidity. I don't know the exact location.

I was put in an empty room alone. When the blindfold was taken off, I realized it was an abandoned school classroom. It must have been in the demilitarized zone. I stayed there for several weeks. They later transported me to several other undisclosed locations, always in the jungle. . . .

My captors didn't communicate with me their demands. I didn't even know if they were in touch with the authorities or with my family. I was treated humanely, though. They fed me at regular hours: breakfast, lunch, and dinner. Once a week, I was able to shower in the bathroom of a private home.

The wave of so-called "express kidnappings" made me believe I would be ransomed soon. Of course, I was also a prominent political figure, which to me meant all arrangements for my freedom would need to take place either secretly with the police or out in the open, with the media fully involved. I preferred the former but I didn't have a choice.

I later found out the government tried to rescue me in 2003. The French government—I have a French passport—was involved in the endeavor. I didn't know anything at the time. But that's about when the FARC forced me to make a video in which I called for the government to surrender and the FARC to assume power. Although I myself was aware of how elusive these demands were, I faked it. I had learned how to fake while working in the Ministry of Finance.

It took a bit for me to realize my high profile had complicated any possibility of dialogue . . . Andrés Pastrana was president when I was taken away. When Álvaro Uribe was elected, his right-wing policies complicated his dialogue with the FARC.

It might have been a year after the kidnapping, maybe sixteen months, when I met Jardiel Poncela. I don't know if he was Yukpa, Bora, or Witoto. He spoke an indigenous language. At least at the beginning.

He was around twenty-five years of age. Handsome, oily hair, in aboriginal clothes. Always well-kept. He had a rifle at his side whenever he was in charge of guarding me. I assume his orders were to make sure I didn't escape. I wouldn't have been able to. I didn't know my way through the jungle. And I was friends with Iñaki (I don't remember his last name), the Vasque photographer. He was brought to the location where I was kept during my second year in bondage.

It wasn't uncommon to talk to our captors; I not only communicated with Jardiel but with several others, Raquel Timaña among them.

Unlike the emotions I experienced with several other captors, I was never intimidated by Jardiel. On the contrary, our exchanges were always friendly, even jovial. Since the beginning, he was cordial—to a fault. He would want to make my stay pleasant, as if he didn't agree with the FARC ideology. But he was a soldier through and through. He would sometimes describe, in frightening detail, military operations he participated in. Or call them terrorist acts: he and his squadron invaded villages looking to recruit young men. He said that when they left the place, there would be several corpses left behind on the sidewalk: "Blood shines when it spills."

I was struck by his writing, too. Every third night, as he was on guard outside my room, he would write in his diary. I asked him about it. He said his involvement with the FARC had changed his life. He understood why Colombia needed change. He said he wasn't a *Green*, like me, but he loved the forest. It was full of spirits. Rivers, every tree, every stone had its own character, its voice. In the middle of the night, if you were quiet you could hear them converse. The amount of wisdom you would acquire would be invaluable. This was especially true during storms because all elements in the jungle become aroused then. "The resin of trees is like semen," he said.

Jardiel's handwriting was indecipherable to me. I assumed he had learned those letters among his tribesmen.

One day, after Jardiel served me breakfast—this wasn't unusual, since my health was a concern to my captors—he started talking in a way I didn't understand. Not that the topics were secret. He had been given orders not to disclose any sensitive information with me. What made the conversation intriguing was that his words sounded like those of a friend I had in childhood, Estersita Rabinovich. Not her per se but her parents and especially her abuelo.

I asked Jardiel what he was saying. I needed help.

"It's in Yiddish!"

I was surprised.

"You speak that language? How did you learn it?"

"We don't speak it among the Quayuubu. It was never spoken by our ancestors. Great Master Quimbaya made his announcements in Quayuubusé."

He paused. Then he told me about Tata Grabinsky.

"He came to visit us one evening. He was old. He said he had a message for us. Most of the tribe ignored him. But I got to talk to him and became his friend. Tata Grabinsky said it was time to resist the colonizers. Colombia was at a crossroads. The aristocrats were taking everything for themselves. The people needed to reclaim what was theirs. He said he had been a businessman in Bogotá but had given up everything to come to the jungle and join the struggle. . . . He spoke to me in Yiddish. I didn't understand anything at first."

In 2006, the French government made a proposal to the FARC for the exchange of prisoners, including me. Foreign Minister Philippe Douste-Blazy stated that it was "up to the Revolutionary Armed Forces of Colombia to show they were serious about releasing former Colombian presidential candidate Ina Betancourt and other detainees."

I was occasionally allowed to listen to radio or watch TV in a restaurant less than a kilometer from where I was kept imprisoned. Those images sometimes made me think of my candidacy. I'm not sure I still want to be president of Colombia.

At any rate, by then my relationship with Jardiel had matured. He had figured out ways to be assigned to me. On a regular day, we would spend five or six hours together. Naturally, we fell in love.

I taught him how to speak French and he taught me Yiddish. He said he and his FARC colleagues weren't terrorists, even though the Colombian government frequently portrayed them that way.

He described how Tata Grabinsky—I believe he was from Uruguay, or perhaps Chile—had been a rabbi. He was involved in arms sales in various countries, including to the Nicaraguan Contras. Jardiel said Tata Grabinsky didn't see any conflict between war and faith. He would pray three times a day. Jardiel said he had never seen a Jew recite liturgy in his life before. He also said that Tata Grabinsky was involved in helping Jews in Bogotá, Caracas, and other cities organize as an army in case the governments of those countries didn't help when there was an anti-Jewish attack.

In July 2007, I saw my daughter Margaret on TV. I became sentimental when I saw her. She was in a press conference in which she announced that the French Embassy in Colombia was in conversations with the FARC because the government wasn't truly collaborating in my release.

I wanted to tell Margaret that I was alive. More than alive, actually. I was pregnant with a baby who would be born in two or three months.

Yes, I gave birth with a midwife. It might have been a member of the FARC too. It was painful. I had the experience of my previous two children, which means I knew what to expect.

[. . .]

I'm sorry: I can't give more specific information about where Jardiel had been trained.

[. . .]

The baby was asleep when one evening, as all other captors were away, Jardiel said he wanted to take Jorgito away for a few days. I was frightened. He told me not to be scared. He wanted to bring him to his tribesmen. It was important that the baby was introduced to the tribe's tradition. Jardiel announced: "To know your past is to sense your future."

That took a total of five days. Jardiel requested permission for me to accompany him but obviously it was denied.

I prepared the baby as best I could. Jardiel got someone to feed him. They were away four days and three nights. I was in a state of desperation because I was sure the FARC had taken my precious son from me. That was a far stronger torment than anything I myself suffered during my captivity. . . .

One of those nights, I dreamed in Yiddish. I was in my house in Bogotá. My parents were with me. They spoke but I didn't hear them. I was annoyed.

When they came back, my sense of relief was enormous. I was joyful to see Jorgito. He had lost almost a pound but he was fine. According to Jardiel, a tribesman had given him nutrients.

It isn't true, as some media outlets have suggested, that Jardiel was an Israeli agent. He has nothing to do with the Mossad. This is said because people think Yiddish is the same as Hebrew.

Sometime later—I don't know how long, though—French president Nicolas Sarkozy personally offered to travel to the Colombian jungle to negotiate with the FARC. I confess that by then, I wasn't sure I wanted to leave. A long time had gone by. I felt close to Jardiel. He was a good father to Jorgito.

We spoke mostly in Yiddish to the boy. It was bizarre. We did it for one single reason: we felt so close to one another, we wanted to feel we were alone in the world. A bit like Robinson Crusoe.

How would my family in Bogotá react when they found out I had a baby at forty-six? And that my son was Jewish?

I don't believe Jardiel Poncela understood the degree with which his actions caused harm to others. He killed people but not because he hated them. He believed it was a means to a better future. He wanted Jorgito to also want a better life for everyone.

Along with fourteen other captives (I didn't know them all), I was rescued on July 2 in what came to be known as Operación Jacque. As Minister of Defense Juan Manuel Santos announced, a series of military operatives—the media is calling them "spies"--had infiltrated the FARC.

The captives, including four Europeans (Jacques Pointiere and Genevieve Bouchet from France, Luiggi Damico from Italy, and Iñaki from Spain) and three US contractors (Thomas Howes, Marc Gonsalves, and Keith Strasell), were in several different locations. By a previously agreed time, the FARC "spies" managed to bring every captive to the same location.

We were all asleep when it happened. A battalion of soldiers arrived at dawn. It must have been around 5:30 a.m. Our guards, including Jardiel, were asleep too. The soldiers knew who was where. They shot them point blank. Jardiel was among them.

I woke up sweating. I thought it was a nightmare. Fortunately, I was able to get Jorge, who was two and a half years old at the time. I held him tightly. My son was rescued with me.

In the jungle, I learned to listen to trees, to follow the light rivers reflect, to be aware of smells. The quiet of the jungle is precious. Modern civilization has forgotten what it means to live in harmony with other creatures.

The Partido Verde Oxígeno is in disarray. I hope it reconfigures itself one day.

My mother and father claim I was raped and the result is Jorgito. It's a lie! My heart breaks apart when thinking Jorge won't have vivid memories of his father. The government said to me yesterday that they recovered Jardiel's notebook "with his scribbles." I demand to have it back.

TRANSLATED BY BERNARD LEVINSON

A Yidisher Bokher in Mexique

ILAN STAVANS

Ilan Stavans (b. 1961), a literary scholar, essayist, and translator, grew up speaking Yiddish and Spanish in Mexico. An immigrant to the United States in the mid-eighties, he teaches at Amherst College. His books include the memoir On Borrowed Words: A Memoir of Language *(2001), the volume of stories* The Disappearance *(2007), the graphic novel* El Iluminado *(2012), and the travel book* The Seventh Heaven: Travels through Jewish Latin America *(2019). His work, adapted into film, theater, and radio, has been translated into multiple languages. He lives in Amherst, Massachusetts.*

ATTENDING A YIDDISH DAY SCHOOL in Mexico, as I did from kindergarten to high school, might seem—I'm aware—like an anachronism. How on earth did *mame-loshn* (Yiddish) thrive in such an unexpected place? Yet for the thousands of students like me at the Alte Yidishe Shule, there was nothing strange about it. Ours was a private school built by indigent Jews, largely Bundists, from shtetlekh and urban centers in the Pale of Settlement who immigrated to the New World seeking a new life. Mexico welcomed them with open arms, while other countries closed the doors. Mexico promised them freedom. The Jews, in turn, were eager to prosper.

The curriculum had two tracks: one in Yiddish, the other in Spanish. The division was straightforward: in Yiddish we learned about our Jewishness; in Spanish, about our Mexicanness. To our teachers, there was no clash, no division, no forking path between these identities. Why opt between them if you could choose both?

Such was the pride in learning that our shule was like a kheyder, a traditional elementary school, or maybe even a yeshive, a Talmudic academy, except that religion was replaced by culture. I don't remember ever having a discussion about my beliefs in God in class. In fact, at a rather early age, I, along with several of my friends, declared ourselves agnostic. Not that it mattered. Since a bunch of our teachers were Holocaust survivors, I suspect they sympathized, having also rebelled against a God who didn't appear to have done much to protect his people in recent times. I don't remember ever seeing a prayer book at school. But maybe I'm misrepresenting them and some of the teachers were believers. In any case, they offered us the same thing Mexico had granted them: freedom.

I hardly remember reading the Torah in school. On the rare occasion we did, it was always as a series of mythical stories: a plotline with characters, good and evil, who behave all the time like the rest of us, trying to find meaning in life when none is available. Years later, when I was already an adult, I remember feeling struck by the religious emphasis in just about every episode. How could I have missed it? My gut feeling is that our teachers were ambivalent about it, too. They liked storytelling, and that's what they stressed. Today I'm grateful to them for introducing me to the Bible not as a Halakhic (legal) manual but as a depository of collective memory. For that reason, my relationship with it isn't tyrannical.

In total, I had approximately eight years of Yiddish at the Alte Yidishe Shule. This formative education provided me not only with the language skills I needed to read the works of Mendele Moykher Sforim, Sholem Aleichem, Yitskhok Leybush Peretz, and the Singer brothers in the original; it also taught me that a life in two languages is a life experienced twice.

At some point in my middle school years there was a change of zeitgeist among Mexican Jews. It was the seventies. Israel was triumphant after the Yom Kippur War. It suddenly became obvious to parents, teachers, and administrators that Hebrew, not Yiddish, needed to be the school's focus. So they started bringing shlikhim (emissaries from Israel), whose assignment it was to train us in the language of Hayim Nahman Bialik and Shmuel Yosef Agnon. To say we began to learn loshn-koydesh (the holy tongue) would be a mistake, for these pedagogical Israeli ambassadors also didn't see religion as their legacy. Be that as it may, the change was dramatic: Yiddish was pushed to a second tier; it became a second-class language, a thing of the past, in a school built on the premise that *mame-loshn* was what made us Jewish.

I wasn't alone in feeling uncomfortable. Not that I didn't like Israel. I had family there. I wanted one day to travel to Jerusalem, to appreciate, with my own eyes, how Jews had transformed the desert. But I resented the way Yiddish was displaced. And that, too, became a lesson, for I understood that a language is a depository of cultural capital. As soon as that capital loses value, the language becomes passé.

After high school, I indeed traveled to the Middle East, then to Europe and Africa. It would take several years for me to recognize the value of the education I had received in Mexico. Since Yiddish had been ostracized by my elders, I relegated it to a remote place of my mind.

Spanish became my principal means of communication, followed by English, which I learned when I immigrated to the United States in the mid-eighties. Today, that equation has been reversed.

It was only when I was a newly arrived Mexican immigrant in New York that I came to terms with Yiddish. It happened in a rather unexpected way, as I became exposed to the mixing of Spanish and English (called Spanglish today) in the subway and on the street, on TV, and on the radio. At first that barbaric hybrid, neither here nor there, made me cringe. My beloved Spanish language was being contaminated by an onslaught of Anglicisms. Should I do something to stop the pollution? However, I soon came to recognize that "a new Yiddish" was emerging in the United States, this time among Latinos, a vehicle of communication that depended on jazzy, never-ending code switching, just as Yiddish had done between Hebrew and German plus a variety of Slavic tongues.

Yiddish automatically regained a dominant place for me. I not only wanted to reclaim its status, for me and others, but also to study its history, its evolution, in order to measure the potential of Spanglish.

Nowadays Yiddish is an essential component of the way I look at the world. I use it to communicate with my mother and other relatives, I translate from it into Spanish and English, and I constantly introduce it in the classroom in courses dealing with the transformation of language and with the shaping of identities. I have a collection of Yiddish lexicons from which I draw whenever I write about the Darwinian way in which words go in and out of fashion.

And, with regularity, I dream in Yiddish. In one recurrent dream, a teacher of mine from Di Alte Yidishe Shule insists I still haven't submitted last week's homework. I tell her I've been working on it. "Es kumt," I assure her.

Camacho's Wedding Feast

ALBERTO GERCHUNOFF

Alberto Gerchunoff (1883–1950) is considered the founder of Jewish Latin American literature. He switched from Yiddish to Spanish after his immigration from Ukraine to Argentina, where he became a writer for La Nación *and other newspapers. Jorge Luis Borges considered him a mentor. Set at the turn of the twentieth century in Rajil, a shtetl-like agricultural town in La Pampa, this lyrical story, first published as part of* The Jewish Gauchos *(1910), evokes the often explosive relationship between gentiles and Jews in the Southern Hemisphere. It fuses the universal theme of the stolen bride with a narrative voice and incident borrowed from* Don Quixote. *Through the tale's folkloristic tone, which finds pleasure in describing the details of pastoral life as well as Jewish rituals and tradition, the Russian-born author, considered the grandfather of Jewish Latin American literature, advances his ill-fated view of Argentina as the true Promised Land. Prudencio de Pereda was the author of three novels,* All the Girls We Loved *(1948),* Fiesta *(1953), and* Windmills in Brooklyn *(1960), and the translator of Alberto Gerchunoff's* Jewish Gauchos of the Pampas *(1959).*

FOR TWO WEEKS NOW, the people of the entire district had been expectantly waiting for Pascual Liske's wedding day. Pascual was the rich Liskes' son. The family lived in Espindola and, naturally enough, the respectable people of the colonies were looking forward to the ceremony and feast. To judge by the early signs, the feast was to be exceptional. It was well-known in Rajil that the groom's family had purchased eight demijohns of wine, a barrel of beer, and numerous bottles of soft drinks. Kelner's wife had discovered this when she happened to come on the Liskes' cart, stopped near the breakwater. The reins had broken, and the Liskes' hired man was working frantically to replace them.

"The soft drinks were rose colored," she told the neighbors. "Yes!" she said, looking directly at the doubting shochet's wife. "Yes, they were rose colored, and each bottle had a waxen seal on it."

Everyone agreed old man Liske's fortune could stand that kind of spending.

In addition to the original land and oxen that he'd gotten from the administration, Liske had many cows and horses. Last year's harvest alone had brought him thousands of pesos, and he could well afford to marry off his son in style without touching his principal.

Everyone further agreed that the bride deserved this kind of a wedding. Raquel was one of the most beautiful girls in the district, if not in the whole world. She was tall, with straw-blond hair so fine and full it suggested mist; her eyes were so blue they made one's breath catch. She was tall and lithe, but her simple print dresses showed the full curving loveliness of a beautiful body. An air of shyness and a certain peevishness became her because they seemed to protect her loveliness.

Many of the colonists had tried to win her—the haughty young clerk of the administration as well as all the young men in Villaguay and thereabouts, but none had achieved a sympathetic response. Pascual Liske had been the most persistent of these suitors, but certainly not the most favored, at first. In spite of his perseverance and his gifts, Raquel did not like him. She felt depressed and bored because Pascual never spoke of anything but seedlings, livestock, and harvests. The only young man she had seemed to favor was a young admirer from the San Gregorio colony, Gabriel Camacho. She had gone out dancing with him during the many times he used to come to visit.

Her family had insisted she accept Pascual and the marriage had been arranged.

On the day of the feast, the invited families had gathered at the breakwater before Espindola. A long line of carts, crowded with men and women, was pointed toward the colony. It was a spring afternoon, and the flowering country looked beautiful in the lowering rays of the sun. Young men rode up and down the line on their spirited ponies, calling and signaling to the girls when the mothers were looking elsewhere. In their efforts to catch a girl's eye, they set their ponies to capering in true gaucho style. In their eagerness, some even proposed races and other contests.

Russian and Jewish songs were being sung in all parts of the caravan, the voices fresh and happy. At other points, the songs of this, their new country, could be heard being sung in a language that few understood.

At last, the caravan moved into the village. The long line of heavy carts, being gently pulled by the oxen, had the look of a primitive procession. The carts stopped at different houses, and the visitors went inside to finish their preparations. Then, at the appointed time, all the invited guests came out together and began to make their way to the groom's house.

Arriving at the Liskes', they found that rumors of the fabulous preparations had not been exaggerated. A wide pavilion stood facing the house with decorative lanterns hanging inside on high poles, masked by flowered branches. Under the canvas roof were long tables covered with white cloths and countless covered dishes and bowls that the flies buzzed about hopelessly. Old Liske wore his black velvet frock coat—a relic of his prosperous years in Bessarabia—as well as a newly added silk scarf of yellow, streaked with blue. With hands in his pockets, he moved from group to group, being conspicuously pleasant to everyone and speaking quite freely of the ostentation and unusual luxury of the feast. To minimize the importance of it all, he would mention the price, in a lowered voice, and then, as if to explain his part in this madness, would shrug his shoulders, saying, "After all, he's my only son."

The Hebrew words ben-yokhed ("only son") express this sentiment very well, and they were heard frequently as many guests expressed their praises of the fat Pascual. Even his bumpkin qualities were cited as assets in the extraordinary rash of praise.

His mother was dressed in a showy frock with winged sleeves and wore a green kerchief spread over her full shoulders. Moving quickly, in spite of her ample roundness, she went from place to place, talking and nodding to everyone in the growing crowd, which was soon becoming as big and fantastic as the fiesta.

Under the side eave of the house, a huge cauldron filled with chickens simmered over a fire, while at the side, in the deeper shadow, hung a row of dripping roasted geese. In front of these were trays with the traditional stuffed fish stacked for cooling. What the guests admired more than the chicken-filled cauldron, the roast geese, stuffed fish, and the calf's ribs that the cooks were preparing were the demijohns of wine, the huge cask of beer, and, above all else, the bottles of soft drinks whose roseate color the sun played on. Yes, it was so. Just as they'd heard in Rajil, there were the bottles of rose-colored soft drinks with red seals on the bottles.

The music was supplied by an accordion and guitar, and the two musicians were already essaying some popular Jewish pieces. Voices in the crowd were tentatively humming along with them.

The bride was preparing for the ceremony in the house next to Liske's. Friends were dressing her, and her crown of sugar was already well smudged from constant rearrangement. Raquel was very sad. No matter how much the other girls reminded her of her wonderful luck—to marry a man like Pascual wasn't something that happened every day—she remained depressed. She was silent most of the time and answered with sighs or short nods. She was normally a shy girl, but today she seemed truly sad. Those eyes that were usually so wide and clear now seemed as clouded as her forehead.

In talking about the guests, someone told Raquel that Gabriel had come with other people from San Gregorio. She grew more depressed at hearing his name and, as she put on the bridal veil, two big tears ran down her cheeks and fell on her satin blouse.

Everyone knew the cause of her weeping. Raquel and Gabriel had come to an understanding months ago, and Jacobo—that wily little know-it-all—had claimed he saw them kissing in the shadow of a paradise tree on the eve of the Day of Atonement.

Pascual's mother finally arrived at the bride's house and, in accordance with custom, congratulated the bride and kissed her noisily. Her voice screeched as she called to let the ceremony begin. Raquel said nothing. She shrugged in despair and stood hopelessly while the group of friends gathered at her back and picked up her lace-bordered train. The future father-in-law arrived with the rabbi and the procession started.

Outside Liske's house, the guests were gathered about the tables, while inside the house Pascual, who was dressed in black, waited with friends and the father of the bride. When they heard the hand-clapping outside, they went out to the grounds and the ceremony began.

Pascual walked over to the canopy, held up by couples of young men and women, and stood under it. He was joined immediately by his betrothed, who came escorted by the two sponsors. Rabbi Nisen began the blessings and offered the ritual cup to the bride and groom. Then the bride began her seven turns around the man, accompanied by the sponsors. As she finished, an old lady called out that there had only been six, and another turn was made. The rabbi read the marriage contract, which conformed entirely with the sacred laws of Israel. He sang the nuptial prayers again. The ceremony ended with the symbolic breaking of the cup. An old man placed it on the ground, and Pascual stepped on it with force enough to break rock.

The crowd pressed in to congratulate the couple. Her friends gathered around the bride, embracing and kissing her, but Raquel was still depressed. She accepted the congratulations and good wishes in silence. Other guests gathered around the long table and began to toast and drink.

Old Liske proposed some dancing before they sat down to supper, and he himself began by moving into the first steps of the characteristic Jewish place, "the happy dance," to the accompaniment of the accordion and guitar. At the head of the long table, the bride and groom stood together and watched the growing bustle without saying a word to each other. Facing them, standing very erect and pale, was Gabriel.

The guests called for the bride and groom to dance. Pascual frowned anxiously and shook his head. He did not dance. The calls and applause receded, and everyone stood waiting in embarrassment. Gabriel stepped forward suddenly and offered his arm to the bride. The accordion and guitar began a popular Jewish polka.

Gabriel tried to outdo himself and he was a superb dancer. At one point he said something to Raquel, and she looked at him in surprise and grew still paler. People were beginning to whisper and move away. Israel Kelner had taken the arm of the shochet as they both stepped away from the watching circle.

"Gabriel shouldn't have done this," Kelner said. "Everybody knows that he's in love with Raquel and that she's not in love with her husband."

The shochet pulled at his beard and smiled. "I don't want to offend anyone," he said. "I'm a friend of Liske's and he's a religious man—but Pascual is a beast. Did you see how mixed up he got when he was repeating the *hare-iad* pledge during the ceremony? Believe me, Rabbi Israel, I feel sorry for the girl. She's so beautiful and fine. . . . "

Little Jacobo took Rebecca aside and talked to her in Argentine criollo—he was the most gaucho of the Jews, as demonstrated now by his complete gaucho dress. Listen, negrita," he began. "Something's going to happen here."

"A fight?" Rebecca whispered with interest.

"Just what I'm telling you. I was in San Gregorio this morning. Met Gabriel there. He asked me if I was going to the wedding—this one, of course. I said yes, I was, and he asked me about doing something later. . . . "

"A race?" Rebecca interrupted. "You mean to say that you made a bet with Gabriel? Oh, you men! And they said that he was heartbroken!"

"Oh, well," Jacobo said. He shrugged his shoulders. "As they say: Men run to races. . . . "

As night began to fall, the paper lanterns were lit, and many guests walked off a distance to see the effect of the lights. It was a special privilege of the rich to have such lights, and the last time they'd been seen here was during the visit of Colonel Goldschmith, a representative of the European Jewish Committee.

The next item was dinner, a banquet that bars description. The guests were seated and the bride and groom served the "golden broth," the consecrative dish of the newlyweds. Then the platters of chicken, duck, and fish began to circulate, and the wine was poured to a complete and unanimous chorus of praise directed to the hostess.

"I've never eaten such tasty stuffed fish."

"Where could you ever get such roast geese as this?" the shochet asked.

Rabbi Moises Ornstein delivered the eulogy and added: "I must say that no one cooks as well as Madam Liske. Whoever tastes her dishes knows that they are a superior person's."

Fritters of meat and rice, wrapped in vine leaves, were served next, while more beer and wine quickened the spirits of the guests. The bride excused herself, saying that she had to change her dress. She left the party accompanied by her friends. Her mother-in-law had started to go with them, but Jacobo stopped her. "Madam Liske!" he said. "Sit down and listen to your praises. Sit down and hear what we think of this wonderful banquet. We'll be mad if you leave," he said, when she seemed reluctant to stop. "We're enjoying ourselves very much and we want to share this with you."

"Let me go, my boy," she said. "I have to help my daughter-in-law."

"Rebecca will help her. Sit down. Sit down. Rebecca!" Jacobo turned to shout. "Go and help the bride!"

The old lady sat down—everyone about had joined in the urging—and Jacobo brought her a glass of wine so that they could drink a toast.

"When one has a son like yours," the shochet said to Madam Liske, "one should be glad."

The toasts were offered and drunk, and this clinking of glasses, lusty singing, and music could be heard over all the grounds. The sky was full of stars, the atmosphere lightly tinged with clover and the scent of hay. In the nearby pasture, the cows mooed and the light wind stirred the leaves. Jacobo got up and excused himself.

"I have to see about my pony," he explained. "I think he might need a blanket."

"I'll look after my mare," Gabriel said, as he stood up to go with him. They moved away from the group, and Jacobo took Gabriel's arm. "Listen, the bay is saddled and waiting by the palisade," he said. "The boyero's kid is watching him and the gate is open. At the first turn there's a sulky all set. The Lame One is watching there. Tell me, have you got a gun?"

Gabriel did not seem to hear this last point. He patted Jacobo's arm and started to walk toward the palisade. After a few steps, he turned to look back. "And how will Raquel get away from the girls in there?"

"Don't worry about that. Rebecca's there."

When the girls who were with the bride did return to the party, Madam Liske asked for her daughter-in-law. "She's coming right away with Rebecca," they told her. Then Rebecca returned alone and gave the old lady still another excuse. Jacobo was doing his best to distract Madam Liske with toasts. Others took it up, and there was a great clinking of glasses and mumblings of toasts.

The musicians continued to play and the guests to eat and drink. The jugs of wine were being refilled continuously, and no one's glass was ever low. Pascual, the groom, looked fat and solemn and said nothing. From time to time, he would dart a quick look at the bride's empty chair. The gallop of a horse was heard at that moment, and then, soon after, the sounds of a sulky starting off.

Jacobo whispered into Rebecca's ear: "That's them, isn't it?"

"Yes," the girl whispered back, "they were leaving when I came away."

The continued absence of the bride was worrying her mother-in-law and, without saying anything, she slipped into the house to see. She came out immediately.

"Rebecca, have you seen Raquel?" she said.

"I left her in the house, Señora. Isn't she there?"

"She's not."

"That's funny. . . . "

The old lady spoke to her husband and to her son, Pascual. The guests were beginning to whisper among themselves. They saw that something had gone wrong. The accordion and guitar went silent. The guests began to stand up; some glasses were tipped over, but no one paid any attention. A few of the guests moved toward the house. Others asked: "Is it the bride? Has something happened to the bride?"

The shochet of Rajil asked his friend and counterpart from Karmel about the point of sacred law, if it was true that the bride had fled.

"Do you think she has?" the shochet of Karmel asked.

"It's possible. Anything is possible in these situations."

"Well, I think that divorce would be the next step. The girl would be free, as would be her husband. It's the common course."

Meanwhile, the excitement was growing all around them. Old Liske grabbed the gaucho's little son. "Did you see anything out there? Out there on the road?" he said.

"Yes. Out there, on the road to San Gregorio. I saw a sulky, with Gabriel—he was driving it—and there was a girl sitting with him."

"He's kidnapped her!" Madam Liske screamed. Her voice was close to hysteria. "Kidnapped her!"

Shouts and quick talking started all over the grounds now. Most of the crowd was genuinely shocked and surprised. When old Liske turned to abuse the father of the gaucho boy, the man stood up to him, and they were soon wrestling and rolling in the center of pushing and shouting guests. The table was overturned, and spilled wine and broken glass added to the excitement.

The shochet of Rajil mounted a chair and shouted for order. What had happened was a disgrace, he said, a punishment from God, but fighting and shouting would not ease it any.

"She's an adulteress!" shouted the enraged Liske, as he sought to break out of restraining hands. "An infamous adulteress!"

"She is not!" the shochet answered him. "She would be," he said, "if she had left her husband after one day, at least, after the marriage; as our law so clearly says it. This is the law of God, you know, and there is no other way but that they be divorced. Pascual is a fine, honorable young man, but if she doesn't love him, she can't be made to live under his roof."

The shochet went on in his usually eloquent and wise way, and he cited similar cases acknowledged by the most illustrious rabbis and scholars. In Jerusalem, the sacred capital, there had occurred a similar case, and Rabbi Hillel had declared in favor of the girl. At the end, the shochet turned to Pascual: "In the name of our laws, Pascual, I ask that you grant a divorce to Raquel and that you declare, here and now, that you accept it for yourself." Pascual scratched his head and looked sad. Then, in a tearful voice, he accepted the shochet's proposal.

The crowd grew quiet and the guests soon began to leave, one by one, some murmuring, some hiding a smile.

Well, as you can see, my patient readers, there are fierce, arrogant gauchos, wife stealers, and Camachos, as well as the most learned and honorable of rabbinical scholars, in the little Jewish colony where I learned to love the Argentine sky and felt a part of its wonderful earth. This story I've told—with more detail than art—is a true one, just as I'm sure the original story of Camacho's feast is true. May I die this instant if I've dared to add the lightest bit of invention to the marvelous story.

I'd like very much to add some verses—as was done to the original Camacho story—but God has denied me that talent. I gave you the tale in its purest truth, and if you want couplets, add them yourself in your most gracious style. Don't forget my name, however—just as our gracious Master Don Miguel de Cervantes Saavedra remembered the name of Cide Hamete Benegeli and gave him all due credit for the original Camacho story.

And if the exact, accurate telling of this tale has pleased you, don't send me any golden doubloons—here, they don't even buy bread and water. Send me some golden drachmas or, if not, I'd appreciate a carafe of Jerusalem wine from the vineyards my ancestors planted as they sang the praises of Jehovah. May He grant you wealth and health, the gifts I ask for myself.

TRANSLATED BY PRUDENCIO DE PEREDA

PERMISSIONS

The editors wish to express their gratitude to editorial assistant Alexandra Kanovsky for her invaluable help. María Aybar and Camilo Toruño at Amherst College, as well as Michael Gerber and Susan Miron, provided support. Thanks also to Aaron Lansky, Susan Bronson, Lisa Newman, and David Mazower at the Yiddish Book Center, and to Annette Hochstein, Arielle Kane, Alison Gore, and Rachael Guynn Wilson at Restless Books. Nathan Rostron shepherded the manuscript through production in outstanding fashion. Scott Bryan Wilson and Yankl Salant provided excellent copyediting. The vast majority of material in this volume first appeared in *Pakn Treger*. (For reasons of clarity, titles have occasionally been changed.) All efforts have been made to contact copyright holders. In case of any inadvertent omissions, please contact the publisher: Restless Books, 232 3rd Street Suite A101, Brooklyn NY 11215, email publisher@restlessbooks.com.

William Gropper: *from* Di goldene medine. First published in *Di goldene medine* [The Golden Land] (Freiheit Publishing Co., 1927).

Daniel Kahn: March of the Jobless Corps, *adapt.* Mordechai Gebirtig. First performed on *Lost Causes* (Oriente Musik, 2010). Used by permission of Daniel Kahn.

Paul Buhle: *Di Freiheit*, A Personal Reflection. First published in *Pakn Treger*, no. 11–12, summer 1989. Used by permission of Paul Buhle.

Bernard Weinstein: *from* The Jewish Unions in America, *trans.* Maurice Wolfthal. First published in *The Jewish Unions in America* (Open Book Publishers, 2018). Used by permission.

Morris Rosenfeld: The Triangle Fire, trans. Leon Stein. First published in *Jewish Daily Forward* (1911).

Sholem Asch: *from* God of Vengeance (Act II), *trans.* Joachim Neugroschel. First published in *Pakn Treger*, no. 23, winter 1996. Used by permission.

Eddy Portnoy: On Zuni Maud. First published in *Pakn Treger*, no. 55, fall 2007. Used by permission of Eddy Portnoy.

Lola: The Bitter Drop. First published in *Der groyser kundes*, December 17, 1915.

Naomi Seidman: Is Hebrew Male and Yiddish Female? First published in *A Marriage Made in Heaven: The Sexual Politics of Hebrew and Yiddish* (University of California Press, 1997). Used by permission of Naomi Seidman.

Aaron Lansky and Gitl Schaechter-Viswanath: The Maximalist's Daughter. First published in *Pakn Treger* no. 75, summer 2017. Used by permission.

Jeffrey Shandler: Looking for Yiddish in Boro Park. First published in *Pakn Treger*, no. 40, fall 2002. Used by permission of Jeffrey Shandler.

Ilan Stavans: O, R*O*S*T*E*N, My R*O*S*T*E*N! First published in *Pakn Treger*, fall 2006. Reprinted in *Singer's Typewriter and Mine: Reflections on Jewish Culture* (University of Nebraska Press, 2012). Used by permission of Ilan Stavans.

Shirley Kumove: A Guide to Yiddish Sayings. First published in *Pakn Treger*, no. 24, spring 1997. Included in *Words Like Arrows: A Collection of*

Yiddish Folk Sayings (Schocken Books, 1985). Used by permission of Shirley Kumove.

Stanley Siegelman: The Artificial Elephant. First published in *Forverts*, January 30, 2006. Reprinted by permission of Peter Siegelman.

Matthew Goodman: Kosher Chinese? First published in *Jewish Food: The World at Table* (William Morrow Cookbooks, 2005). Republished in *Pakn Treger*, no. 61, spring 2010. Used by permission of Matthew Goodman.

Aaron Lansky: A Little Taste. First published in *Outwitting History: The Amazing Adventures of a Man Who Rescued a Million Yiddish Books* (Algonquin Books, 2004). Used by permission of Aaron Lansky.

Arthur Klein, Alice Ahart, Lisa Newman, Albert Berkowitz, Daniel Okrent: Carp, Rugelach, Egg Creams. First published in *Pakn Treger*, no. 67, summer 2013. Used by permission.

Kadya Molodowsky: The Baker and the Beggar, *trans.* Miriam Udel. Used by permission of Miriam Udel.

Asya Vaisman Schulman: On Bagels, Gefilte Fish, and Cholent. First published in *Pakn Treger*, no. 68, fall 2013, and no. 69, summer 2014. Used by permission.

Procter & Gamble: Crisco Recipes for the Jewish Housewife. First published in *Crisco Recipes for the Jewish Housewife* (Procter and Gamble, 1933). Republished in *Pakn Treger*, no. 67, fall 2013.

Alison Sparks: Holy Mole and Kamish! This is partially its first publication. The recipe for latkes with mole first appeared in *The Jewish Identity Project*, Susan Chernow and Joanna Lindenbaum, eds. (Yale University Press, 2005). Used by permission of Alison Sparks.

Isadore Lillian: Hering mit pateytes, *trans.* Jane Peppler. First published in *Pakn Treger*, no. 67, summer 2013. Used by permission of Jane Peppler. Please visit http://yiddishpennysongs.com.

Isaac Bashevis Singer: The Cafeteria, *trans.* Dorothea Straus. First published in *The New Yorker*, December 1968. Used by permission of Susan Schulman Literary Agency LLC on behalf of the Isaac Bashevis Singer estate.

Isaac Bashevis Singer: How Does It Feel to Be a Yiddish Writer in America? First published in *Forverts* (1965). Republished in *Pakn Treger*, no. 77, summer 2018. Reprinted by permission of Susan Schulman Literary Agency LLC on behalf of the Isaac Bashevis Singer estate.

Janet Hadda, Kenneth Turan, Anita Norich, Aaron Lansky, Ilan Stavans, Rivka Galchen: Literature, It's Like Orgasm! First published in *Pakn Treger*, no. 24, spring 1997. Used by permission.

Anna Margolin: Epitaph, *trans.* Shirley Kumove. Used by permission of Shirley Kumove. My Home, Girls on Crotona Park, *and* Unhappy, *trans.* Maia Evrona. First published in In Translation, brooklynrail. org, February 2015. Used by permission of Maia Evrona.

Celia Dropkin: I Will Run Away, *trans.* Gene Zeiger. Used by permission. White as the Snow on the Alps *and* I Beam, You're Beaming, *trans.* Maia Evrona. First published in the Jewish Women Archive's website: https://jwa.org. Used by permission of Maia Evrona.

Jacob Glatstein: Summoned Home, *trans.* Maier Deshell. First published in *Pakn Treger*, no. 55, fall 2007. Included in *The Glatstein Chronicles* (Yale University Press, 2010), ed. Ruth R. Wisse, translated by Maier Deshell and Norbert Guterman. Used by permission.

Moyshe-Leyb Halpern: Madame, *trans.* Aaron Rubinstein. First published in *Pakn Treger*, no. 47, spring 2005. Used by permission of Aaron Rubinstein.

Peretz Hirshbein: *from* Across America, *trans.* Jessica Kirzane. First published in *Pakn Treger*, no. 67, summer 2013. Used by permission of Jessica Kirzane.

Blume Lempel: Oedipus in Brooklyn, *trans.* Ellen Cassedy and Yermiyahu Ahron Taub. Translation first published in *Oedipus in Brooklyn and Other Stories* (Mandel Vilar Press and Dryad Press, 2016). Used by permission of Ellen Cassedy and Yermiyahu Ahron Taub.

Rokhl Korn: The New House, *trans.* Seymour Levitan. First published in *Pakn Treger*, no. 35, winter 2001. Included in *Paper Roses: Selected Poems of Rokhl Korn* (Aya Press, 1985).

Chaim Grade: Woe Is Me that My City Is Now Only a Memory, *trans.*

467

by permission of the author's granddaughter Harriet Goodman Hoffman on behalf of the author's estate.

Isaac Berliner: Popocatépetl, *trans.* Ilan Stavans. First published in Asymptote, July 2019. Used by permission of Ilan Stavans.

Claudia Mirelstein: The Yiddish Terrorist, *trans.* Bernard Levinson. First published in *La rabia del alacrán*, by Claudia Mirelman (Bogota: Alfaguara, 2017). Used by permission of Claudia Mirelstein and Bernard Levinson.

Goldie Morgentaler: Bontshe Shvayg in Lethbridge. First published in *Pakn Treger*, no. 62, winter 2010. Used by permission of Goldie Morgentaler.

Ilan Stavans: A Yidisher Bokher in Mexique. First published in *Pakn Treger*, no. 68, fall 2013. Used by permission of Ilan Stavans.

Alberto Gerchunoff: Camacho's Wedding Feast, *trans.* Prudencio de Pereda. First published in *The Jewish Gauchos of the Pampas* (Abelard-Schuman, 1959). Reprinted in *Oy, Caramba! An Anthology of Jewish Stories from Latin America*, ed. Ilan Stavans (University of New Mexico Press, 2016).

INDEX

ABOUT THE EDITORS

ILAN STAVANS is the publisher of Restless Books and the Lewis-Sebring Professor of Humanities and Latin American and Latino Culture at Amherst College. His books, translated into twenty languages, include *On Borrowed Words, Spanglish, Dictionary Days,* and *A Critic's Journey.* He has edited the *Norton Anthology of Latino Literature,* the three-volume set *Isaac Bashevis Singer: Collected Stories,* and *The Poetry of Pablo Neruda,* among dozens of other volumes. A cofounder of the Great Books Summer Program, he is the host of the NPR podcast *In Contrast.*

JOSH LAMBERT is the Academic Director of the Yiddish Book Center and a Visiting Assistant Professor of English at the University of Massachusetts, Amherst. He is the author of *American Jewish Fiction: A JPS Guide* and *Unclean Lips: Obscenity, Jews, and American Culture,* which received a Jordan Schnitzer Book Award from the Association of Jewish Studies and a Canadian Jewish Book Award. His reviews and essays have been published by the *New York Times Book Review,* the *Los Angeles Times, Haaretz, Tablet,* the *Forward,* and many others.

RESTLESS BOOKS is an independent, nonprofit publisher devoted to championing essential voices from around the world whose stories speak to us across linguistic and cultural borders. We seek extraordinary international literature for adults and young readers that feeds our restlessness: our hunger for new perspectives, passion for other cultures and languages, and eagerness to explore beyond the confines of the familiar.

Through cultural programming, we aim to celebrate immigrant writing and bring literature to underserved communities. We believe that immigrant stories are a vital component of our cultural consciousness; they help to ensure awareness of our communities, build empathy for our neighbors, and strengthen our democracy.

Visit us at restlessbooks.org